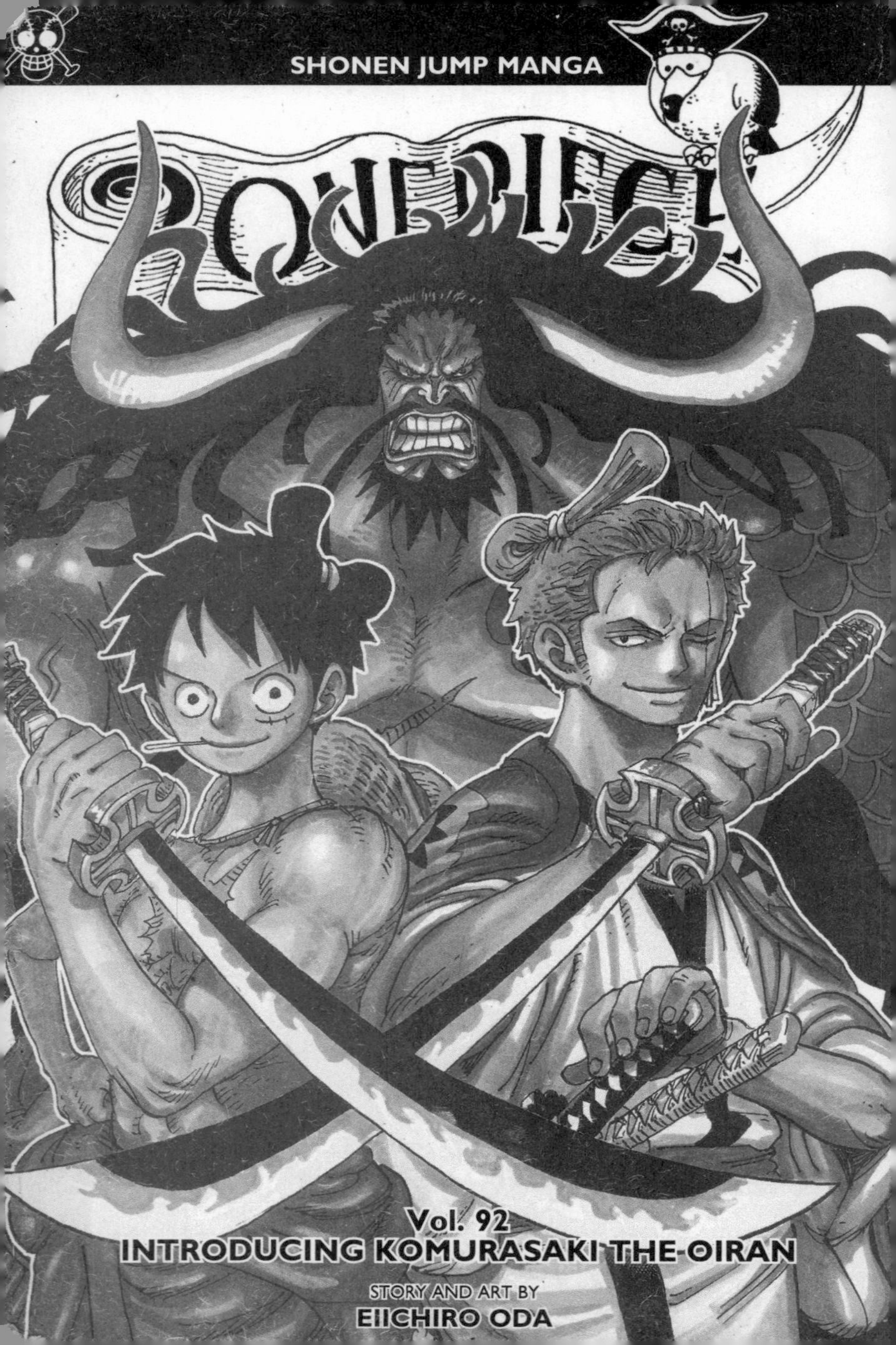
SHONEN JUMP MANGA
ONE PIECE
Vol. 92
INTRODUCING KOMURASAKI THE OIRAN
STORY AND ART BY
EIICHIRO ODA

尾田栄一郎

"Forty-eight browns and 100 grays!!"
This is a figurative saying that indicates there are
a multitude of shades of brown and gray in Japan.
In the old days, the common people were instructed
not to wear flashy colors, and so they developed
a wealth of plain colors to use instead. I bet they
wish they could have worn all kinds of rainbow hues
though. Well, the Wano Arc is going to be wild and
flashy! Can't wait to see this animated too!!
Let volume 92 beginneth!!!

-Eiichiro Oda, 2019

E iichiro Oda began his manga career at the age of
17, when his one-shot cowboy manga **Wanted!**
won second place in the coveted Tezuka manga
awards. Oda went on to work as an assistant to
some of the biggest manga artists in the industry,
including Nobuhiro Watsuki, before winning the
Hop Step Award for new artists. His pirate
adventure **One Piece**, which debuted in
Weekly Shonen Jump in 1997, quickly became
one of the most popular manga in Japan.

The story of ONE PIECE 1»92

Characters

The Straw Hat Crew

Chopperemon [Ninja]
Tony Tony Chopper

Studied powerful medicines in the Birdie Kingdom as he waited to rejoin the crew.

Ship's Doctor, Bounty: 100 berries

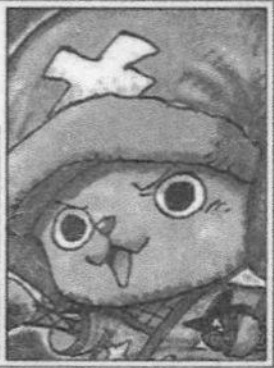

Luffytaro [Ronin]
Monkey D. Luffy

A young man dreaming of being the Pirate King. After two years of training he rejoins his friends in search of the New World!

Captain, Bounty: 1.5 billion berries

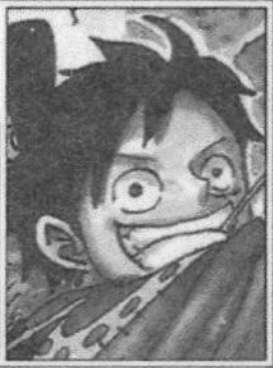

Orobi [Geisha]
Nico Robin

Spent time on the island of Baltigo with Dragon, Luffy's father and leader of the Revolutionary Army.

Archeologist, Bounty: 130 million berries

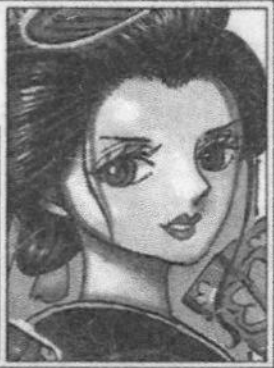

Zolojuro [Ronin]
Roronoa Zolo

Swallowed his pride on Gloom Island and trained under Mihawk before rejoining Luffy.

Fighter, Bounty: 320 million berries

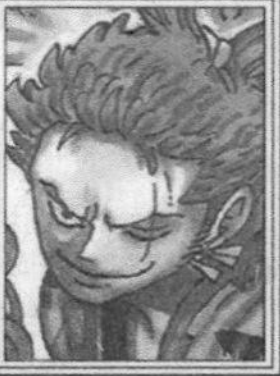

Franosuke [Carpenter]
Franky

Upgraded himself into "Armored Franky" in the Future Land, Baldimore.

Shipwright, Bounty: 94 million berries

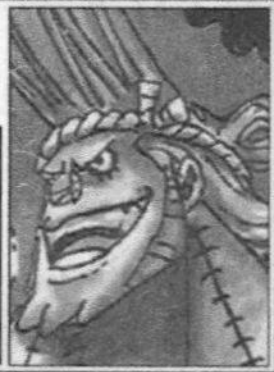

Onami [Kunoichi]
Nami

Learned about the climates of the New World on Weatheria, a Sky Island that studies the atmosphere.

Navigator, Bounty: 66 million berries

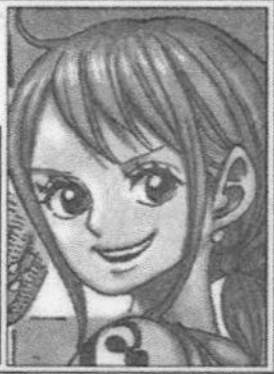

Bonekichi [Ghost]
Brook

Originally captured by Long-Arm bandits for a freak show, he is now the mega-star "Soul King" Brook.

Musician, Bounty: 83 million berries

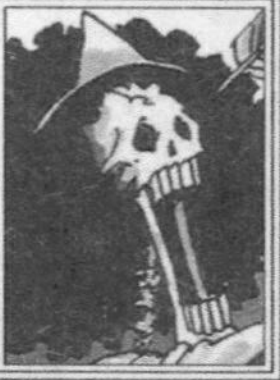

Usohachi [Toad Oil Salesman]
Usopp

Received Heraclesun's lessons on the Bowin Islands in his quest to be the "king of the snipers."

Sniper, Bounty: 200 million berries

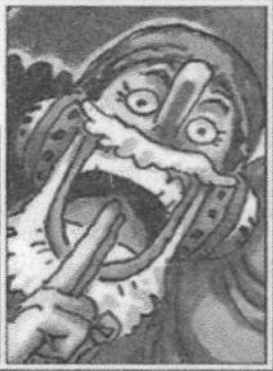

Shanks

One of the Four Emperors. Waits for Luffy in the "New World," the second half of the Grand Line.

Captain of the Red-Haired Pirates

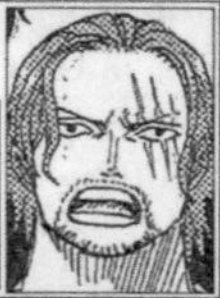

Sangoro [Soba Cook]
Sanji

Honed his skills fighting with the masters of Newcomer Kenpo in the Kamabakka Kingdom.

Cook, Bounty: 330 million berries

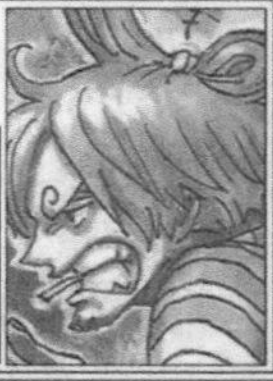

Ninja-Pirate-Mink-Samurai Alliance

Heart Pirates

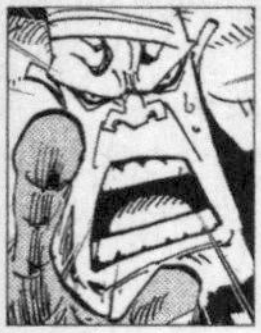
Jean Bart
Crew, Heart Pirates

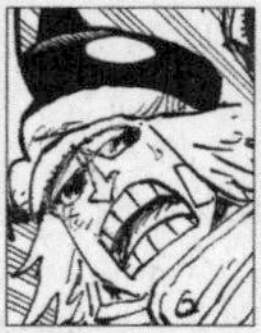
Shachi
Crew, Heart Pirates

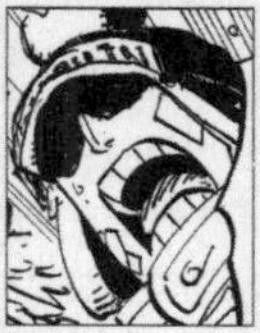
Penguin
Crew, Heart Pirates

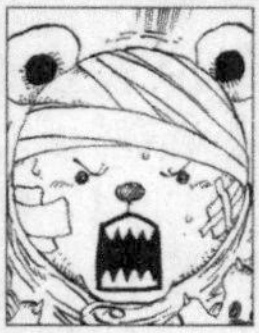
Bepo
Navigator, Heart Pirates

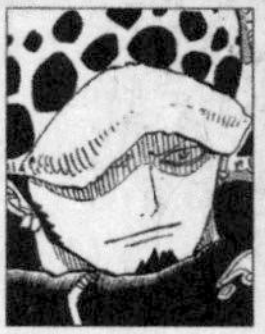
Trafalgar Law
Captain, Heart Pirates

Mokomo Dukedom

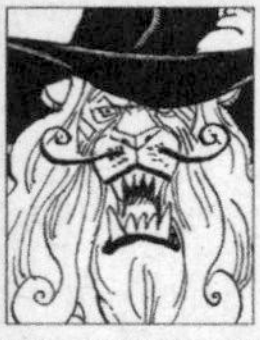
Full-Power Shishilian (Lion Mink)
Captain, Dogstorm Musketeers

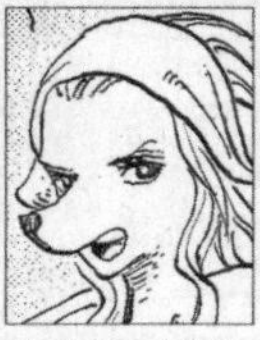
Wanda (Dog Mink)
Battlebeast Tribe, Kingsbird

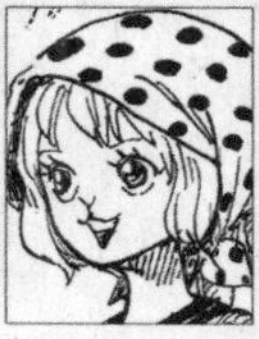
Carrot (Bunny Mink)
Battlebeast Tribe, Kingsbird

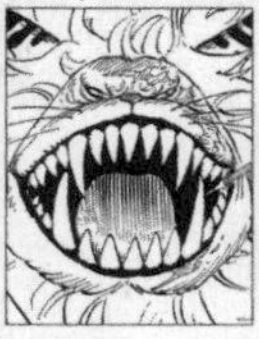
Cat Viper
King of the Night, Mokomo

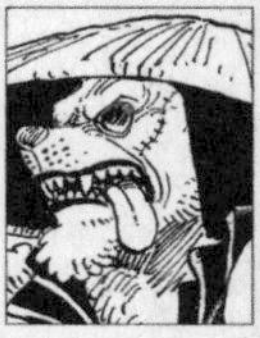
Duke Dogstorm
King of the Day, Mokomo

Wano

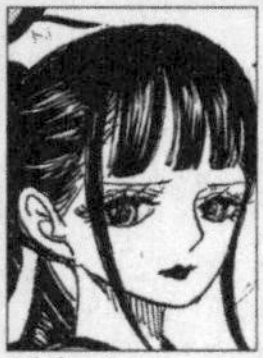
Okiku
Samurai of Wano

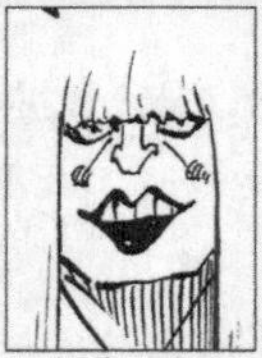
Evening Shower Kanjuro
Samurai of Wano

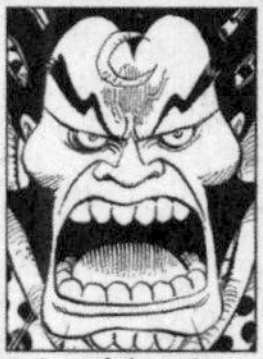
Raizo of the Mist
Ninja of Wano

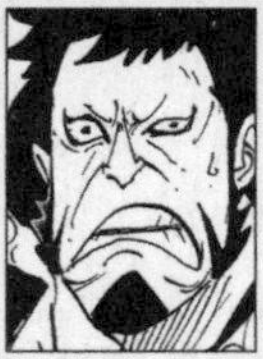
Foxfire Kin'emon
Samurai of Wano

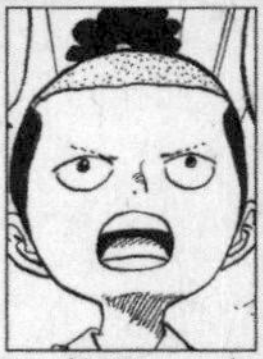
Kozuki Momonosuke
Daimyo (Heir) to Kuri in Wano

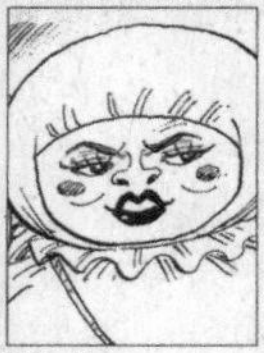
Shinobu
Veteran Kunoichi

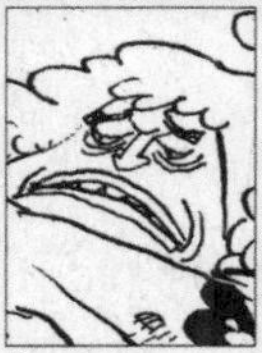
Shutenmaru
Chief, Atamayama Thieves Brigade

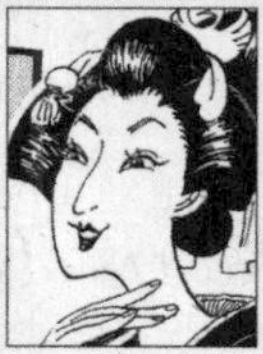
Otsuru (Kin'emon's Wife)
Tea Shop Owner

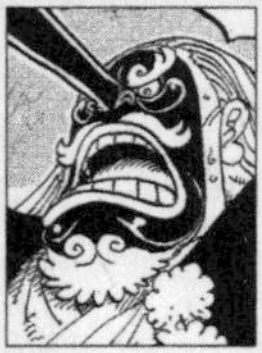
Tenguyama Hitetsu
Katana Blacksmith

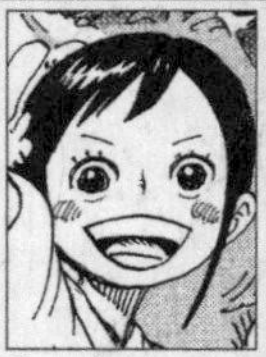
Otama
Child of Kuri in Wano

clandestine work to prepare for the coming battle. But when Luffy saves Otama from Kaido's followers, the enemy side learns of his presence and chases after him! Later, he meets up with Kin'emon and learns that Momonosuke and the samurai have actually jumped through time from the Wano of 20 years ago! The plan is made to complete Oden's desire and strike down Kaido at Onigashima, the island of ogres, in two weeks' time! Just then, Kaido himself appears in the form of a gigantic dragon!

Animal Kingdom Pirates

Kaido, King of the Beasts (Emperor of the Sea)

A pirate known as the "strongest creature alive." Despite numerous tortures and death sentences, none have been able to kill him.

Captain, Animal Kingdom Pirates

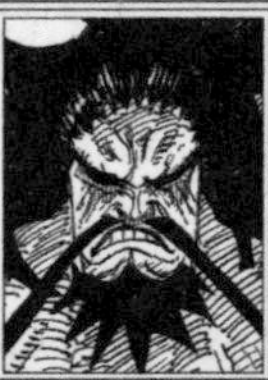

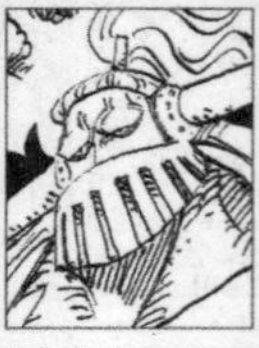

Jack the Drought

Lead Performer, Animal Kingdom Pirates

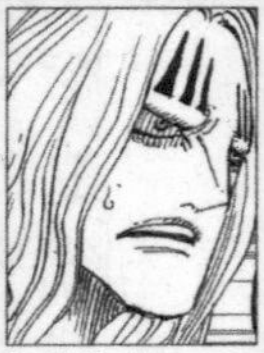

Basil Hawkins

Headliner, Animal Kingdom Pirates

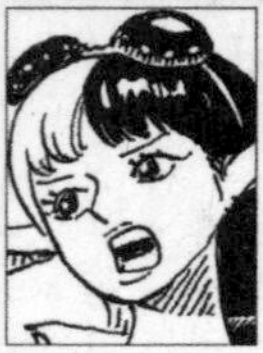

Speed

Headliner, Animal Kingdom Pirates

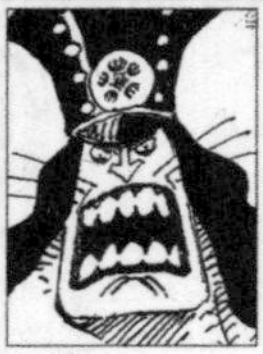

Holdem

Headliner, Animal Kingdom Pirates

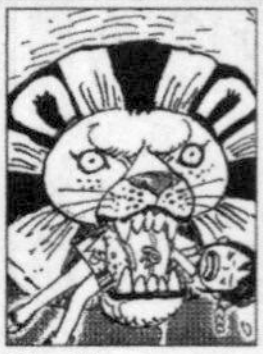

Kamijiro

Holdem's Tummy

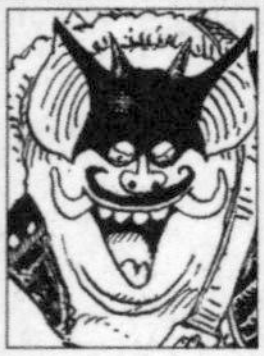

Bat-man

Gifter, Animal Kingdom Pirates

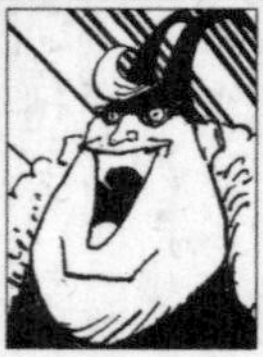

Gazelle-man

Gifter, Animal Kingdom Pirates

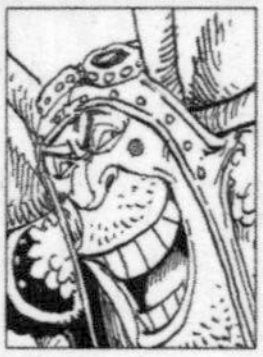

Mouse-man

Gifter, Animal Kingdom Pirates

?

Kurozumi Orochi

Shogun of Wano

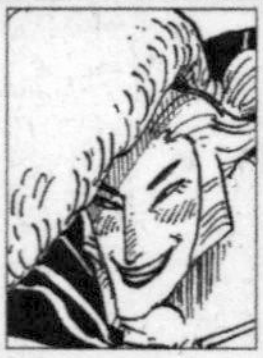

Napping Kyoshiro

Money Changer for the Kurozumi Clan

Story

After two years of hard training, the Straw Hat pirates are back together, first at the Sabaody Archipelago and then through Fish-Man Island to their next stage: the New World!!

Luffy and crew defeat Doflamingo, then get through a scuffle with the Emperor of the Sea, Big Mom, on their way to Wano for the purpose of taking down Kaido. The lead party of Robin, Usopp and Franky have been undertaking

Vol. 92
INTRODUCING KOMURASAKI THE OIRAN

CONTENTS

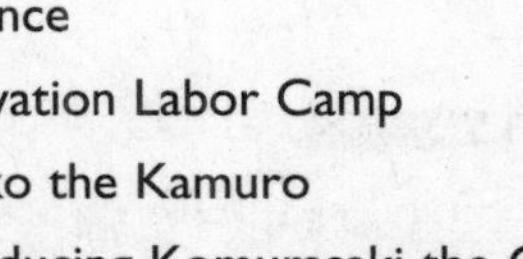

Chapter 922:
SUPREME COMMANDER KAIDO OF THE ANIMAL KINGDOM PIRATES

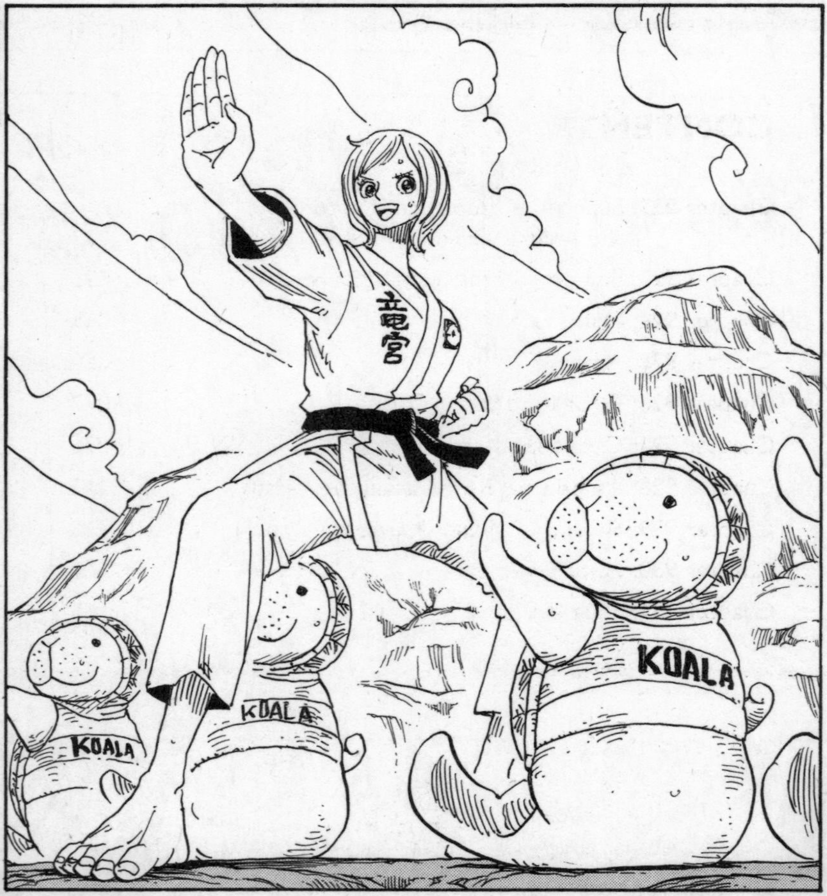
*SHIRT RYUGU
竜宮
KOALA
KOALA
KOALA

REQUEST: "KOALA TEACHING KUNG-FU DUGONGS THE WAYS OF FISH-MAN KARATE" BY MEHH FROM SAKU

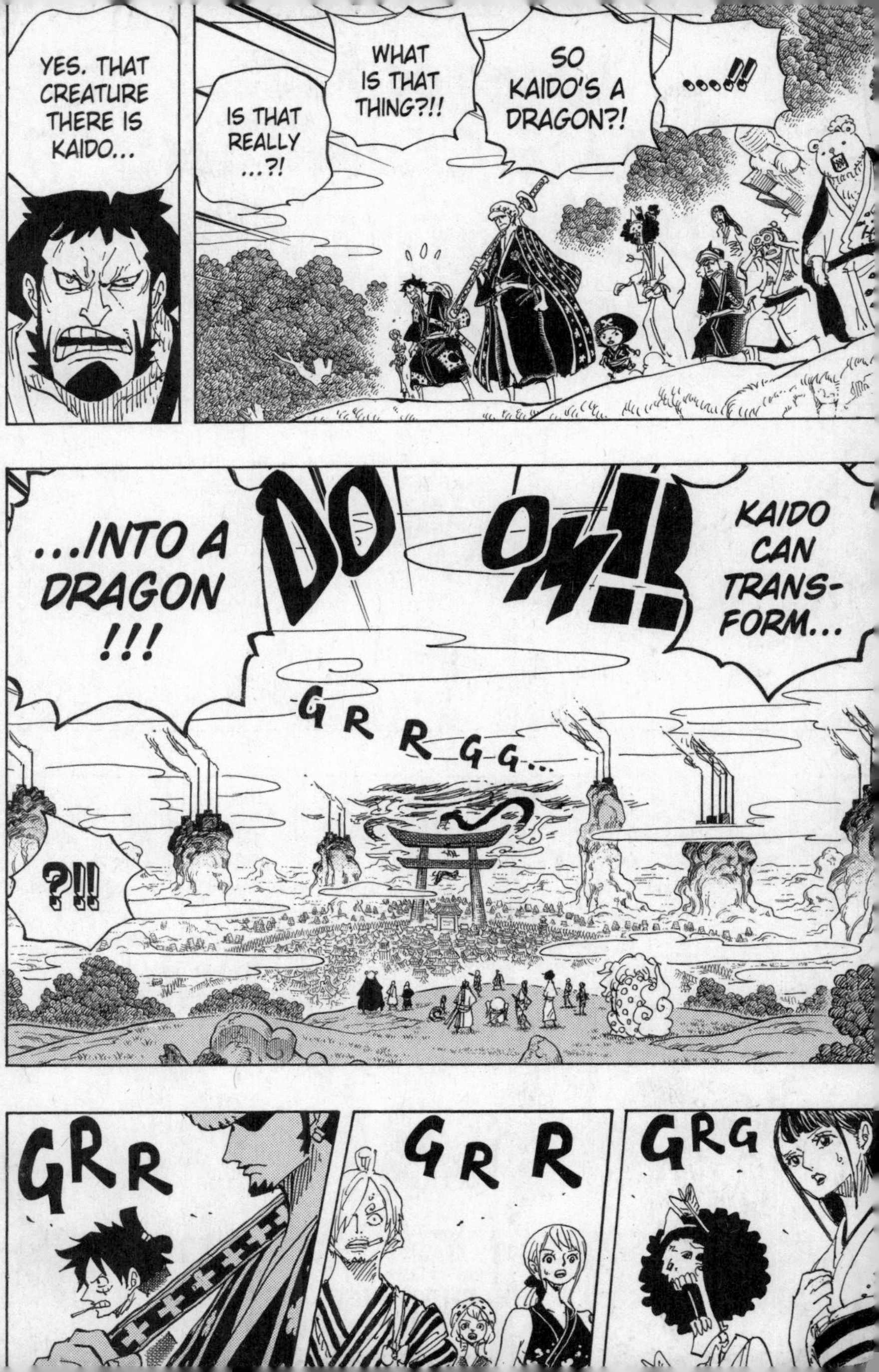
....!!
SO KAIDO'S A DRAGON?!
WHAT IS THAT THING?!!
IS THAT REALLY ...?!
YES. THAT CREATURE THERE IS KAIDO...
KAIDO CAN TRANS-FORM...
DOOM!!
...INTO A DRAGON !!!
GRRRGG...
?!!
GRG
GRR
GRR

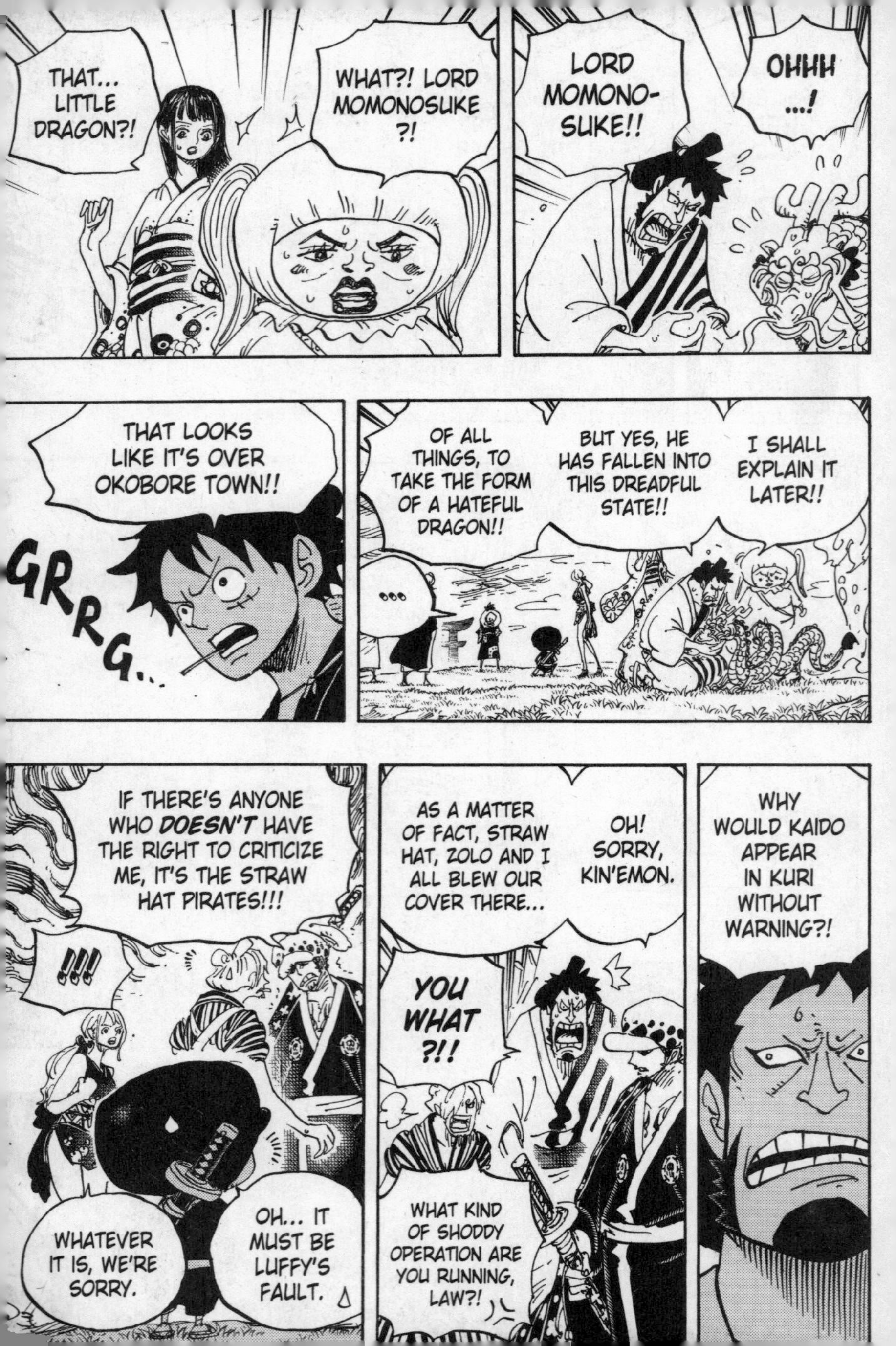
OHHH ...!
LORD MOMONOSUKE!!
WHAT?! LORD MOMONOSUKE ?!
THAT... LITTLE DRAGON?!
I SHALL EXPLAIN IT LATER!!
BUT YES, HE HAS FALLEN INTO THIS DREADFUL STATE!!
OF ALL THINGS, TO TAKE THE FORM OF A HATEFUL DRAGON!!
...
THAT LOOKS LIKE IT'S OVER OKOBORE TOWN!!
GRRG...
WHY WOULD KAIDO APPEAR IN KURI WITHOUT WARNING?!
OH! SORRY, KIN'EMON.
AS A MATTER OF FACT, STRAW HAT, ZOLO AND I ALL BLEW OUR COVER THERE...
YOU WHAT?!!
WHAT KIND OF SHODDY OPERATION ARE YOU RUNNING, LAW?!
IF THERE'S ANYONE WHO *DOESN'T* HAVE THE RIGHT TO CRITICIZE ME, IT'S THE STRAW HAT PIRATES!!!
!!!
OH... IT MUST BE LUFFY'S FAULT.
WHATEVER IT IS, WE'RE SORRY.

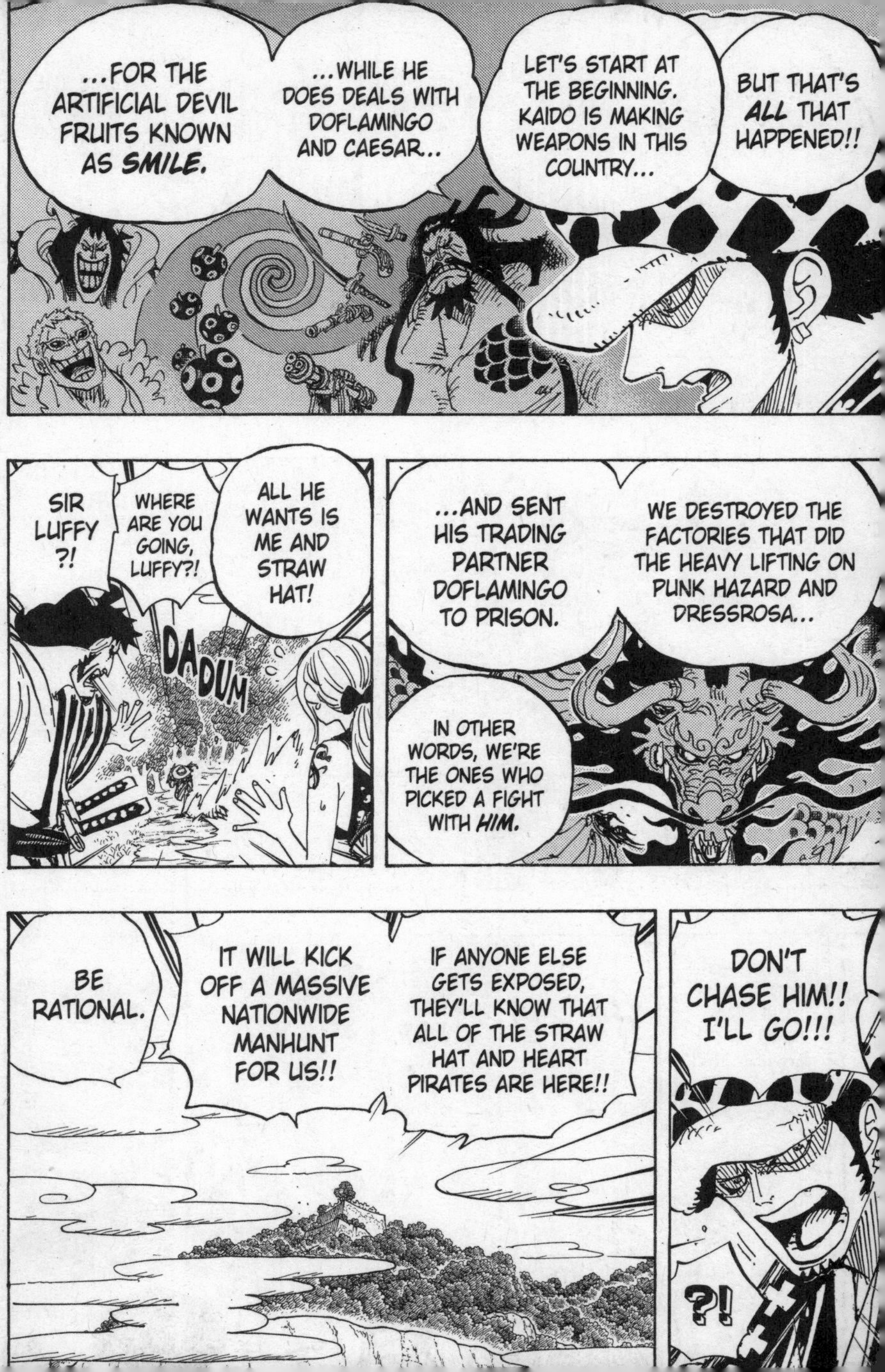
BUT THAT'S ALL THAT HAPPENED!!
LET'S START AT THE BEGINNING. KAIDO IS MAKING WEAPONS IN THIS COUNTRY...
...WHILE HE DOES DEALS WITH DOFLAMINGO AND CAESAR...
...FOR THE ARTIFICIAL DEVIL FRUITS KNOWN AS SMILE.
WE DESTROYED THE FACTORIES THAT DID THE HEAVY LIFTING ON PUNK HAZARD AND DRESSROSA...
...AND SENT HIS TRADING PARTNER DOFLAMINGO TO PRISON.
IN OTHER WORDS, WE'RE THE ONES WHO PICKED A FIGHT WITH HIM.
ALL HE WANTS IS ME AND STRAW HAT!
WHERE ARE YOU GOING, LUFFY?!
SIR LUFFY?!
DADUM
DON'T CHASE HIM!! I'LL GO!!!
?!
IF ANYONE ELSE GETS EXPOSED, THEY'LL KNOW THAT ALL OF THE STRAW HAT AND HEART PIRATES ARE HERE!!
IT WILL KICK OFF A MASSIVE NATIONWIDE MANHUNT FOR US!!
BE RATIONAL.

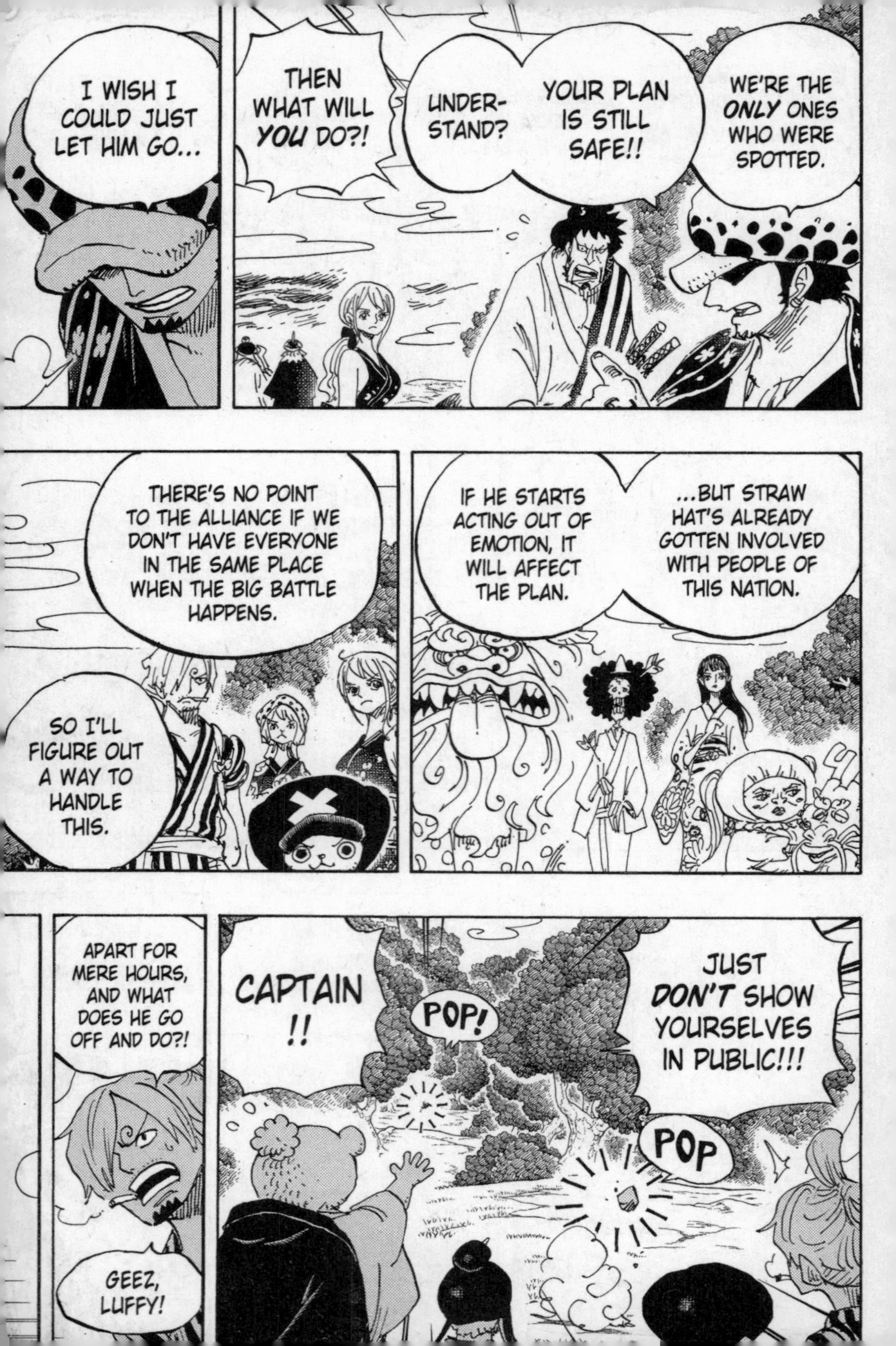
WE'RE THE ONLY ONES WHO WERE SPOTTED.
YOUR PLAN IS STILL SAFE!!
UNDER-STAND?
THEN WHAT WILL YOU DO?!
I WISH I COULD JUST LET HIM GO...
...BUT STRAW HAT'S ALREADY GOTTEN INVOLVED WITH PEOPLE OF THIS NATION.
IF HE STARTS ACTING OUT OF EMOTION, IT WILL AFFECT THE PLAN.
THERE'S NO POINT TO THE ALLIANCE IF WE DON'T HAVE EVERYONE IN THE SAME PLACE WHEN THE BIG BATTLE HAPPENS.
SO I'LL FIGURE OUT A WAY TO HANDLE THIS.
JUST DON'T SHOW YOURSELVES IN PUBLIC!!!
CAPTAIN !!
POP!
POP
APART FOR MERE HOURS, AND WHAT DOES HE GO OFF AND DO?!
GEEZ, LUFFY!

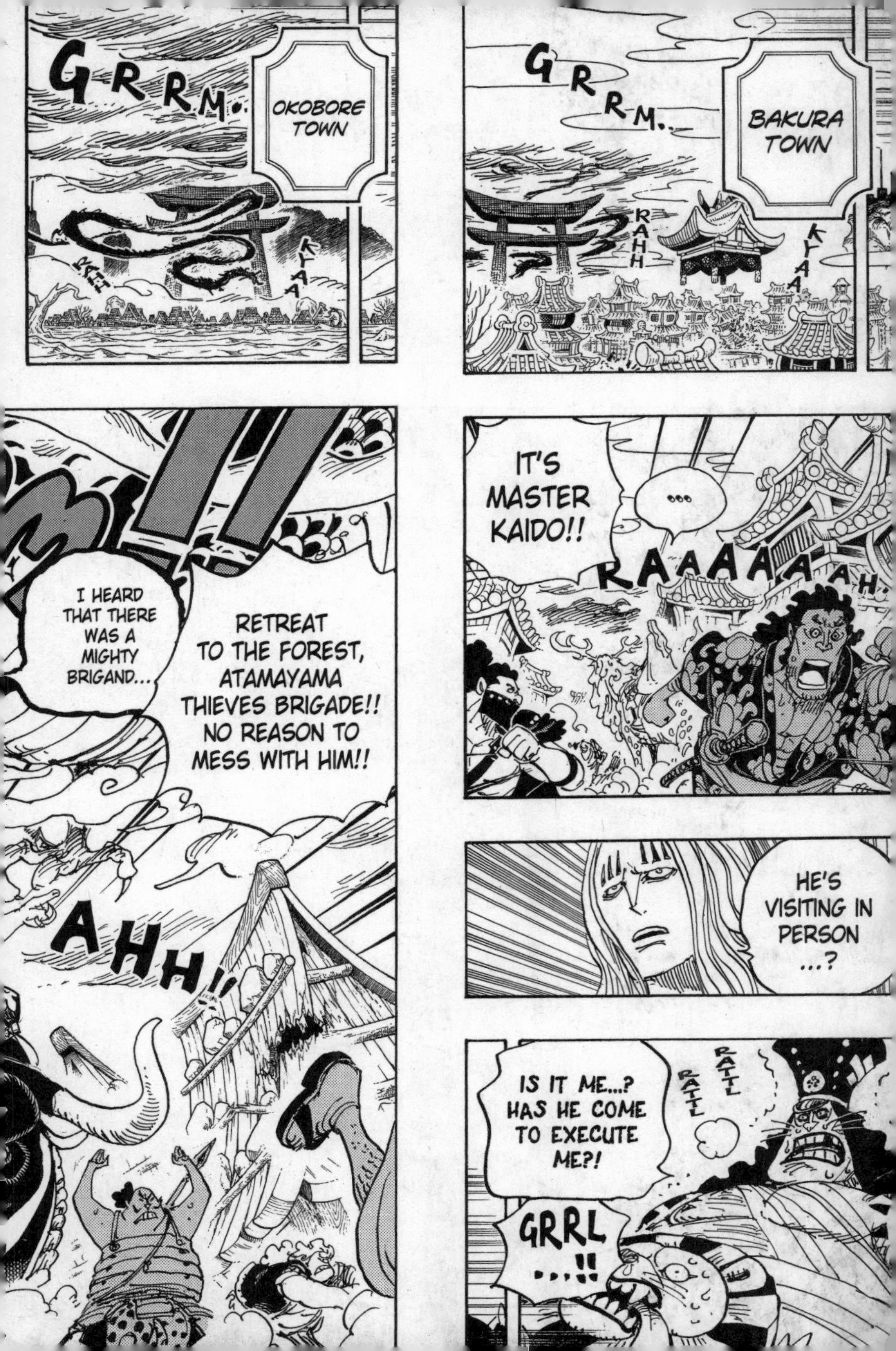
GRRRM..
BAKURA TOWN
RAHH
KYAA
GRRRM..
OKOBORE TOWN
RAHH
KYAA
IT'S MASTER KAIDO!!
...
RAAAAAAH.
HE'S VISITING IN PERSON ...?
IS IT ME...? HAS HE COME TO EXECUTE ME?!
RATTL
RATTL
GRRL ...!!
RETREAT TO THE FOREST, ATAMAYAMA THIEVES BRIGADE!! NO REASON TO MESS WITH HIM!!
I HEARD THAT THERE WAS A MIGHTY BRIGAND...
AHH!!

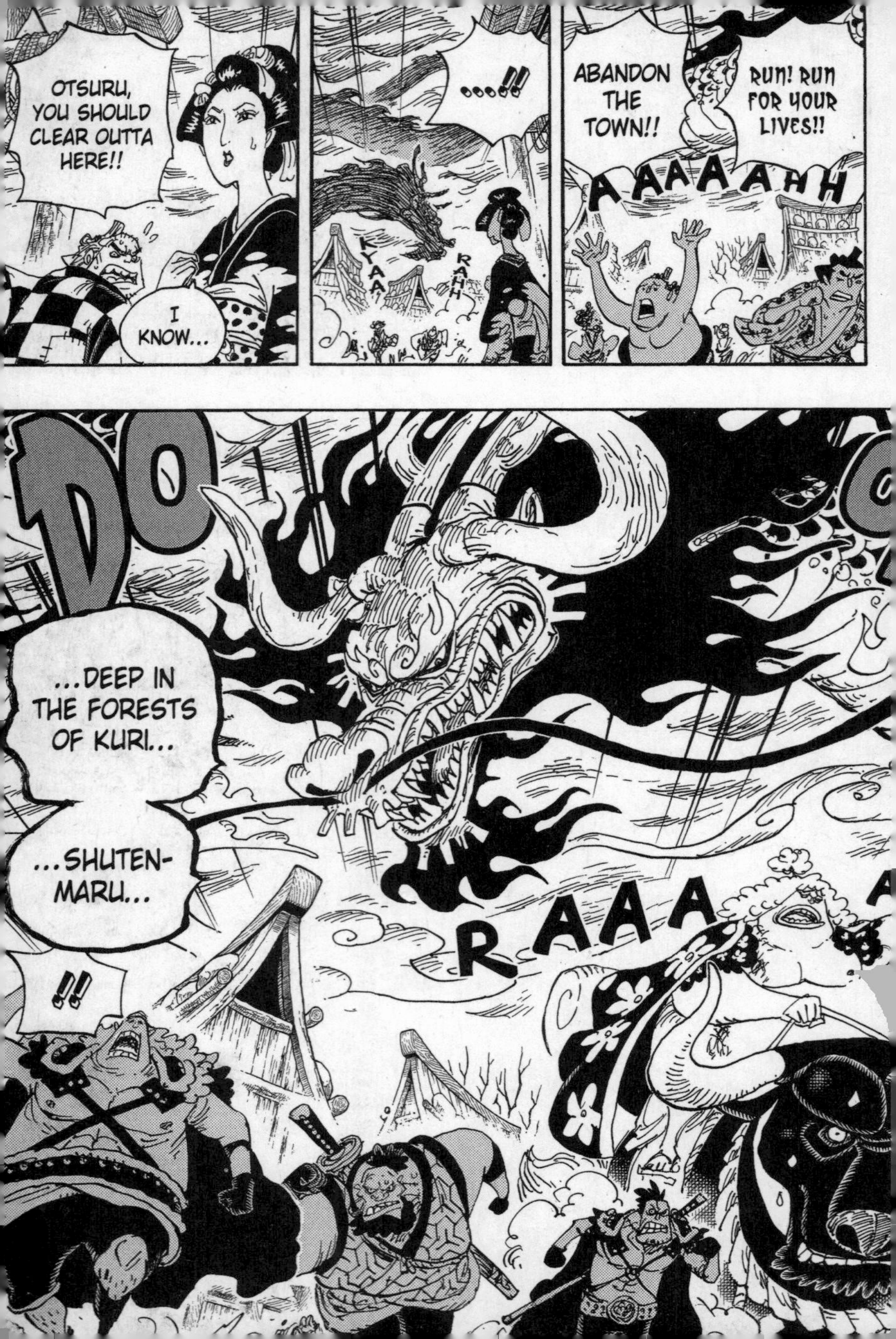
RUN! RUN FOR YOUR LIVES!!
ABANDON THE TOWN!!
AAAAAHH
....!!
KYAA
RAHH
OTSURU, YOU SHOULD CLEAR OUTTA HERE!!
I KNOW...
DO
...DEEP IN THE FORESTS OF KURI...
...SHUTEN-MARU...
!!
RAAA

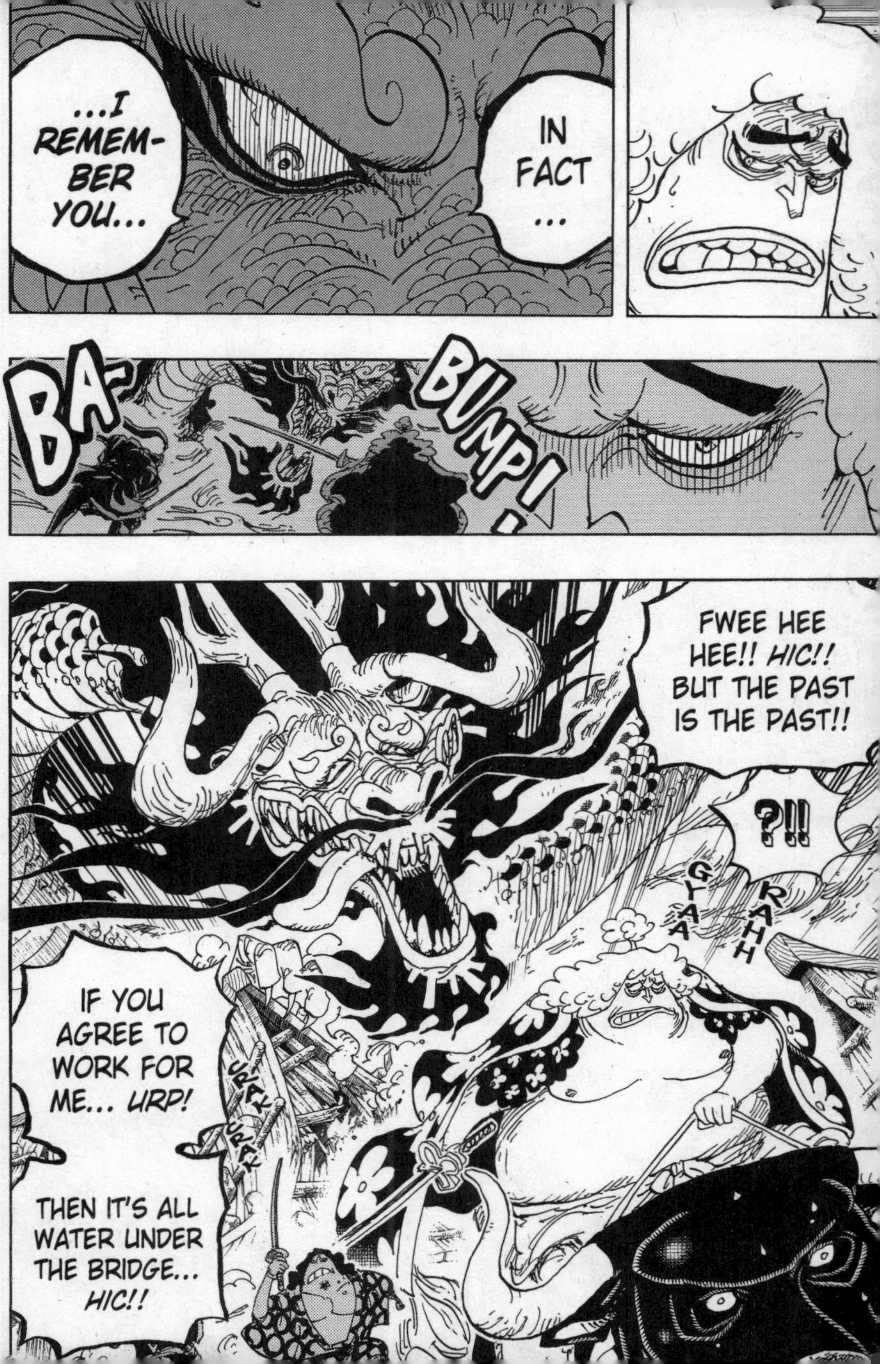
...I REMEMBER YOU...
IN FACT ...
BA-BUMP!!
FWEE HEE HEE!! HIC!! BUT THE PAST IS THE PAST!!
?!!
GYAAA
RAHHH
IF YOU AGREE TO WORK FOR ME... URP!
URAK URAK
THEN IT'S ALL WATER UNDER THE BRIDGE... HIC!!

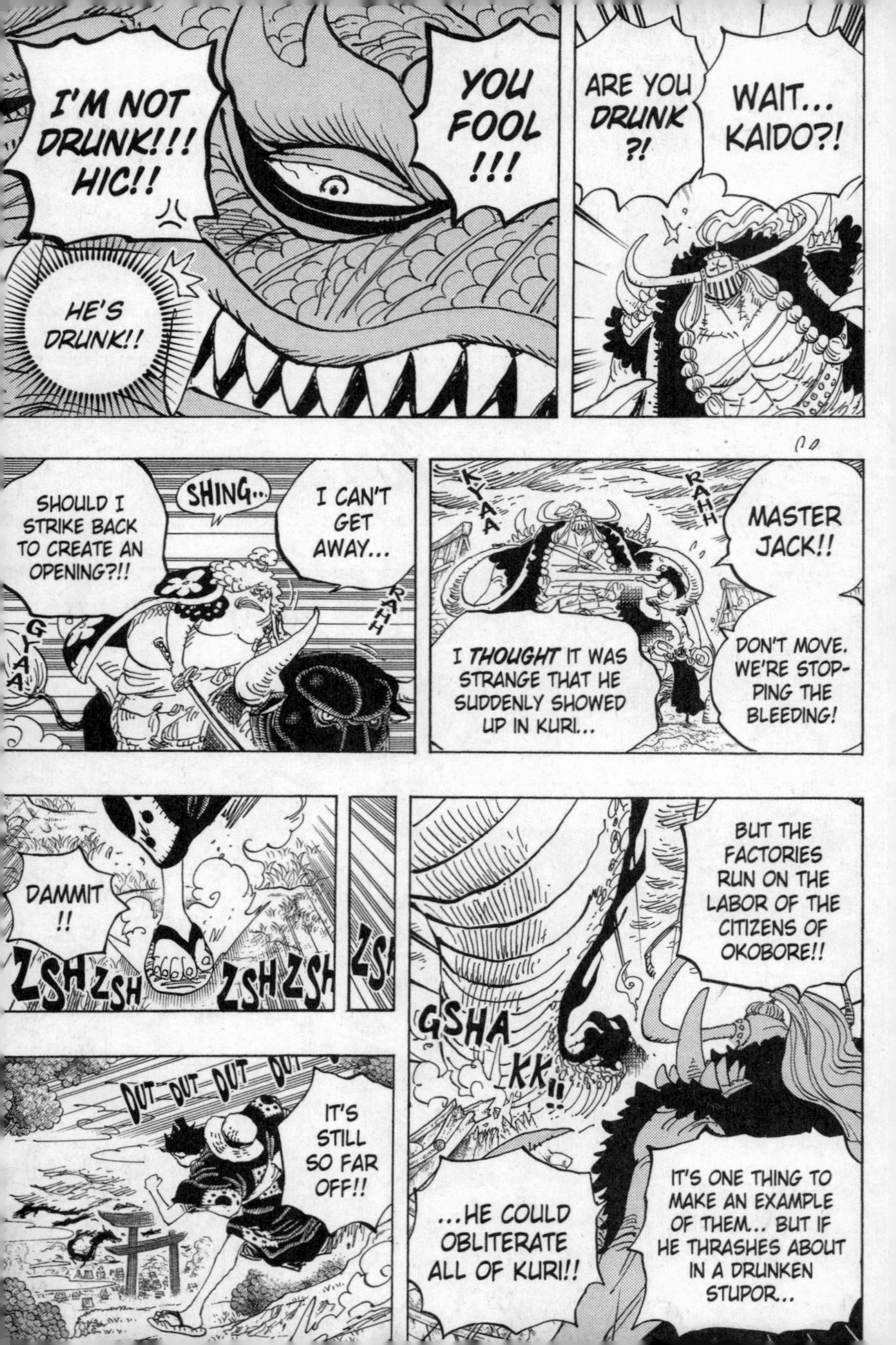
WAIT... KAIDO?!
ARE YOU DRUNK?!
YOU FOOL!!!
I'M NOT DRUNK!!! HIC!!
HE'S DRUNK!!
RAHH
KYAA
MASTER JACK!!
DON'T MOVE. WE'RE STOPPING THE BLEEDING!
I THOUGHT IT WAS STRANGE THAT HE SUDDENLY SHOWED UP IN KURI...
I CAN'T GET AWAY...
SHING...
SHOULD I STRIKE BACK TO CREATE AN OPENING?!!
RAHH
GYAA
BUT THE FACTORIES RUN ON THE LABOR OF THE CITIZENS OF OKOBORE!!
GSHAKK!!
IT'S ONE THING TO MAKE AN EXAMPLE OF THEM.. BUT IF HE THRASHES ABOUT IN A DRUNKEN STUPOR..
...HE COULD OBLITERATE ALL OF KURI!!
ZSH
DAMMIT!!
ZSH ZSH ZSH ZSH
DUT DUT DUT DUT
IT'S STILL SO FAR OFF!!

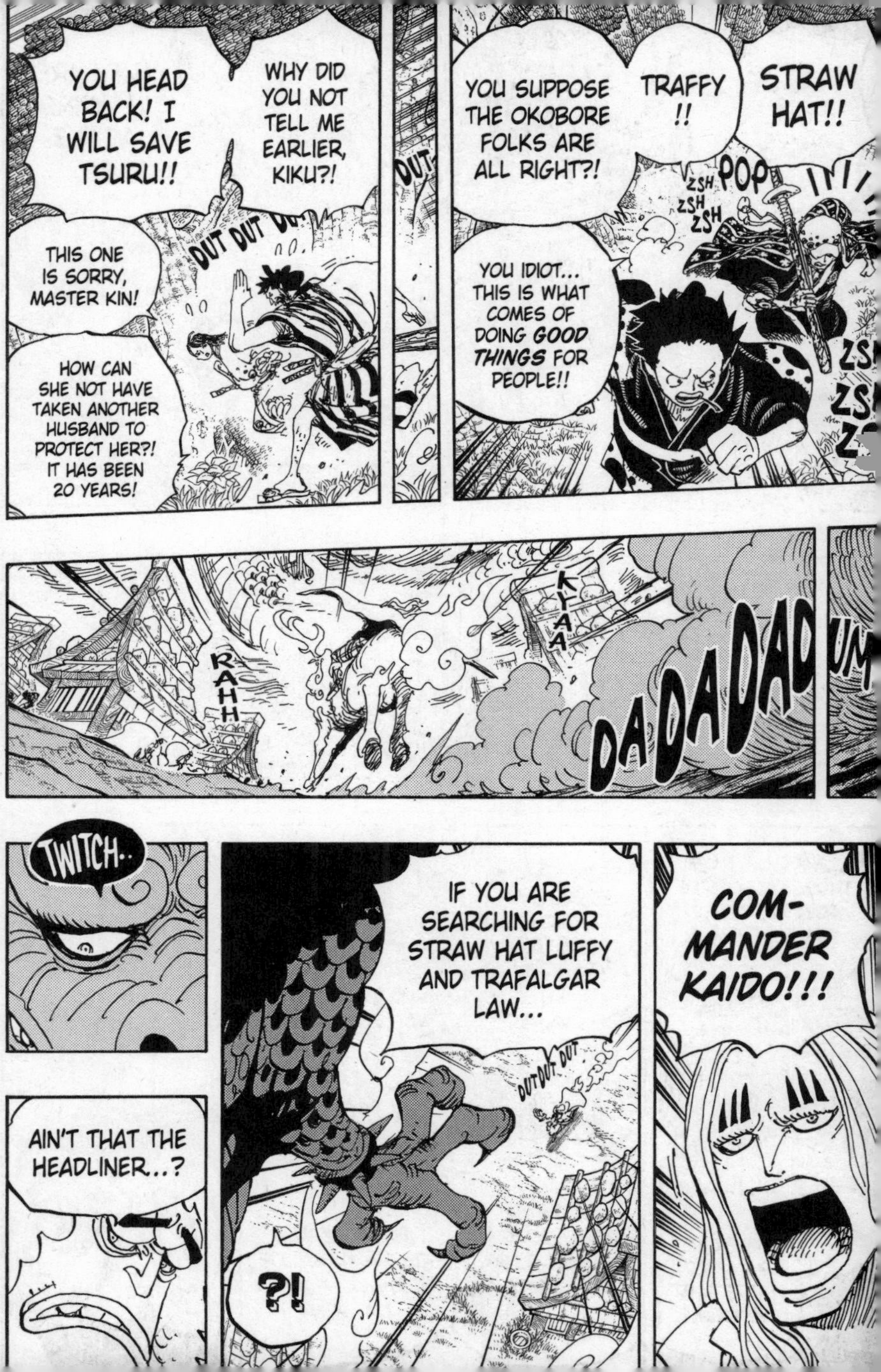
STRAW HAT!!
TRAFFY !!
YOU SUPPOSE THE OKOBORE FOLKS ARE ALL RIGHT?!
POP
ZSH ZSH ZSH
YOU IDIOT... THIS IS WHAT COMES OF DOING GOOD THINGS FOR PEOPLE!!
DUT
WHY DID YOU NOT TELL ME EARLIER, KIKU?!
YOU HEAD BACK! I WILL SAVE TSURU!!
DUT DUT DU
THIS ONE IS SORRY, MASTER KIN!
HOW CAN SHE NOT HAVE TAKEN ANOTHER HUSBAND TO PROTECT HER?! IT HAS BEEN 20 YEARS!
DADADADUM
KYAAA
RAHHH
COM-MANDER KAIDO!!!
IF YOU ARE SEARCHING FOR STRAW HAT LUFFY AND TRAFALGAR LAW...
DUT DUT DUT
?!
TWITCH..
AIN'T THAT THE HEADLINER...?

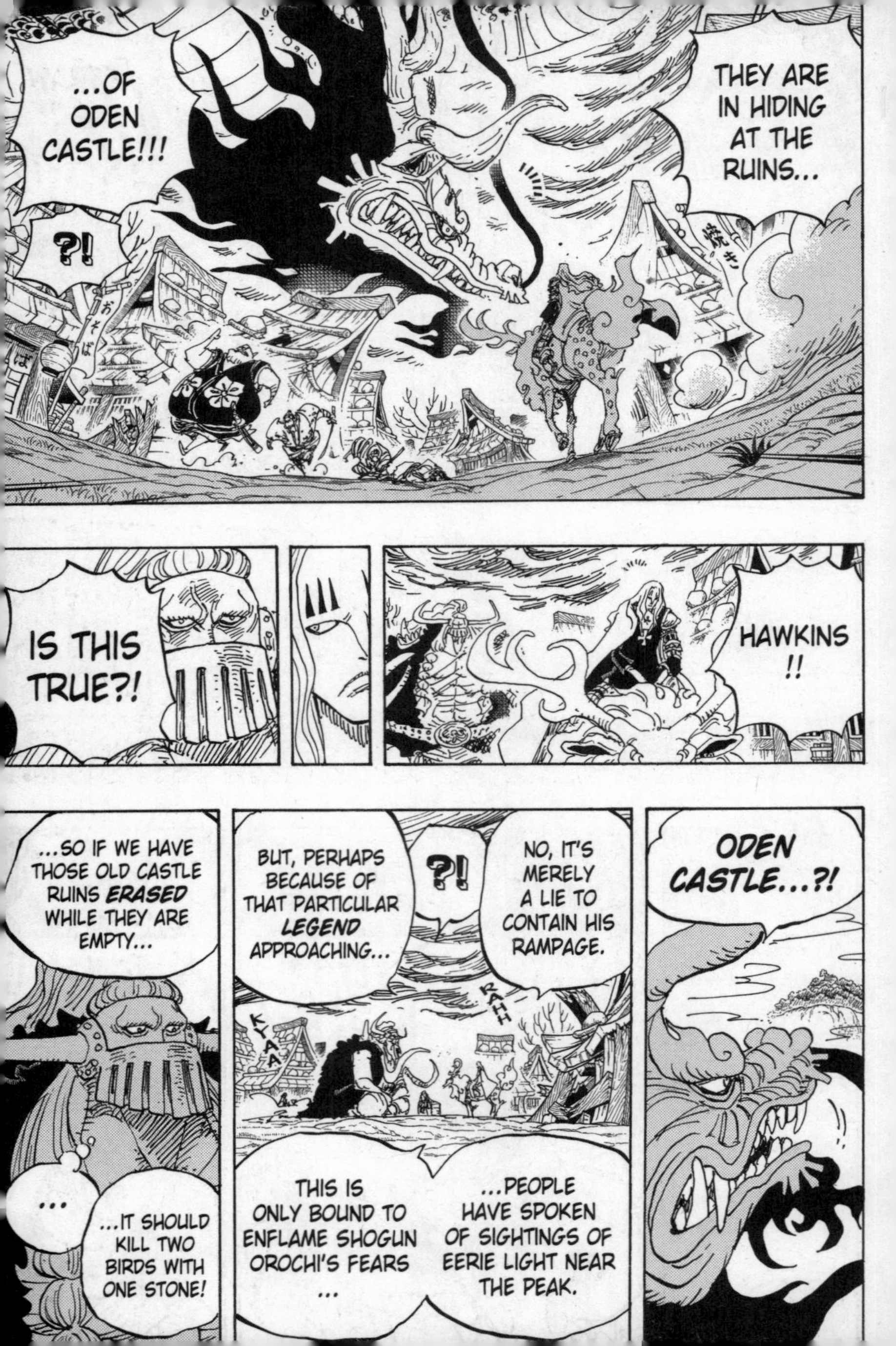

THEY ARE IN HIDING AT THE RUINS...
...OF ODEN CASTLE!!!
?!
HAWKINS !!
IS THIS TRUE?!
ODEN CASTLE...?!
NO, IT'S MERELY A LIE TO CONTAIN HIS RAMPAGE.
?!
BUT, PERHAPS BECAUSE OF THAT PARTICULAR *LEGEND* APPROACHING...
RAHH
KYAA
...PEOPLE HAVE SPOKEN OF SIGHTINGS OF EERIE LIGHT NEAR THE PEAK.
THIS IS ONLY BOUND TO ENFLAME SHOGUN OROCHI'S FEARS ...
...SO IF WE HAVE THOSE OLD CASTLE RUINS *ERASED* WHILE THEY ARE EMPTY...
...
...IT SHOULD KILL TWO BIRDS WITH ONE STONE!

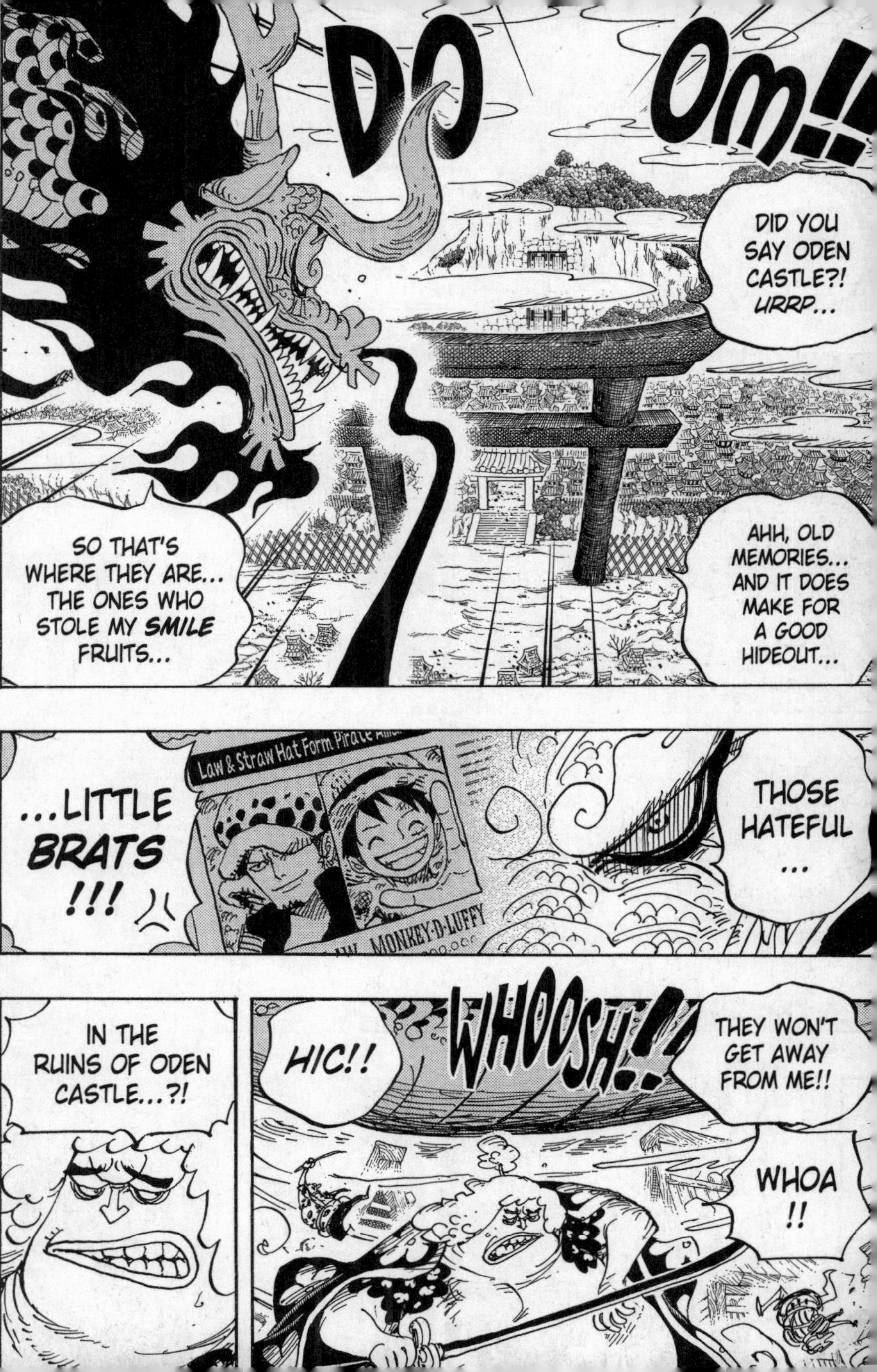
DOOM!!
DID YOU SAY ODEN CASTLE?! URRP...
AHH, OLD MEMORIES... AND IT DOES MAKE FOR A GOOD HIDEOUT...
SO THAT'S WHERE THEY ARE... THE ONES WHO STOLE MY SMILE FRUITS...
THOSE HATEFUL ...
Law & Straw Hat Form Pirate
MONKEY·D·LUFFY
...LITTLE BRATS !!!
THEY WON'T GET AWAY FROM ME!!
WHOOSH!!
HIC!!
WHOA !!
IN THE RUINS OF ODEN CASTLE...?!

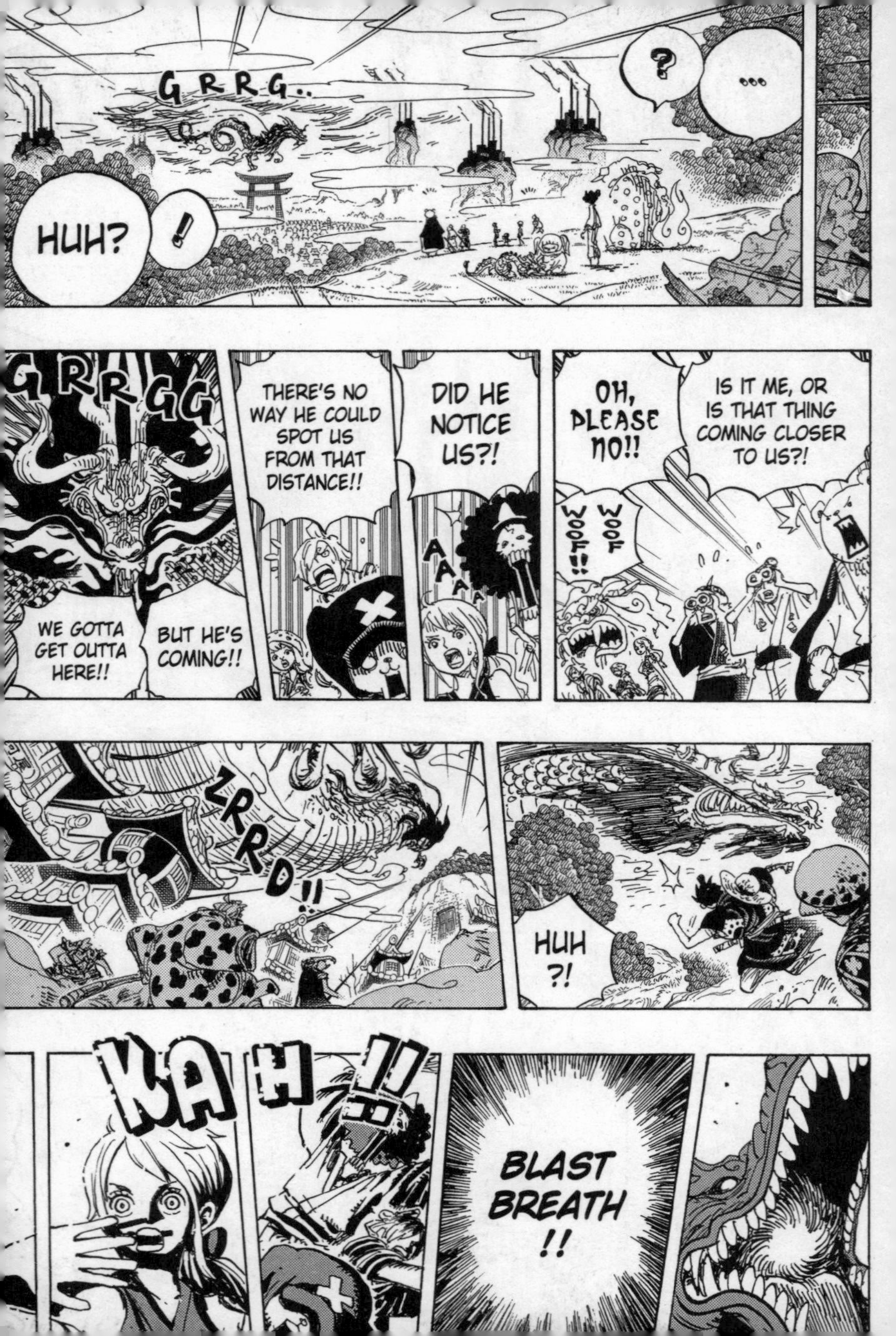
?
...
GRRG..
!
HUH?
IS IT ME, OR IS THAT THING COMING CLOSER TO US?!
OH, PLEASE NO!!
WOOF
WOOF!!
DID HE NOTICE US?!
AAAA
THERE'S NO WAY HE COULD SPOT US FROM THAT DISTANCE!!
GRRRGG
BUT HE'S COMING!!
WE GOTTA GET OUTTA HERE!!
HUH ?!
ZRRRD!!
BLAST BREATH !!
KAH!!

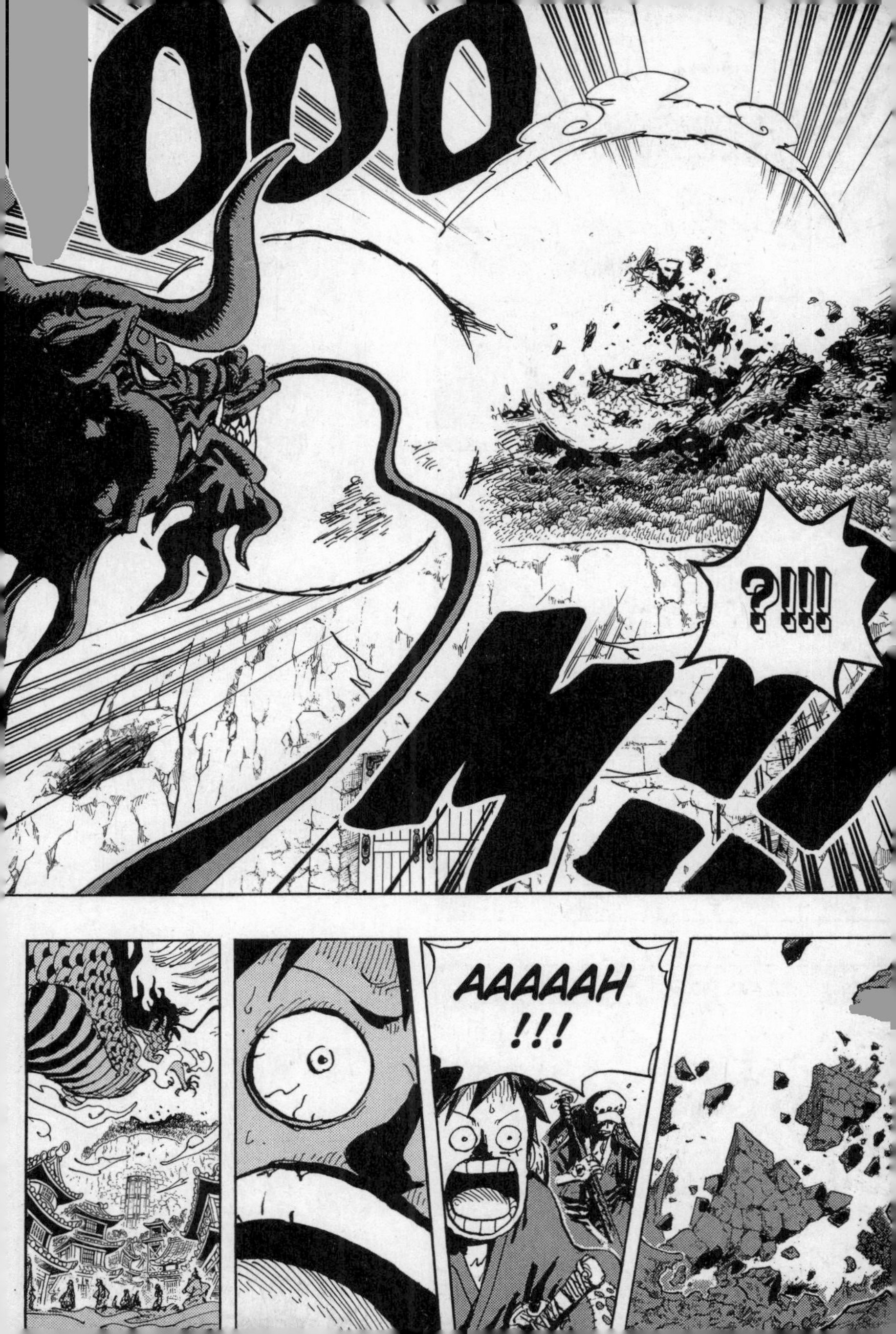
OOO
?!!!
AAAAAH
!!!

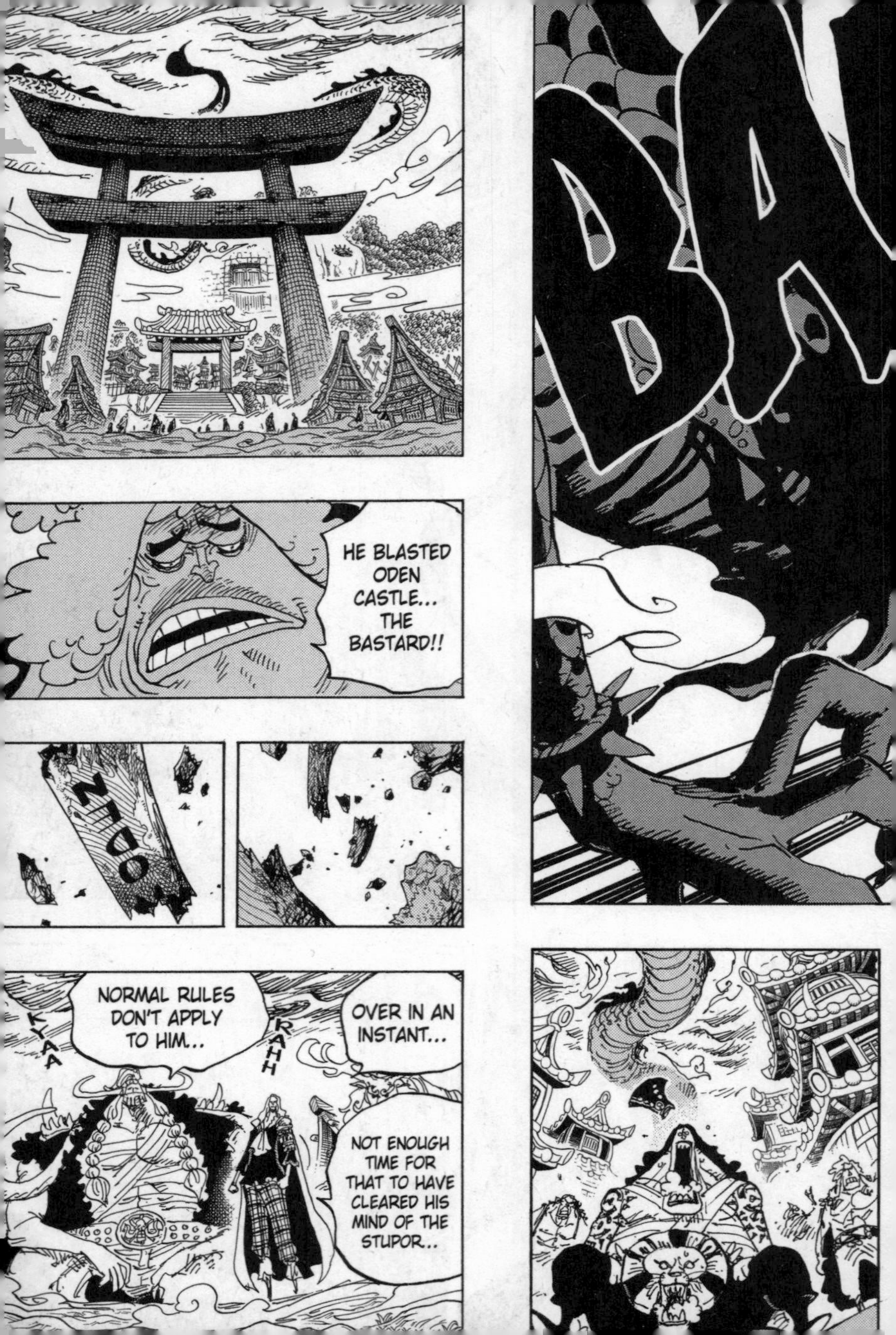
DAN
HE BLASTED ODEN CASTLE... THE BASTARD!!
ODEN
OVER IN AN INSTANT...
NOT ENOUGH TIME FOR THAT TO HAVE CLEARED HIS MIND OF THE STUPOR...
RAHH
NORMAL RULES DON'T APPLY TO HIM...
KYAA

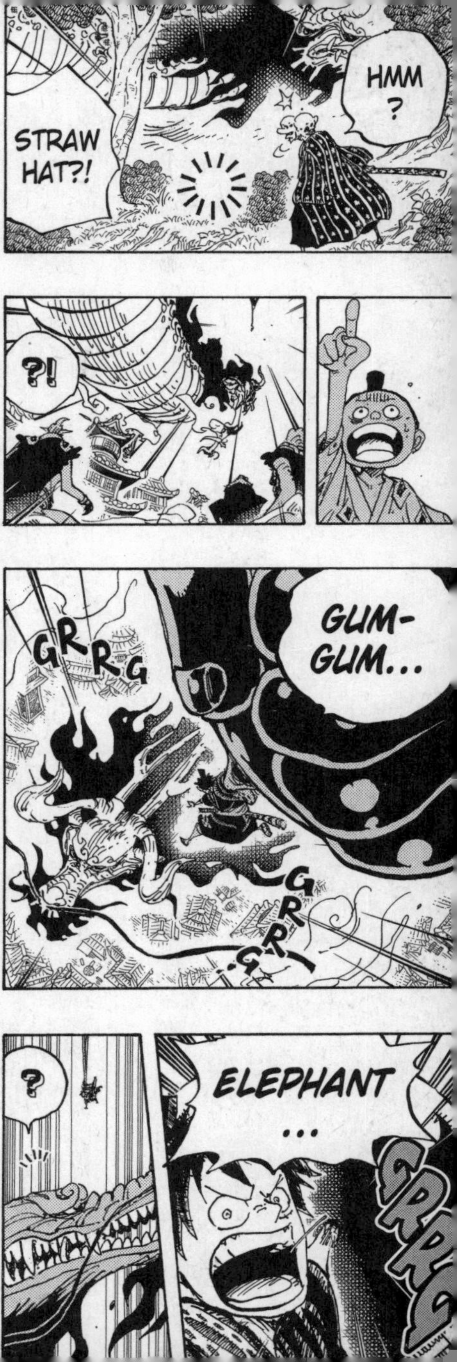
HMM ?
STRAW HAT?!
?!
GUM-GUM...
GRRG
GRRRG
ELEPHANT ...
?

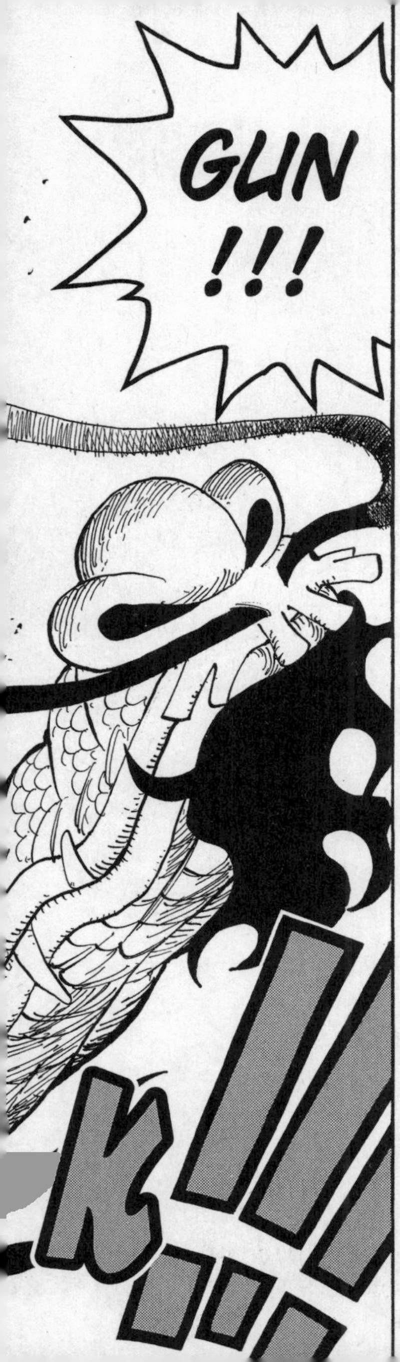
GUN !!!

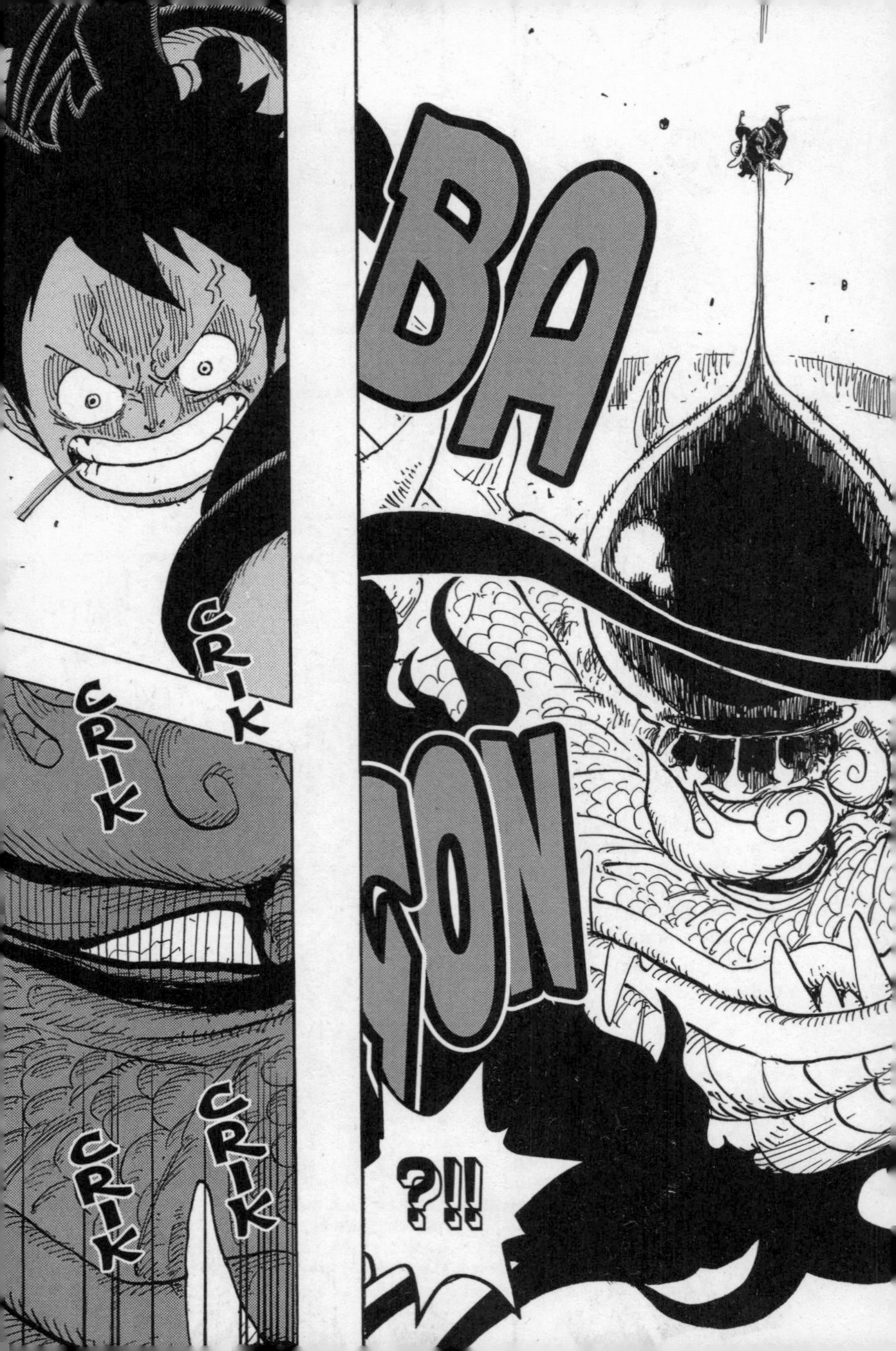

BA
GON
?!!
CRIK
CRIK
CRIK
CRIK

SBS Question Corner

(420 Land, Hong Kong)

A: Ooh, the radio show's starting!

Q: "...with a listener request from a young man by the name of Eiichiro Oda! And the name of the song is Start the SBS...Ssz...szt...zzktzkz...Beeeeep!!"

--Michi Nakahara

A: They started my segment over the radio!!!

Q: My question is, why do you use all those "beng" and "be-beng" sound effects in Wano?

--Be-be-beng

A: It's different, right? Before I would only write "doom" or "boom" or "da-doom." In my mind, it's the sound of a stringed instrument called the Biwa. But in the art, the character is playing a shamisen, which is a bit lighter-sounding. I'm hoping that in the anime, they'll find a way to blend the sounds a bit. I'm looking at you, Toei!!

Q: Normally, the women you draw have rather large breasts, but when the women of Wano are in kimonos, it's not noticeable at all, right? Are you saying Japanese women don't need to have a large chest??

--Chi-chan

A: As a matter of fact, I didn't know much about the kimono in the past, and drew a woman wearing one with the chest accentuated, like I usually do, and I got a letter from a reader who was a professional when it comes to kimonos. They taught me that the beauty of the kimono's form is in smoothing out the curves to form a graceful silhouette, even for people with large chests. Of course, people are free to wear them how they like, but since I learned how to appreciate the ideal beauty of the kimono, I've been drawing them without accentuating the chest! Trust me, she's still got it underneath!!

24

Chapter 923:
EMPEROR OF THE SEA KAIDO VS. LUFFY

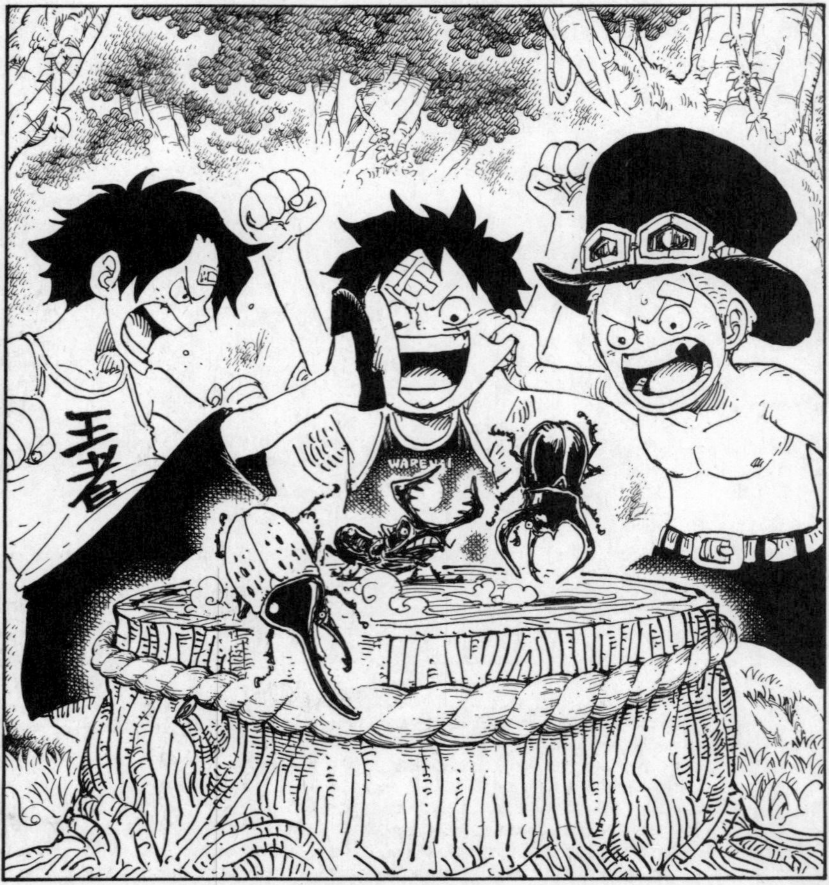
王者
*RULER

REQUEST: "CHILD LUFFY, ACE AND SABO HAVING A CONTEST WITH ATLAS, HERCULES AND MIYAMA BEETLES" BY HONEY LICKER

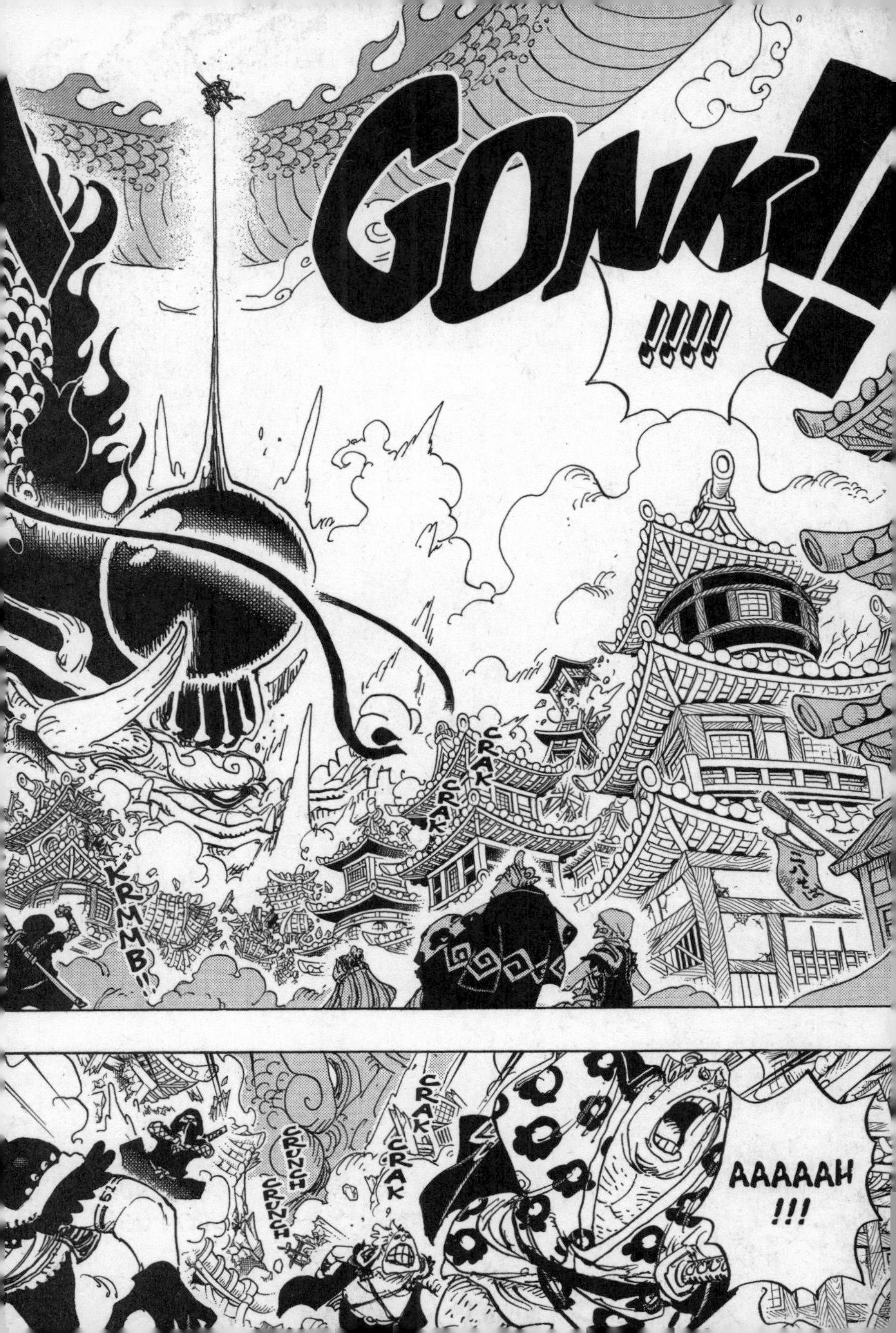
GONK!!
!!!!
CRAK
CRAK
KRMMB!!
AAAAAH!!!
CRAK
CRAK
CRUNCH
CRUNCH

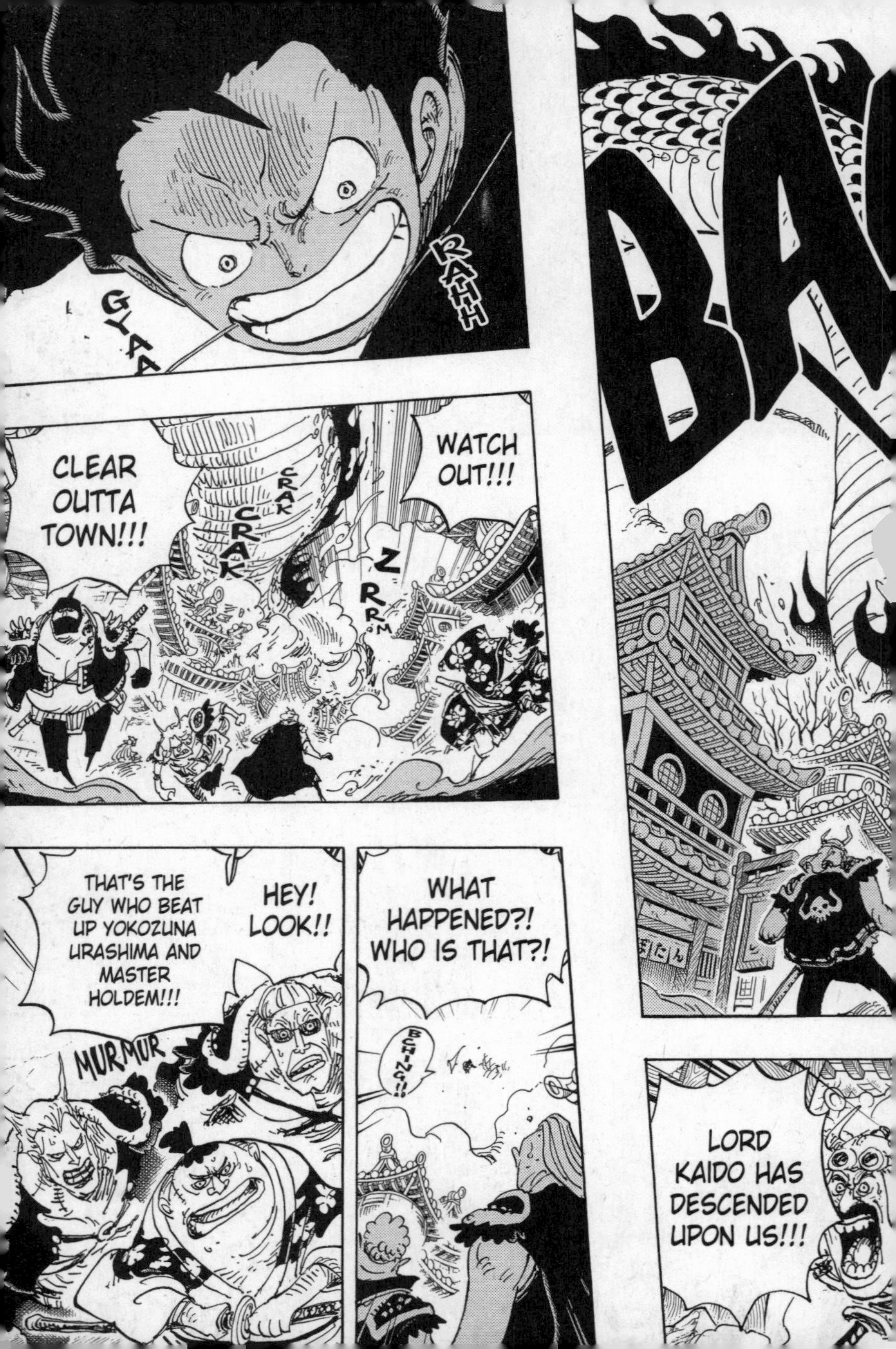
BA
RAAHH
GYAA
WATCH OUT!!!
CRAK
CRAK
CLEAR OUTTA TOWN!!!
ZRRROM
LORD KAIDO HAS DESCENDED UPON US!!!
WHAT HAPPENED?! WHO IS THAT?!
BCHING!!
HEY! LOOK!!
THAT'S THE GUY WHO BEAT UP YOKOZUNA URASHIMA AND MASTER HOLDEM!!!
MURMUR

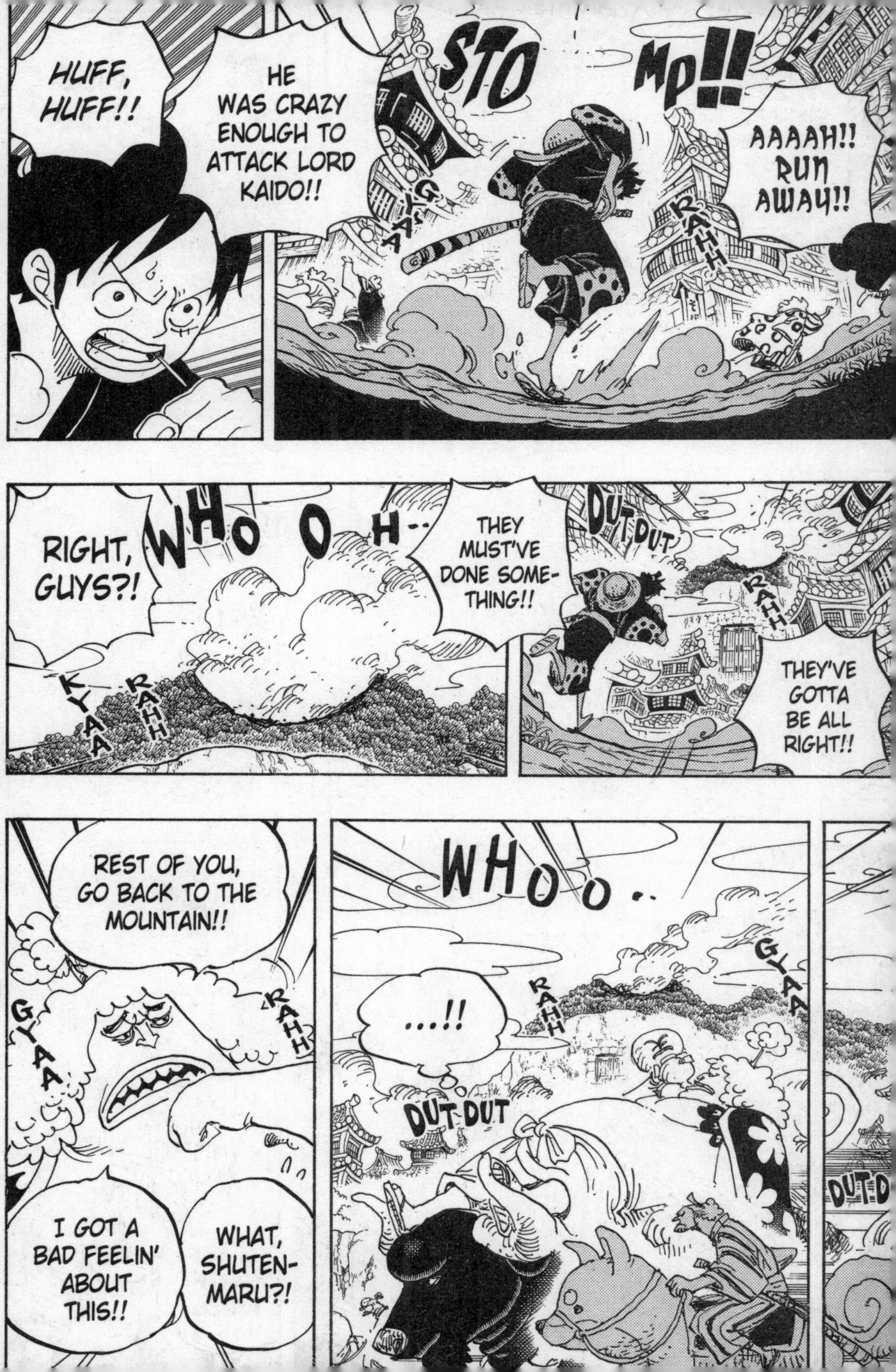
STOMP!!
AAAAH!! RUN AWAY!!
RAHH
GYAA
HE WAS CRAZY ENOUGH TO ATTACK LORD KAIDO!!
HUFF, HUFF!!
DUT DUT
RAHH
THEY'VE GOTTA BE ALL RIGHT!!
THEY MUST'VE DONE SOME-THING!!
WHOOOH..
RIGHT, GUYS?!
RAHH
KYAA
DUT D
WHOOO..
GYAA
RAHH
...!!
DUT DUT
REST OF YOU, GO BACK TO THE MOUNTAIN!!
RAHH
GYAA
WHAT, SHUTEN-MARU?!
I GOT A BAD FEELIN' ABOUT THIS!!

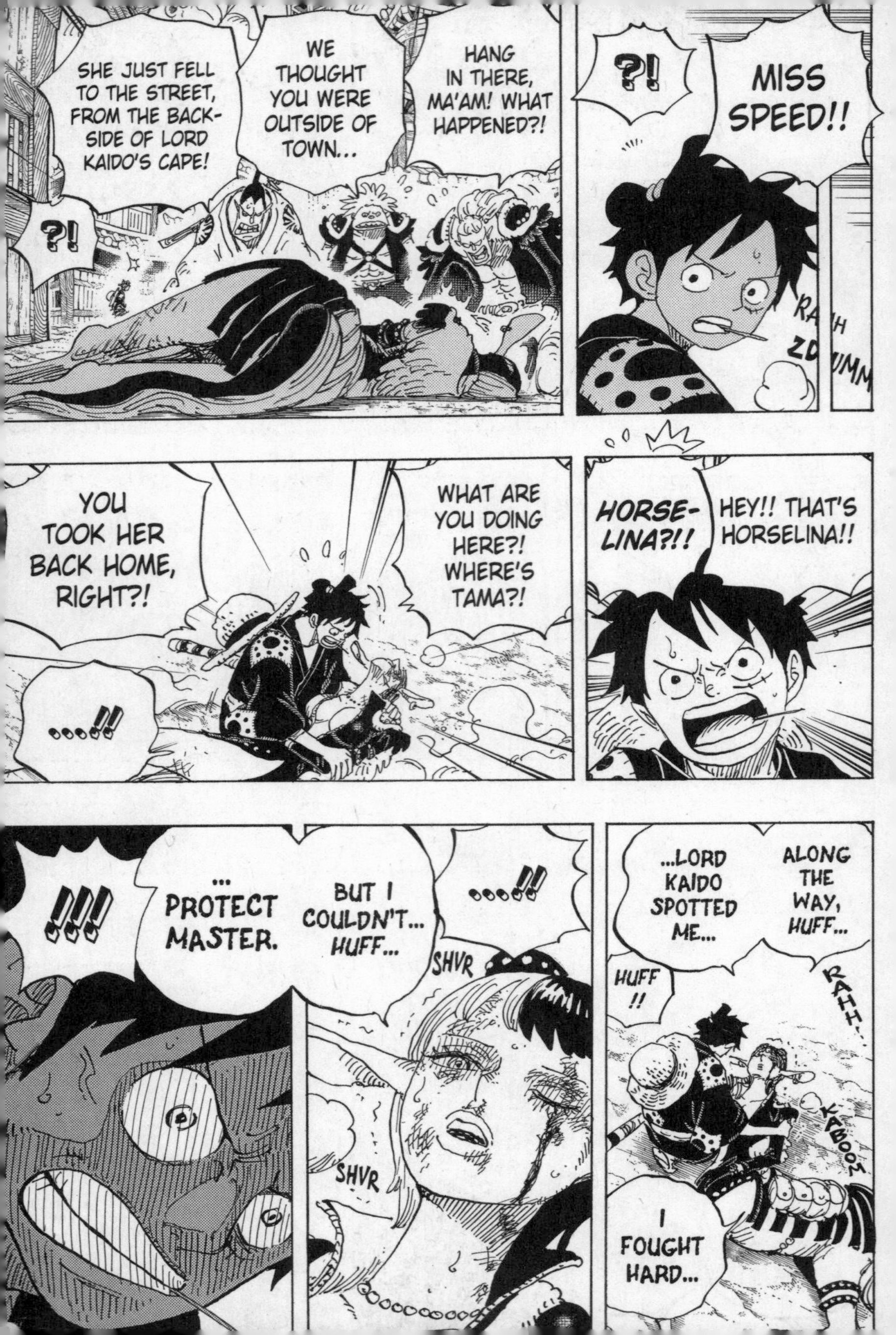
?!
MISS SPEED!!
HANG IN THERE, MA'AM! WHAT HAPPENED?!
WE THOUGHT YOU WERE OUTSIDE OF TOWN...
SHE JUST FELL TO THE STREET, FROM THE BACK-SIDE OF LORD KAIDO'S CAPE!
?!
HEY!! THAT'S HORSELINA!!
HORSE-LINA?!!
WHAT ARE YOU DOING HERE?! WHERE'S TAMA?!
YOU TOOK HER BACK HOME, RIGHT?!
...!!
ALONG THE WAY, HUFF...
...LORD KAIDO SPOTTED ME...
HUFF !!
RAHH
KABOOM
I FOUGHT HARD...
...!!
SHVR
BUT I COULDN'T... HUFF...
SHVR
... PROTECT MASTER.
!!!

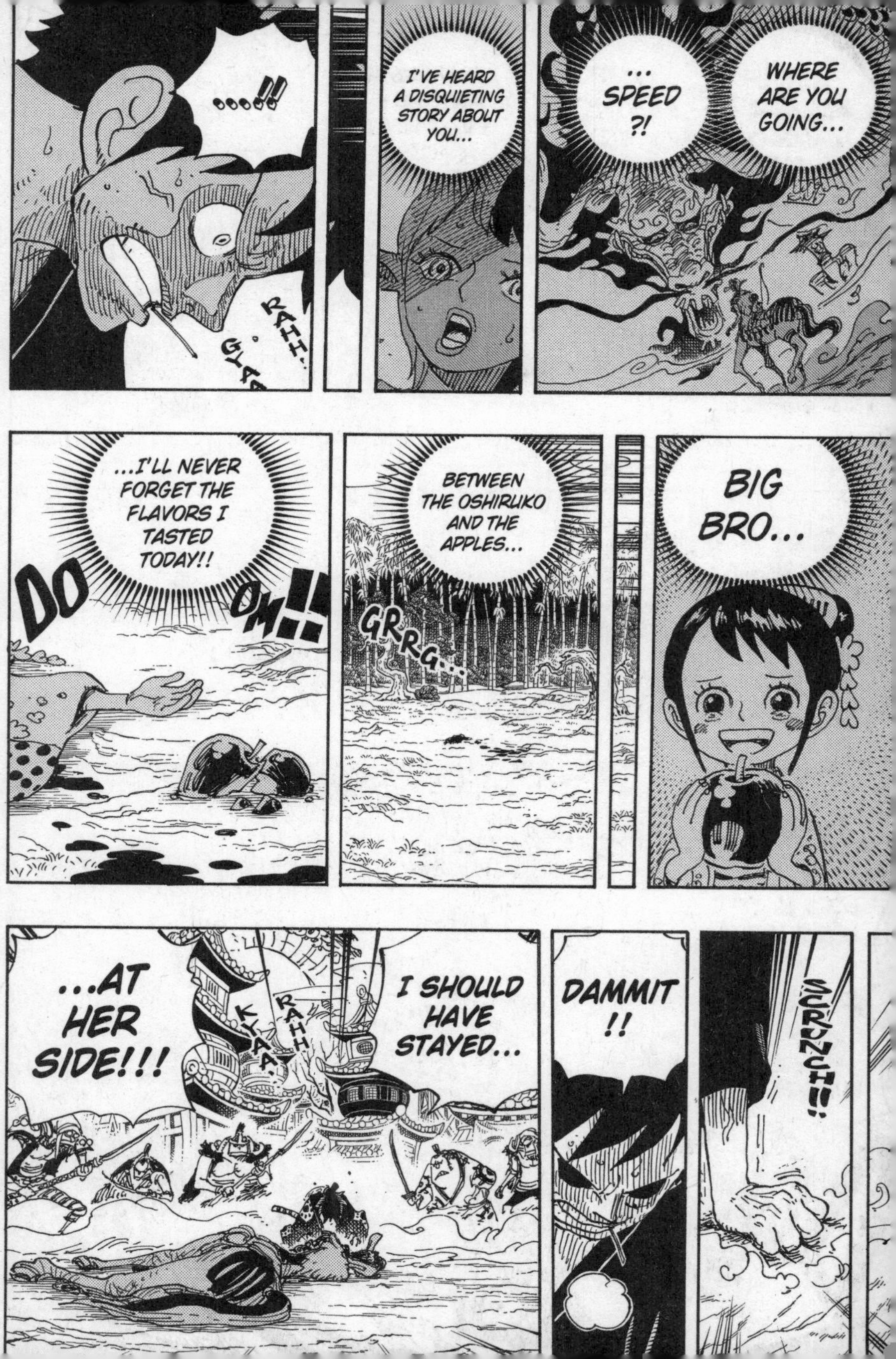
WHERE ARE YOU GOING...
...SPEED?!
I'VE HEARD A DISQUIETING STORY ABOUT YOU...
.....!!
RAHH
GYAA
BIG BRO...
BETWEEN THE OSHIRUKO AND THE APPLES...
GRRG...
...I'LL NEVER FORGET THE FLAVORS I TASTED TODAY!!
DOOM!!
SCRUNCH!!
DAMMIT!!
I SHOULD HAVE STAYED...
...AT HER SIDE!!!
RAHH
KYAA

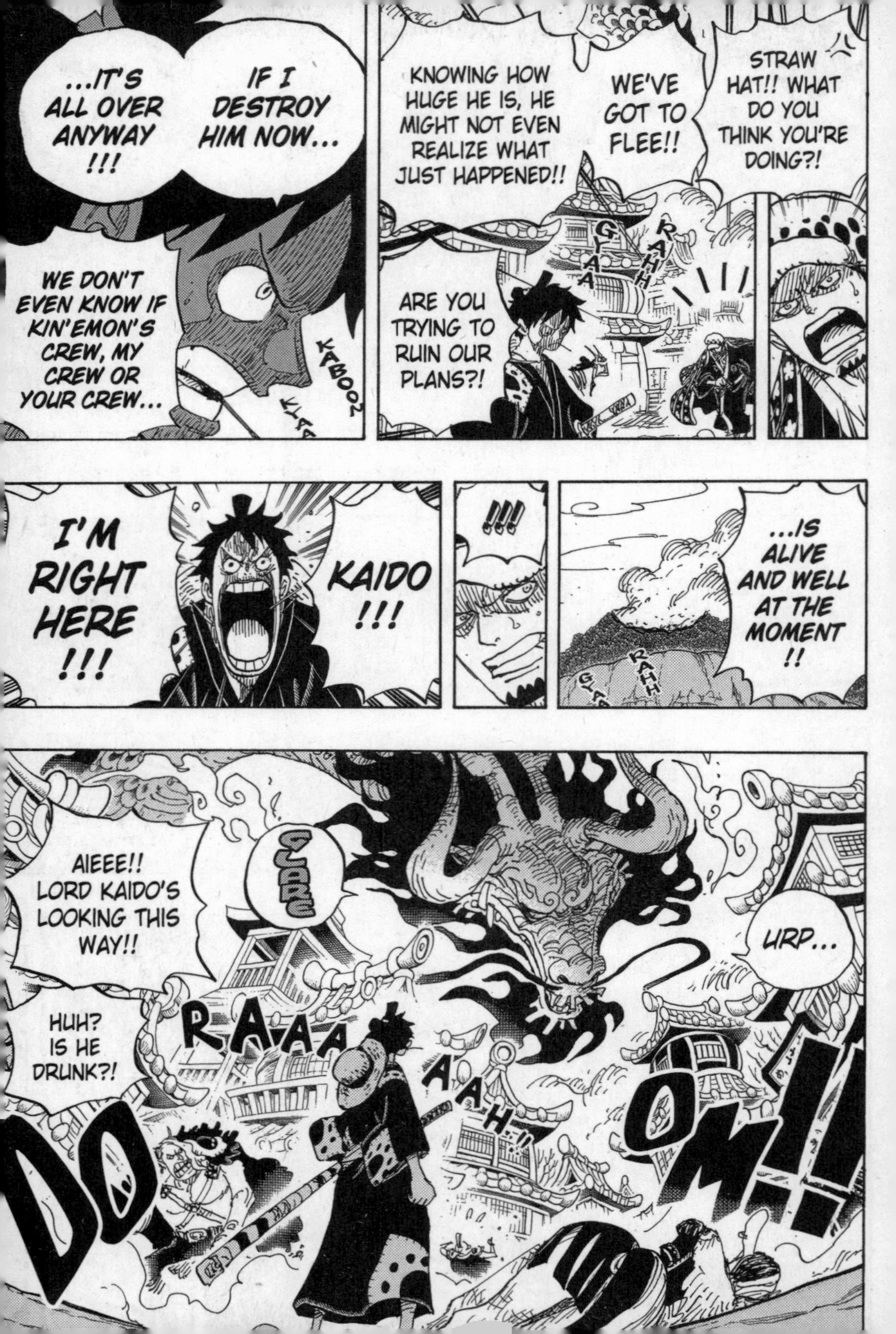
STRAW HAT!! WHAT DO YOU THINK YOU'RE DOING?!
WE'VE GOT TO FLEE!!
KNOWING HOW HUGE HE IS, HE MIGHT NOT EVEN REALIZE WHAT JUST HAPPENED!!
RAHH
GYAA
ARE YOU TRYING TO RUIN OUR PLANS?!
IF I DESTROY HIM NOW...
...IT'S ALL OVER ANYWAY !!!
KABOOM
WE DON'T EVEN KNOW IF KIN'EMON'S CREW, MY CREW OR YOUR CREW...
...IS ALIVE AND WELL AT THE MOMENT !!
RAHH
!!!
KAIDO !!!
I'M RIGHT HERE !!!
URP...
GLARE
AIEEE!! LORD KAIDO'S LOOKING THIS WAY!!
HUH? IS HE DRUNK?!
RAAAAAH!!
DOOM!!

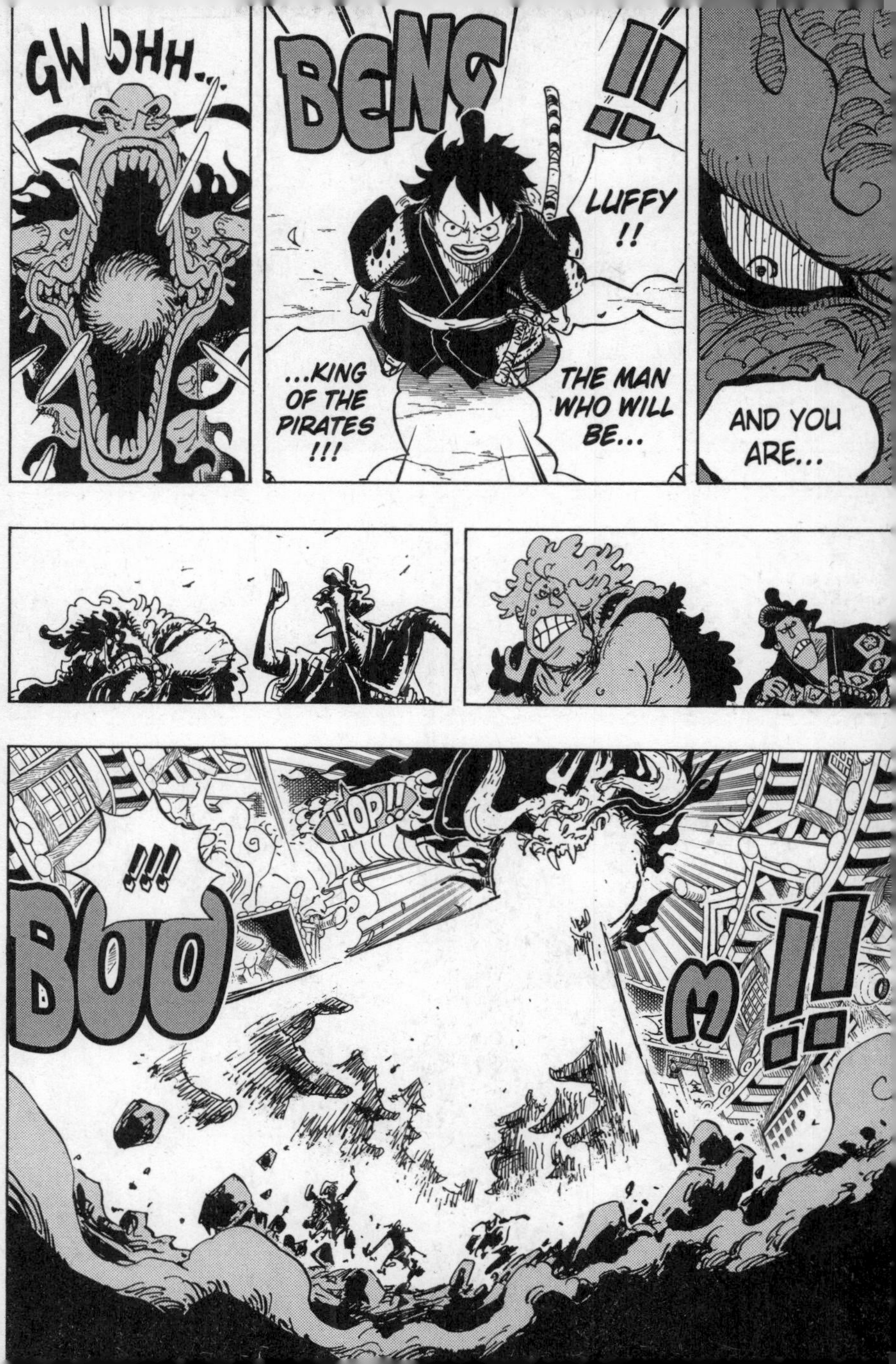
AND YOU ARE...
BENG!!
LUFFY !!
THE MAN WHO WILL BE...
...KING OF THE PIRATES !!!
GWOHH...
HOP!!
!!!
BOOM!!

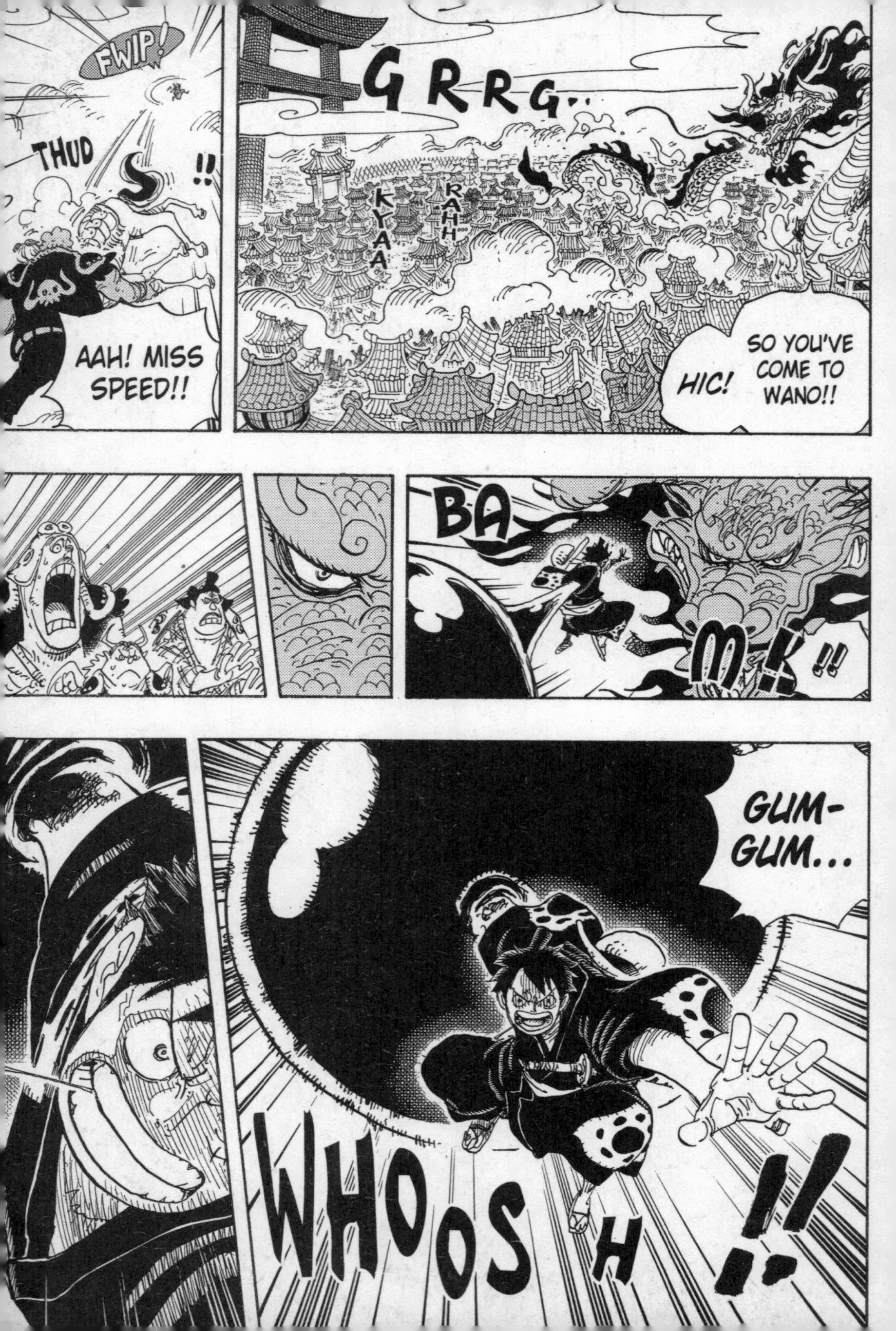
GRRG..
KYAA
RAHH...
SO YOU'VE COME TO WANO!!
HIC!
FWIP!
THUD
!!
AAH! MISS SPEED!!
BA
MK!!
GUM-GUM...
WHOOSH!!

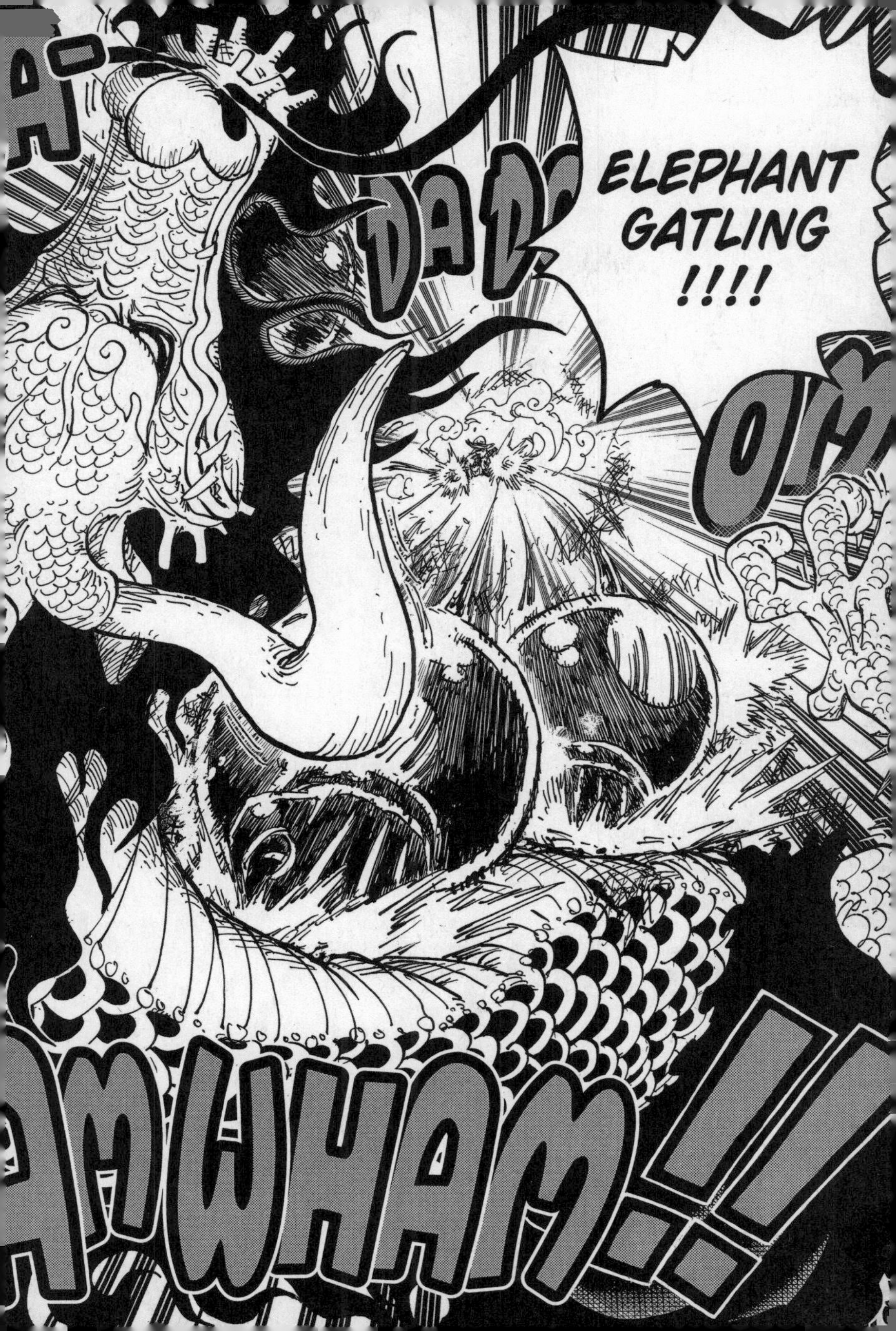
ELEPHANT
GATLING
!!!!
DA
WHAM!!

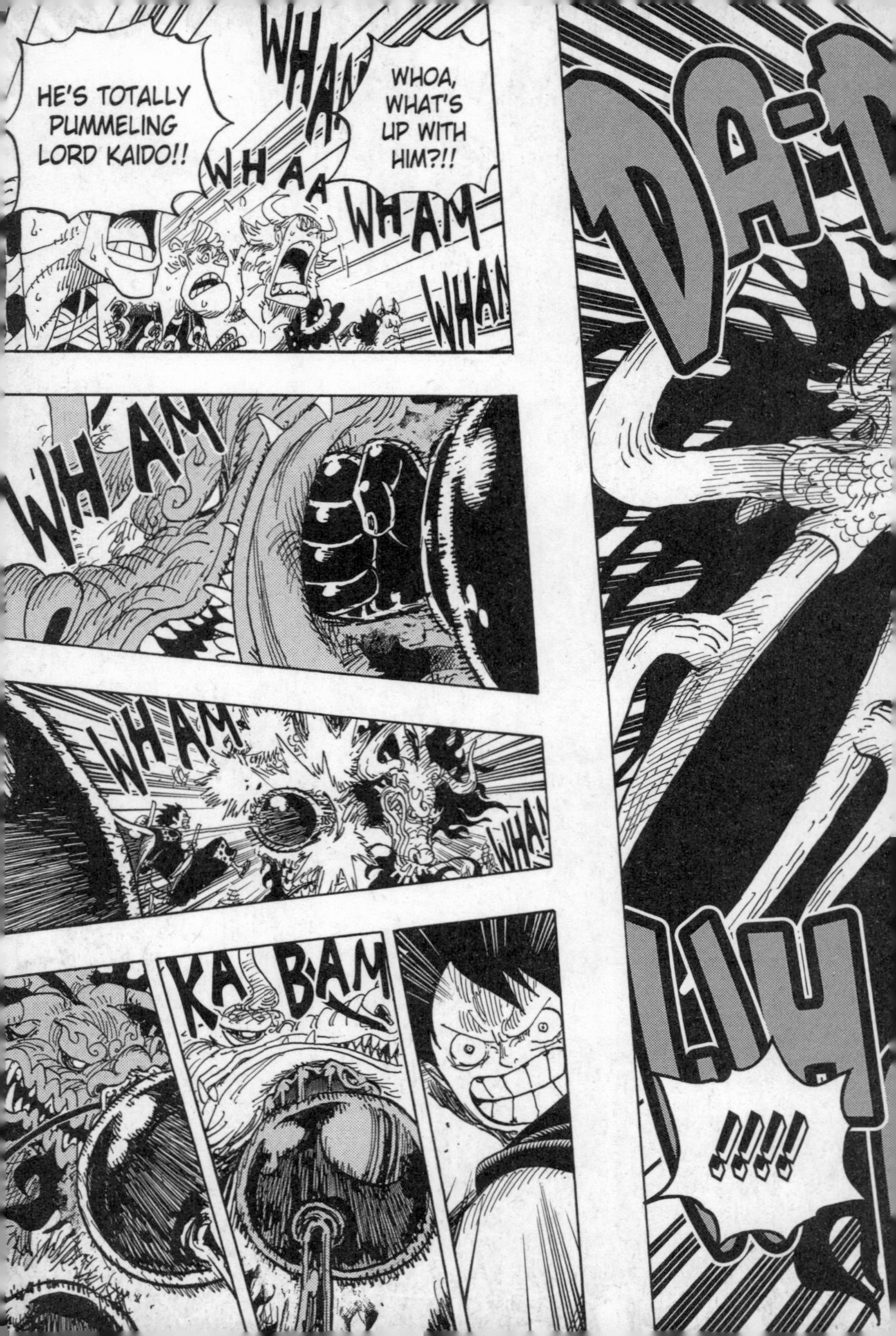
!!!!
WHOA, WHAT'S UP WITH HIM?!!
HE'S TOTALLY PUMMELING LORD KAIDO!!
WHAM
WHAM
WHAM
KA-BAM

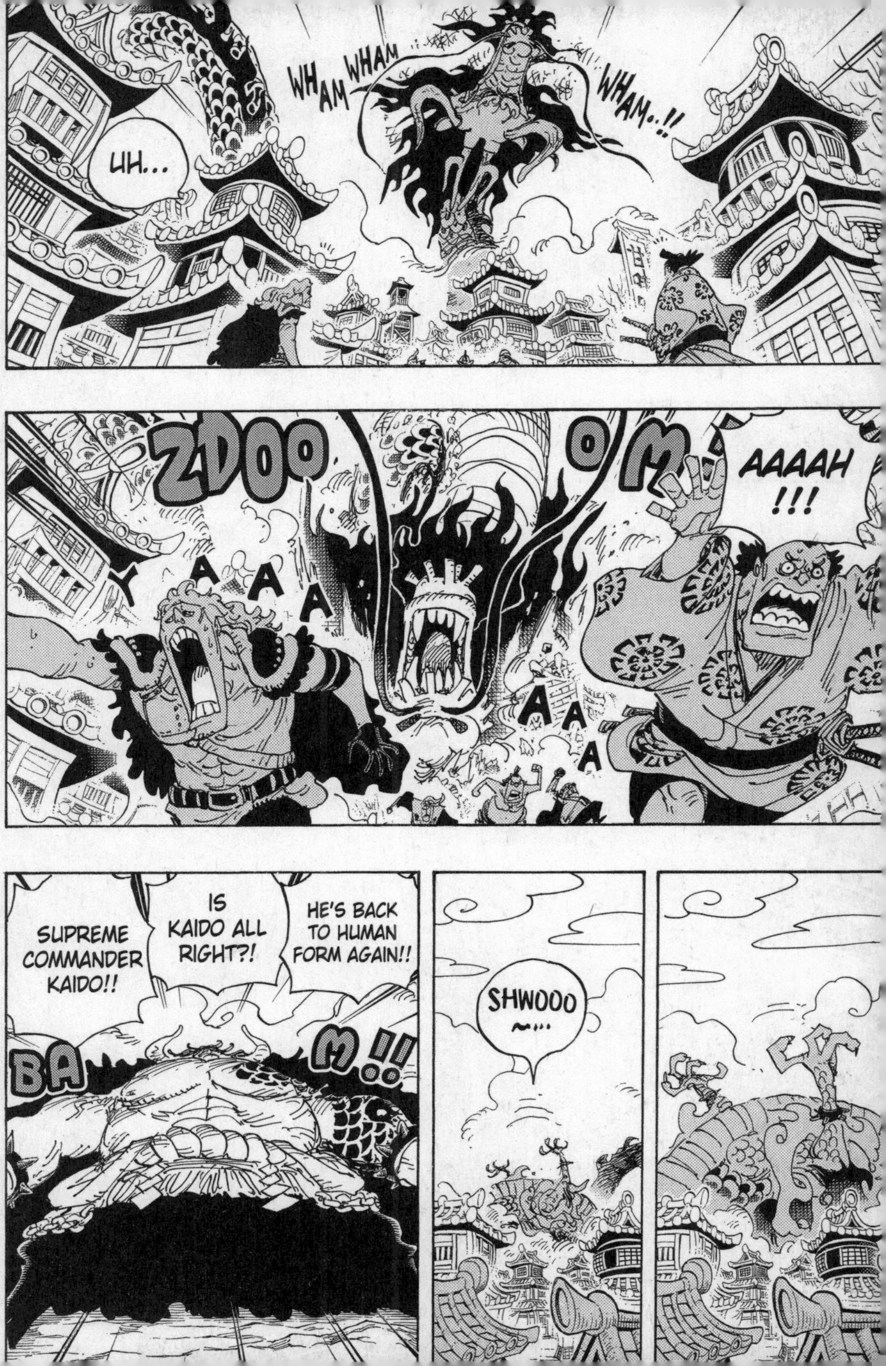
WHAM..!!
WHAM WHAM
UH...
AAAAH!!!
ZDOOOM
AAA
AAA
SHWOOO ~...
HE'S BACK TO HUMAN FORM AGAIN!!
IS KAIDO ALL RIGHT?!
SUPREME COMMANDER KAIDO!!
BAM!!

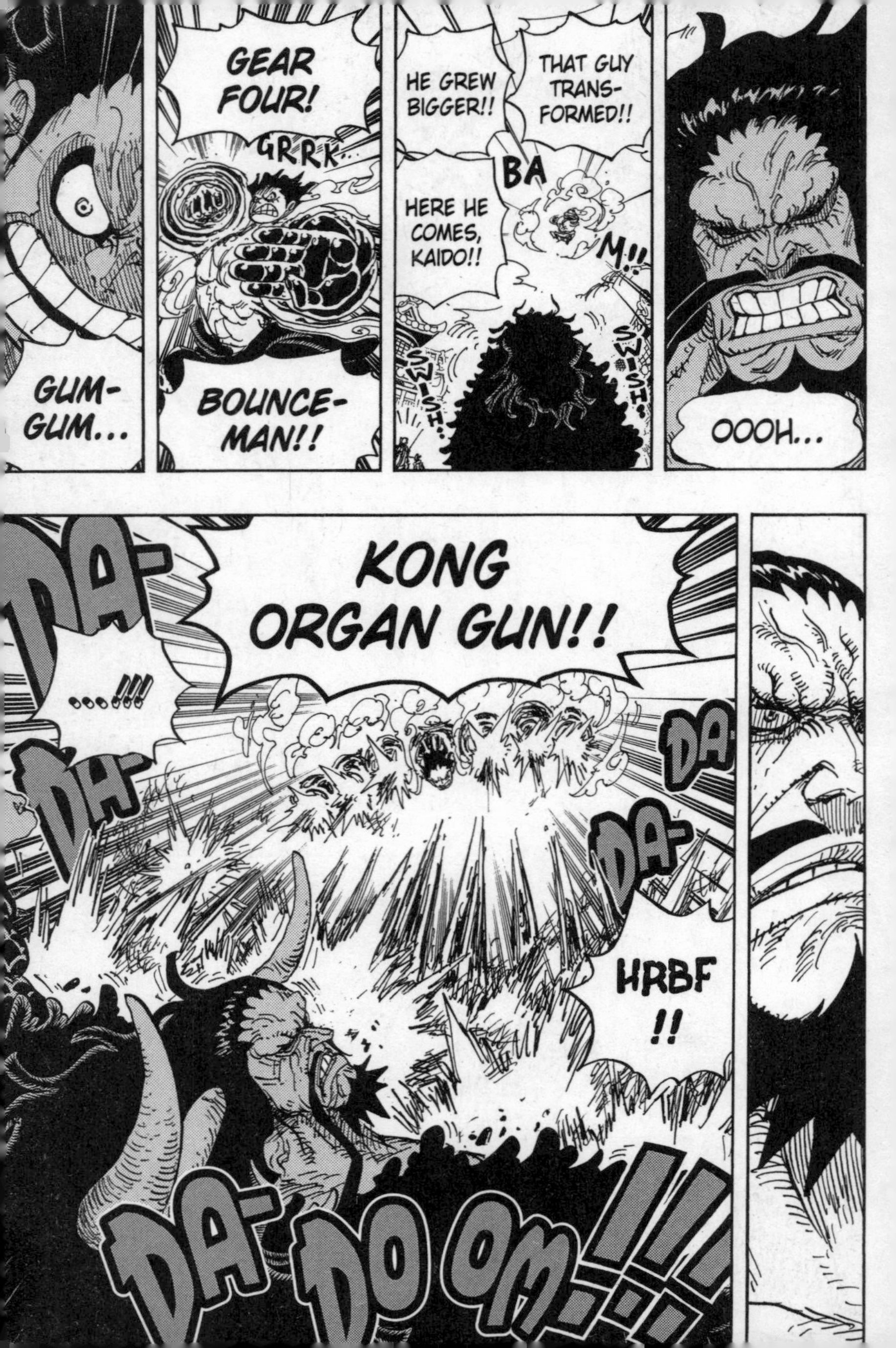
OOOH...
THAT GUY TRANS-FORMED!!
HE GREW BIGGER!!
BA
M!!
HERE HE COMES, KAIDO!!
SWISH!
SWISH!
GEAR FOUR!
GRRK
BOUNCE-MAN!!
GUM-GUM...
KONG ORGAN GUN!!
DA-
DA-
DA-
...!!!
DA-
HRBF !!
DA-DO OM!!!

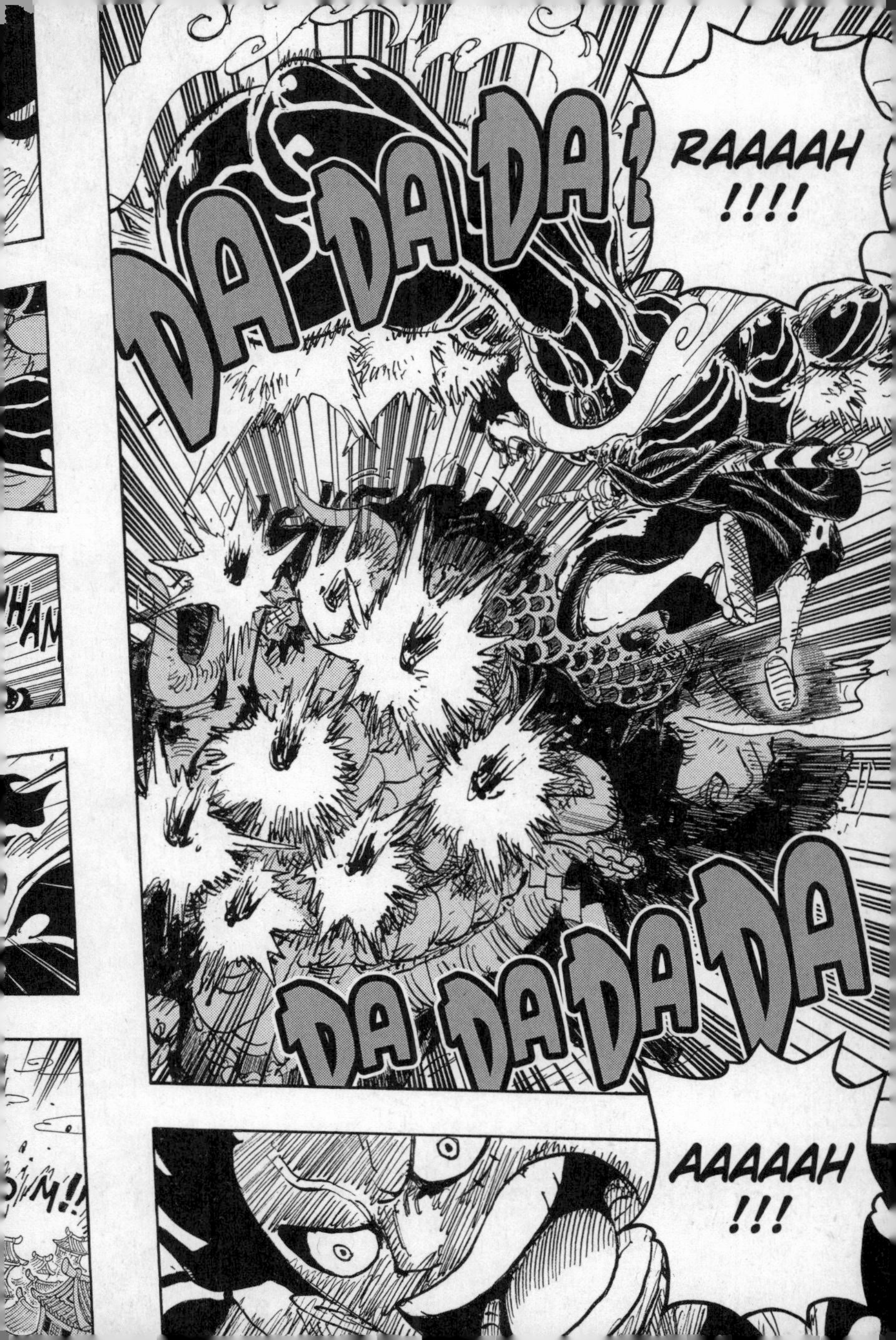
RAAAAH !!!!
DA DA DA!
DA DA DA DA
AAAAAH !!!

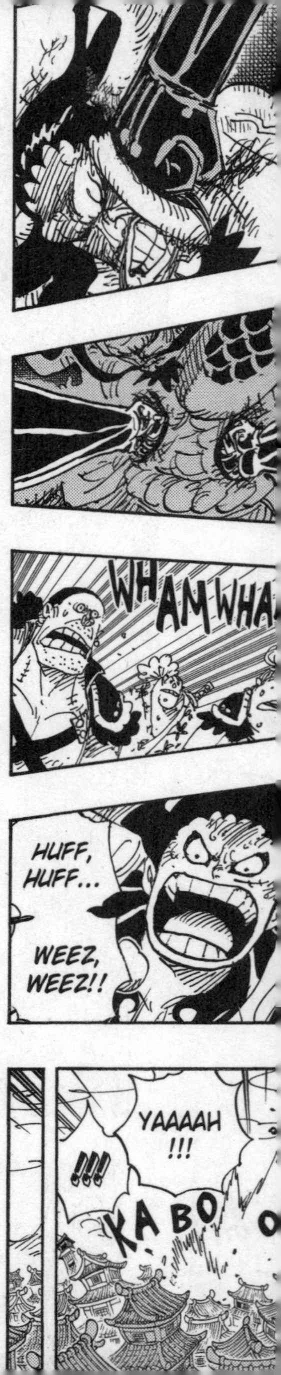
WHAM WHA
HUFF, HUFF...
WEEZ, WEEZ!!
YAAAAH !!!
!!!
KA BO
O

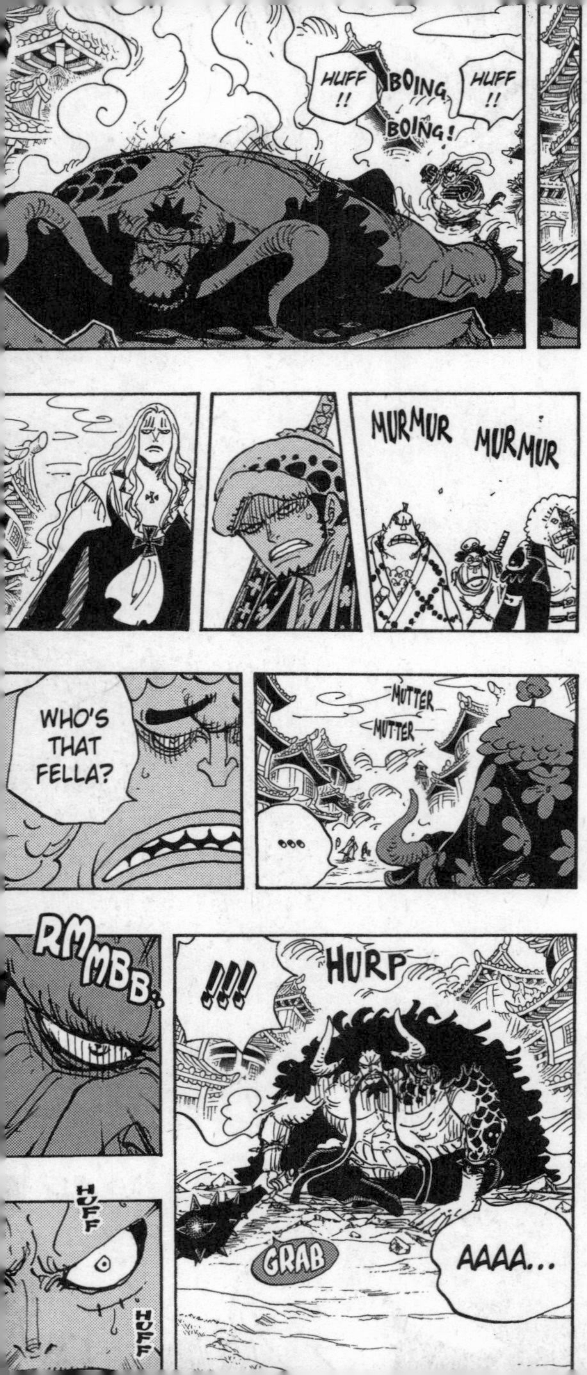
HUFF !!
BOING BOING!
HUFF !!
MURMUR
MURMUR
MUTTER
MUTTER
...
WHO'S THAT FELLA?
HURP
!!!
AAAA...
GRAB
RMMBB..
HUFF
HUFF

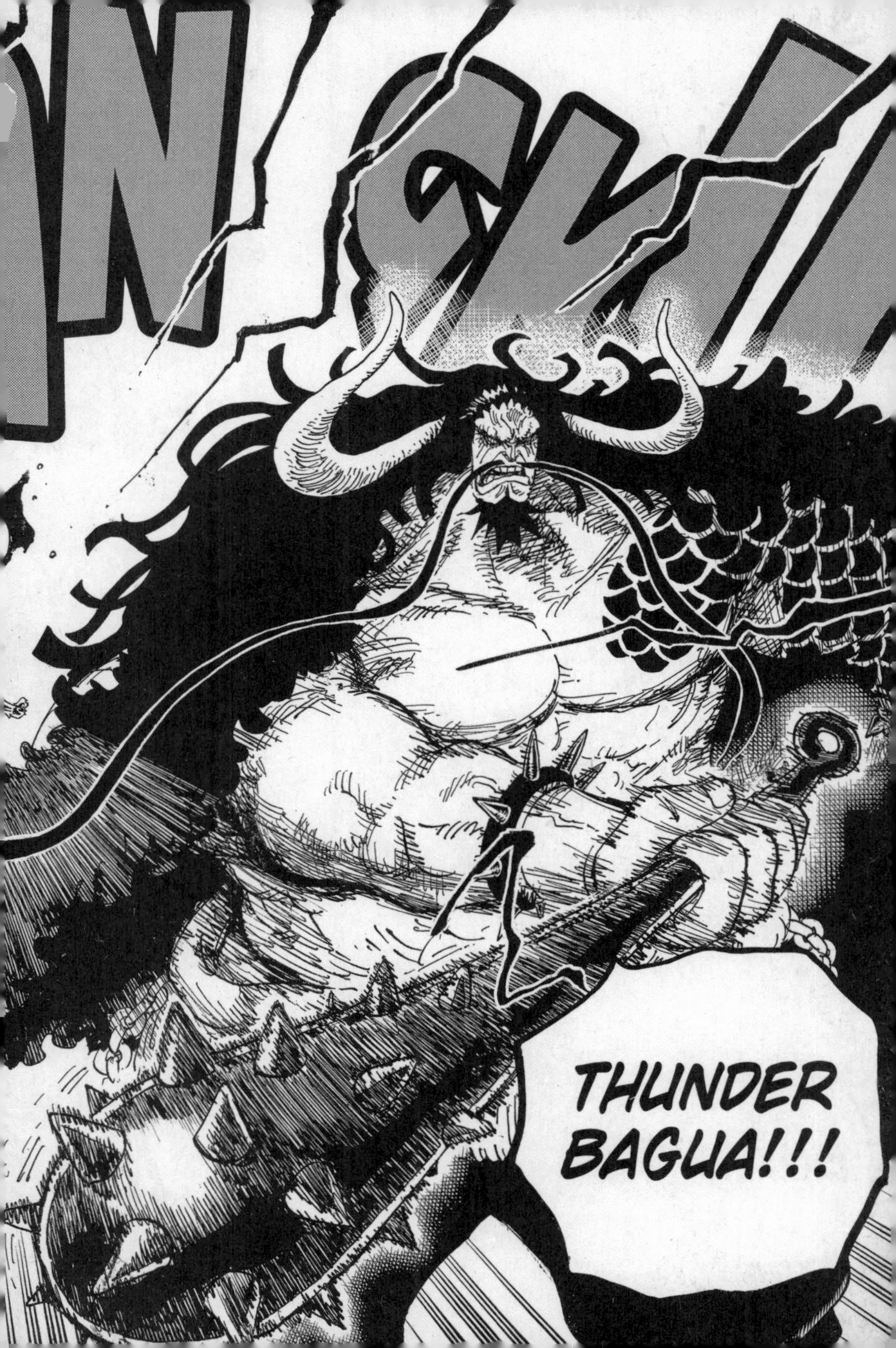
THUNDER BAGUA!!!

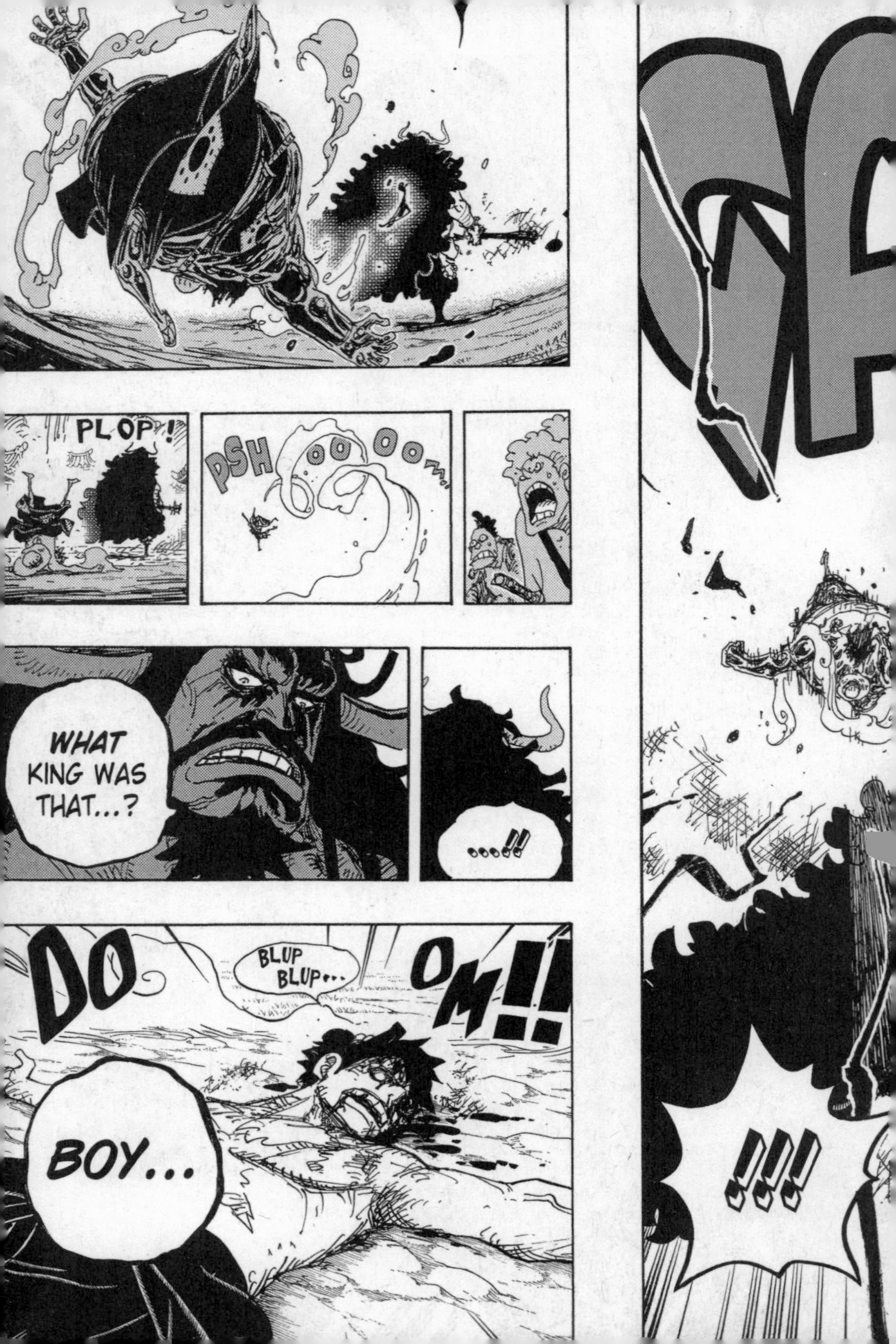
!!!
PSHOOOOOM
PLOP!
....!!
WHAT KING WAS THAT...?
OM!!
BLUP BLUP...
DO
BOY...

質問コーナー
Wanna fry up Odacchi...
エス
ビー
エス

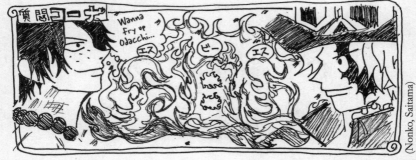

(Nonko, Saitama)

Q: Question for you, Sir Odacchi!! The buildings in Wano are rounded and warped and very full of character, but I must ask... Is that little roof over the sumo ring just... hanging in thin air?!?

BAKURA TOWN, KURI, WANO
RAAA AAAH...!!
DAMMIT !!
SUMO EVENT IN PROGRESS

A
AA

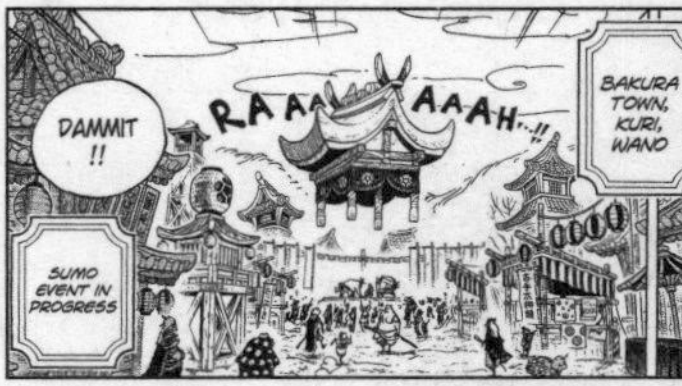

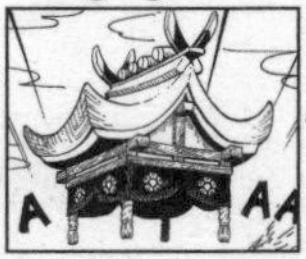

--Buchonosuke

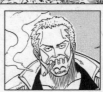

A: That's right. It's floating. Er, it's flying. It's a kite. When you see sumo events held indoors, they hang this tsuriyane roof over the ring from the ceiling above, but since the sumo in Bakura Town is outside, they fly it instead. It looks heavy, but it's actually very light. The part about it being a kite is kind of complicated, so just think of it as a kind of balloon!

Q: Odacchi!! I noticed something. In chapter 916, volume 91, when Luffy beats Yokozuna Urashima, one of the banners there reads "Mougan Ono-zeki." (Fierce Rock Axe Sumo). Or should that be "Axe-Hand Morgan," like the character from chapter 4?! Is it possible that former Captain Morgan will appear in Wano?! Am I right about that?!

--Takashi

猛岩斧関

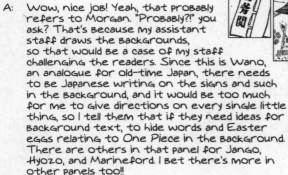

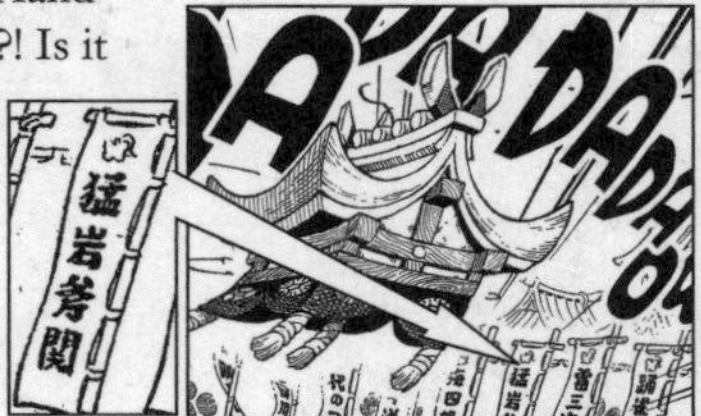

A: Wow, nice job! Yeah, that probably refers to Morgan. "Probably?!" you ask? That's because my assistant staff draws the backgrounds, so that would be a case of my staff challenging the readers. Since this is Wano, an analogue for old-time Japan, there needs to be Japanese writing on the signs and such in the background, and it would be too much for me to give directions on every single little thing, so I tell them that if they need ideas for background text, to hide words and Easter eggs relating to One Piece in the background. There are others in that panel for Jango, Hyozo, and Marineford. I bet there's more in other panels too!!

Chapter 924:

HUH

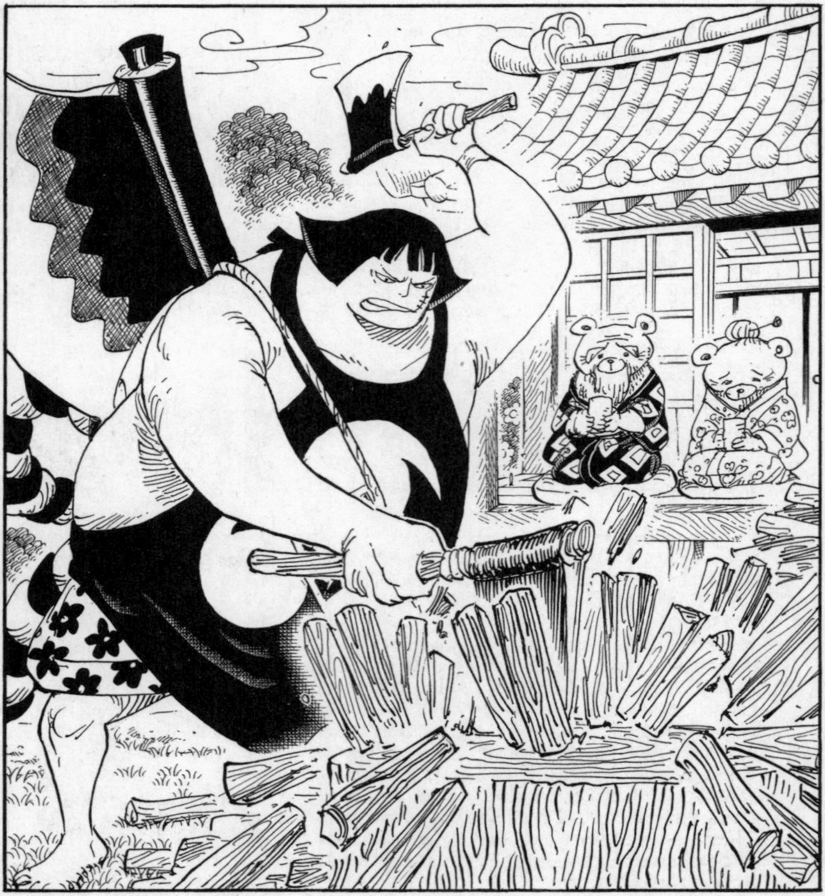

REQUEST: "SENTOMARU SPLITTING LOGS FOR AN ELDERLY BEAR COUPLE" BY SANADACCHI

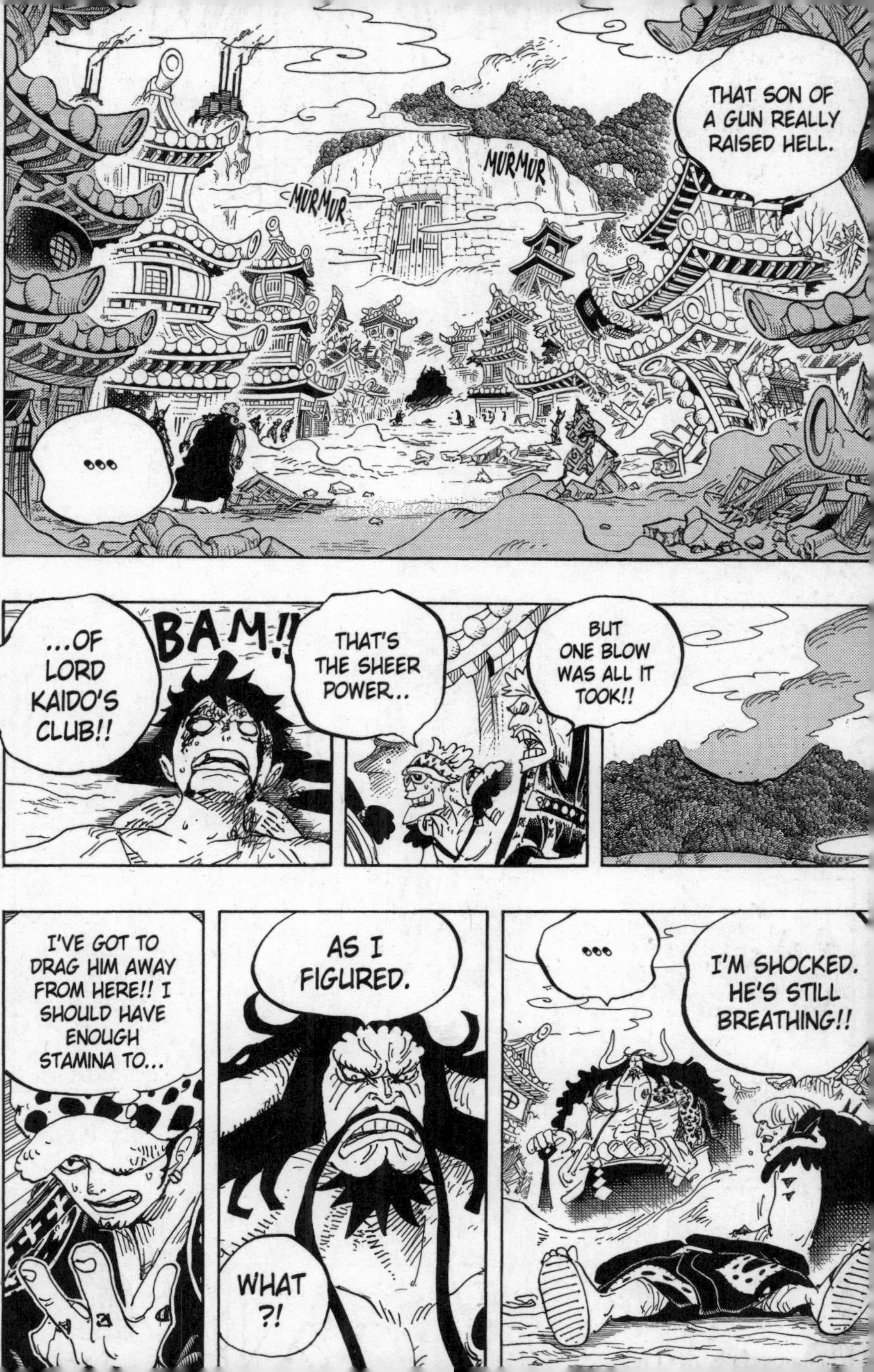

THAT SON OF A GUN REALLY RAISED HELL.
MURMUR
MURMUR
...
BUT ONE BLOW WAS ALL IT TOOK!!
THAT'S THE SHEER POWER...
BAM!!
...OF LORD KAIDO'S CLUB!!
I'M SHOCKED. HE'S STILL BREATHING!!
...
AS I FIGURED.
WHAT ?!
I'VE GOT TO DRAG HIM AWAY FROM HERE!! I SHOULD HAVE ENOUGH STAMINA TO...

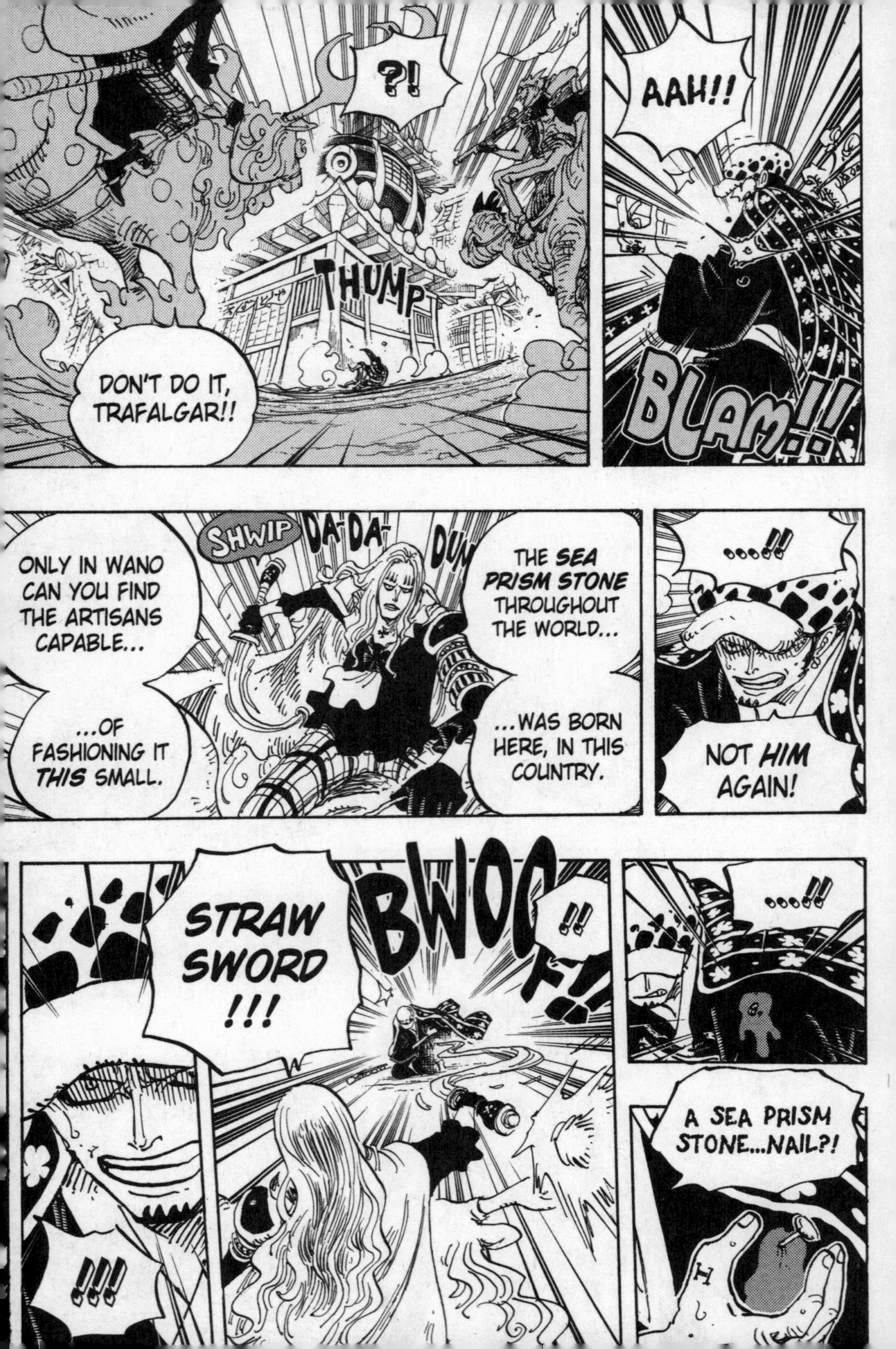
AAH!!
BLAM!!!
?!
THUMP
DON'T DO IT, TRAFALGAR!!
...!!
NOT HIM AGAIN!
THE SEA PRISM STONE THROUGHOUT THE WORLD...
...WAS BORN HERE, IN THIS COUNTRY.
DA-DA-DUN
SHWIP
ONLY IN WANO CAN YOU FIND THE ARTISANS CAPABLE...
...OF FASHIONING IT THIS SMALL.
...!!
A SEA PRISM STONE...NAIL?!
BWOOF!!
!!
STRAW SWORD !!!
!!!

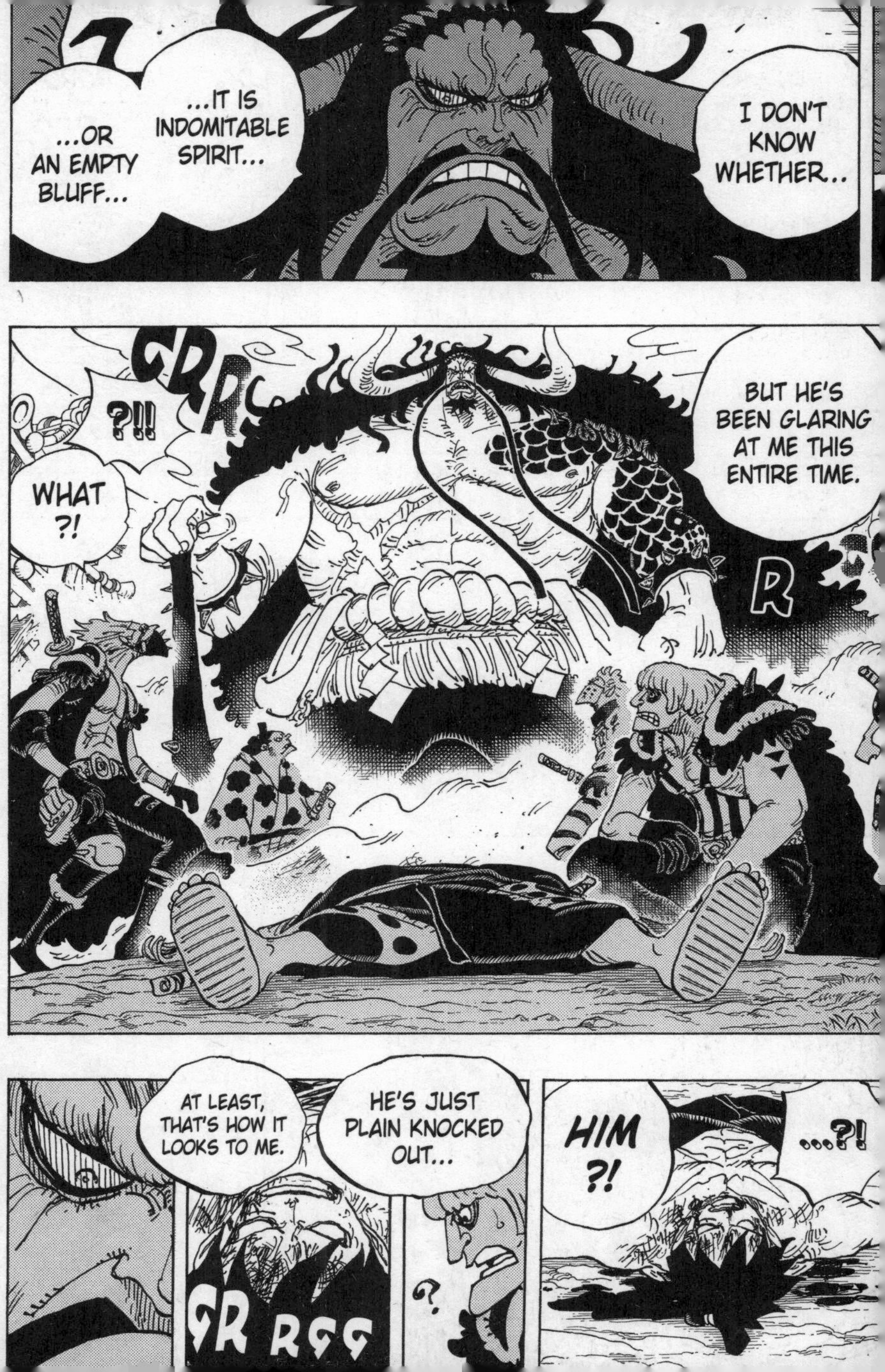
I DON'T KNOW WHETHER...
...IT IS INDOMITABLE SPIRIT...
...OR AN EMPTY BLUFF...
BUT HE'S BEEN GLARING AT ME THIS ENTIRE TIME.
R
GRR
?!!
WHAT ?!
...?!
HIM ?!
HE'S JUST PLAIN KNOCKED OUT...
?
AT LEAST, THAT'S HOW IT LOOKS TO ME.
GR RGG

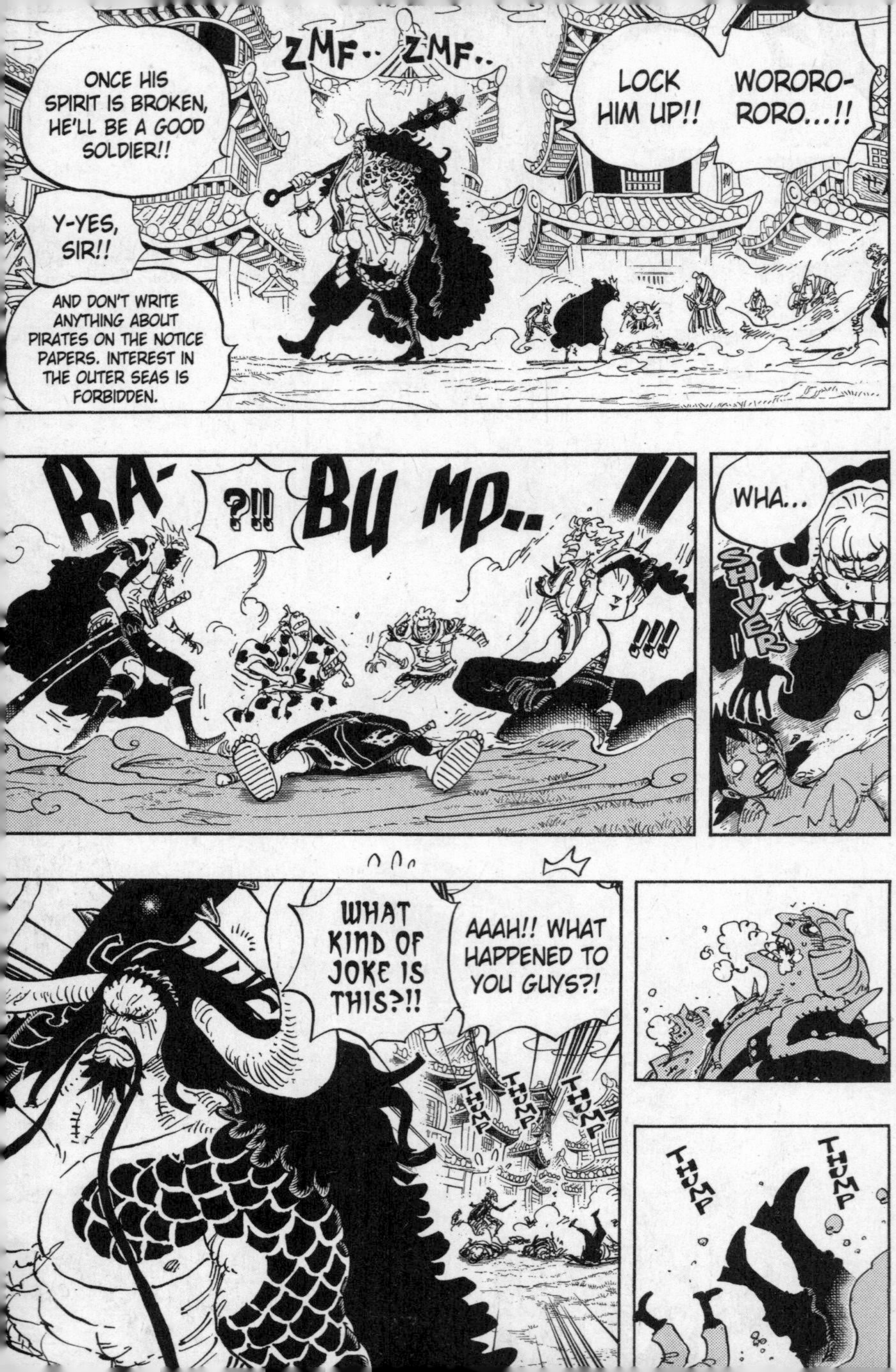
WORORO-RORO...!!
LOCK HIM UP!!
ZMF.. ZMF..
ONCE HIS SPIRIT IS BROKEN, HE'LL BE A GOOD SOLDIER!!
Y-YES, SIR!!
AND DON'T WRITE ANYTHING ABOUT PIRATES ON THE NOTICE PAPERS. INTEREST IN THE OUTER SEAS IS FORBIDDEN.
WHA...
SHIVER
!!
BU MP..
?!!
RA-
!!!
THUMP
THUMP
AAAH!! WHAT HAPPENED TO YOU GUYS?!
WHAT KIND OF JOKE IS THIS?!!
THUMP
THUMP
THUMP

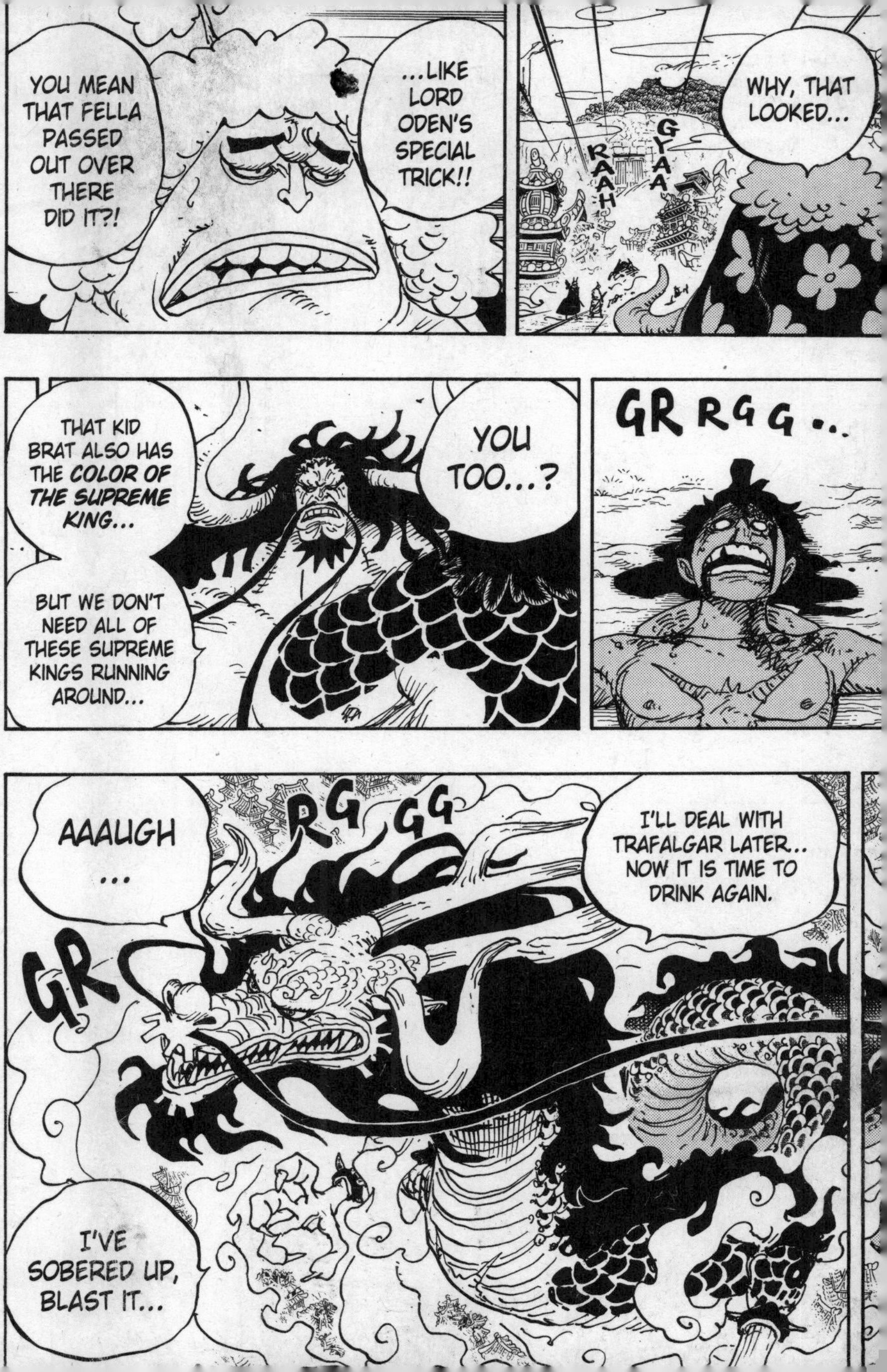
WHY, THAT LOOKED...
GYAA
RAAH
...LIKE LORD ODEN'S SPECIAL TRICK!!
YOU MEAN THAT FELLA PASSED OUT OVER THERE DID IT?!
GR RGG...
YOU TOO...?
THAT KID BRAT ALSO HAS THE COLOR OF THE SUPREME KING...
BUT WE DON'T NEED ALL OF THESE SUPREME KINGS RUNNING AROUND...
I'LL DEAL WITH TRAFALGAR LATER.. NOW IT IS TIME TO DRINK AGAIN.
RG GG
AAAUGH ...
GR
I'VE SOBERED UP, BLAST IT...

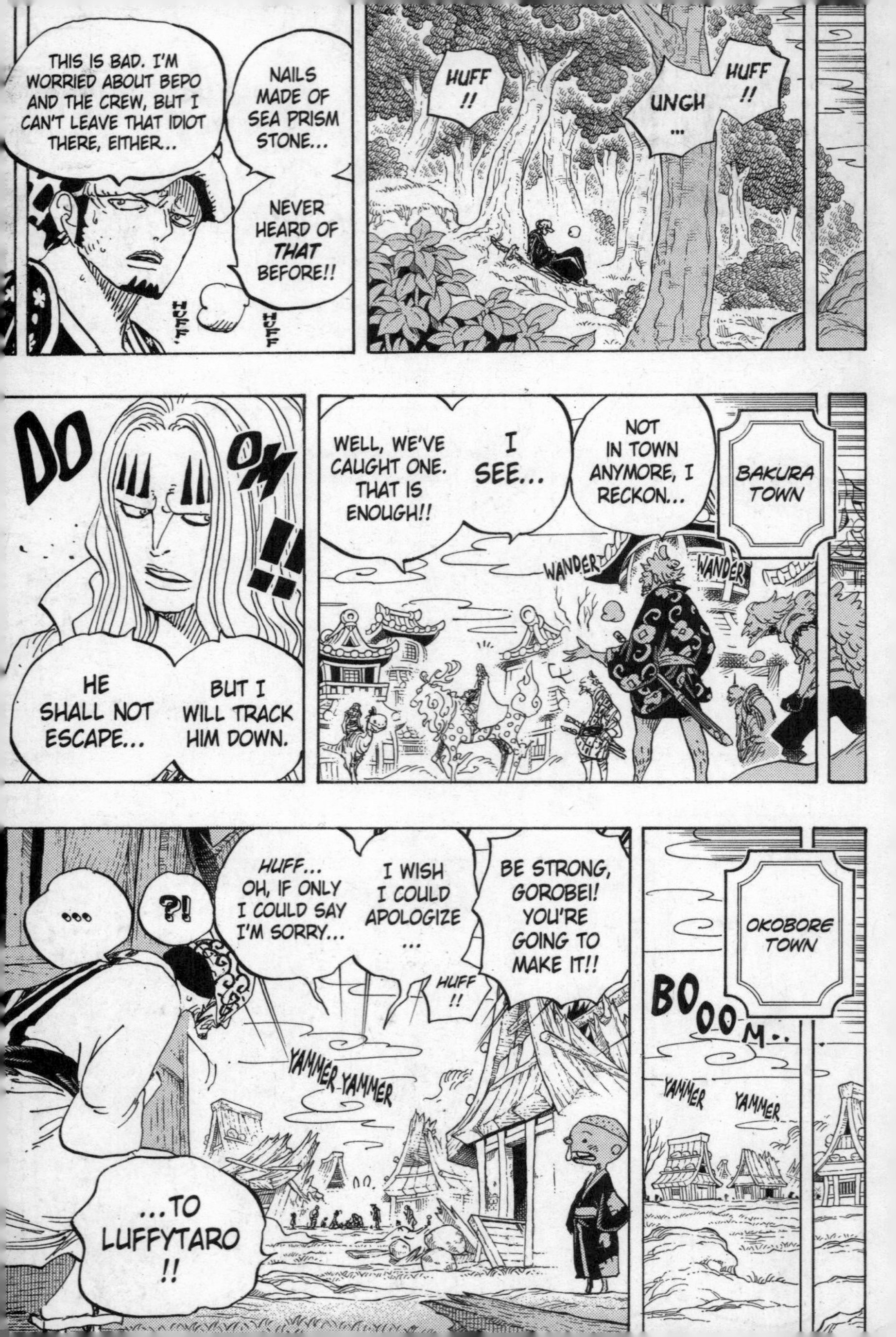
HUFF !!
UNGH ...
HUFF !!
NAILS MADE OF SEA PRISM STONE...
NEVER HEARD OF *THAT* BEFORE!!
THIS IS BAD. I'M WORRIED ABOUT BEPO AND THE CREW, BUT I CAN'T LEAVE THAT IDIOT THERE, EITHER...
HUFF
HUFF
BAKURA TOWN
NOT IN TOWN ANYMORE, I RECKON...
I SEE...
WELL, WE'VE CAUGHT ONE. THAT IS ENOUGH!!
WANDER
WANDER
DOOM!!
BUT I WILL TRACK HIM DOWN.
HE SHALL NOT ESCAPE...
OKOBORE TOWN
BOOOM..
YAMMER
YAMMER
BE STRONG, GOROBEI! YOU'RE GOING TO MAKE IT!!
I WISH I COULD APOLOGIZE ...
HUFF... OH, IF ONLY I COULD SAY I'M SORRY...
HUFF !!
?!
...
YAMMER YAMMER
...TO LUFFYTARO !!

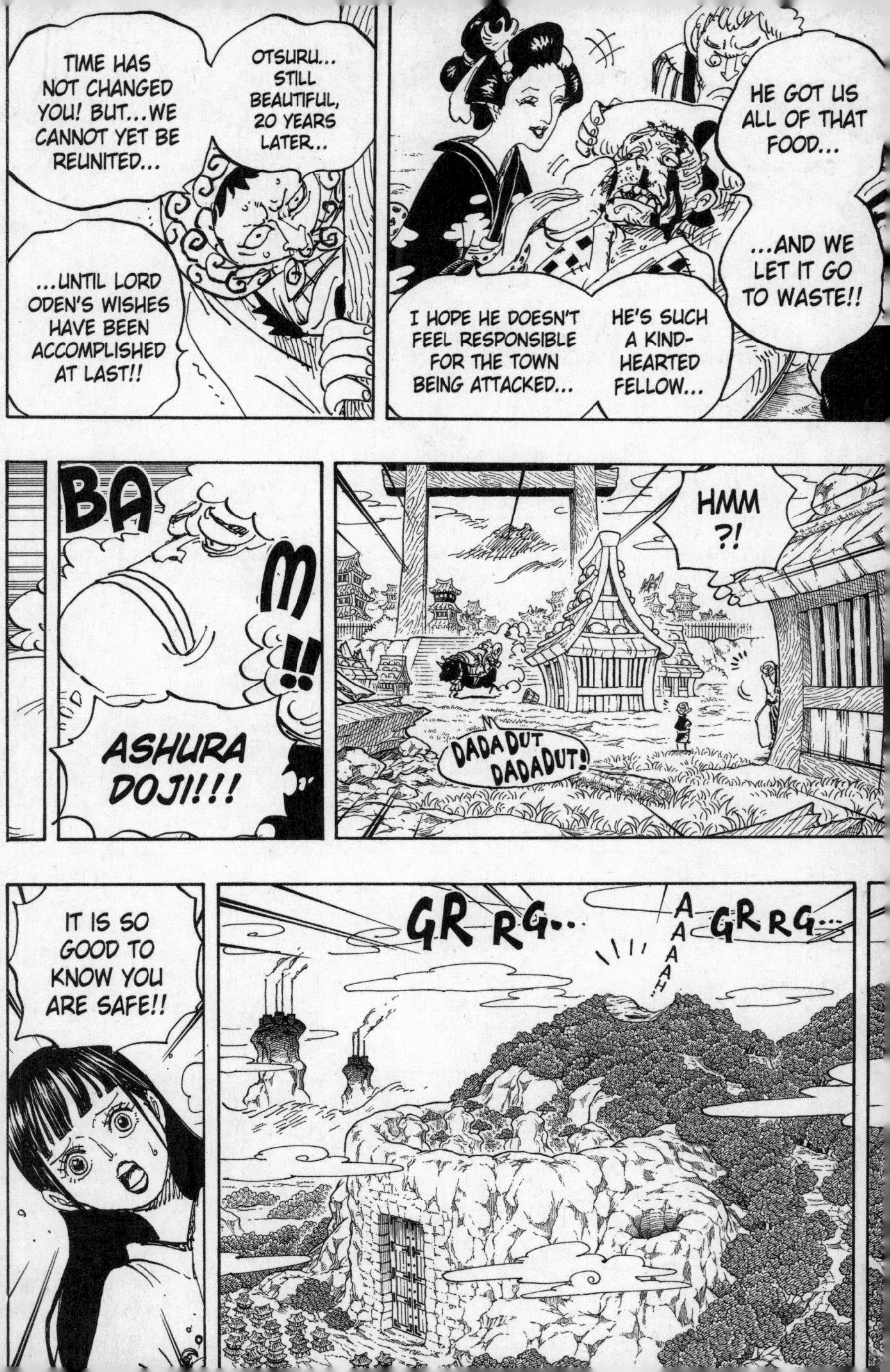
HE GOT US ALL OF THAT FOOD...
...AND WE LET IT GO TO WASTE!!
HE'S SUCH A KIND-HEARTED FELLOW...
I HOPE HE DOESN'T FEEL RESPONSIBLE FOR THE TOWN BEING ATTACKED...
OTSURU... STILL BEAUTIFUL, 20 YEARS LATER...
TIME HAS NOT CHANGED YOU! BUT...WE CANNOT YET BE REUNITED...
...UNTIL LORD ODEN'S WISHES HAVE BEEN ACCOMPLISHED AT LAST!!
HMM ?!
DADADUT DADADUT!
BAM!!
ASHURA DOJI!!!
GRRG...
AAAAAH!!
GR RG..
IT IS SO GOOD TO KNOW YOU ARE SAFE!!

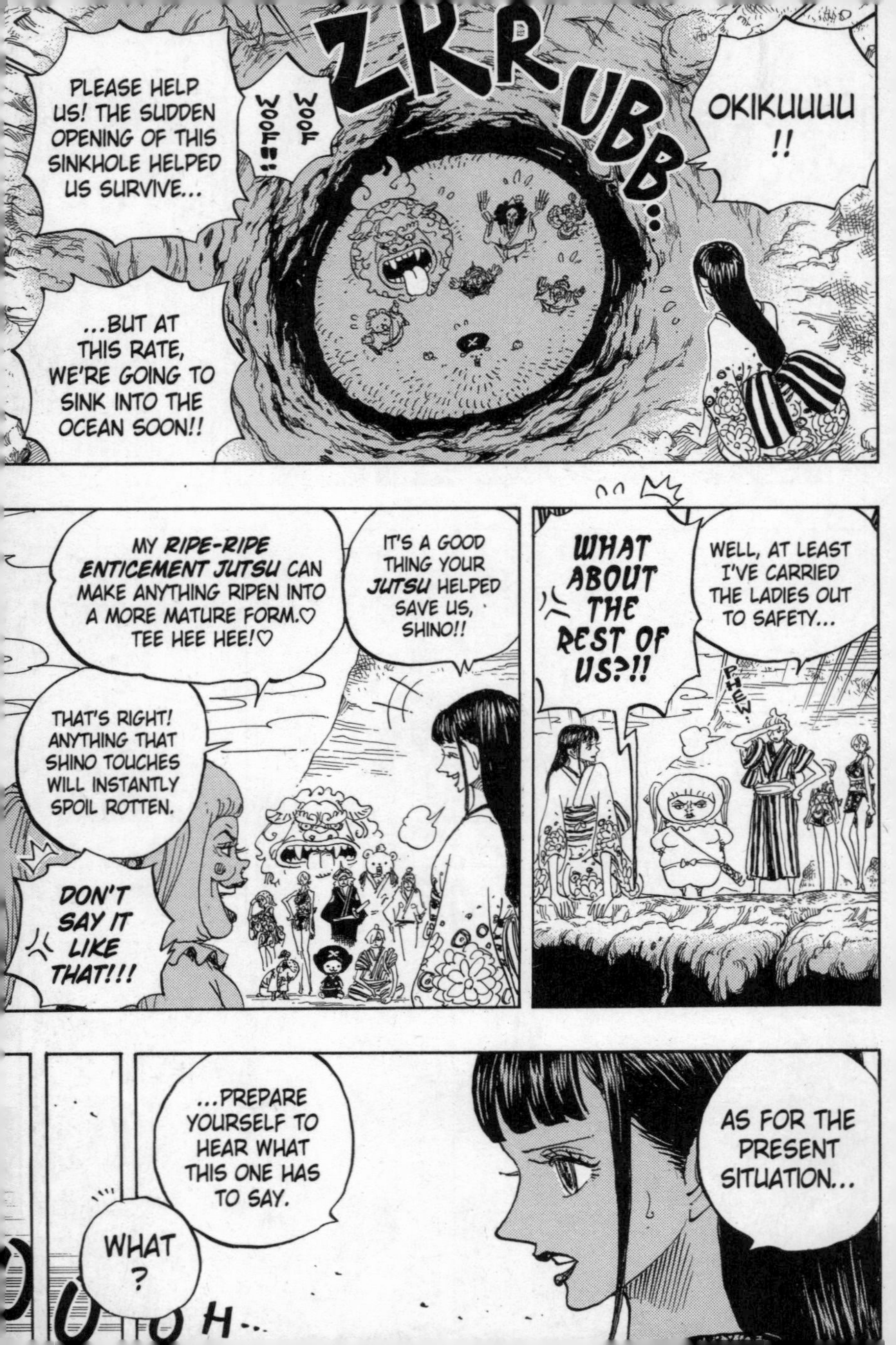
OKIKUUUU !!
ZKRUBB..
WOOF WOOF!!
PLEASE HELP US! THE SUDDEN OPENING OF THIS SINKHOLE HELPED US SURVIVE...
...BUT AT THIS RATE, WE'RE GOING TO SINK INTO THE OCEAN SOON!!
WELL, AT LEAST I'VE CARRIED THE LADIES OUT TO SAFETY...
PHEW
WHAT ABOUT THE REST OF US?!!
IT'S A GOOD THING YOUR JUTSU HELPED SAVE US, SHINO!!
MY RIPE-RIPE ENTICEMENT JUTSU CAN MAKE ANYTHING RIPEN INTO A MORE MATURE FORM.♡ TEE HEE HEE!♡
THAT'S RIGHT! ANYTHING THAT SHINO TOUCHES WILL INSTANTLY SPOIL ROTTEN.
DON'T SAY IT LIKE THAT!!!
AS FOR THE PRESENT SITUATION...
...PREPARE YOURSELF TO HEAR WHAT THIS ONE HAS TO SAY.
WHAT ?
OOOH...

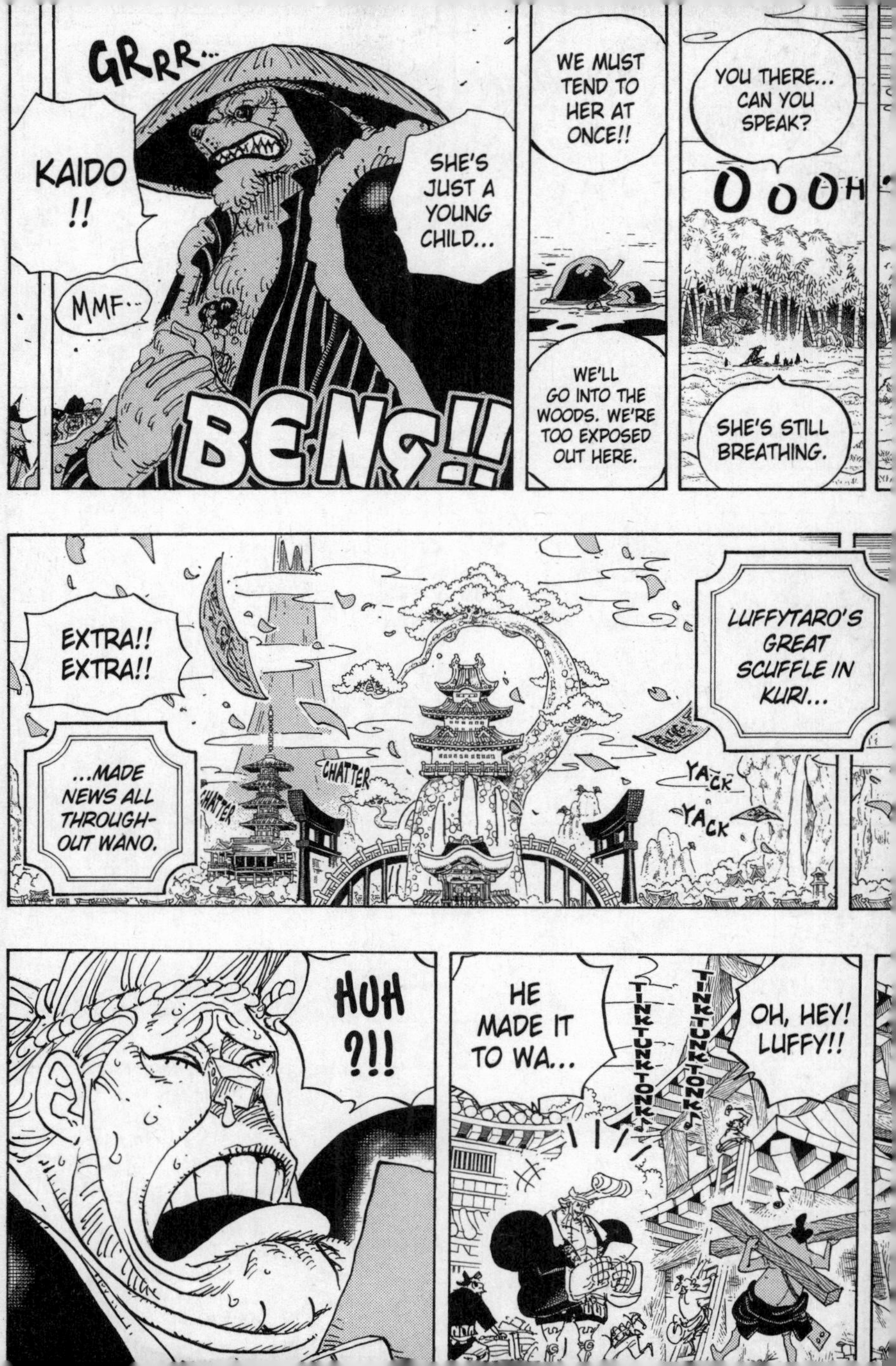
YOU THERE... CAN YOU SPEAK?
OOOH
SHE'S STILL BREATHING.
WE MUST TEND TO HER AT ONCE!!
WE'LL GO INTO THE WOODS. WE'RE TOO EXPOSED OUT HERE.
SHE'S JUST A YOUNG CHILD...
GRRR...
KAIDO!!
MMF...
BENG!!
LUFFYTARO'S GREAT SCUFFLE IN KURI...
EXTRA!! EXTRA!!
...MADE NEWS ALL THROUGHOUT WANO.
YACK
YACK
CHATTER
CHATTER
OH, HEY! LUFFY!!
TINKTUNKTONK
TINKTUNKTONK
HE MADE IT TO WA...
HUH?!!

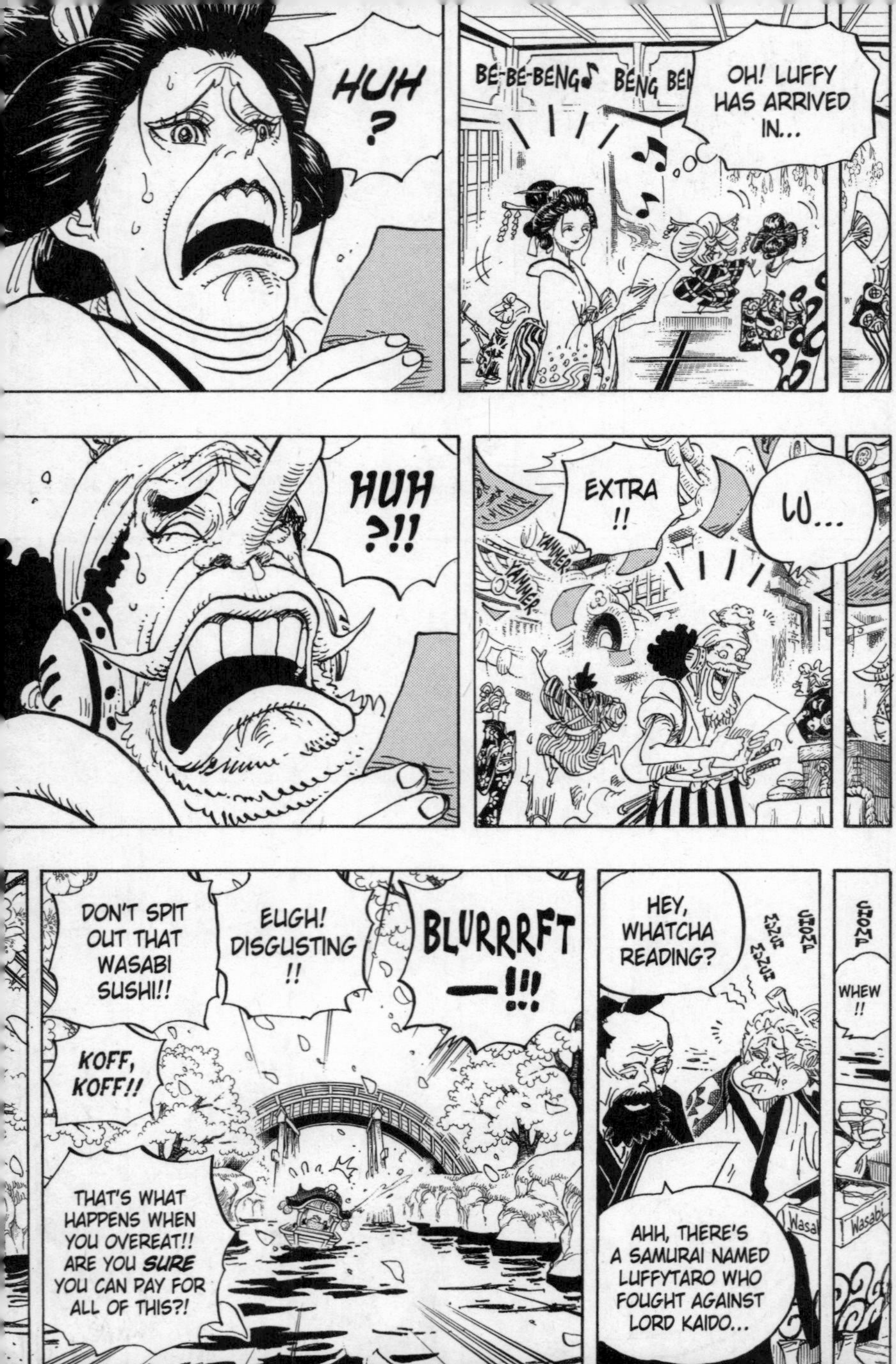

OH! LUFFY HAS ARRIVED IN...
BE-BE-BENG♪ BENG BEN
HUH ?
LU...
EXTRA !!
YAMMER
YAMMER
HUH ?!!
CHOMP
WHEW !!
HEY, WHATCHA READING?
CHOMP
MUNCH MUNCH
AHH, THERE'S A SAMURAI NAMED LUFFYTARO WHO FOUGHT AGAINST LORD KAIDO...
Wasabi
Wasabi
BLURRRFT —!!!
EUGH! DISGUSTING !!
DON'T SPIT OUT THAT WASABI SUSHI!!
KOFF, KOFF!!
THAT'S WHAT HAPPENS WHEN YOU OVEREAT!! ARE YOU ***SURE*** YOU CAN PAY FOR ALL OF THIS?!

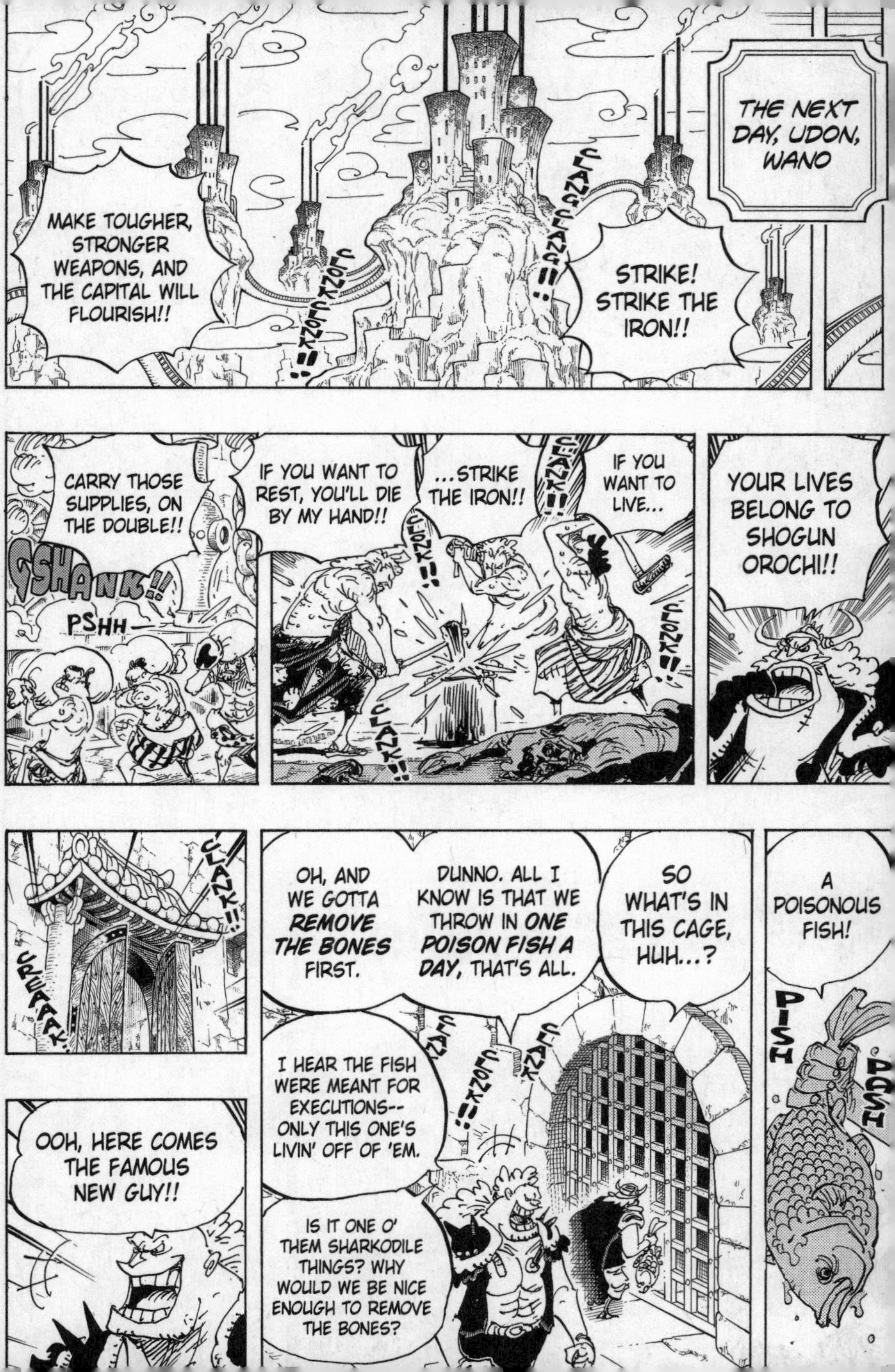
THE NEXT DAY, UDON, WANO
STRIKE! STRIKE THE IRON!!
CLANG CLANG!!
CLONK CLONK!!
MAKE TOUGHER, STRONGER WEAPONS, AND THE CAPITAL WILL FLOURISH!!
YOUR LIVES BELONG TO SHOGUN OROCHI!!
IF YOU WANT TO LIVE...
CLANK!!
...STRIKE THE IRON!!
IF YOU WANT TO REST, YOU'LL DIE BY MY HAND!!
CLONK!!
CLONK!!
CLANK!!
CARRY THOSE SUPPLIES, ON THE DOUBLE!!
GSHANK!!
PSHH
A POISONOUS FISH!
PISH
PASH
SO WHAT'S IN THIS CAGE, HUH...?
DUNNO. ALL I KNOW IS THAT WE THROW IN *ONE POISON FISH A DAY,* THAT'S ALL.
OH, AND WE GOTTA *REMOVE THE BONES* FIRST.
CLANK
CLONK!!
CLANK
I HEAR THE FISH WERE MEANT FOR EXECUTIONS-- ONLY THIS ONE'S LIVIN' OFF OF 'EM.
IS IT ONE O' THEM SHARKODILE THINGS? WHY WOULD WE BE NICE ENOUGH TO REMOVE THE BONES?
CLANK!!
CREAAAK...
OOH, HERE COMES THE FAMOUS NEW GUY!!

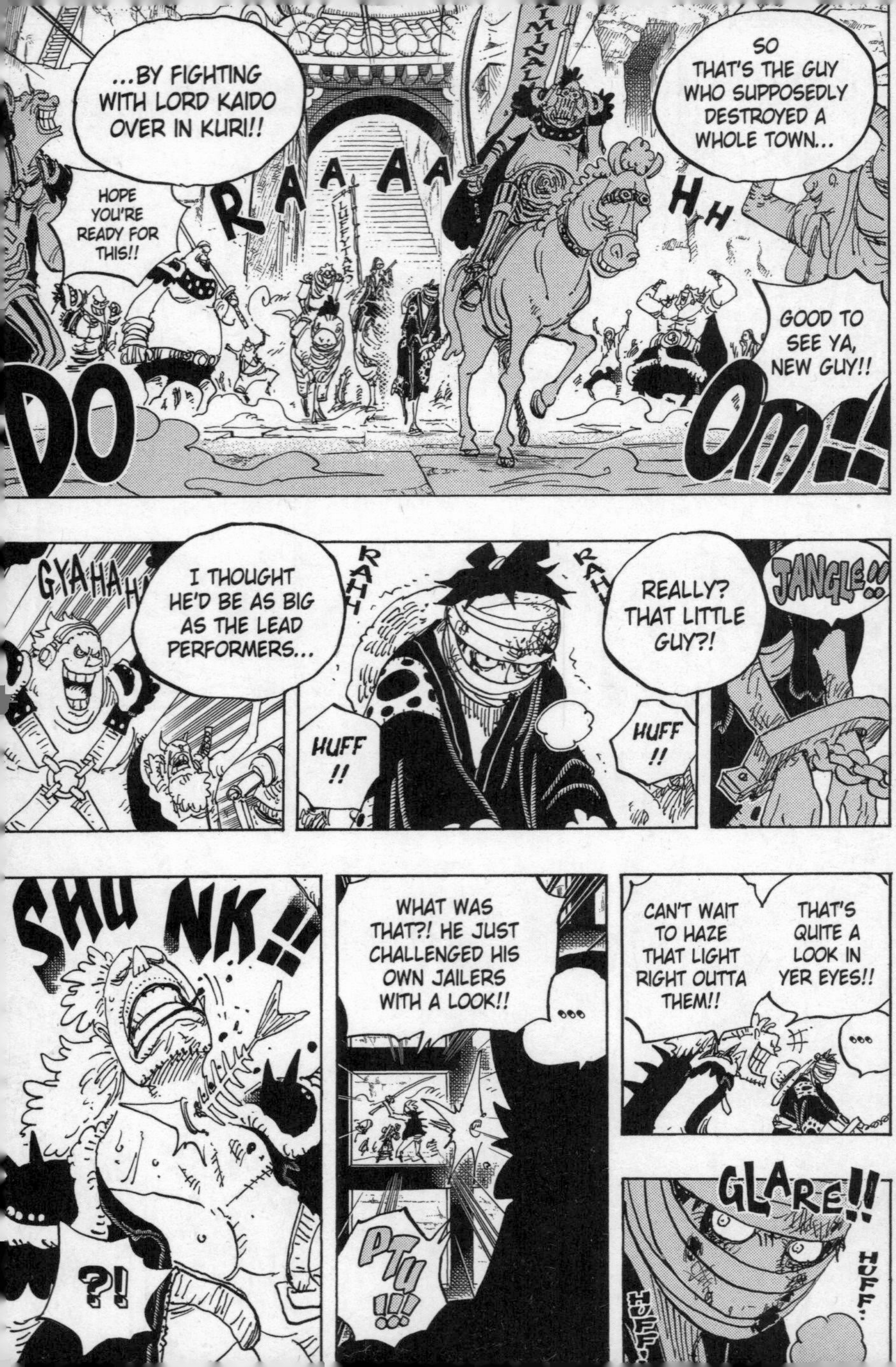
SO THAT'S THE GUY WHO SUPPOSEDLY DESTROYED A WHOLE TOWN...
...BY FIGHTING WITH LORD KAIDO OVER IN KURI!!
RAAAAHH
GOOD TO SEE YA, NEW GUY!!
HOPE YOU'RE READY FOR THIS!!
DOOM!!
JANGLE!!
RAHH
REALLY? THAT LITTLE GUY?!
HUFF !!
RAHH
HUFF !!
I THOUGHT HE'D BE AS BIG AS THE LEAD PERFORMERS...
GYAHAHH
THAT'S QUITE A LOOK IN YER EYES!!
CAN'T WAIT TO HAZE THAT LIGHT RIGHT OUTTA THEM!!
...
GLARE!!
HUFF..
HUFF..
WHAT WAS THAT?! HE JUST CHALLENGED HIS OWN JAILERS WITH A LOOK!!
...
PTU!!!
SHUNK!!
?!

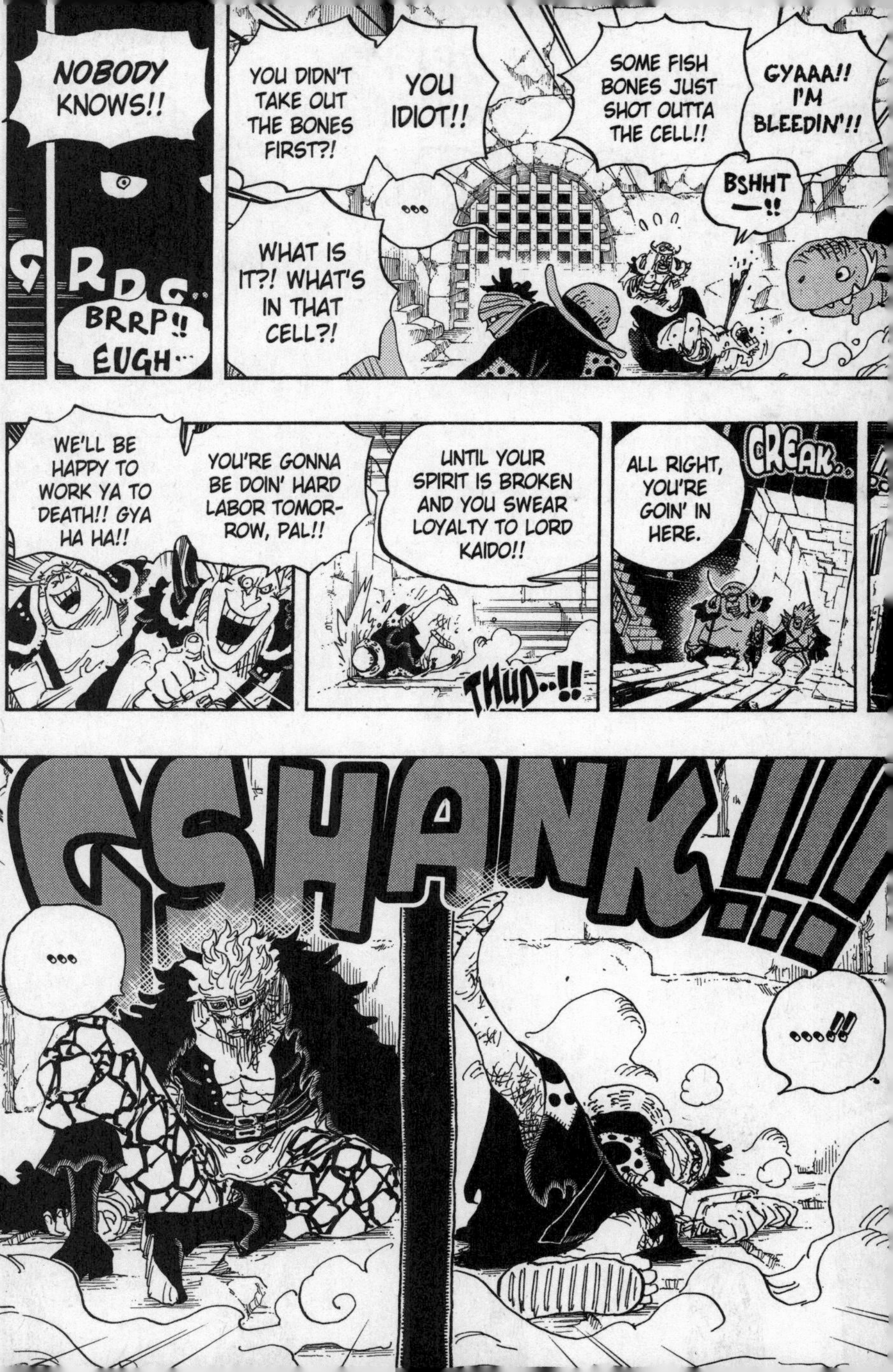
GYAAA!! I'M BLEEDIN'!!
SOME FISH BONES JUST SHOT OUTTA THE CELL!!
YOU IDIOT!!
YOU DIDN'T TAKE OUT THE BONES FIRST?!
BSHHT—!!
...
WHAT IS IT?! WHAT'S IN THAT CELL?!
NOBODY KNOWS!!
GRDG...
BRRP!! EUGH...
CREAK..
ALL RIGHT, YOU'RE GOIN' IN HERE.
UNTIL YOUR SPIRIT IS BROKEN AND YOU SWEAR LOYALTY TO LORD KAIDO!!
THUD..!!
YOU'RE GONNA BE DOIN' HARD LABOR TOMORROW, PAL!!
WE'LL BE HAPPY TO WORK YA TO DEATH!! GYA HA HA!!
GSHANK!!!
...!!
...

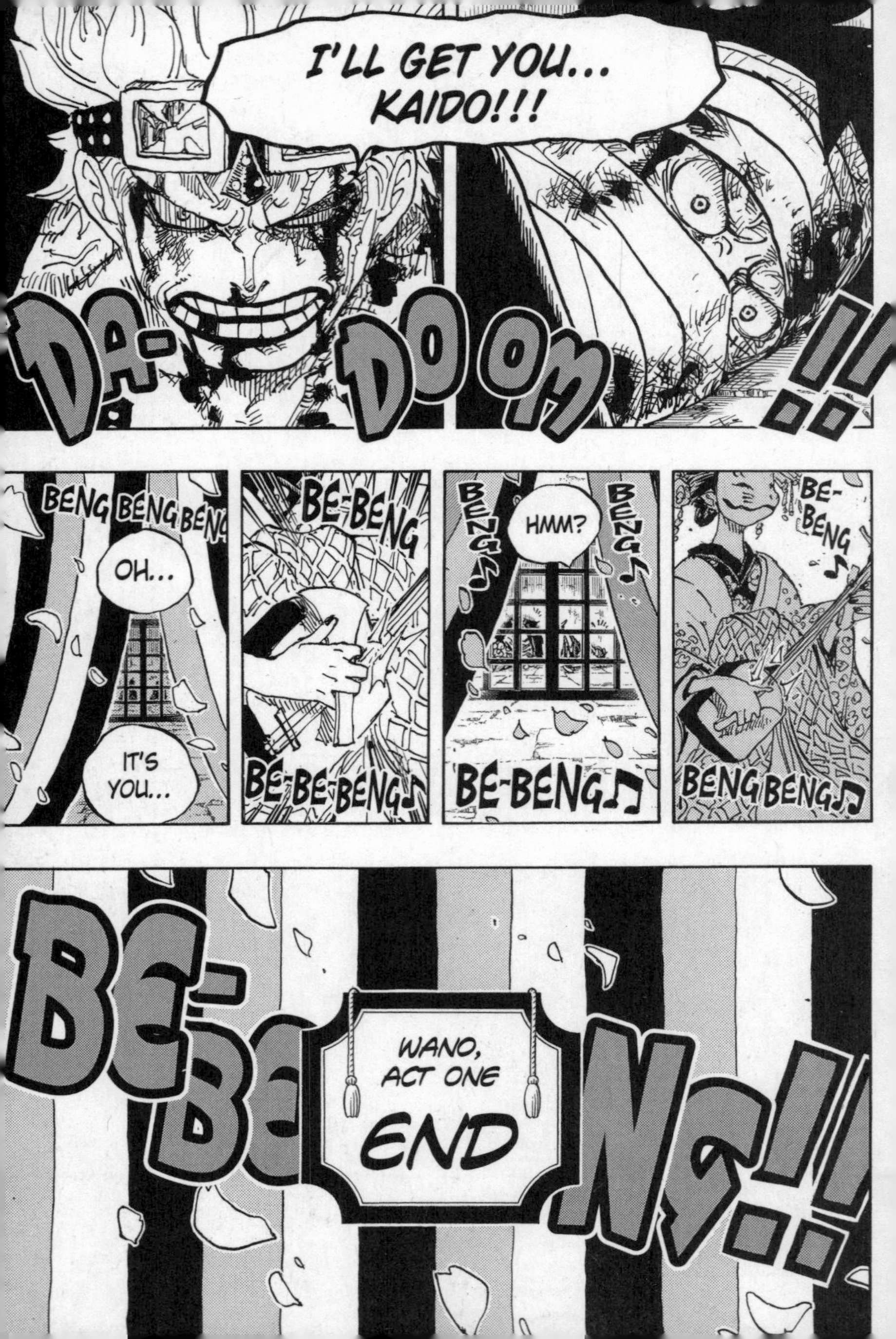
I'LL GET YOU... KAIDO!!!
DA-DOOM!!
BE-BENG♪
BENG BENG♫
BENG♪
BENG♪
HMM?
BE-BENG♫
BE-BENG
BE-BE-BENG♪
BENG BENG BENG
OH...
IT'S YOU...
BE-BE-BENG!!
WANO, ACT ONE
END

SBS Question Corner

(Sasaaki, Okinawa)

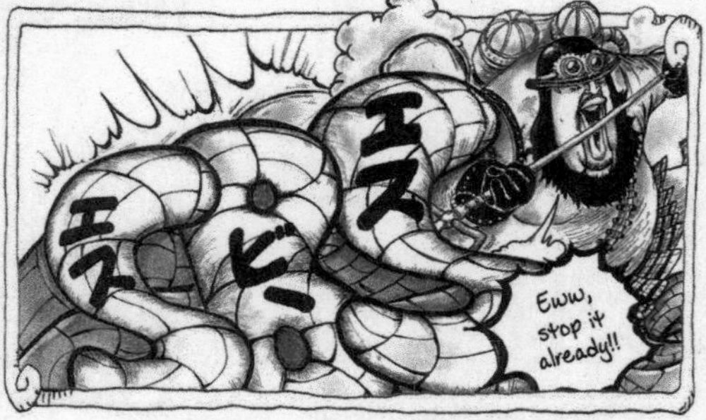

エス
ビー
エス
Eww, stop it already!!

A: We've got a "spot the differences" game from a reader named Yucchan Papa! Thank you so much! The answers are at the bottom of the page, so cover them up as you solve it!

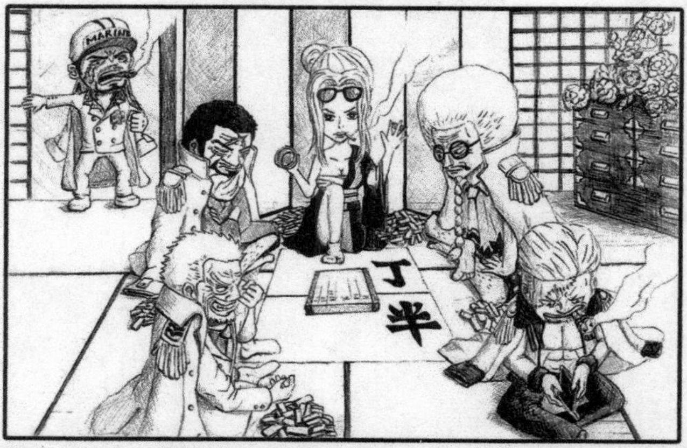

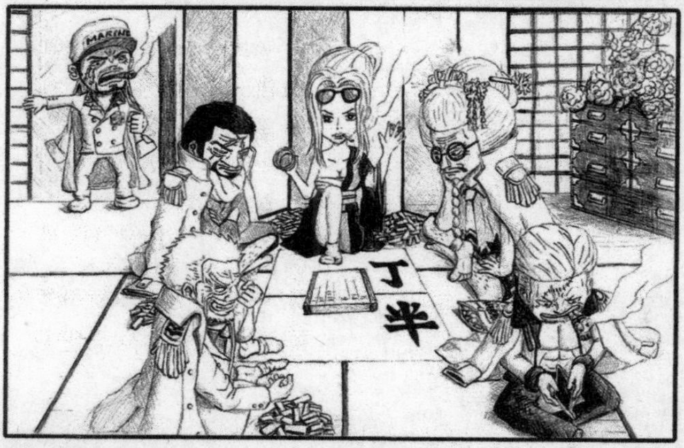

MARINE

Answer

① Lines on Sakazuki's hat
② Length of Fujitora's epaulettes
③ Fujitora's scarf knot
④ Garp's socks half off
⑤ Position of Hina's bun
⑥ Sengoku's wedding headdress
⑦ Length of Sengoku's beard
⑧ Navy Crackers near Sengoku's knee
⑨ Smoker's jacket cuffs

Chapter 925:
ABSENCE

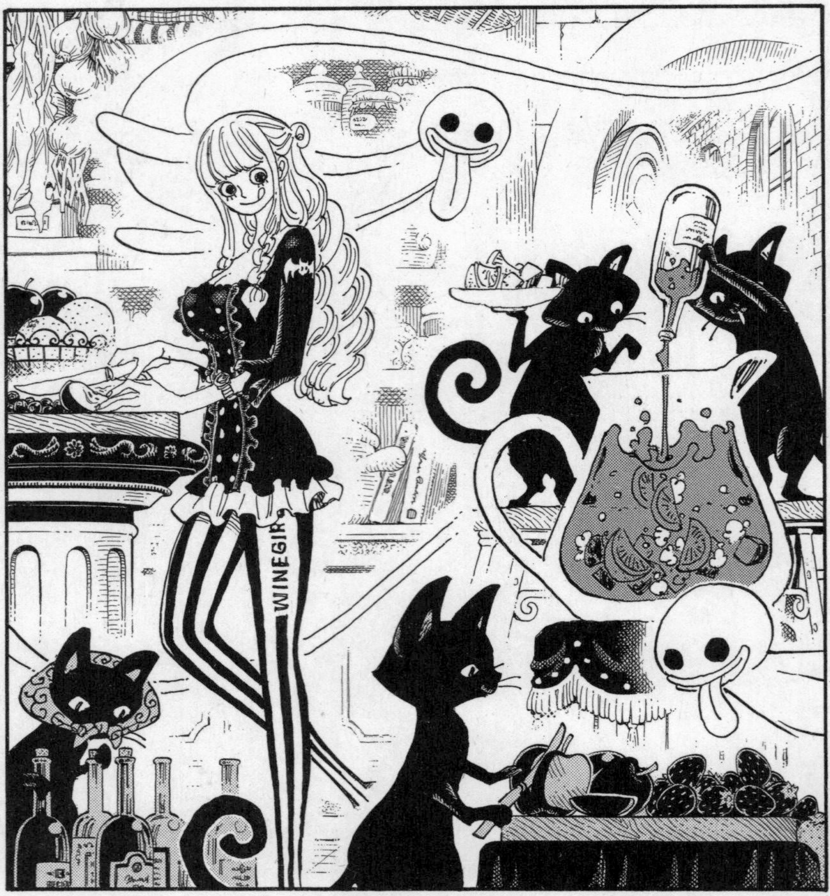
WINEGIR

REQUEST: "PERONA AND BLACK CATS SECRETLY MAKING SANGRIA WITH MIHAWK'S WINE" BY NODA SKYWALKER

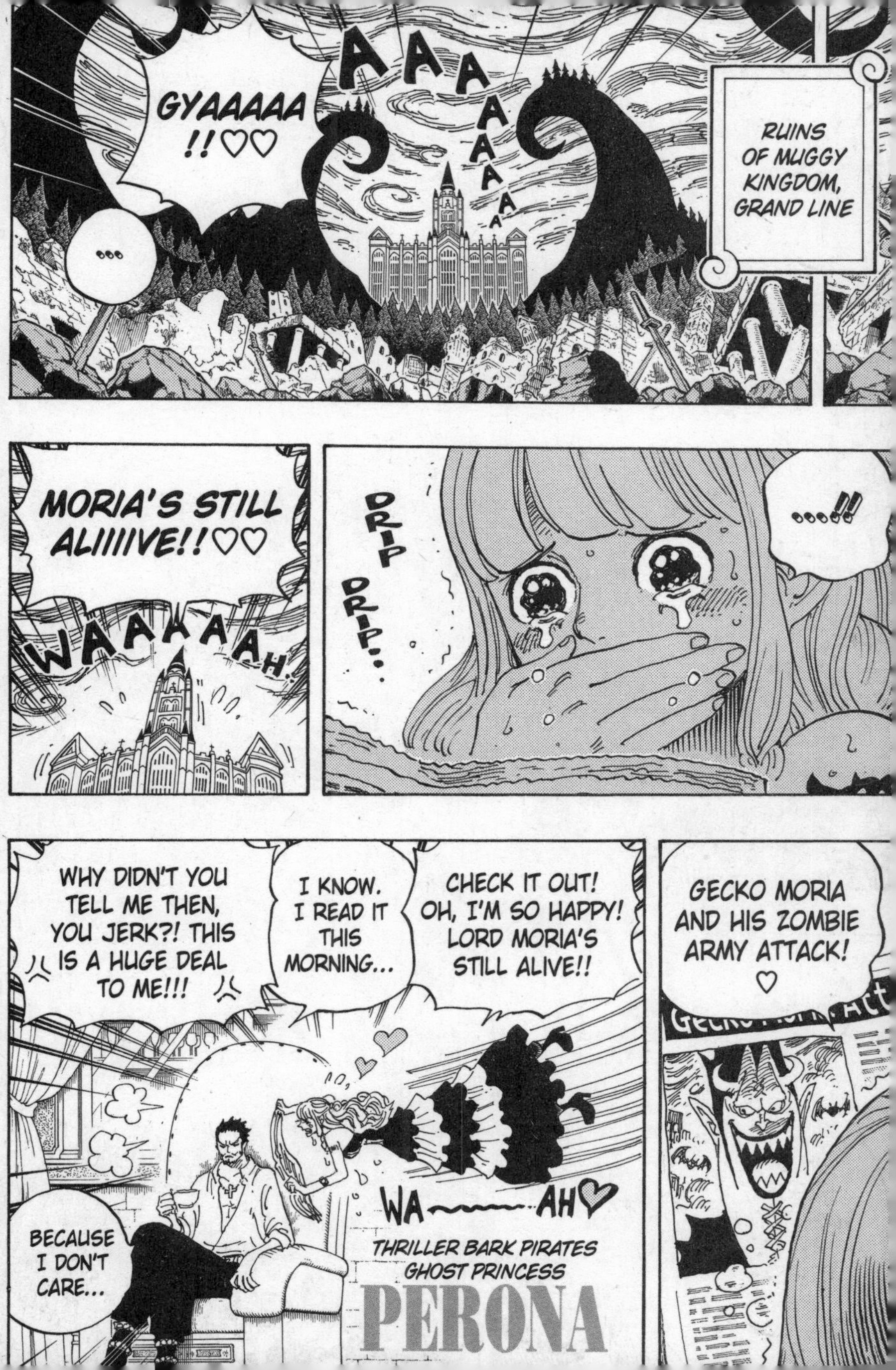
RUINS OF MUGGY KINGDOM, GRAND LINE
AAAAAAAA
GYAAAAA !!♡♡
...
...!!
DRIP DRIP...
MORIA'S STILL ALIIIIVE!!♡♡
WAAAAAH.
GECKO MORIA AND HIS ZOMBIE ARMY ATTACK! ♡
CHECK IT OUT! OH, I'M SO HAPPY! LORD MORIA'S STILL ALIVE!!
WA~~AH♡
I KNOW. I READ IT THIS MORNING...
WHY DIDN'T YOU TELL ME THEN, YOU JERK?! THIS IS A HUGE DEAL TO ME!!!
BECAUSE I DON'T CARE...
THRILLER BARK PIRATES GHOST PRINCESS
PERONA

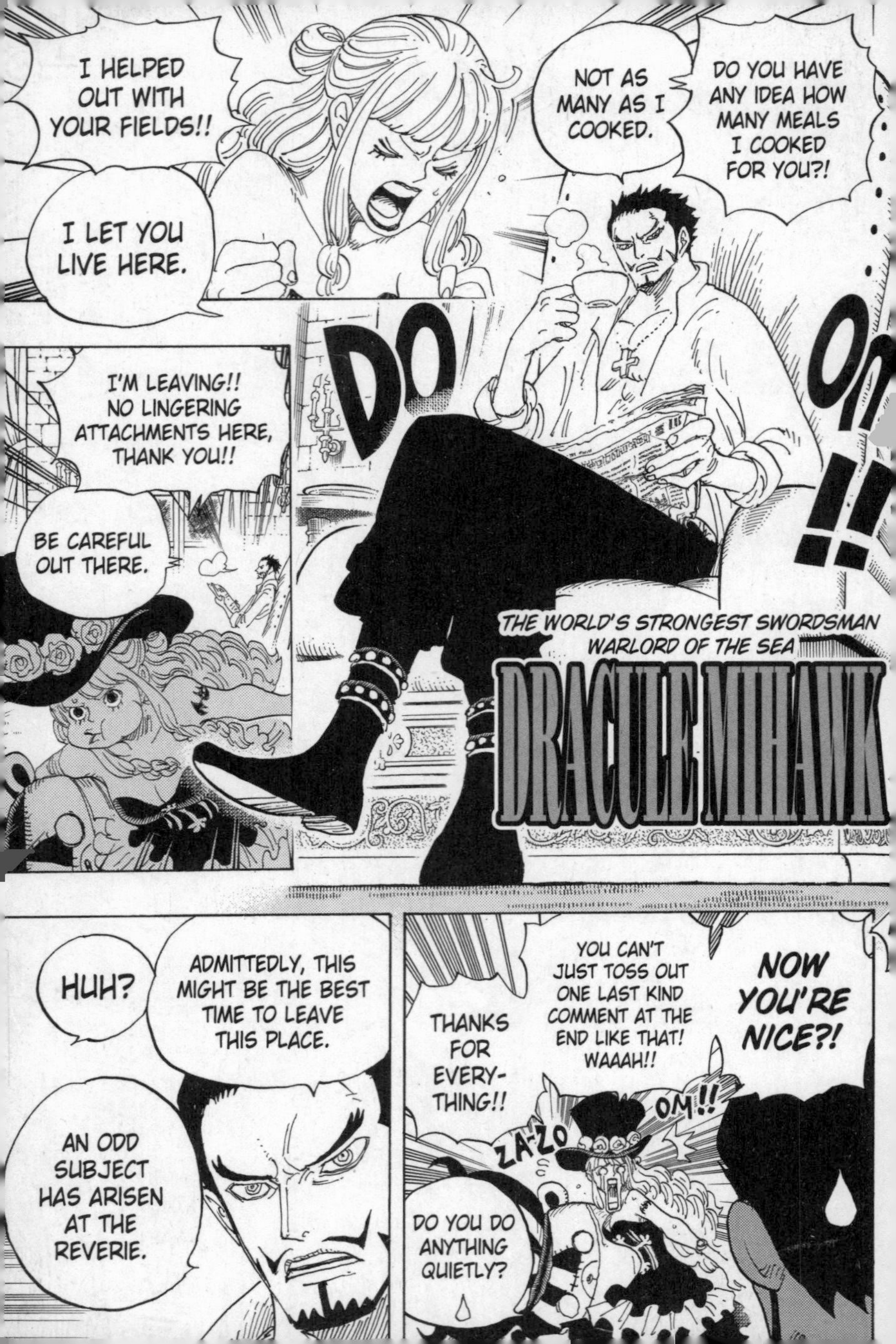
DO YOU HAVE ANY IDEA HOW MANY MEALS I COOKED FOR YOU?!
NOT AS MANY AS I COOKED.
I HELPED OUT WITH YOUR FIELDS!!
I LET YOU LIVE HERE.
DO
ON!!
THE WORLD'S STRONGEST SWORDSMAN WARLORD OF THE SEA
DRACULE MIHAWK
I'M LEAVING!! NO LINGERING ATTACHMENTS HERE, THANK YOU!!
BE CAREFUL OUT THERE.
NOW YOU'RE NICE?!
YOU CAN'T JUST TOSS OUT ONE LAST KIND COMMENT AT THE END LIKE THAT! WAAAH!!
THANKS FOR EVERY-THING!!
OM!!
ZA-ZO
DO YOU DO ANYTHING QUIETLY?
ADMITTEDLY, THIS MIGHT BE THE BEST TIME TO LEAVE THIS PLACE.
HUH?
AN ODD SUBJECT HAS ARISEN AT THE REVERIE.

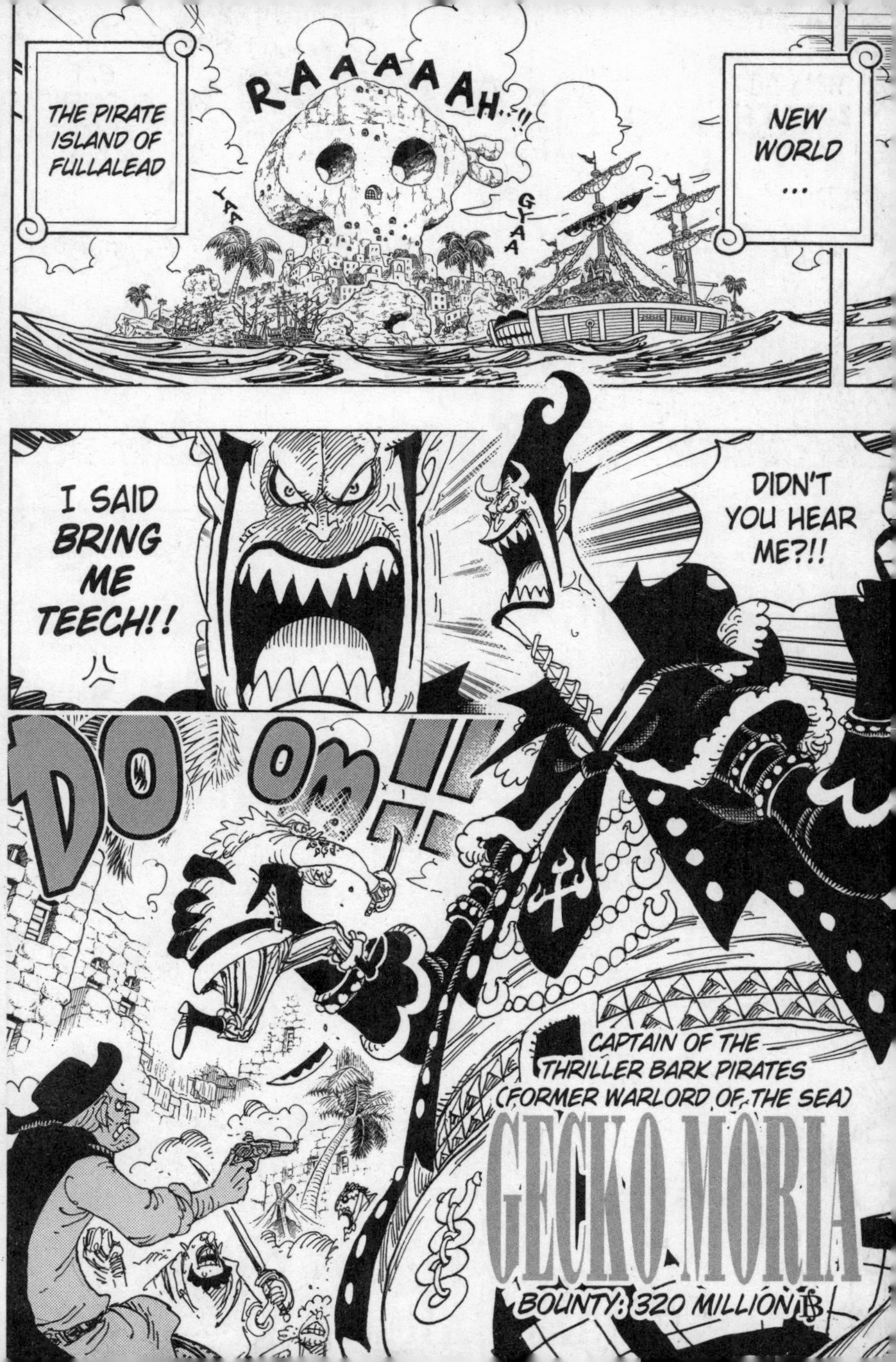
NEW WORLD ...
RAAAAAAH...!!
THE PIRATE ISLAND OF FULLALEAD
GYAA
YAA
DIDN'T YOU HEAR ME?!!
I SAID BRING ME TEECH!!
DOOM!!
CAPTAIN OF THE THRILLER BARK PIRATES (FORMER WARLORD OF THE SEA)
GECKO MORIA
BOUNTY: 320 MILLION

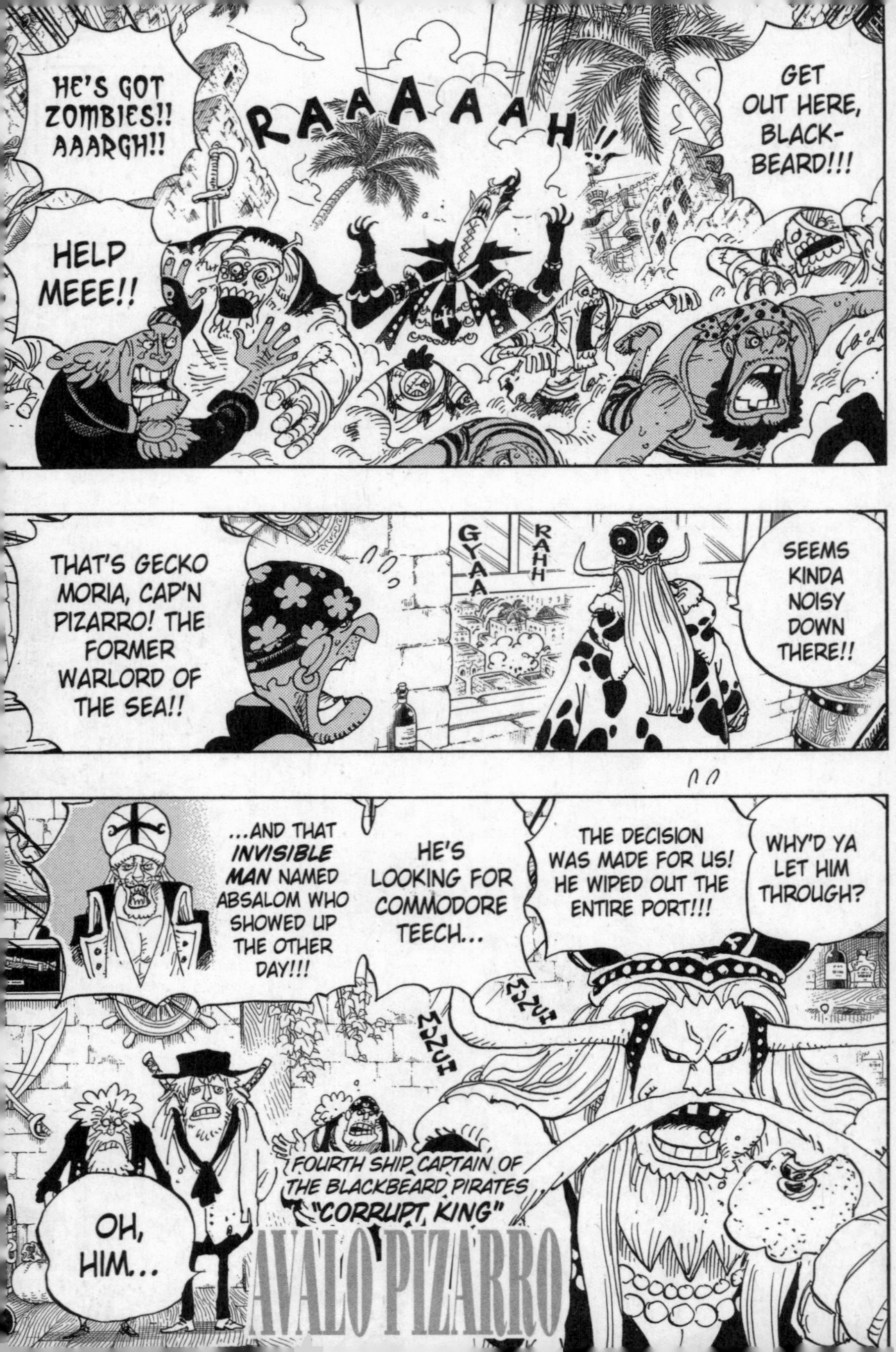
GET OUT HERE, BLACK-BEARD!!!
RAAAAAAH!!
HE'S GOT ZOMBIES!! AAARGH!!
HELP MEEE!!
SEEMS KINDA NOISY DOWN THERE!!
RAHH
GYAAA
THAT'S GECKO MORIA, CAP'N PIZARRO! THE FORMER WARLORD OF THE SEA!!
WHY'D YA LET HIM THROUGH?
THE DECISION WAS MADE FOR US! HE WIPED OUT THE ENTIRE PORT!!!
HE'S LOOKING FOR COMMODORE TEECH...
...AND THAT *INVISIBLE MAN* NAMED ABSALOM WHO SHOWED UP THE OTHER DAY!!!
FOURTH SHIP CAPTAIN OF THE BLACKBEARD PIRATES "CORRUPT KING"
AVALO PIZARRO
OH, HIM...

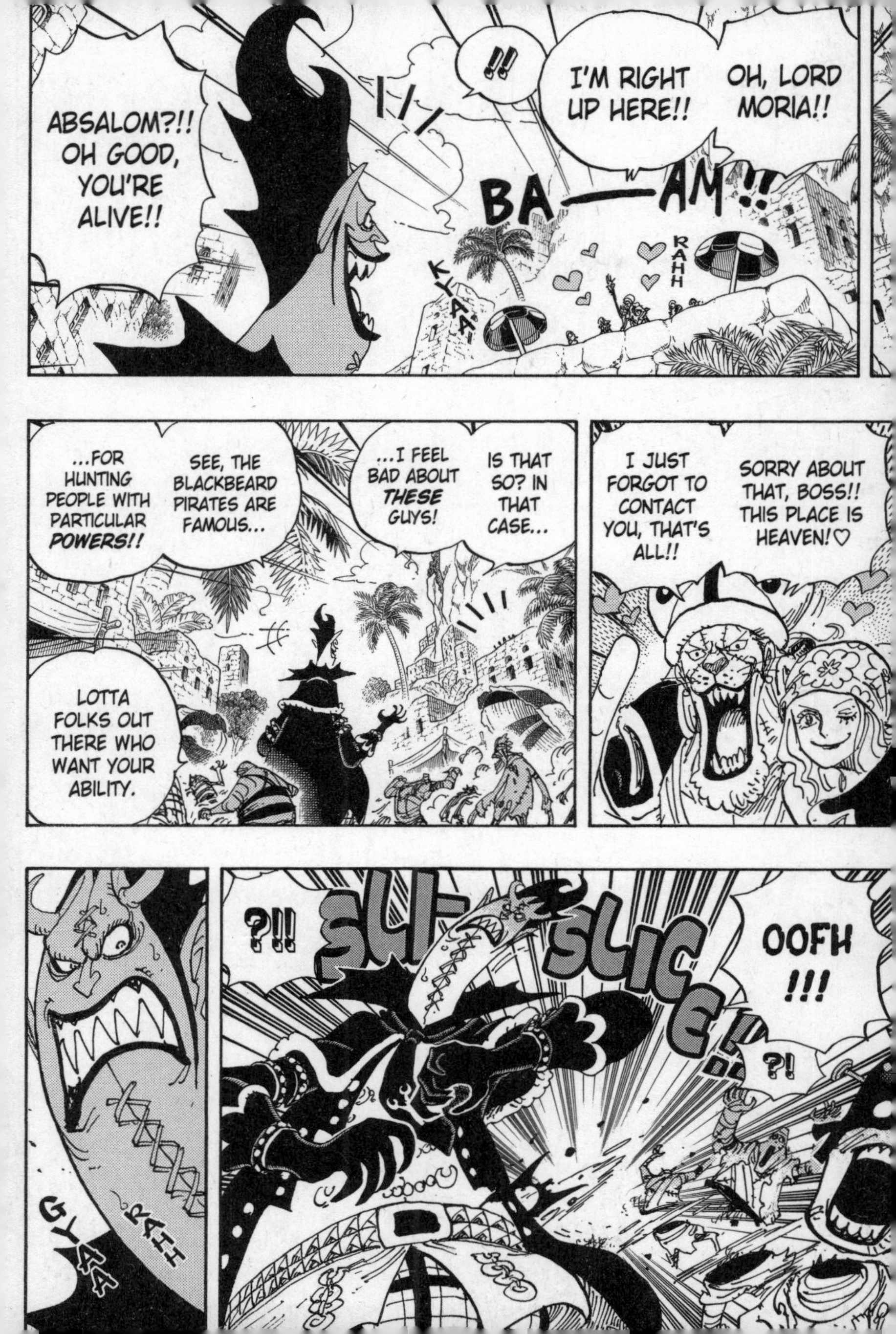
OH, LORD MORIA!!
I'M RIGHT UP HERE!!
!!
BA—AM!!
RAHH
KYAAA
ABSALOM?!! OH GOOD, YOU'RE ALIVE!!
SORRY ABOUT THAT, BOSS!! THIS PLACE IS HEAVEN!♡
I JUST FORGOT TO CONTACT YOU, THAT'S ALL!!
IS THAT SO? IN THAT CASE...
...I FEEL BAD ABOUT *THESE* GUYS!
SEE, THE BLACKBEARD PIRATES ARE FAMOUS...
...FOR HUNTING PEOPLE WITH PARTICULAR *POWERS!!*
LOTTA FOLKS OUT THERE WHO WANT YOUR ABILITY.
OOFH!!!
SLI- SLICE!!
?!
?!!
RAHH
GYAA

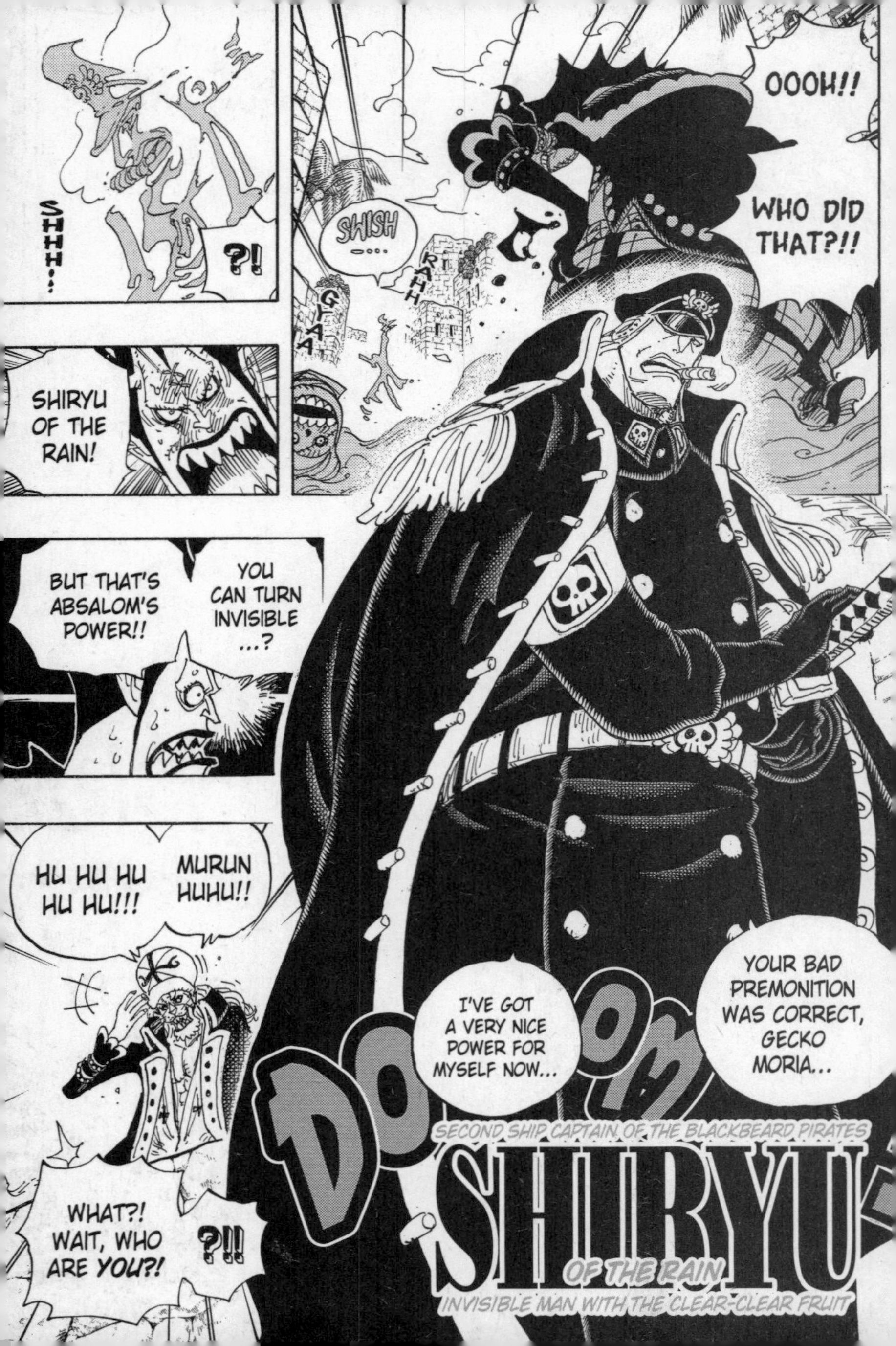
OOOH!!
WHO DID THAT?!!
SWISH —...
RAHH
GYAA
YOUR BAD PREMONITION WAS CORRECT, GECKO MORIA...
I'VE GOT A VERY NICE POWER FOR MYSELF NOW...
DOOOM
SECOND SHIP CAPTAIN OF THE BLACKBEARD PIRATES
SHIRYU OF THE RAIN
INVISIBLE MAN WITH THE CLEAR-CLEAR FRUIT
SHHH!!
?!
SHIRYU OF THE RAIN!
YOU CAN TURN INVISIBLE ...?
BUT THAT'S ABSALOM'S POWER!!
MURUN HUHU!!
HU HU HU HU HU!!!
?!!
WHAT?! WAIT, WHO ARE YOU?!

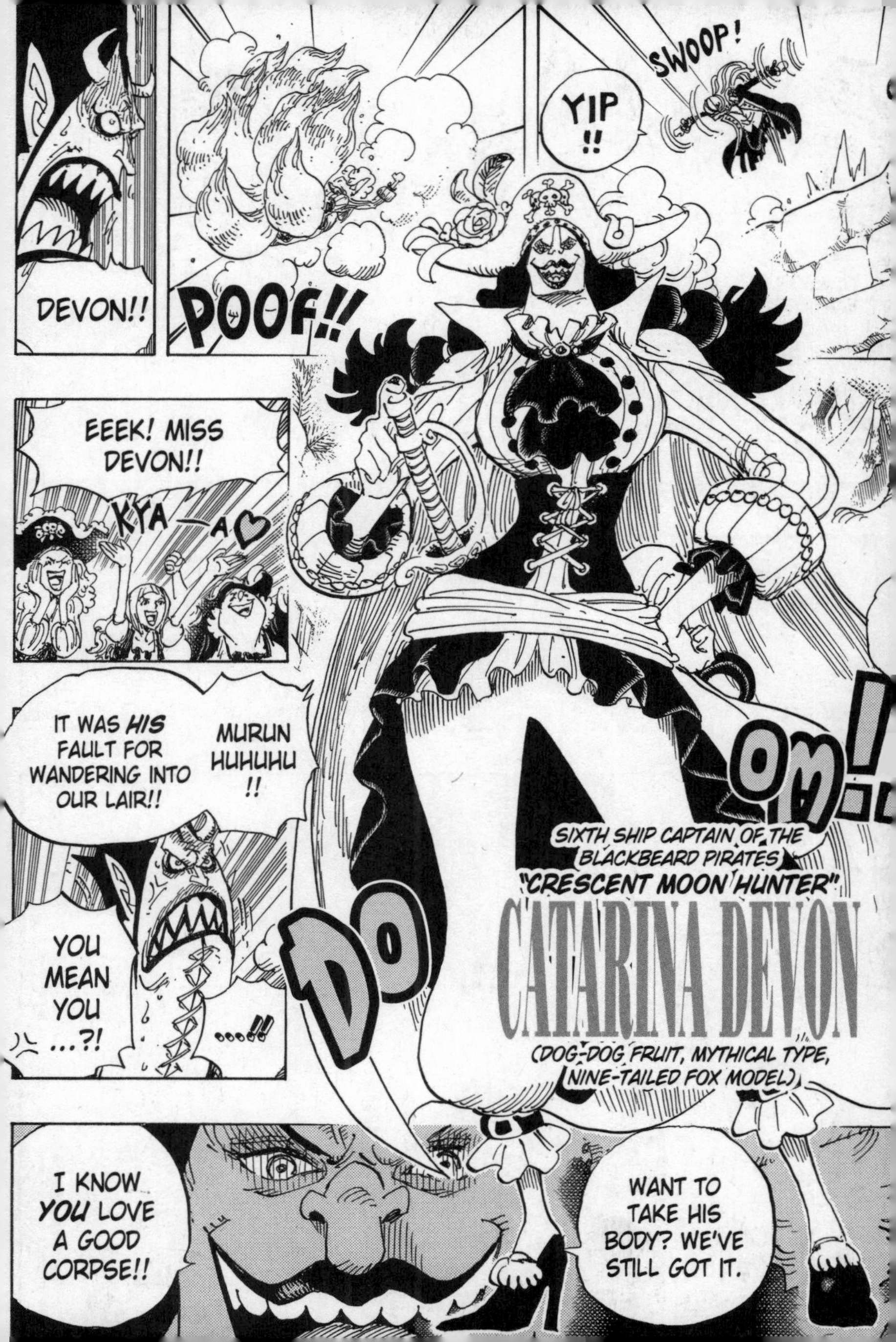
SWOOP!
YIP!!
POOF!!
DEVON!!
DOOM!!
SIXTH SHIP CAPTAIN OF THE BLACKBEARD PIRATES
"CRESCENT MOON HUNTER"
CATARINA DEVON
(DOG-DOG FRUIT, MYTHICAL TYPE, NINE-TAILED FOX MODEL)
EEEK! MISS DEVON!!
KYA—A♥
MURUN HUHUHU!!
IT WAS *HIS* FAULT FOR WANDERING INTO OUR LAIR!!
...!!
YOU MEAN YOU ...?!
WANT TO TAKE HIS BODY? WE'VE STILL GOT IT.
I KNOW *YOU* LOVE A GOOD CORPSE!!

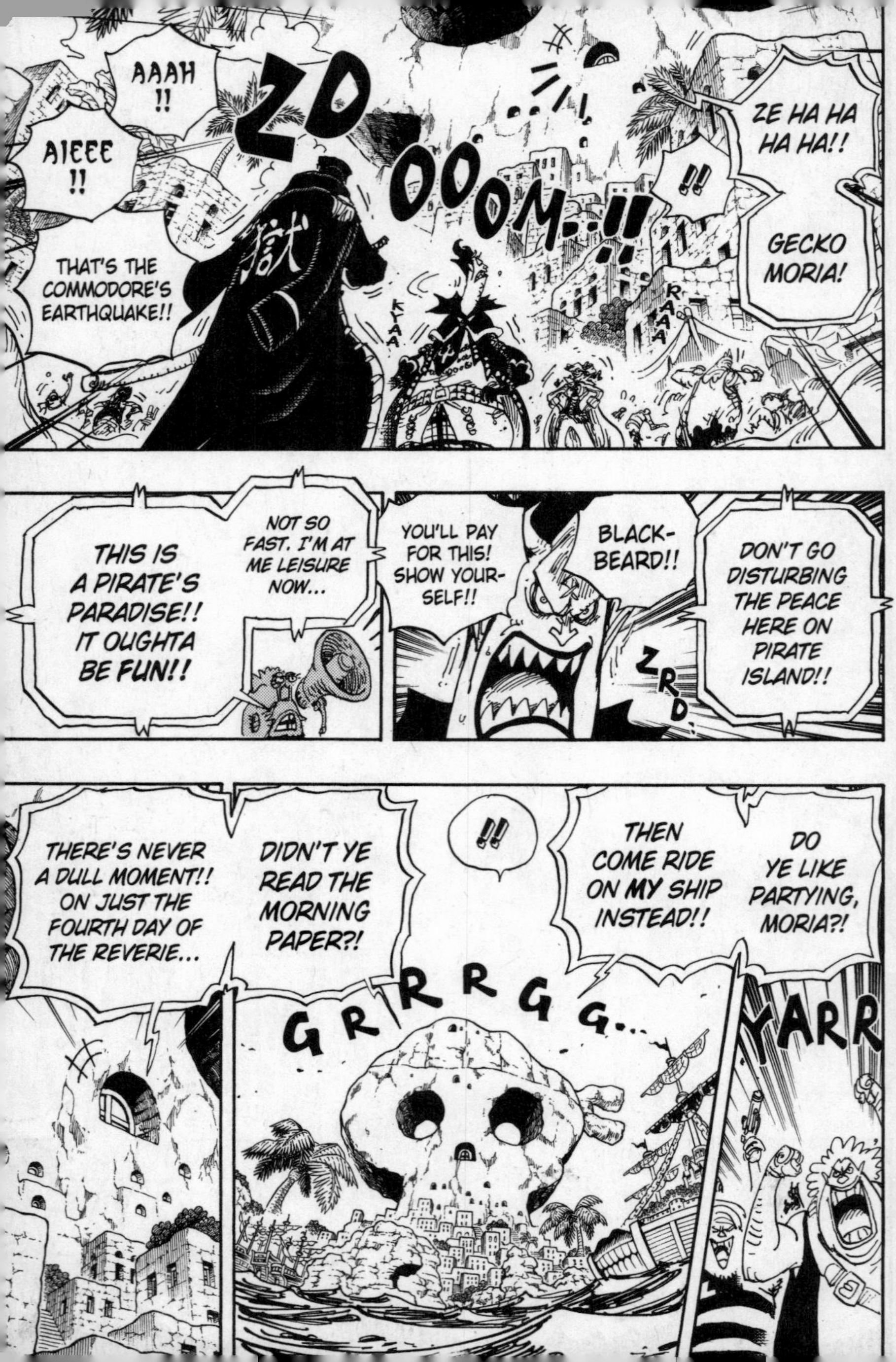
ZE HA HA HA HA!!
GECKO MORIA!
!!
ZDOOOOM..!!
AAAH !!
AIEEE !!
THAT'S THE COMMODORE'S EARTHQUAKE!!
KYAA
RAAA
DON'T GO DISTURBING THE PEACE HERE ON PIRATE ISLAND!!
BLACK-BEARD!!
YOU'LL PAY FOR THIS! SHOW YOUR-SELF!!
ZRD
NOT SO FAST. I'M AT ME LEISURE NOW...
THIS IS A PIRATE'S PARADISE!! IT OUGHTA BE FUN!!
DO YE LIKE PARTYING, MORIA?!
THEN COME RIDE ON MY SHIP INSTEAD!!
YARR
!!
DIDN'T YE READ THE MORNING PAPER?!
GRRRGG...
THERE'S NEVER A DULL MOMENT!! ON JUST THE FOURTH DAY OF THE REVERIE...

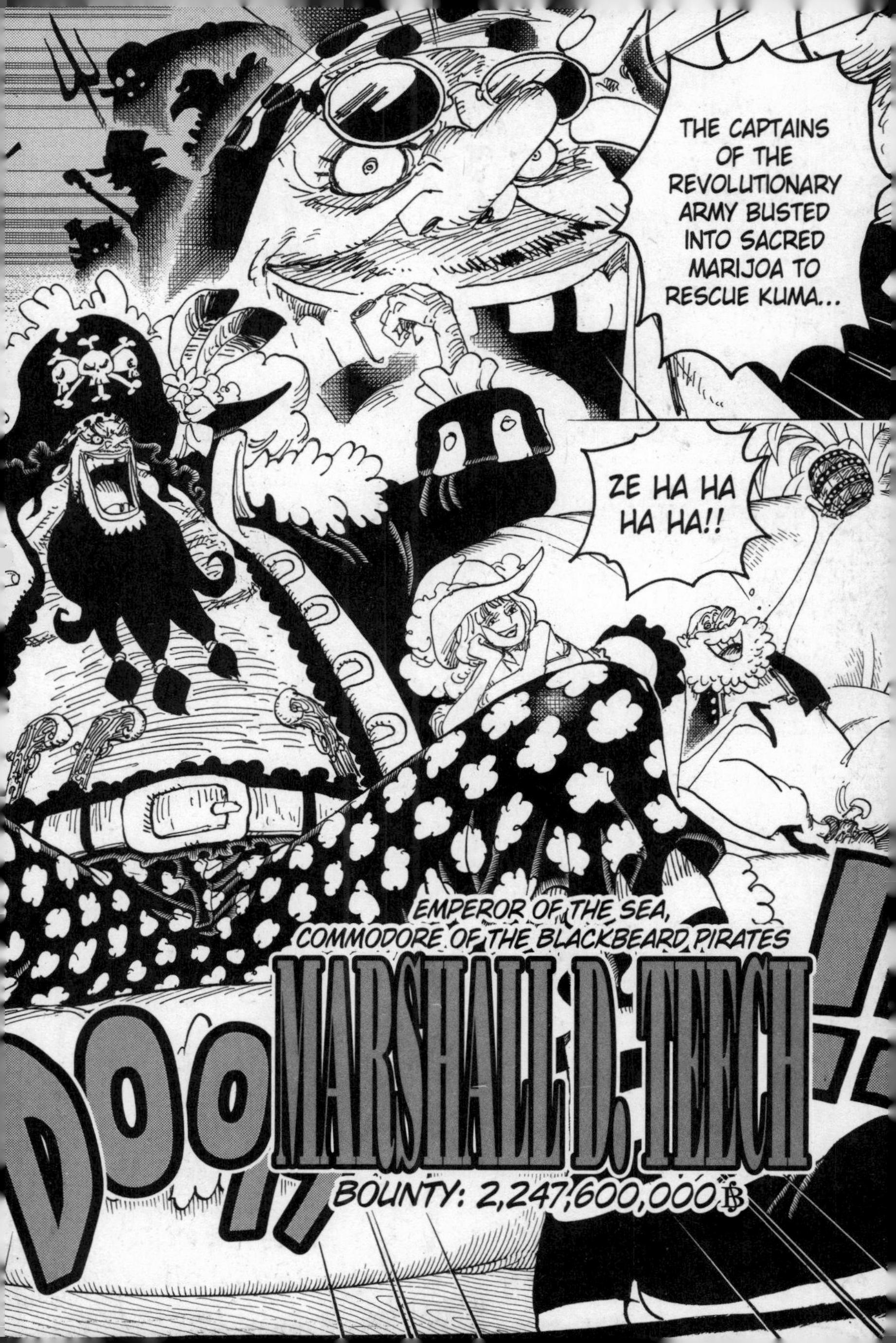
THE CAPTAINS OF THE REVOLUTIONARY ARMY BUSTED INTO SACRED MARIJOA TO RESCUE KUMA...
ZE HA HA HA HA!!
EMPEROR OF THE SEA, COMMODORE OF THE BLACKBEARD PIRATES
MARSHALL D. TEECH
BOUNTY: 2,247,600,000 ฿
DOO

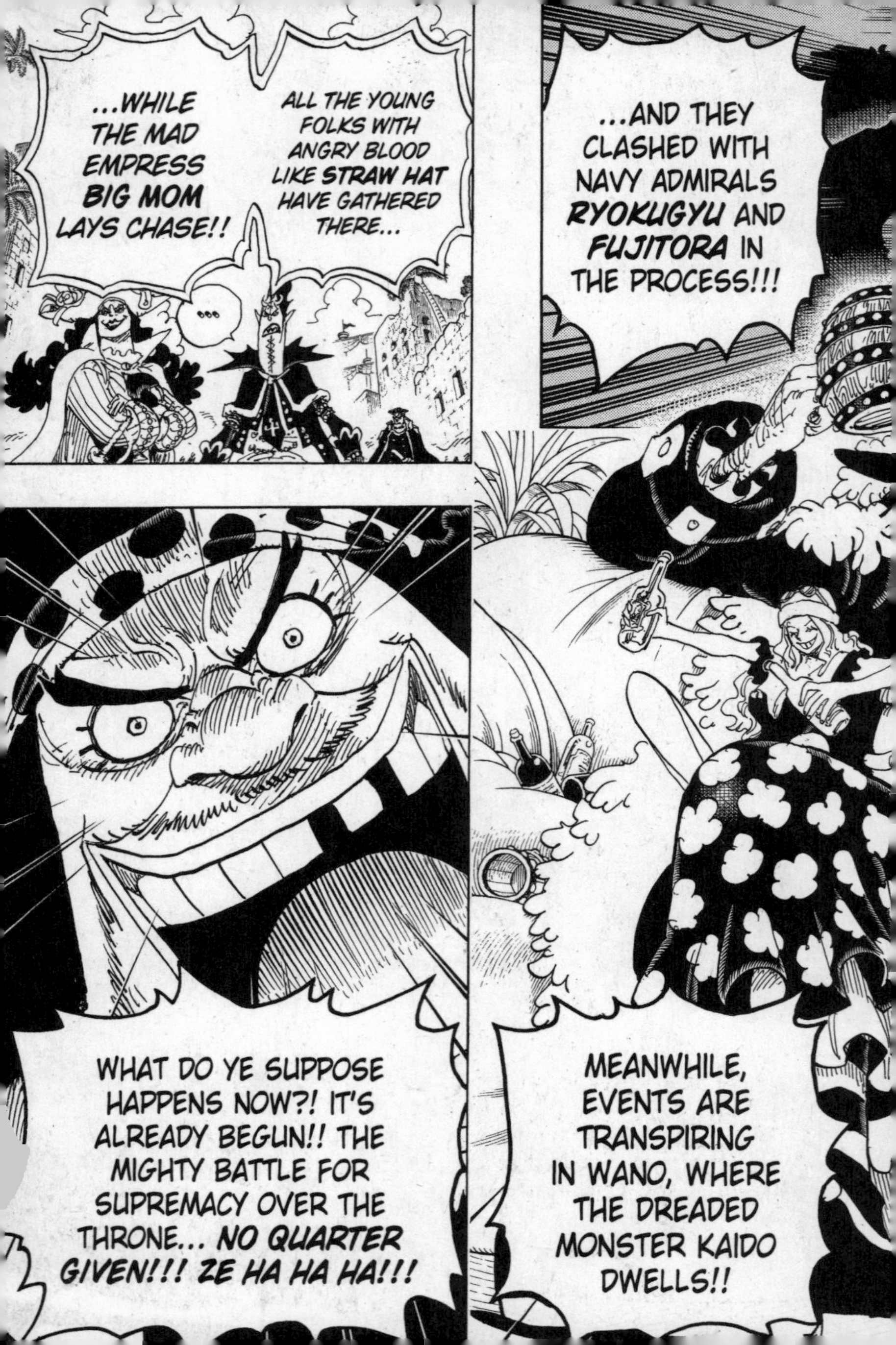
...AND THEY CLASHED WITH NAVY ADMIRALS **RYOKUGYU** AND **FUJITORA** IN THE PROCESS!!!
ALL THE YOUNG FOLKS WITH ANGRY BLOOD LIKE **STRAW HAT** HAVE GATHERED THERE...
...WHILE THE MAD EMPRESS **BIG MOM** LAYS CHASE!!
...
MEANWHILE, EVENTS ARE TRANSPIRING IN WANO, WHERE THE DREADED MONSTER KAIDO DWELLS!!
WHAT DO YE SUPPOSE HAPPENS NOW?! IT'S ALREADY BEGUN!! THE MIGHTY BATTLE FOR SUPREMACY OVER THE THRONE... ***NO QUARTER GIVEN!!! ZE HA HA HA!!!***

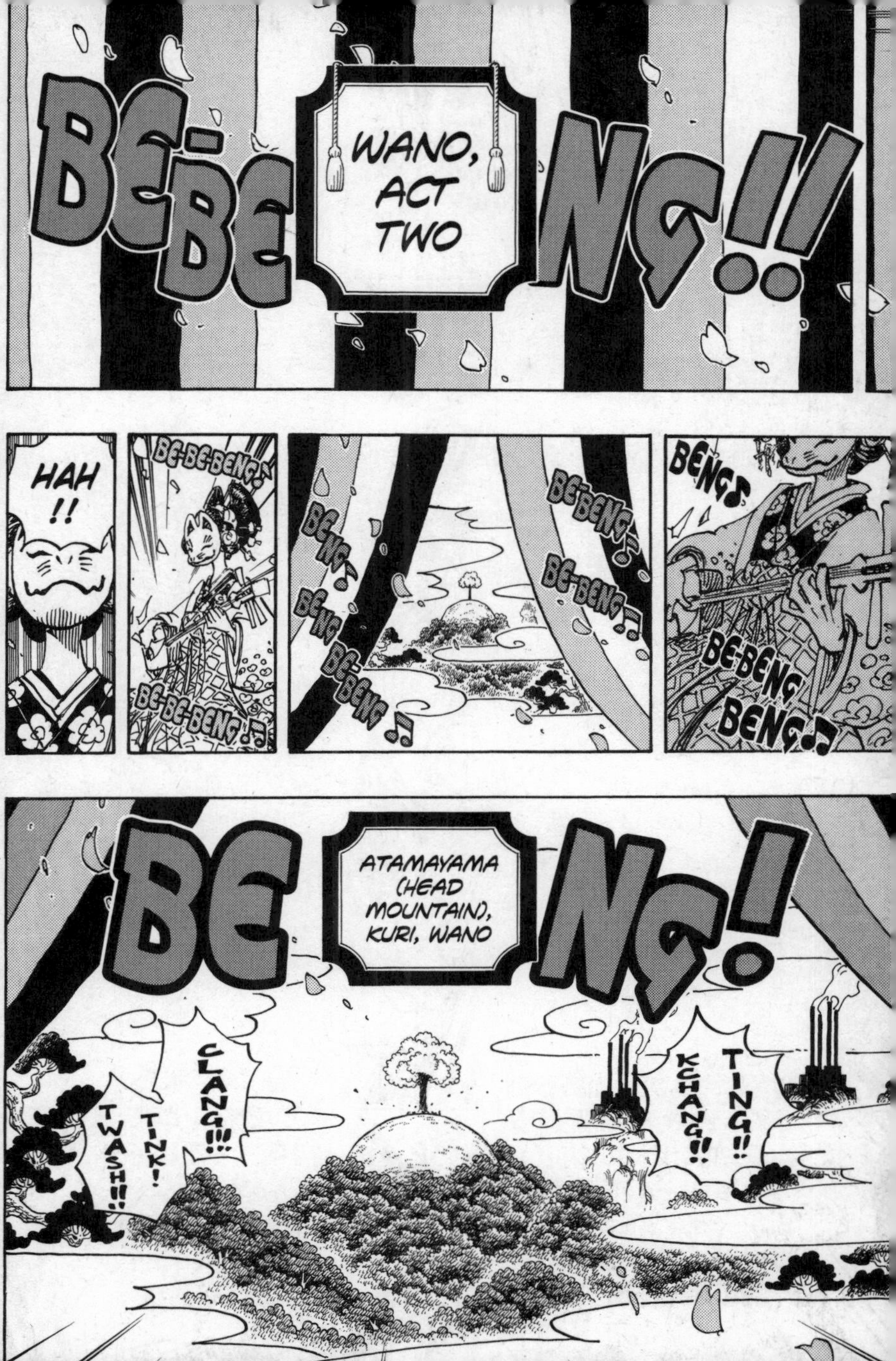
BE-BE-
WANO, ACT TWO
NG!!
BENG♪
BE-BENG BENG♪♪
BE-BENG♪
BE-BENG♪♪
BE-NG♪
BE-NG
BE-BENG♪♪
BE-BE-BENG♪
BE-BE-BENG♪♪
HAH !!
BE
ATAMAYAMA (HEAD MOUNTAIN), KURI, WANO
NG!
TING!!
KCHANG!!
CLANG!!!
TINK!
TWASH!!!

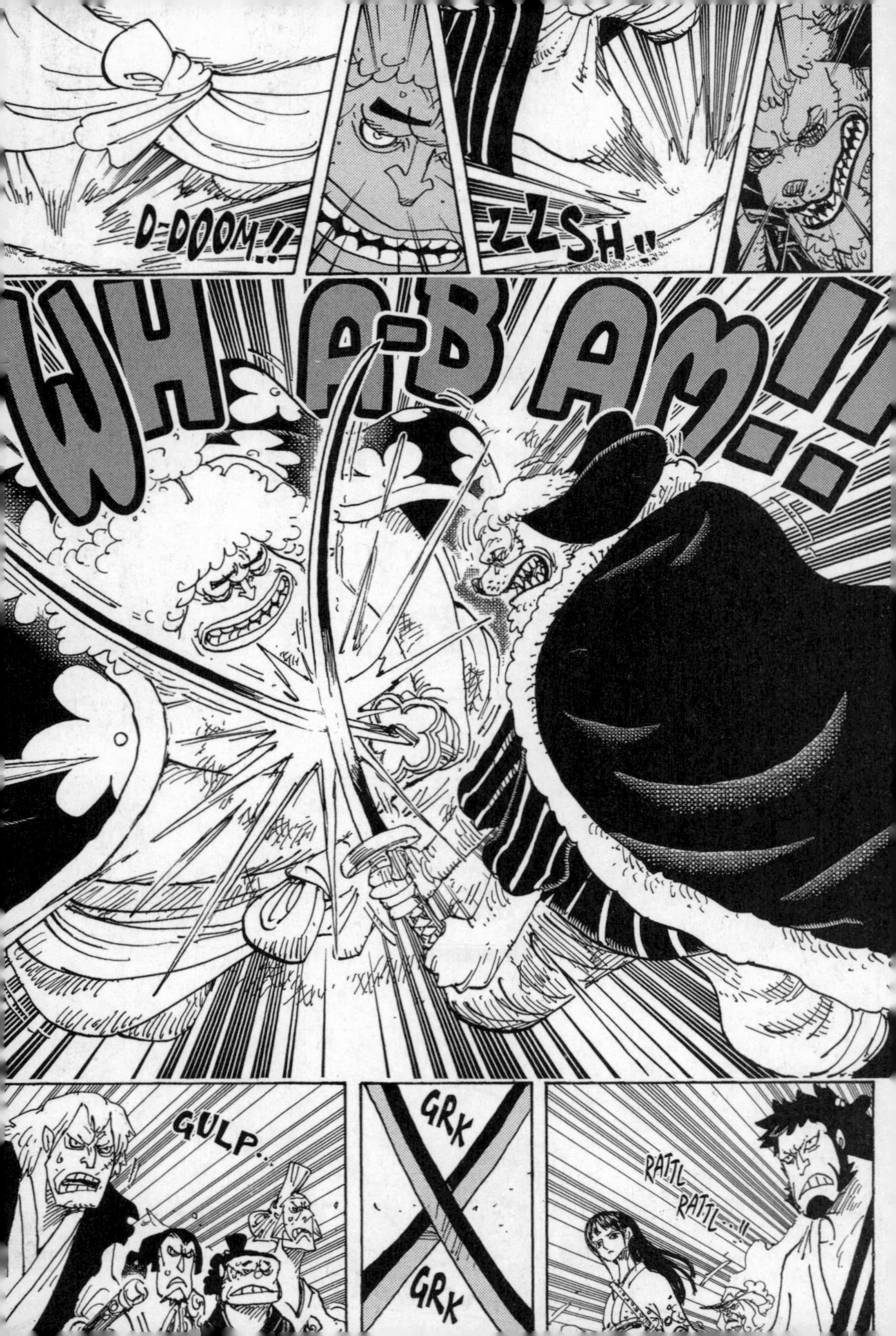
ZZSH!!
D-DOOM!!
WHA-BAM!!
RATTL RATTL...!!
GRK
GRK
GULP..

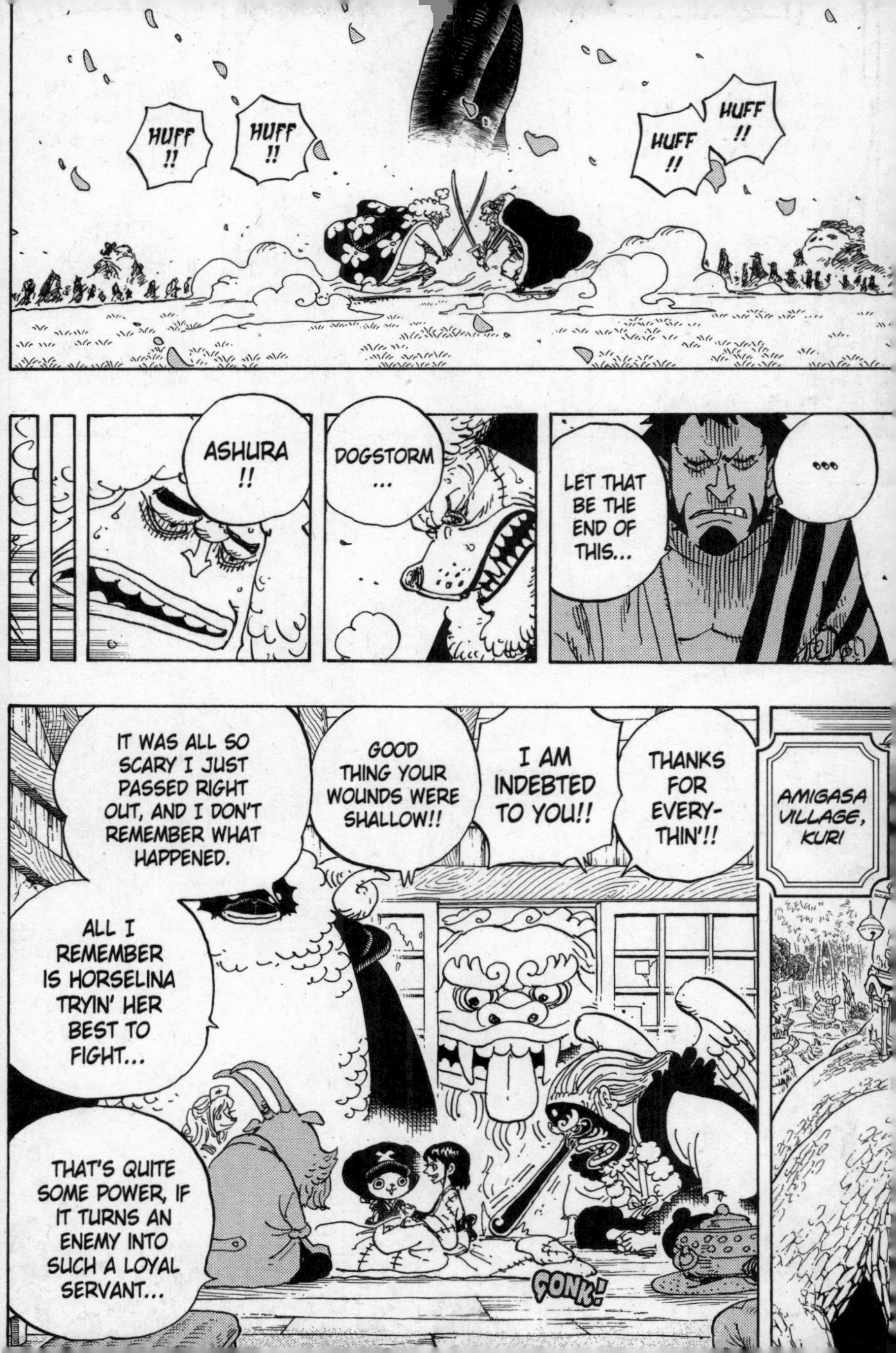
HUFF !!
HUFF !!
HUFF !!
HUFF !!
...
LET THAT BE THE END OF THIS...
DOGSTORM ...
ASHURA !!
AMIGASA VILLAGE, KURI
THANKS FOR EVERY-THIN'!!
I AM INDEBTED TO YOU!!
GOOD THING YOUR WOUNDS WERE SHALLOW!!
IT WAS ALL SO SCARY I JUST PASSED RIGHT OUT, AND I DON'T REMEMBER WHAT HAPPENED.
ALL I REMEMBER IS HORSELINA TRYIN' HER BEST TO FIGHT...
THAT'S QUITE SOME POWER, IF IT TURNS AN ENEMY INTO SUCH A LOYAL SERVANT...
GONK!

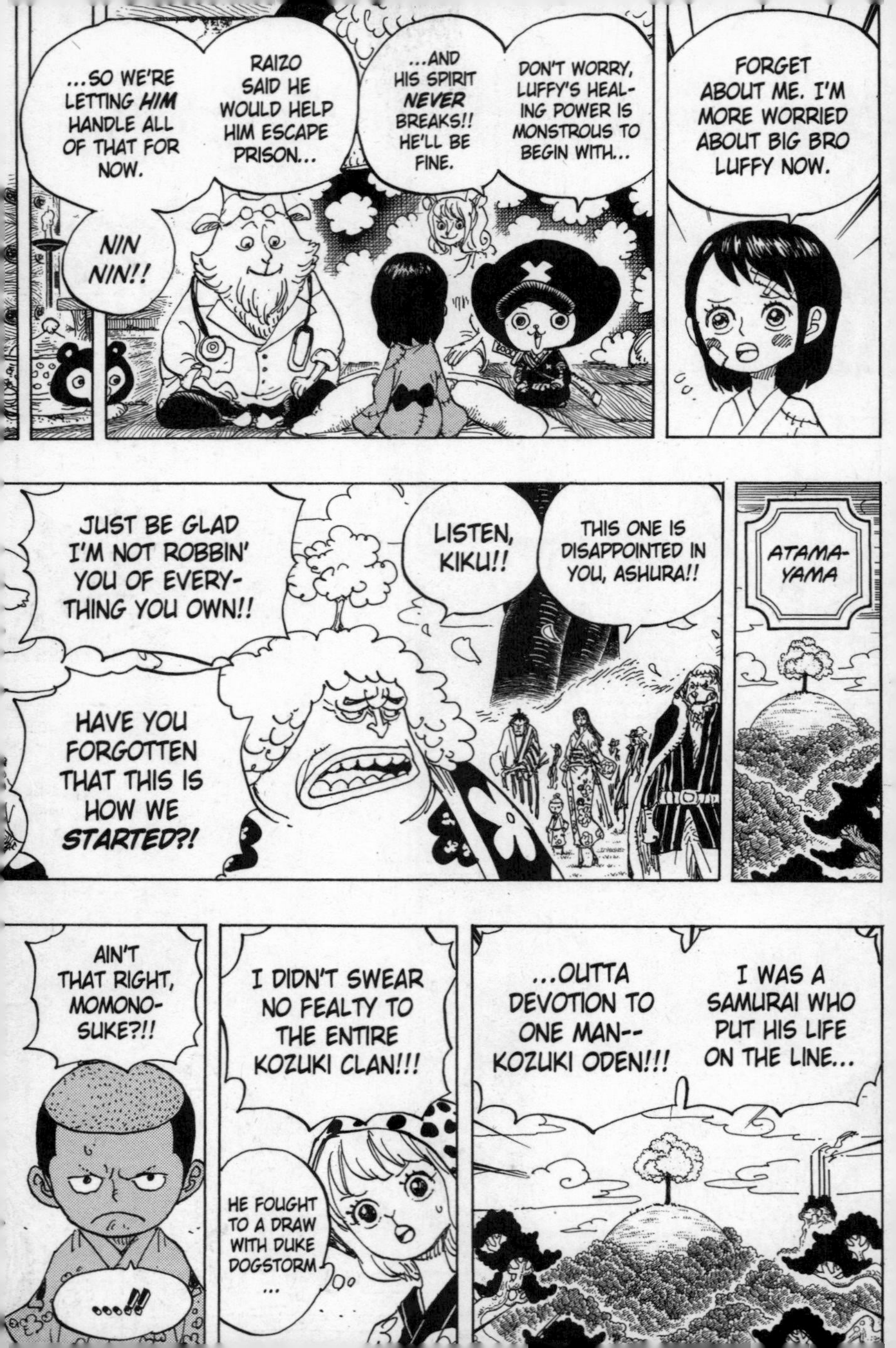
FORGET ABOUT ME. I'M MORE WORRIED ABOUT BIG BRO LUFFY NOW.
DON'T WORRY, LUFFY'S HEAL-ING POWER IS MONSTROUS TO BEGIN WITH...
...AND HIS SPIRIT *NEVER* BREAKS!! HE'LL BE FINE.
RAIZO SAID HE WOULD HELP HIM ESCAPE PRISON...
...SO WE'RE LETTING *HIM* HANDLE ALL OF THAT FOR NOW.
NIN NIN!!
ATAMA-YAMA
THIS ONE IS DISAPPOINTED IN YOU, ASHURA!!
LISTEN, KIKU!!
JUST BE GLAD I'M NOT ROBBIN' YOU OF EVERY-THING YOU OWN!!
HAVE YOU FORGOTTEN THAT THIS IS HOW WE *STARTED?!*
I WAS A SAMURAI WHO PUT HIS LIFE ON THE LINE...
...OUTTA DEVOTION TO ONE MAN-- KOZUKI ODEN!!!
I DIDN'T SWEAR NO FEALTY TO THE ENTIRE KOZUKI CLAN!!!
HE FOUGHT TO A DRAW WITH DUKE DOGSTORM ...
AIN'T THAT RIGHT, MOMONO-SUKE?!!
....!!

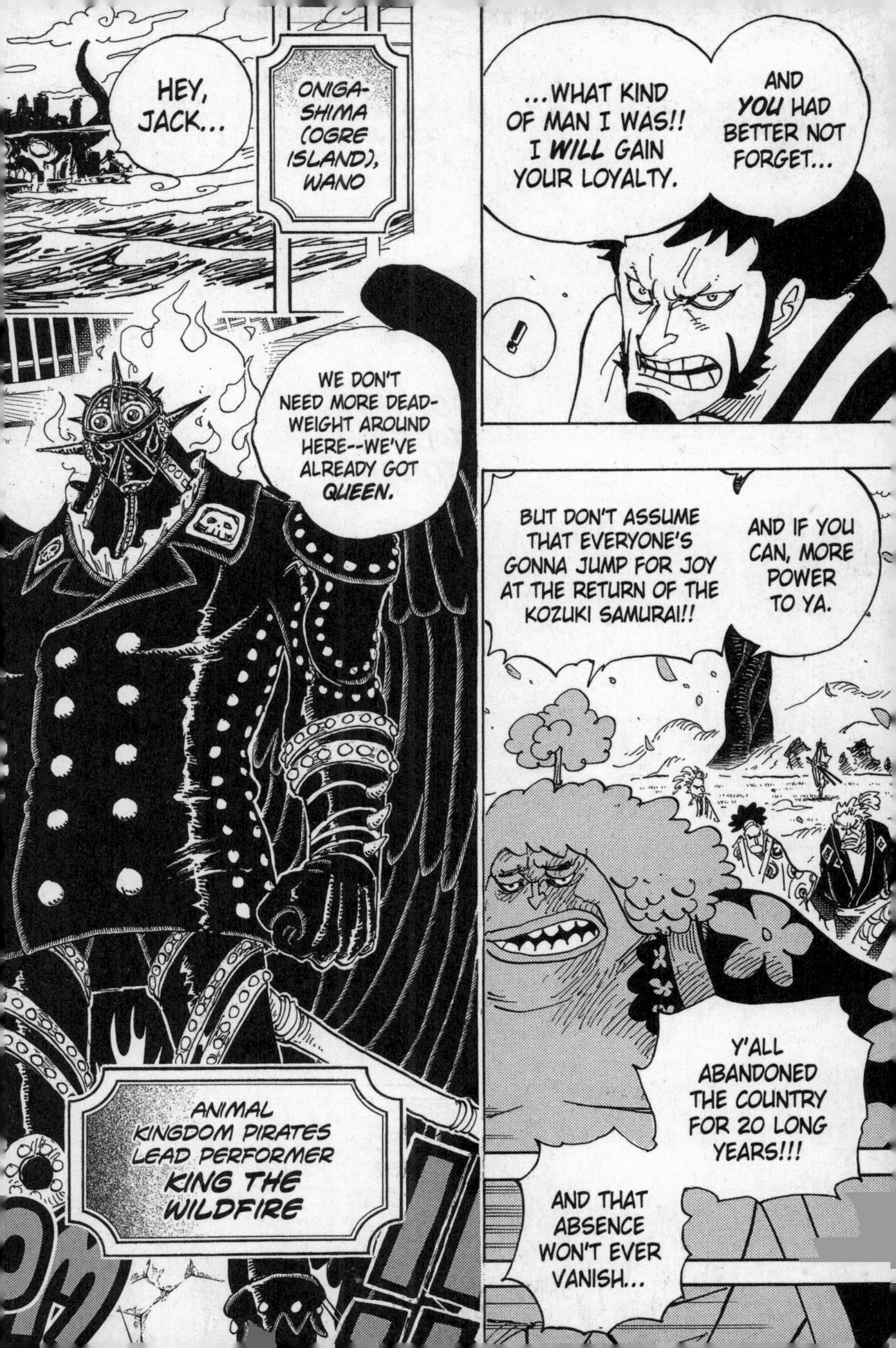
AND YOU HAD BETTER NOT FORGET...
...WHAT KIND OF MAN I WAS!! I WILL GAIN YOUR LOYALTY.
!
AND IF YOU CAN, MORE POWER TO YA.
BUT DON'T ASSUME THAT EVERYONE'S GONNA JUMP FOR JOY AT THE RETURN OF THE KOZUKI SAMURAI!!
Y'ALL ABANDONED THE COUNTRY FOR 20 LONG YEARS!!!
AND THAT ABSENCE WON'T EVER VANISH...
ONIGA-SHIMA (OGRE ISLAND), WANO
HEY, JACK...
WE DON'T NEED MORE DEAD-WEIGHT AROUND HERE--WE'VE ALREADY GOT QUEEN.
ANIMAL KINGDOM PIRATES LEAD PERFORMER KING THE WILDFIRE

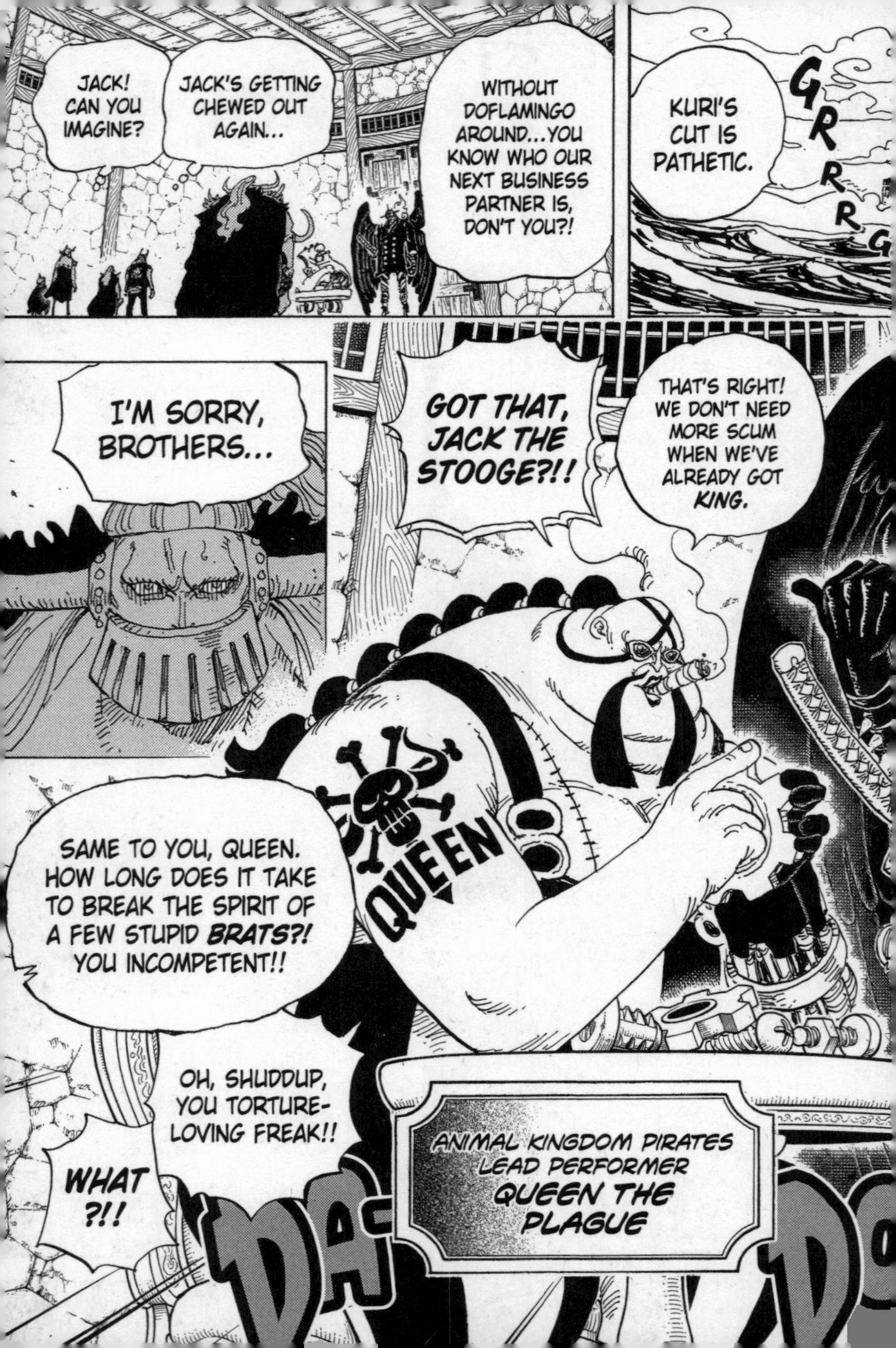
KURI'S CUT IS PATHETIC.
GRRRRG
WITHOUT DOFLAMINGO AROUND...YOU KNOW WHO OUR NEXT BUSINESS PARTNER IS, DON'T YOU?!
JACK'S GETTING CHEWED OUT AGAIN...
JACK! CAN YOU IMAGINE?
THAT'S RIGHT! WE DON'T NEED MORE SCUM WHEN WE'VE ALREADY GOT KING.
GOT THAT, JACK THE STOOGE?!!
QUEEN
I'M SORRY, BROTHERS...
SAME TO YOU, QUEEN. HOW LONG DOES IT TAKE TO BREAK THE SPIRIT OF A FEW STUPID BRATS?! YOU INCOMPETENT!!
ANIMAL KINGDOM PIRATES LEAD PERFORMER QUEEN THE PLAGUE
OH, SHUDDUP, YOU TORTURE-LOVING FREAK!!
WHAT ?!!

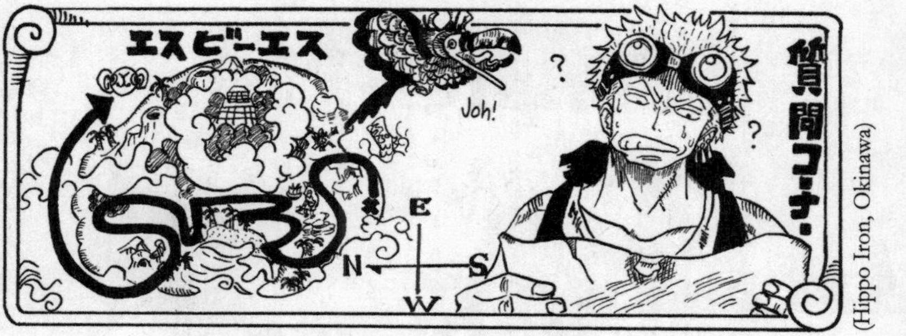
エスビーエス
質問コーナー
SBS
Joh!
E
N
S
W
(Hippo Iron, Okinawa)

A: Well everyone, I've got another announcement. At the New Year's party for *Weekly Shonen Jump*, it was revealed that I have another Usopp Gallery fan-art comrade! As of March 2019, the *Jump* series known as *neO;lation*, drawn by Mizuki Yoda, told me, "Oh, I was in the Usopp Gallery section." I was like, "Really?!"

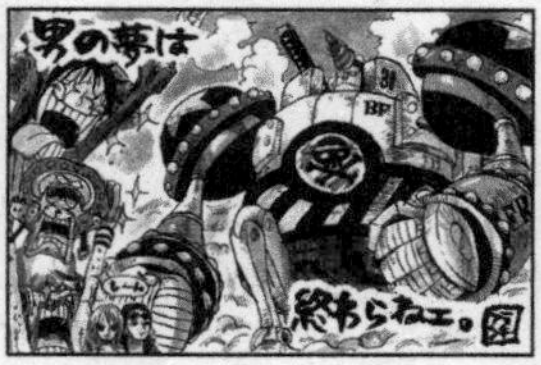
男の夢は
終わらねエ。

⬅ Here it is! From Yodacchi of Tokyo in volume 65.

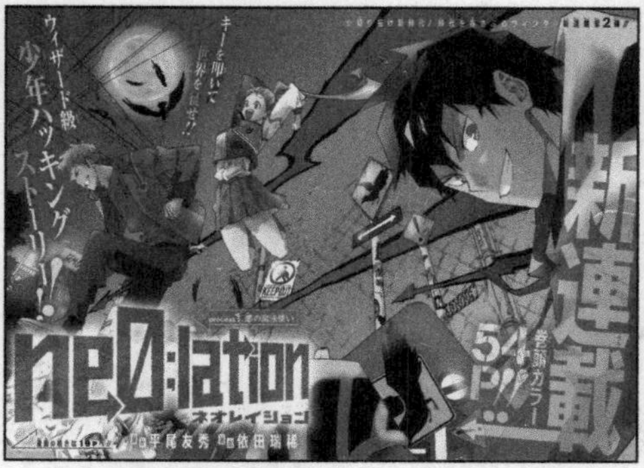
新連載
巻頭カラー
54P!!
キーを叩いて世界を驚かせ!!
ウィザード級
少年ハッキングストーリー!!
neO:lation
ネオレイション
平尾友秀
依田瑞稀

And this is the series! ➡ Another professional has graduated from the section! At this point, the Usopp Gallery Pirates are like a rite of passage to going pro! Well, isn't that just grand?!

Read Mizuki Yoda's *neO;lation*!!

It's a manga about a genius hacker kid. Check it out! And good luck!

Q: Hello, Oda Sensei!! This is my first submission to the SBS!! If Zolo's three swords (Wado Ichimonji, Kitetsu III, Shusui) took human form, what would they look like? (In other words, draw them anthropomorphized!)

--Katsuki

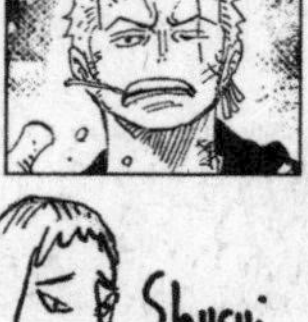

A: I see.

➡

There you are. This has been a smashing success.

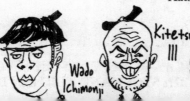

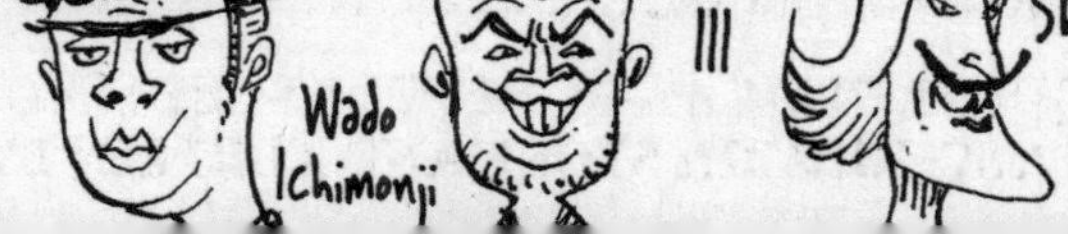
Wado Ichimonji
Kitetsu III
Shusui

Chapter 926:
EXCAVATION LABOR CAMP

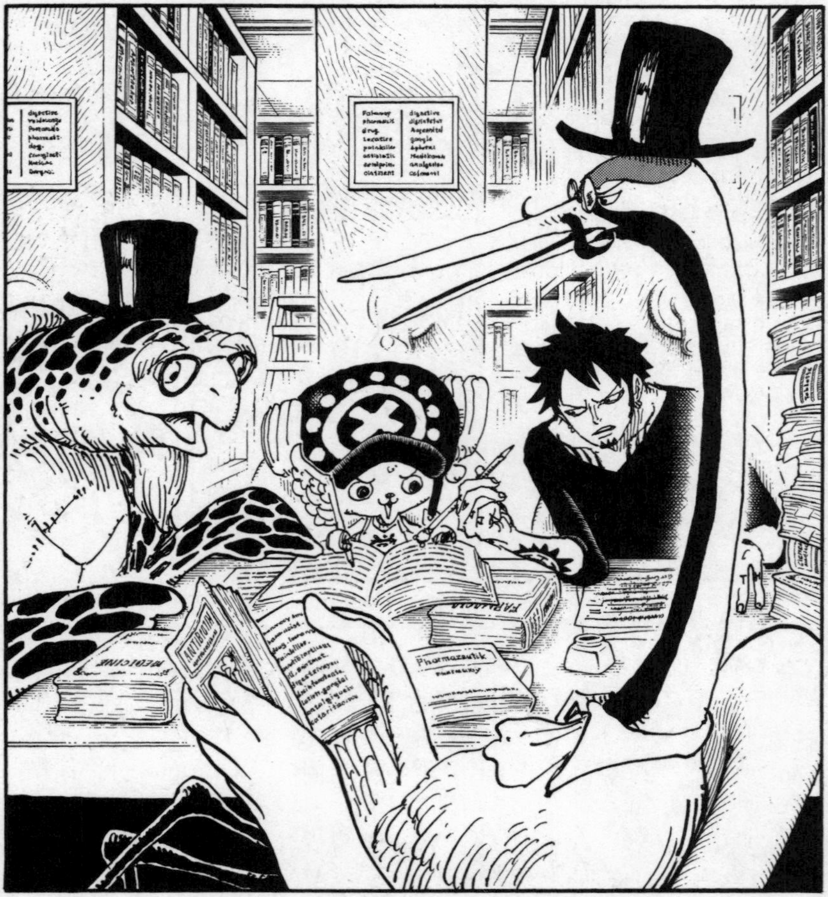
Pharmazeutik

REQUEST: "LAW AND CHOPPER STUDYING MEDICINE WITH A SCHOLARLY STORK AND TURTLE" BY ONANTURE

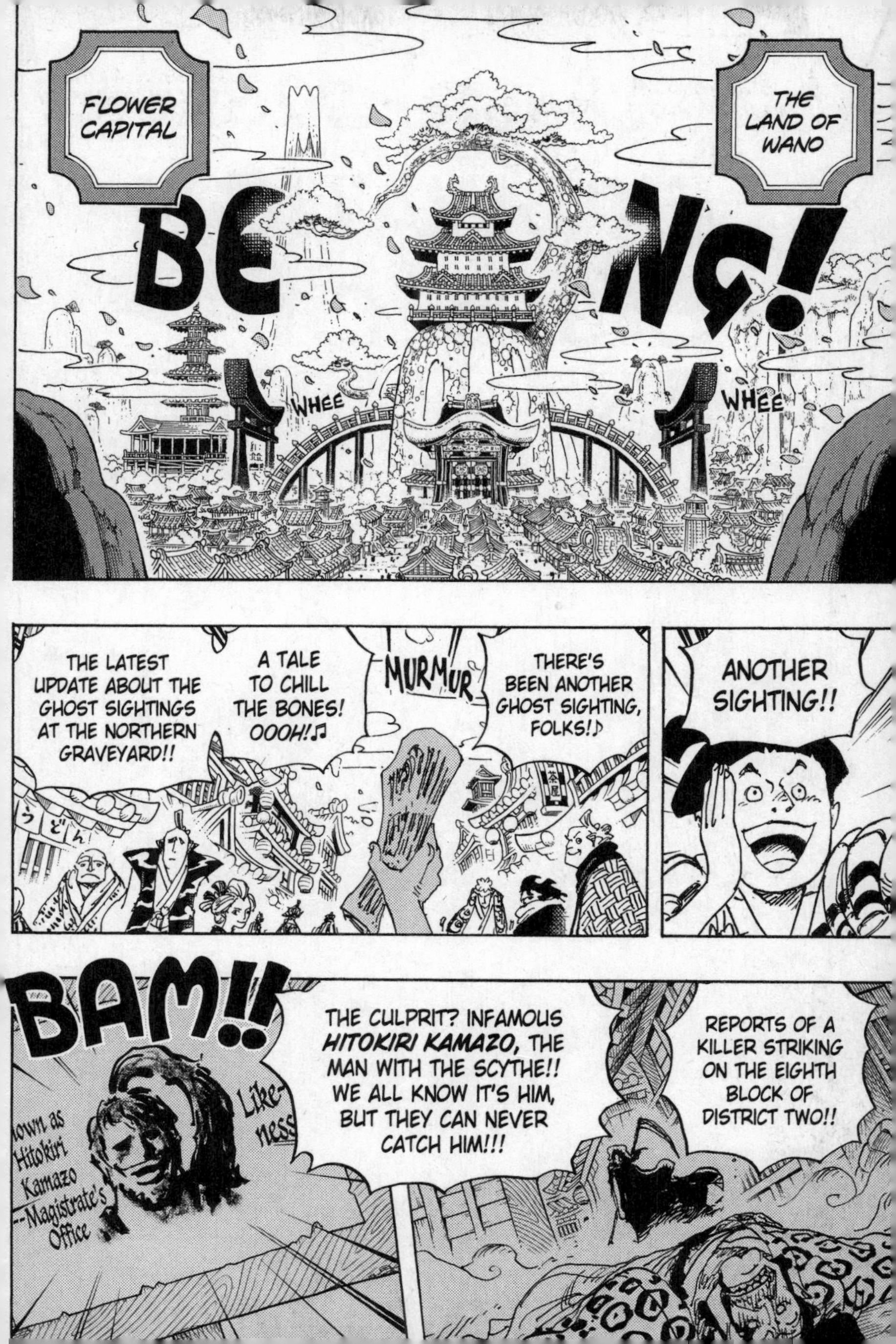
THE LAND OF WANO
FLOWER CAPITAL
BONG!
WHEE
WHEE
ANOTHER SIGHTING!!
THERE'S BEEN ANOTHER GHOST SIGHTING, FOLKS!♪
MURMUR
A TALE TO CHILL THE BONES! OOOH!♫
THE LATEST UPDATE ABOUT THE GHOST SIGHTINGS AT THE NORTHERN GRAVEYARD!!
REPORTS OF A KILLER STRIKING ON THE EIGHTH BLOCK OF DISTRICT TWO!!
THE CULPRIT? INFAMOUS HITOKIRI KAMAZO, THE MAN WITH THE SCYTHE!! WE ALL KNOW IT'S HIM, BUT THEY CAN NEVER CATCH HIM!!!
Likeness
BAM!!
own as Hitokiri Kamazo --Magistrate's Office

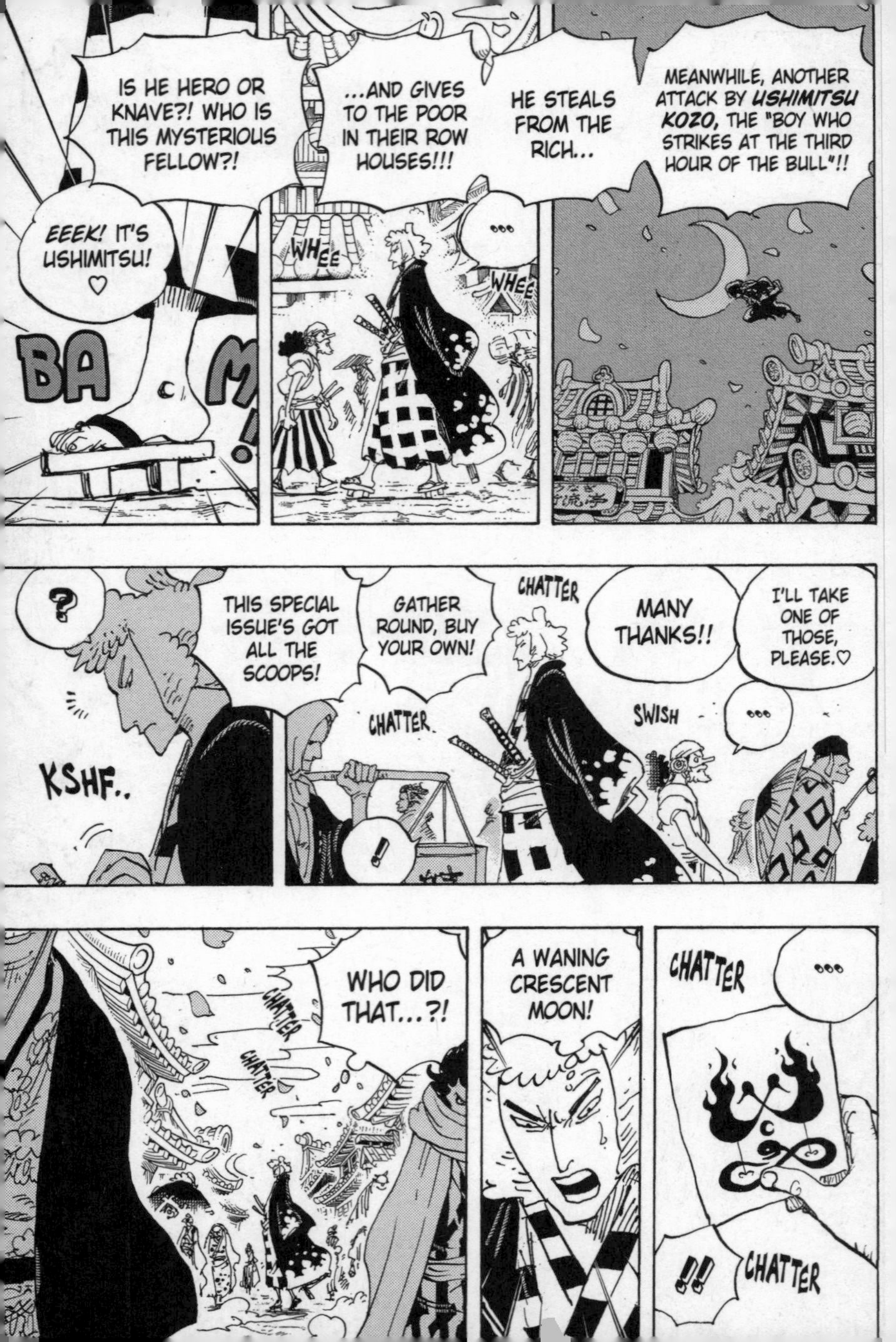

MEANWHILE, ANOTHER ATTACK BY USHIMITSU KOZO, THE "BOY WHO STRIKES AT THE THIRD HOUR OF THE BULL"!!
HE STEALS FROM THE RICH...
...AND GIVES TO THE POOR IN THEIR ROW HOUSES!!!
...
WHEE
WHEE
IS HE HERO OR KNAVE?! WHO IS THIS MYSTERIOUS FELLOW?!
EEEK! IT'S USHIMITSU! ♡
BAM!
I'LL TAKE ONE OF THOSE, PLEASE.♡
MANY THANKS!!
CHATTER
GATHER ROUND, BUY YOUR OWN!
THIS SPECIAL ISSUE'S GOT ALL THE SCOOPS!
SWISH
...
CHATTER
!
?
KSHF..
...
CHATTER
!!
CHATTER
A WANING CRESCENT MOON!
WHO DID THAT...?!
CHATTER
CHATTER

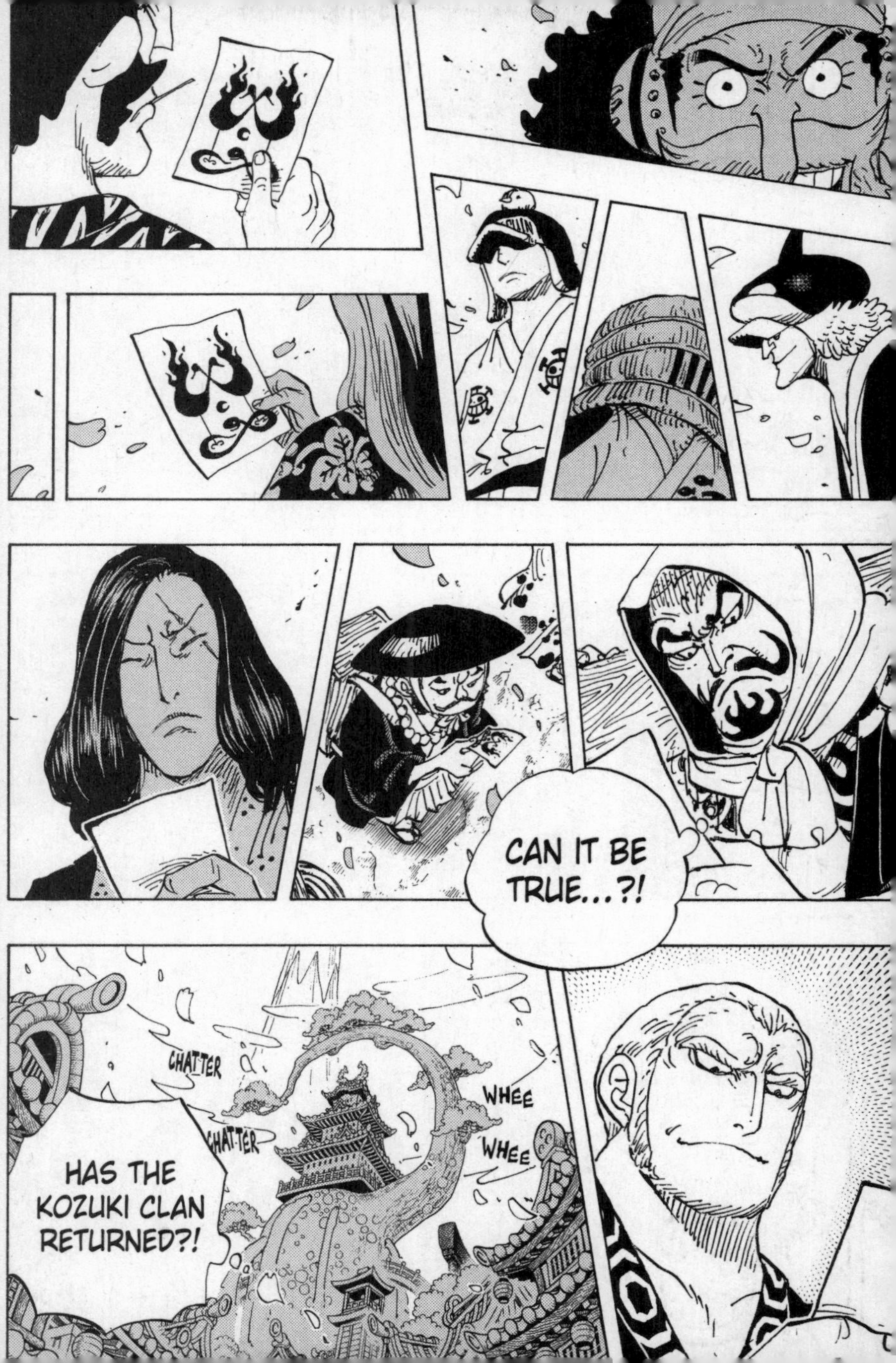
CAN IT BE TRUE...?!
CHAT-TER
WHEE
CHAT-TER
WHEE
HAS THE KOZUKI CLAN RETURNED?!

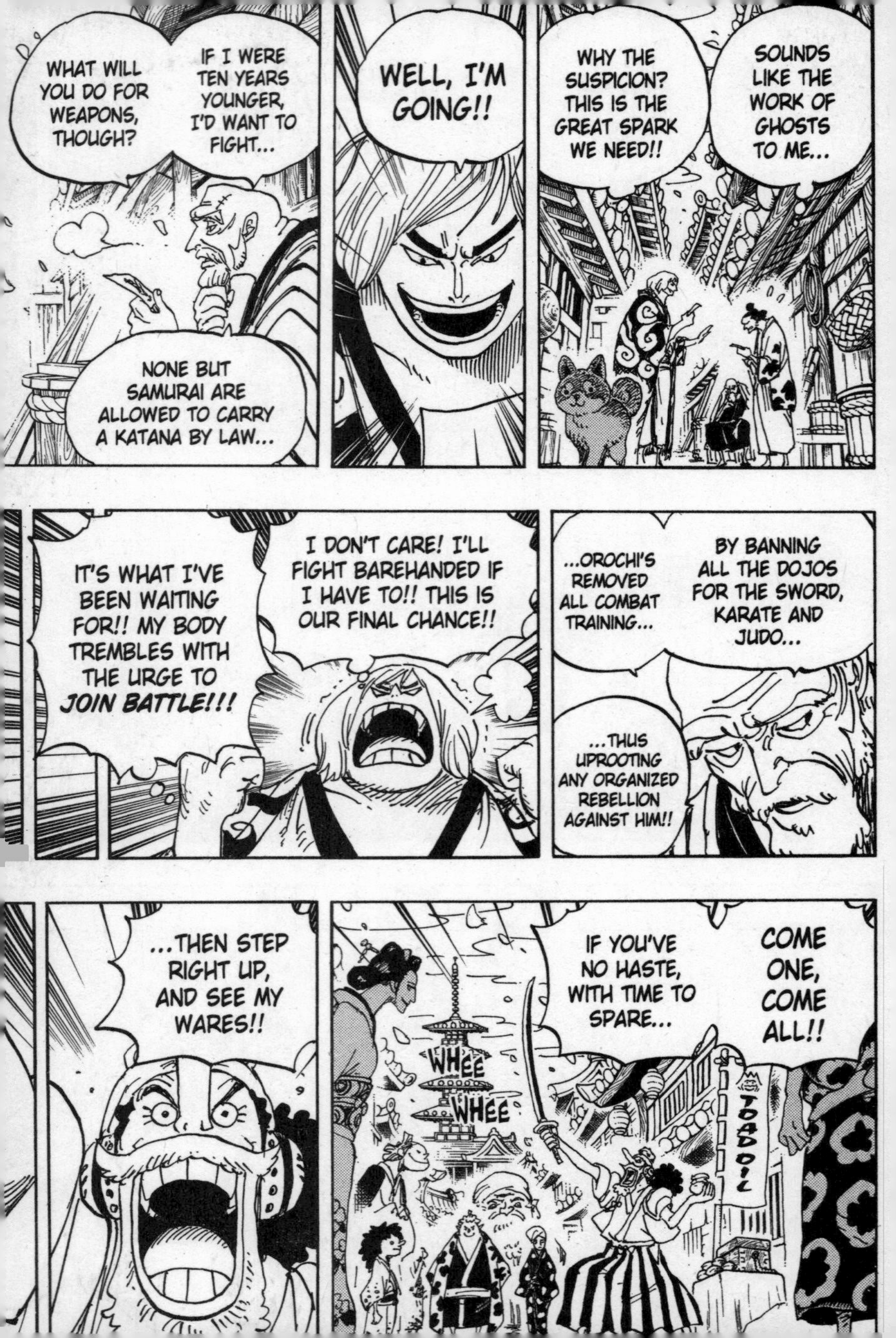
SOUNDS LIKE THE WORK OF GHOSTS TO ME...
WHY THE SUSPICION? THIS IS THE GREAT SPARK WE NEED!!
WELL, I'M GOING!!
IF I WERE TEN YEARS YOUNGER, I'D WANT TO FIGHT...
WHAT WILL YOU DO FOR WEAPONS, THOUGH?
NONE BUT SAMURAI ARE ALLOWED TO CARRY A KATANA BY LAW...
BY BANNING ALL THE DOJOS FOR THE SWORD, KARATE AND JUDO...
...OROCHI'S REMOVED ALL COMBAT TRAINING...
...THUS UPROOTING ANY ORGANIZED REBELLION AGAINST HIM!!
I DON'T CARE! I'LL FIGHT BAREHANDED IF I HAVE TO!! THIS IS OUR FINAL CHANCE!!
IT'S WHAT I'VE BEEN WAITING FOR!! MY BODY TREMBLES WITH THE URGE TO *JOIN BATTLE!!!*
COME ONE, COME ALL!!
IF YOU'VE NO HASTE, WITH TIME TO SPARE...
TOAD OIL
WHEE
WHEE
...THEN STEP RIGHT UP, AND SEE MY WARES!!

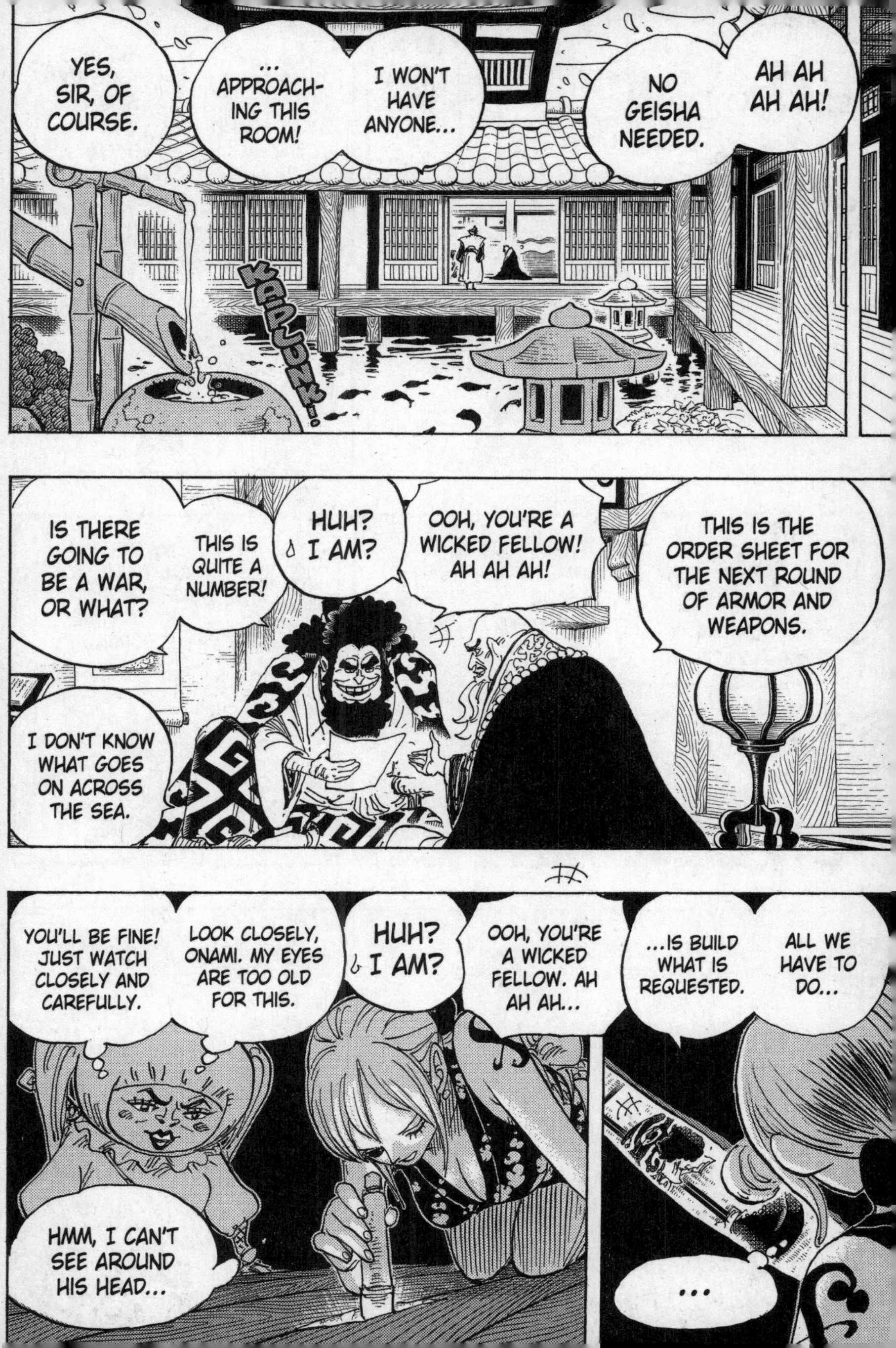
AH AH AH AH!
NO GEISHA NEEDED.
I WON'T HAVE ANYONE...
...APPROACHING THIS ROOM!
YES, SIR, OF COURSE.
KAPLUNK!
THIS IS THE ORDER SHEET FOR THE NEXT ROUND OF ARMOR AND WEAPONS.
OOH, YOU'RE A WICKED FELLOW! AH AH AH!
HUH? I AM?
THIS IS QUITE A NUMBER!
IS THERE GOING TO BE A WAR, OR WHAT?
I DON'T KNOW WHAT GOES ON ACROSS THE SEA.
ALL WE HAVE TO DO...
...IS BUILD WHAT IS REQUESTED.
...
OOH, YOU'RE A WICKED FELLOW. AH AH AH...
HUH? I AM?
LOOK CLOSELY, ONAMI. MY EYES ARE TOO OLD FOR THIS.
YOU'LL BE FINE! JUST WATCH CLOSELY AND CAREFULLY.
HMM, I CAN'T SEE AROUND HIS HEAD...

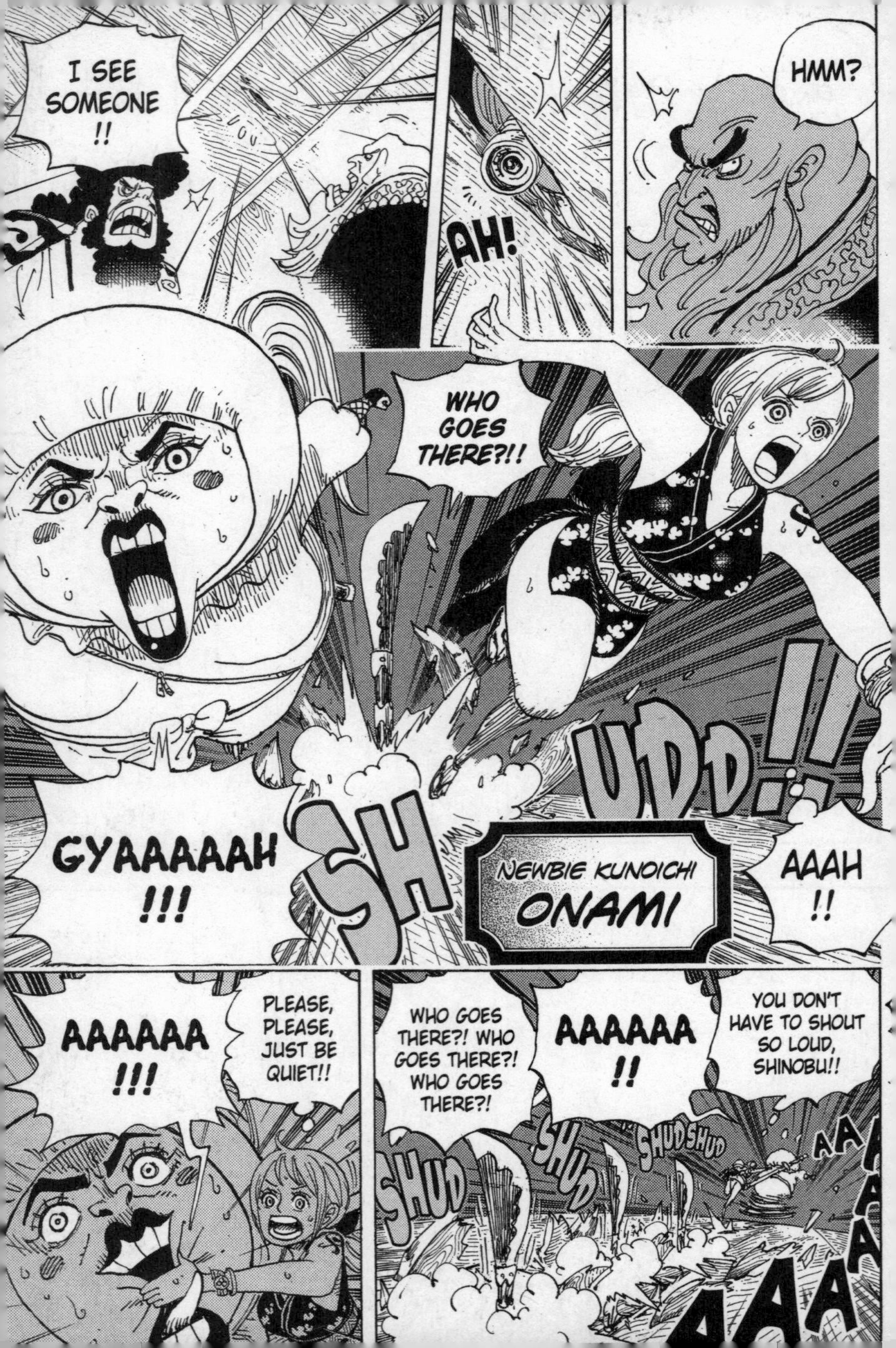
HMM?
AH!
I SEE SOMEONE !!
WHO GOES THERE?!!
SHUDD!!
AAAH !!
NEWBIE KUNOICHI ONAMI
GYAAAAAH !!!
YOU DON'T HAVE TO SHOUT SO LOUD, SHINOBU!!
AAAAAA !!
WHO GOES THERE?! WHO GOES THERE?! WHO GOES THERE?!
SHUDSHUD
SHUD
SHUD
PLEASE, PLEASE, JUST BE QUIET!!
AAAAAA !!!

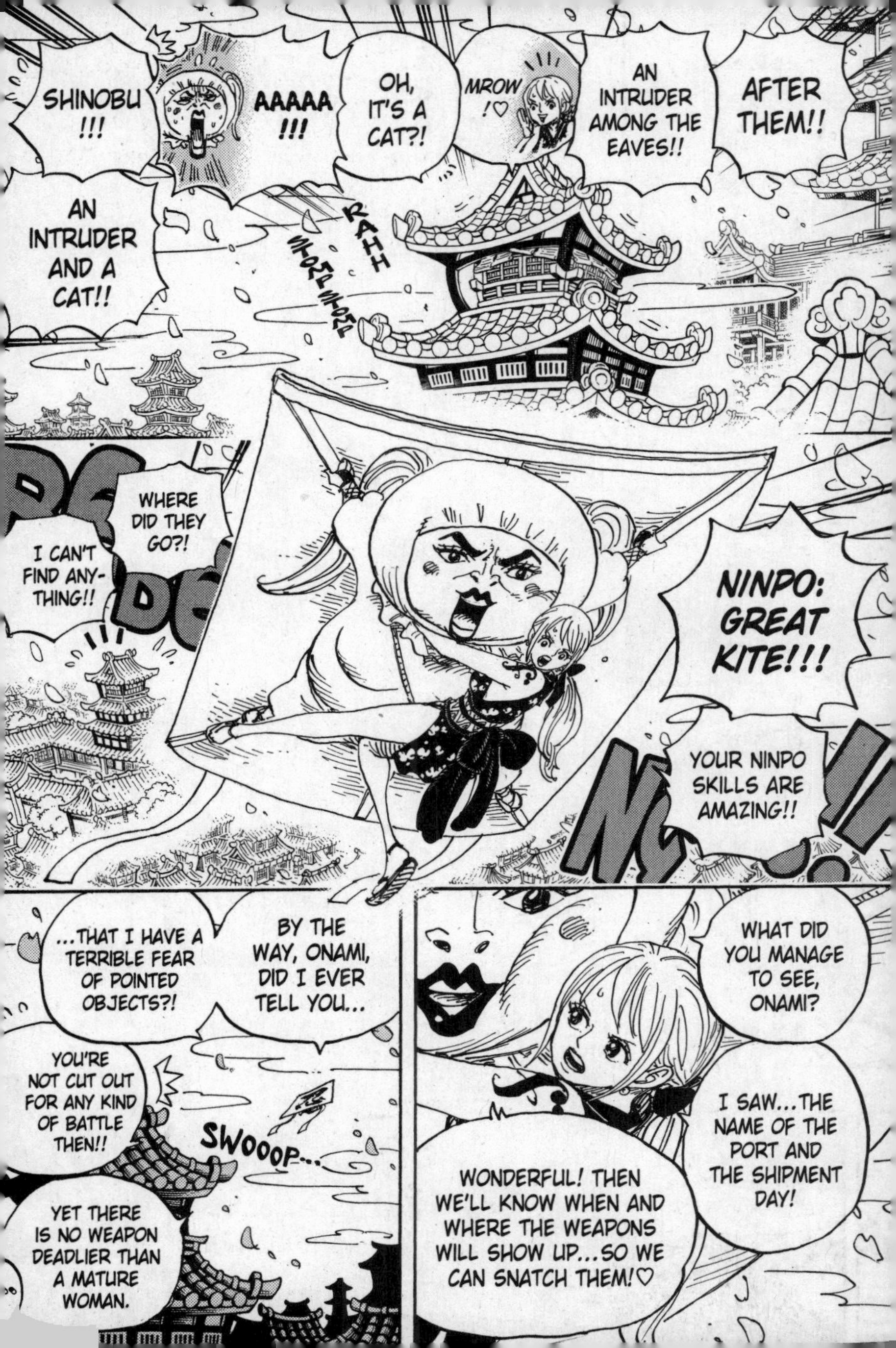
AFTER THEM!!
AN INTRUDER AMONG THE EAVES!!
MROW !♡
OH, IT'S A CAT?!
AAAAA !!!
SHINOBU !!!
AN INTRUDER AND A CAT!!
RAHH
STOMP STOMP
NINPO: GREAT KITE!!!
YOUR NINPO SKILLS ARE AMAZING!!
WHERE DID THEY GO?!
I CAN'T FIND ANY-THING!!
WHAT DID YOU MANAGE TO SEE, ONAMI?
I SAW...THE NAME OF THE PORT AND THE SHIPMENT DAY!
WONDERFUL! THEN WE'LL KNOW WHEN AND WHERE THE WEAPONS WILL SHOW UP...SO WE CAN SNATCH THEM!♡
BY THE WAY, ONAMI, DID I EVER TELL YOU...
...THAT I HAVE A TERRIBLE FEAR OF POINTED OBJECTS?!
YOU'RE NOT CUT OUT FOR ANY KIND OF BATTLE THEN!!
SWOOOP...
YET THERE IS NO WEAPON DEADLIER THAN A MATURE WOMAN.

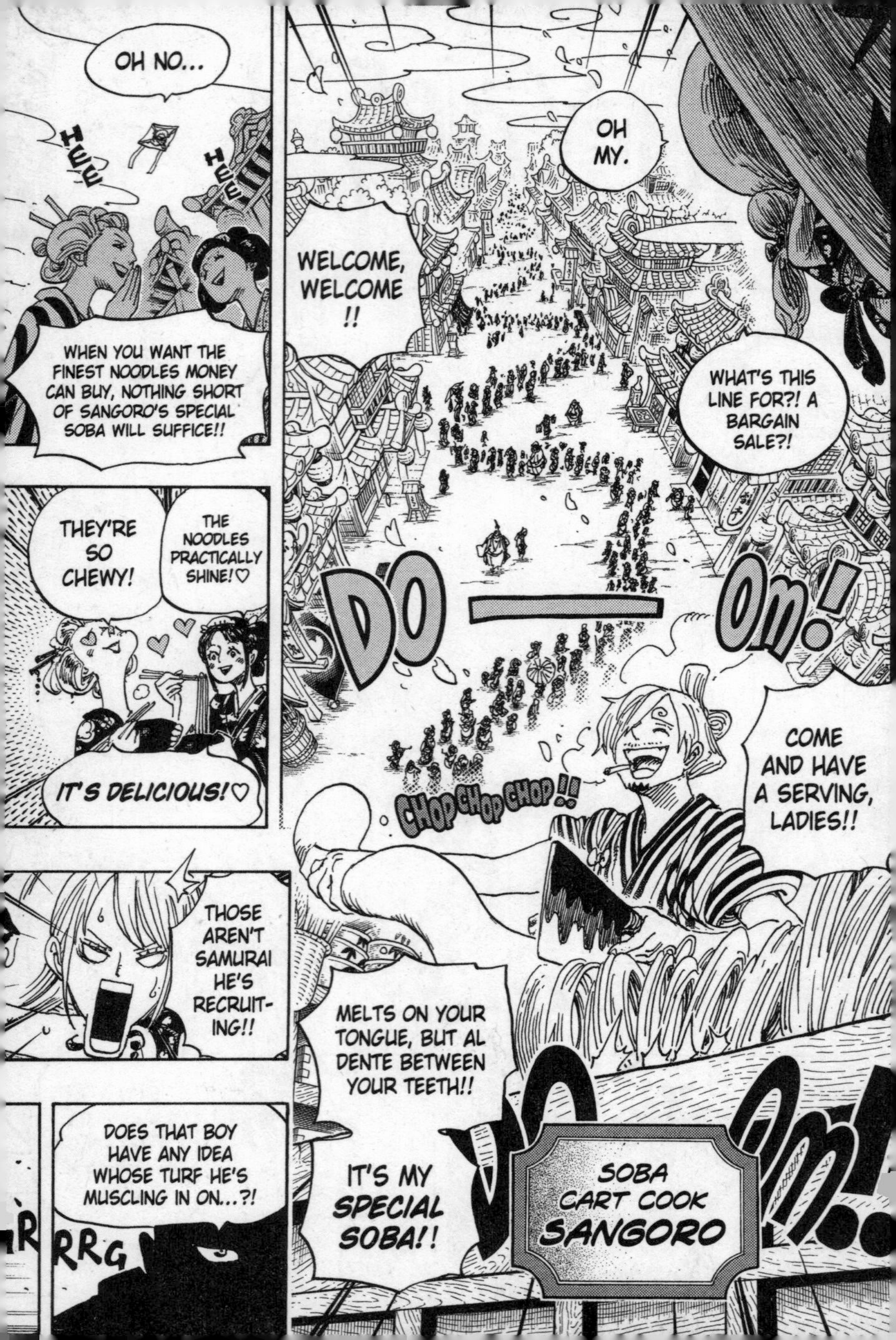
OH MY.
WHAT'S THIS LINE FOR?! A BARGAIN SALE?!
WELCOME, WELCOME !!
DO—OM!
CHOP CHOP CHOP!!
COME AND HAVE A SERVING, LADIES!!
MELTS ON YOUR TONGUE, BUT AL DENTE BETWEEN YOUR TEETH!!
IT'S MY SPECIAL SOBA!!
SOBA CART COOK SANGORO
OH NO...
HEE HEE
HEE HEE
WHEN YOU WANT THE FINEST NOODLES MONEY CAN BUY, NOTHING SHORT OF SANGORO'S SPECIAL SOBA WILL SUFFICE!!
THE NOODLES PRACTICALLY SHINE!♡
THEY'RE SO CHEWY!
IT'S DELICIOUS!♡
THOSE AREN'T SAMURAI HE'S RECRUIT-ING!!
DOES THAT BOY HAVE ANY IDEA WHOSE TURF HE'S MUSCLING IN ON...?!
RRG

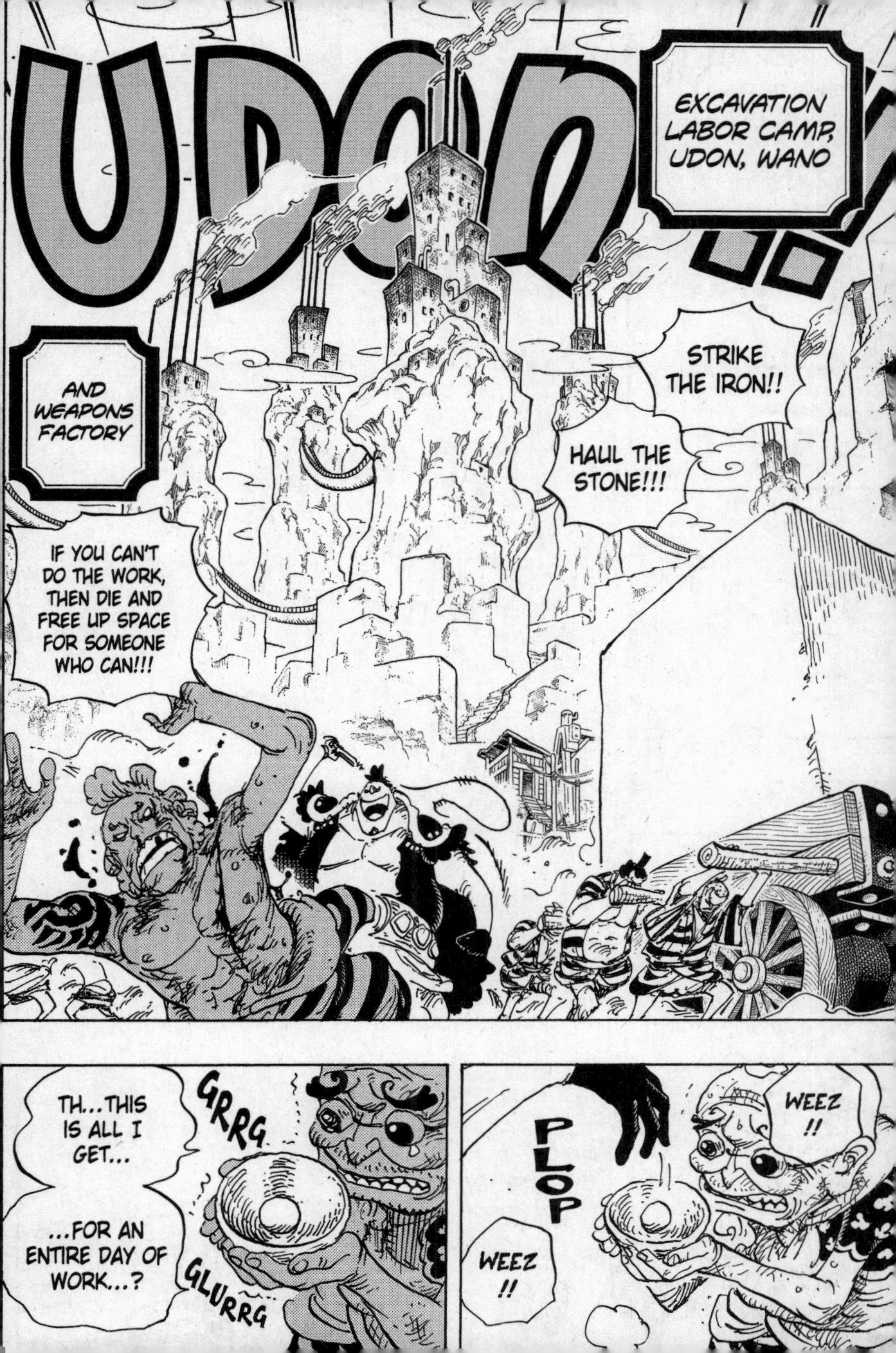
UDON!!
EXCAVATION LABOR CAMP, UDON, WANO
AND WEAPONS FACTORY
STRIKE THE IRON!!
HAUL THE STONE!!!
IF YOU CAN'T DO THE WORK, THEN DIE AND FREE UP SPACE FOR SOMEONE WHO CAN!!!
WEEZ !!
PLOP
WEEZ !!
TH...THIS IS ALL I GET...
GRRG
...FOR AN ENTIRE DAY OF WORK...?
GLURRG

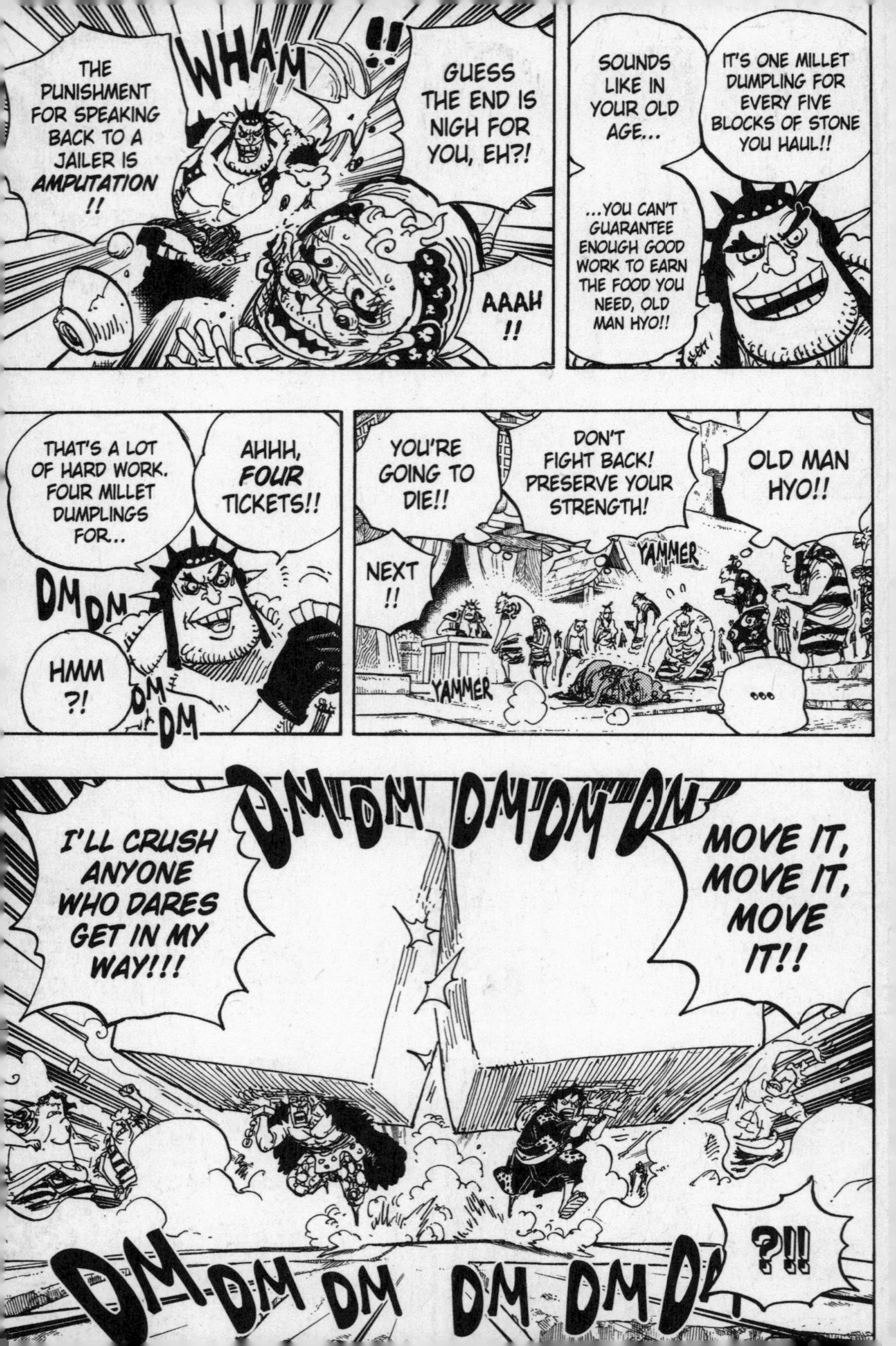
IT'S ONE MILLET DUMPLING FOR EVERY FIVE BLOCKS OF STONE YOU HAUL!!
SOUNDS LIKE IN YOUR OLD AGE...
...YOU CAN'T GUARANTEE ENOUGH GOOD WORK TO EARN THE FOOD YOU NEED, OLD MAN HYO!!
GUESS THE END IS NIGH FOR YOU, EH?!
WHAM!!
THE PUNISHMENT FOR SPEAKING BACK TO A JAILER IS *AMPUTATION*!!
AAAH!!
OLD MAN HYO!!
DON'T FIGHT BACK! PRESERVE YOUR STRENGTH!
YOU'RE GOING TO DIE!!
YAMMER
NEXT!!
YAMMER
...
AHHH, *FOUR* TICKETS!!
THAT'S A LOT OF HARD WORK. FOUR MILLET DUMPLINGS FOR...
DM DM
HMM?!
DM DM
DM DM DM DM DM
MOVE IT, MOVE IT, MOVE IT!!
I'LL CRUSH ANYONE WHO DARES GET IN MY WAY!!!
?!!
DM DM DM DM DM DM

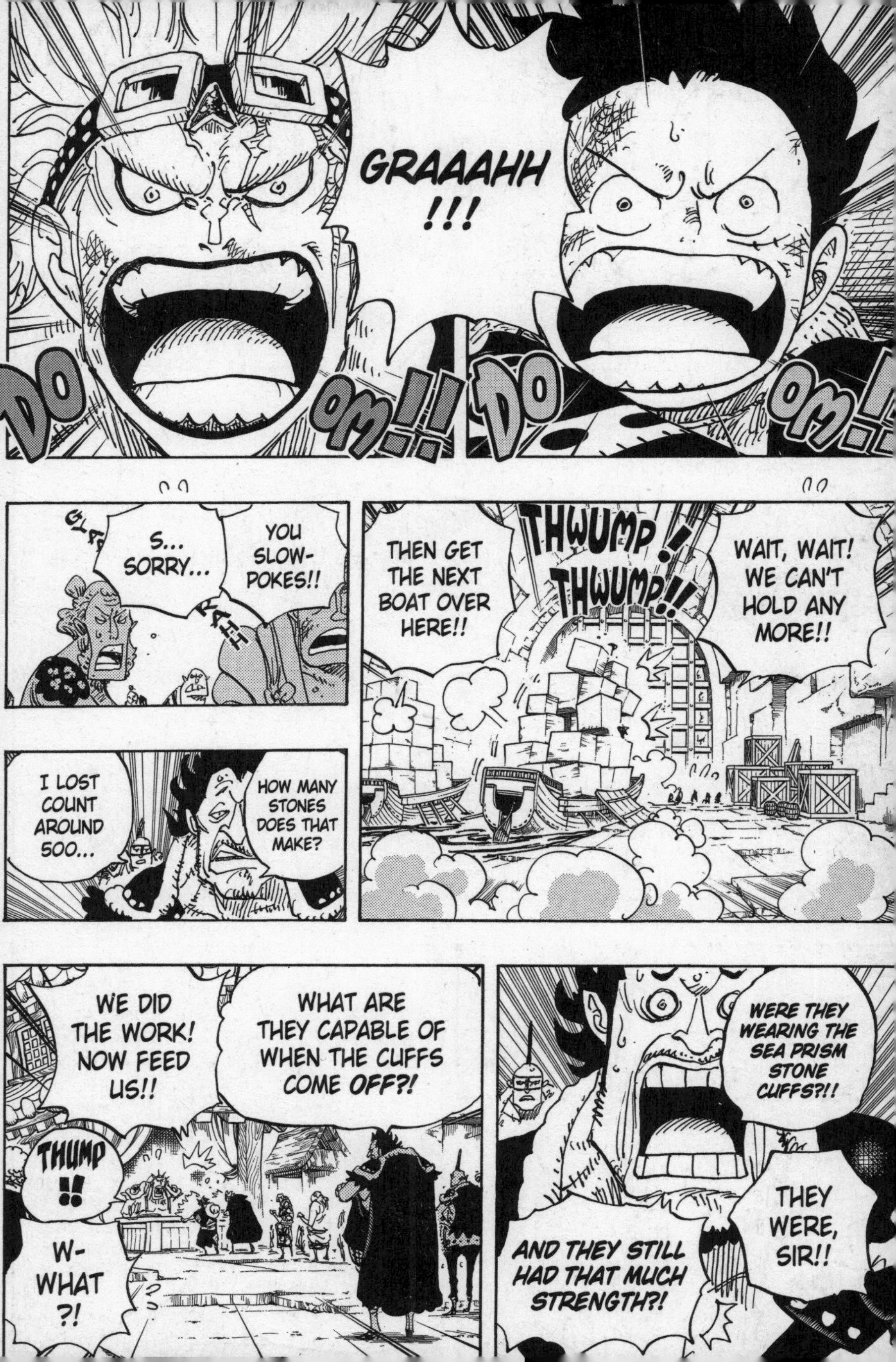
DOOM!!
GRAAAHH!!!
DOOM!!
WAIT, WAIT! WE CAN'T HOLD ANY MORE!!
THWUMP! THWUMP!!
THEN GET THE NEXT BOAT OVER HERE!!
YOU SLOW-POKES!!
S... SORRY...
HOW MANY STONES DOES THAT MAKE?
I LOST COUNT AROUND 500...
WERE THEY WEARING THE SEA PRISM STONE CUFFS?!!
THEY WERE, SIR!!
AND THEY STILL HAD THAT MUCH STRENGTH?!
WHAT ARE THEY CAPABLE OF WHEN THE CUFFS COME OFF?!
WE DID THE WORK! NOW FEED US!!
THUMP!!
W-WHAT?!

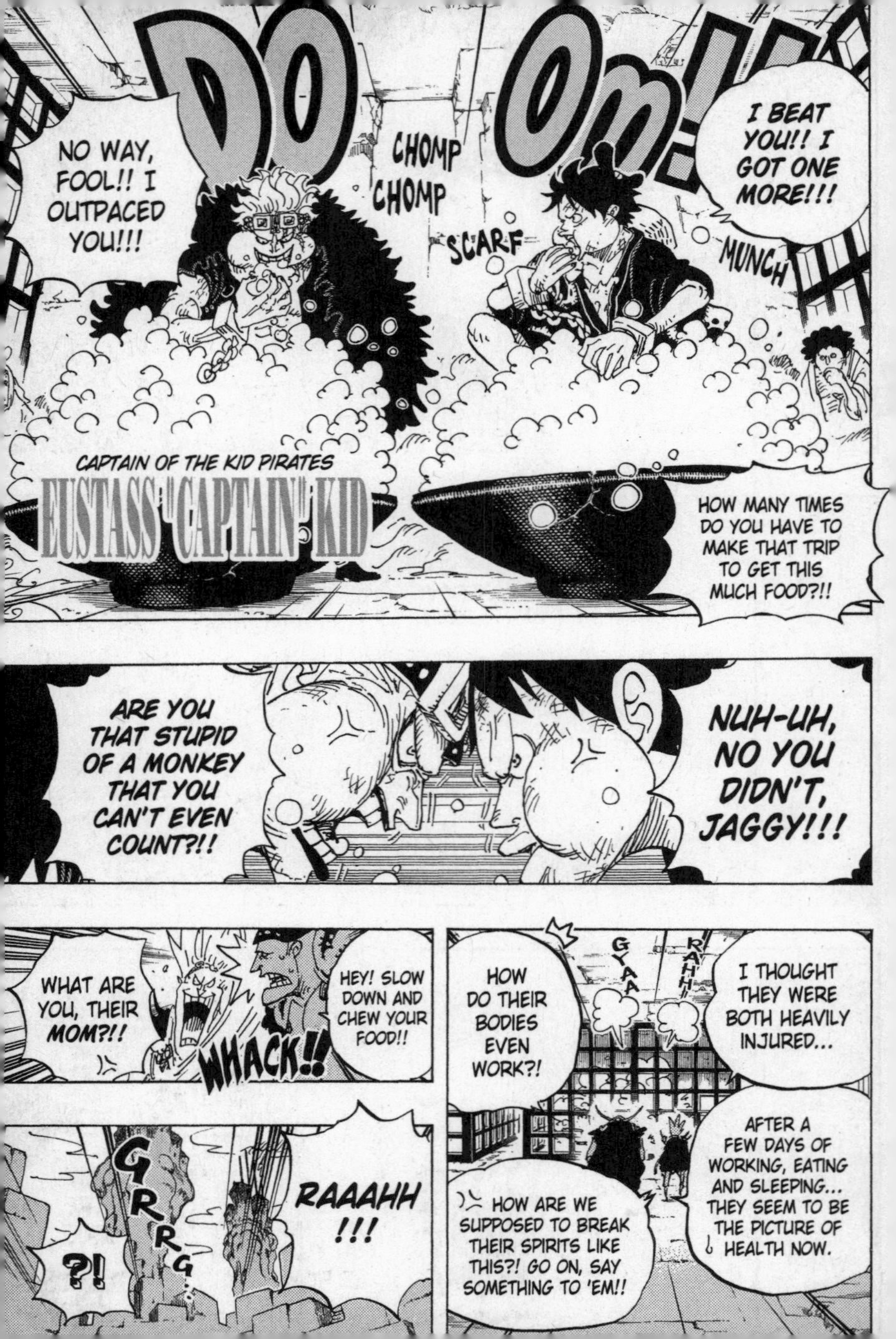
DO-OM!!
I BEAT YOU!! I GOT ONE MORE!!!
MUNCH
SCARF
CHOMP CHOMP
NO WAY, FOOL!! I OUTPACED YOU!!!
CAPTAIN OF THE KID PIRATES
EUSTASS "CAPTAIN" KID
HOW MANY TIMES DO YOU HAVE TO MAKE THAT TRIP TO GET THIS MUCH FOOD?!!
NUH-UH, NO YOU DIDN'T, JAGGY!!!
ARE YOU THAT STUPID OF A MONKEY THAT YOU CAN'T EVEN COUNT?!!
I THOUGHT THEY WERE BOTH HEAVILY INJURED...
RAHH
GYAA
HOW DO THEIR BODIES EVEN WORK?!
AFTER A FEW DAYS OF WORKING, EATING AND SLEEPING... THEY SEEM TO BE THE PICTURE OF HEALTH NOW.
HOW ARE WE SUPPOSED TO BREAK THEIR SPIRITS LIKE THIS?! GO ON, SAY SOMETHING TO 'EM!!
HEY! SLOW DOWN AND CHEW YOUR FOOD!!
WHACK!!
WHAT ARE YOU, THEIR MOM?!!
RAAAHH!!!
GRRRG...
?!

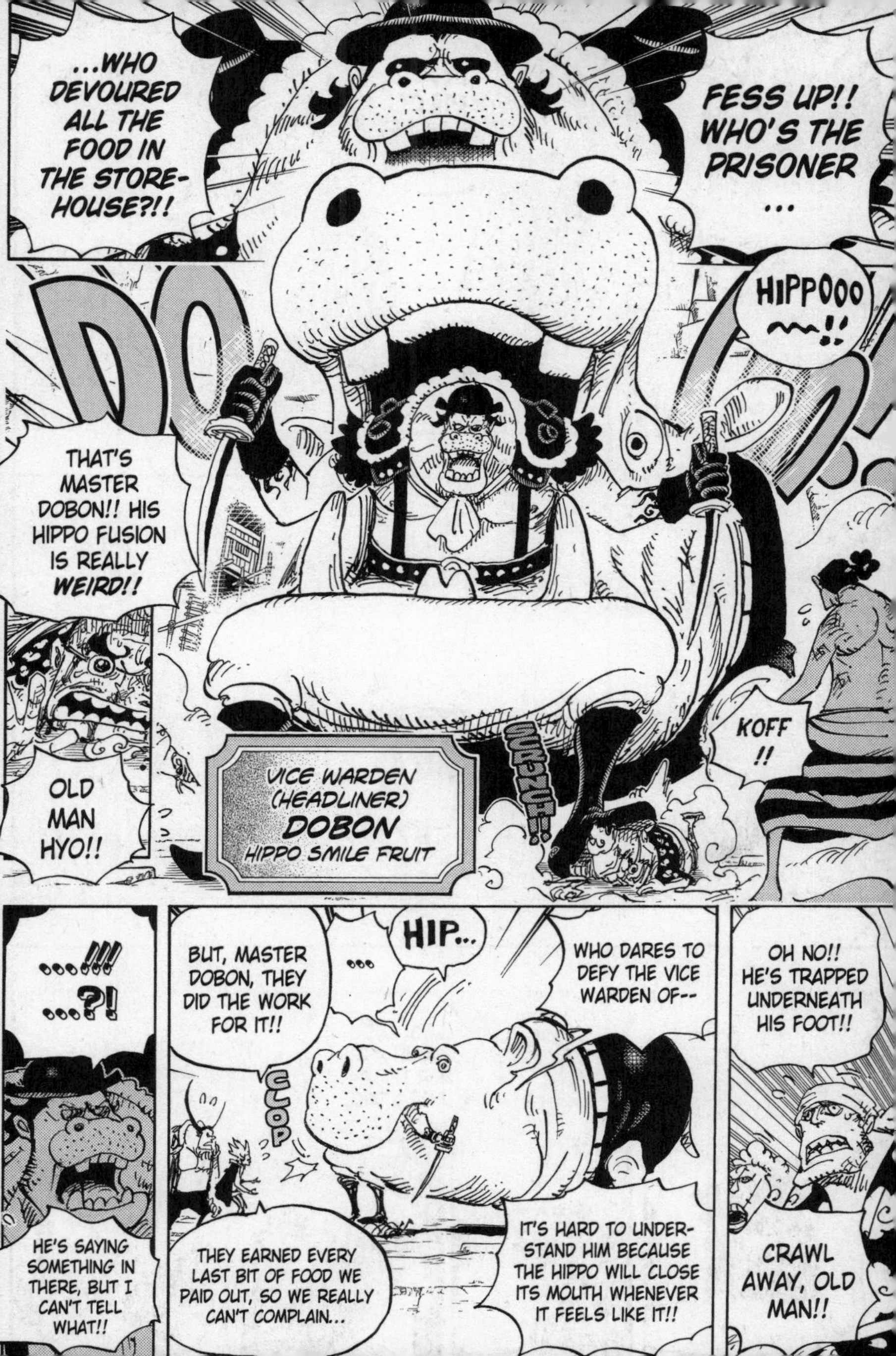
FESS UP!! WHO'S THE PRISONER ...
...WHO DEVOURED ALL THE FOOD IN THE STORE-HOUSE?!!
HIPPOOO ~~!!
DO
KOFF !!
THAT'S MASTER DOBON!! HIS HIPPO FUSION IS REALLY WEIRD!!
SCRUNCH!!
VICE WARDEN (HEADLINER) DOBON HIPPO SMILE FRUIT
OLD MAN HYO!!
OH NO!! HE'S TRAPPED UNDERNEATH HIS FOOT!!
CRAWL AWAY, OLD MAN!!
WHO DARES TO DEFY THE VICE WARDEN OF--
HIP...
...
BUT, MASTER DOBON, THEY DID THE WORK FOR IT!!
CLOP
IT'S HARD TO UNDERSTAND HIM BECAUSE THE HIPPO WILL CLOSE ITS MOUTH WHENEVER IT FEELS LIKE IT!!
THEY EARNED EVERY LAST BIT OF FOOD WE PAID OUT, SO WE REALLY CAN'T COMPLAIN...
...!!!
...?!
HE'S SAYING SOMETHING IN THERE, BUT I CAN'T TELL WHAT!!

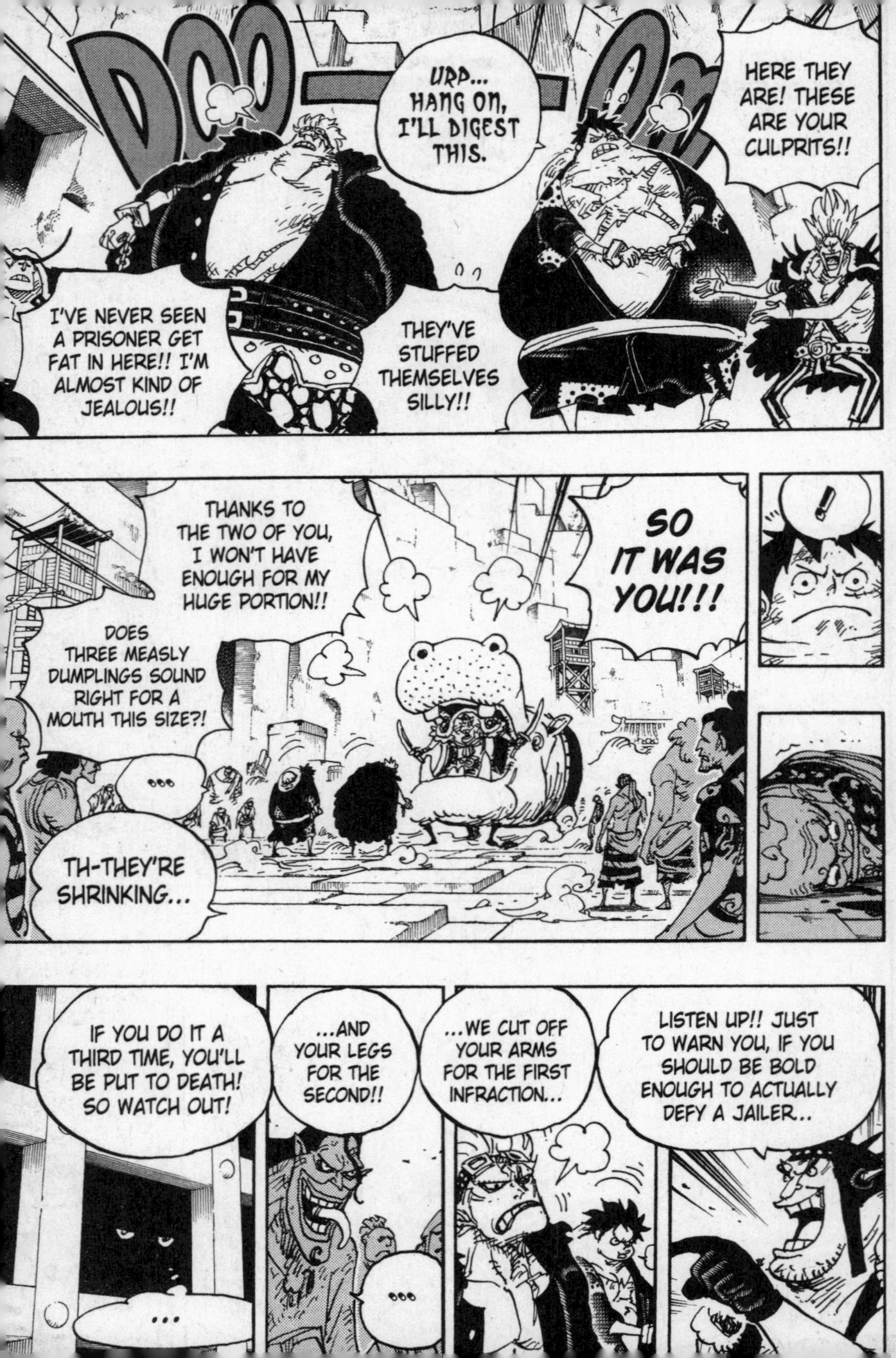
HERE THEY ARE! THESE ARE YOUR CULPRITS!!
URP... HANG ON, I'LL DIGEST THIS.
THEY'VE STUFFED THEMSELVES SILLY!!
I'VE NEVER SEEN A PRISONER GET FAT IN HERE!! I'M ALMOST KIND OF JEALOUS!!
!
...
SO IT WAS YOU!!!
THANKS TO THE TWO OF YOU, I WON'T HAVE ENOUGH FOR MY HUGE PORTION!!
DOES THREE MEASLY DUMPLINGS SOUND RIGHT FOR A MOUTH THIS SIZE?!
...
TH-THEY'RE SHRINKING...
LISTEN UP!! JUST TO WARN YOU, IF YOU SHOULD BE BOLD ENOUGH TO ACTUALLY DEFY A JAILER...
...WE CUT OFF YOUR ARMS FOR THE FIRST INFRACTION...
...AND YOUR LEGS FOR THE SECOND!!
...
IF YOU DO IT A THIRD TIME, YOU'LL BE PUT TO DEATH! SO WATCH OUT!
...

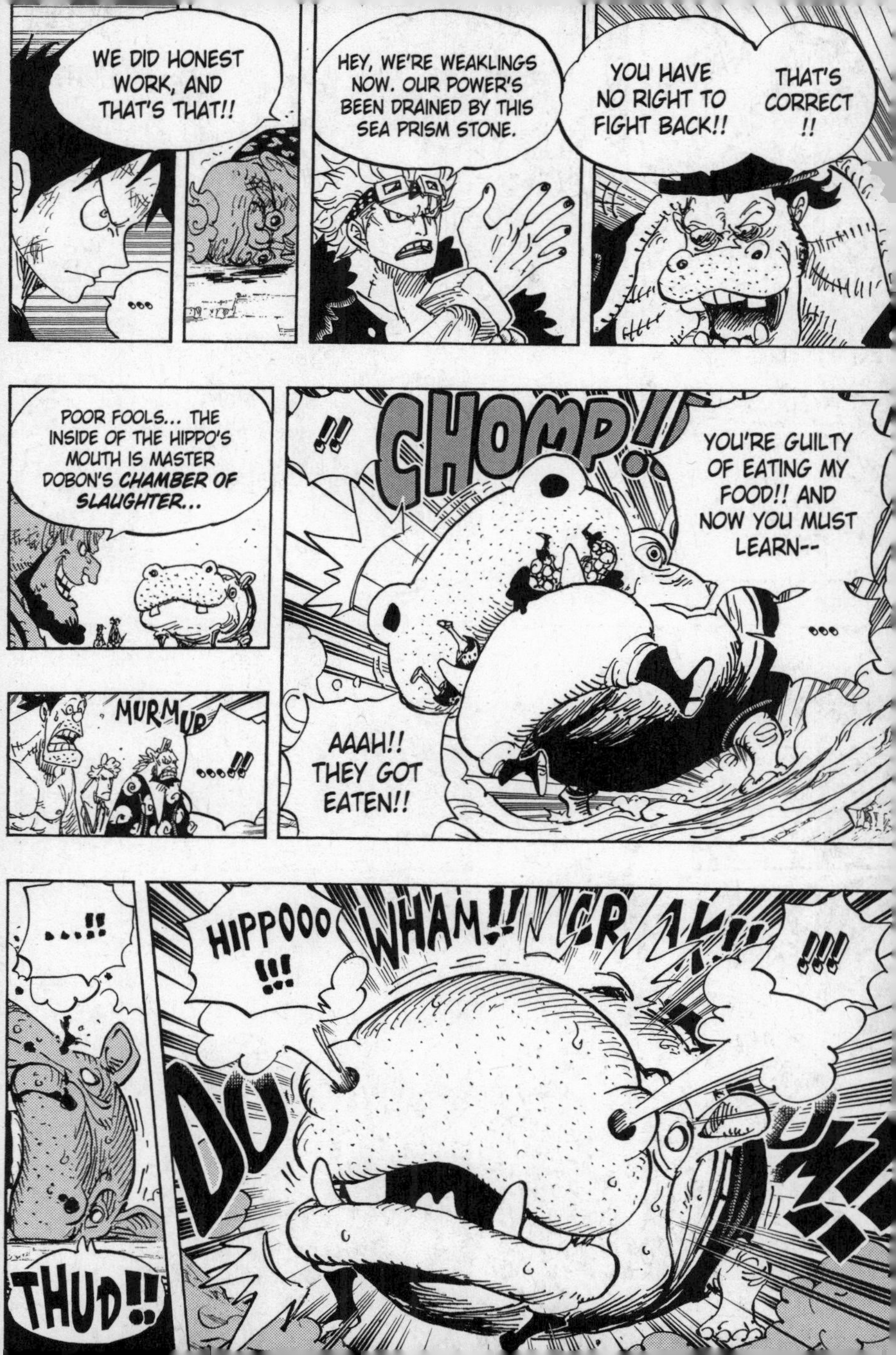
THAT'S CORRECT !!
YOU HAVE NO RIGHT TO FIGHT BACK!!
HEY, WE'RE WEAKLINGS NOW. OUR POWER'S BEEN DRAINED BY THIS SEA PRISM STONE.
WE DID HONEST WORK, AND THAT'S THAT!!
...
YOU'RE GUILTY OF EATING MY FOOD!! AND NOW YOU MUST LEARN--
CHOMP!!
!!
...
AAAH!! THEY GOT EATEN!!
POOR FOOLS... THE INSIDE OF THE HIPPO'S MOUTH IS MASTER DOBON'S CHAMBER OF SLAUGHTER...
MURMUR
...!!
!!!
WHAM!!
HIPPOOO !!!
...!!
THUD!!

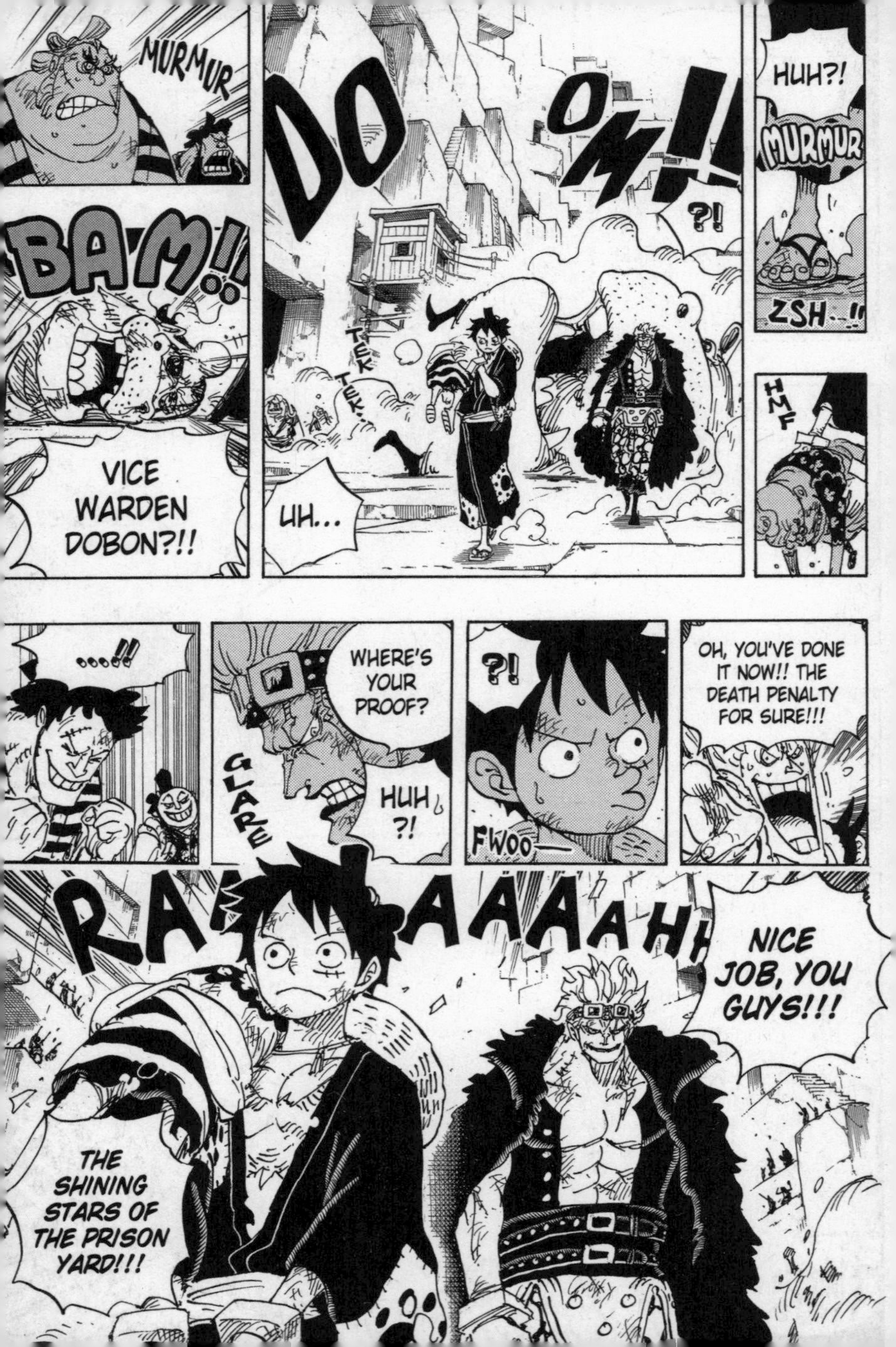
HUH?!
MURMUR
ZSH...!!
HMF
DO
OM!!
?!
TEK TEK...
UH...
MURMUR
BAM!!
VICE WARDEN DOBON?!!
OH, YOU'VE DONE IT NOW!! THE DEATH PENALTY FOR SURE!!!
?!
FWOO—
WHERE'S YOUR PROOF?
HUH ?!
GLARE
....!!
NICE JOB, YOU GUYS!!!
RAAAAAAH
THE SHINING STARS OF THE PRISON YARD!!!

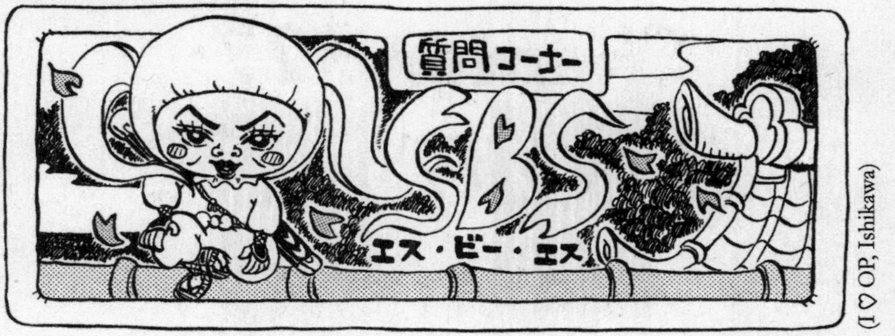
質問コーナー
SBS
エス・ビー・エス

(I ♡ OP, Ishikawa)

Q: In the Zou arc, Momonosuke claimed to have met Roger, so I started wondering if he was somehow an adult who'd been turned back into a child, and was abusing his perceived age to snuggle with Nami and Robin. Since it's been revealed that he's an actual eight-year-old who traveled through time, does that mean he's just a pervy little kid?

--Takumiso

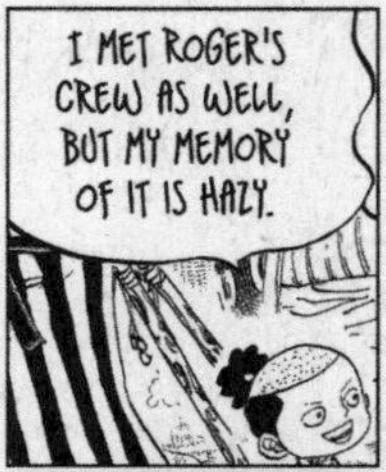
I MET ROGER'S CREW AS WELL, BUT MY MEMORY OF IT IS HAZY.

A: Think about when you were eight years old. Yeah, you were a perv. All boys are pervs!!

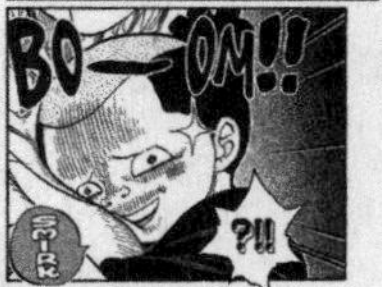
BO—OM!!
?!!

Q: I have a healthy question for you! I think I've finally figured out why all the men want to be Nami's followers. It's because she has two big millet dumplings, right?

--Sanadacchi

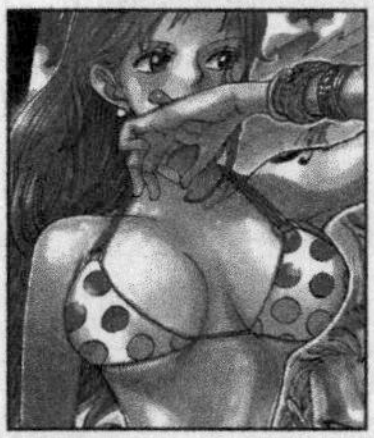

A: Get lost, Sanada.

Q: Is the boss carpenter who appears in Wano in chapter 909 the same "Minatomo" the carpenter who was mentioned way back in the SBS segment of volume 7?

--Yacchi

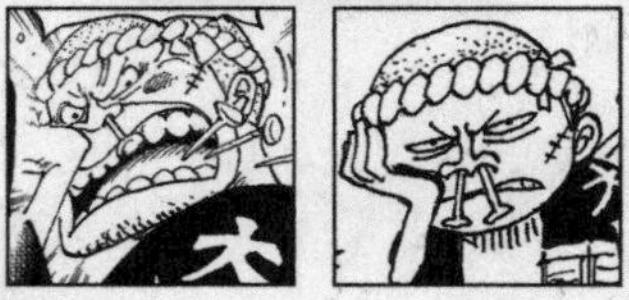

A: That's right!! You're talking about Minatomo the carpenter, who was first introduced when the door to the bar in Windmill Village was fixed again after being broken, and everybody wondered, "Who fixed it?!" And now he's in the closed nation of Wano in the New World! Isn't that weird?! That's because they're not the same person! But their family name is the same, and they are related. It would seem that decades ago, a ship from Wano reached the distant stretches of the East Blue. And among the descendants of the people on that ship is a very familiar character to all of you... But I might cover this in the manga, so I won't say any more. It's not part of the main plot, just a little side story.

Chapter 927:
OTOKO THE KAMURO

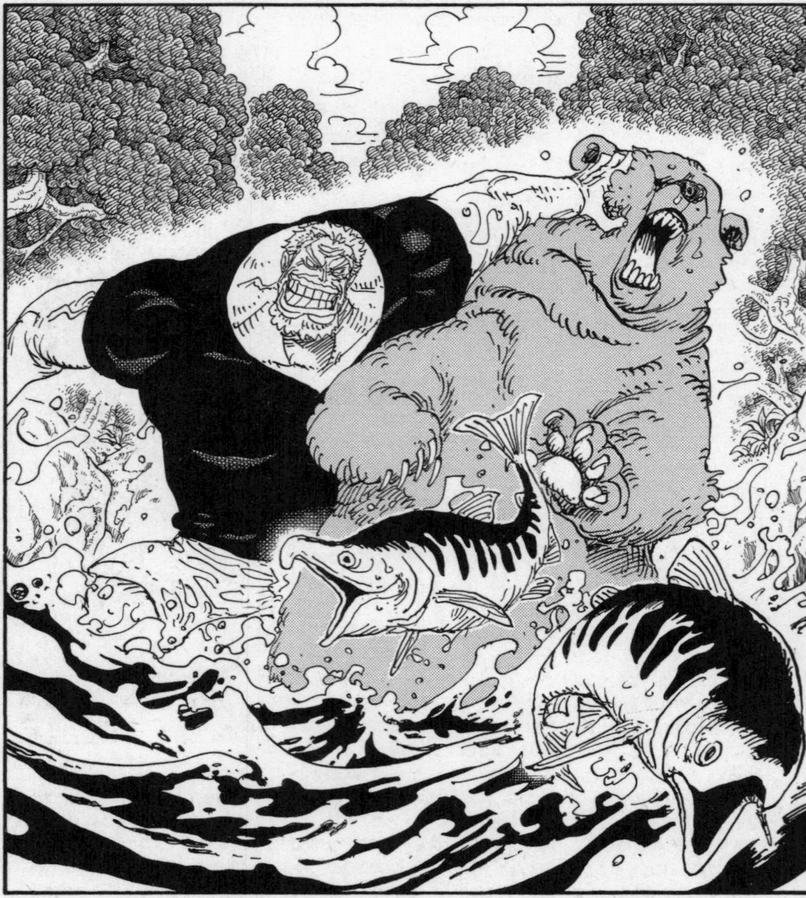

REQUEST: "GARP FIGHTING WITH A BEAR OVER SALMON" BY NODA SKYWALKER

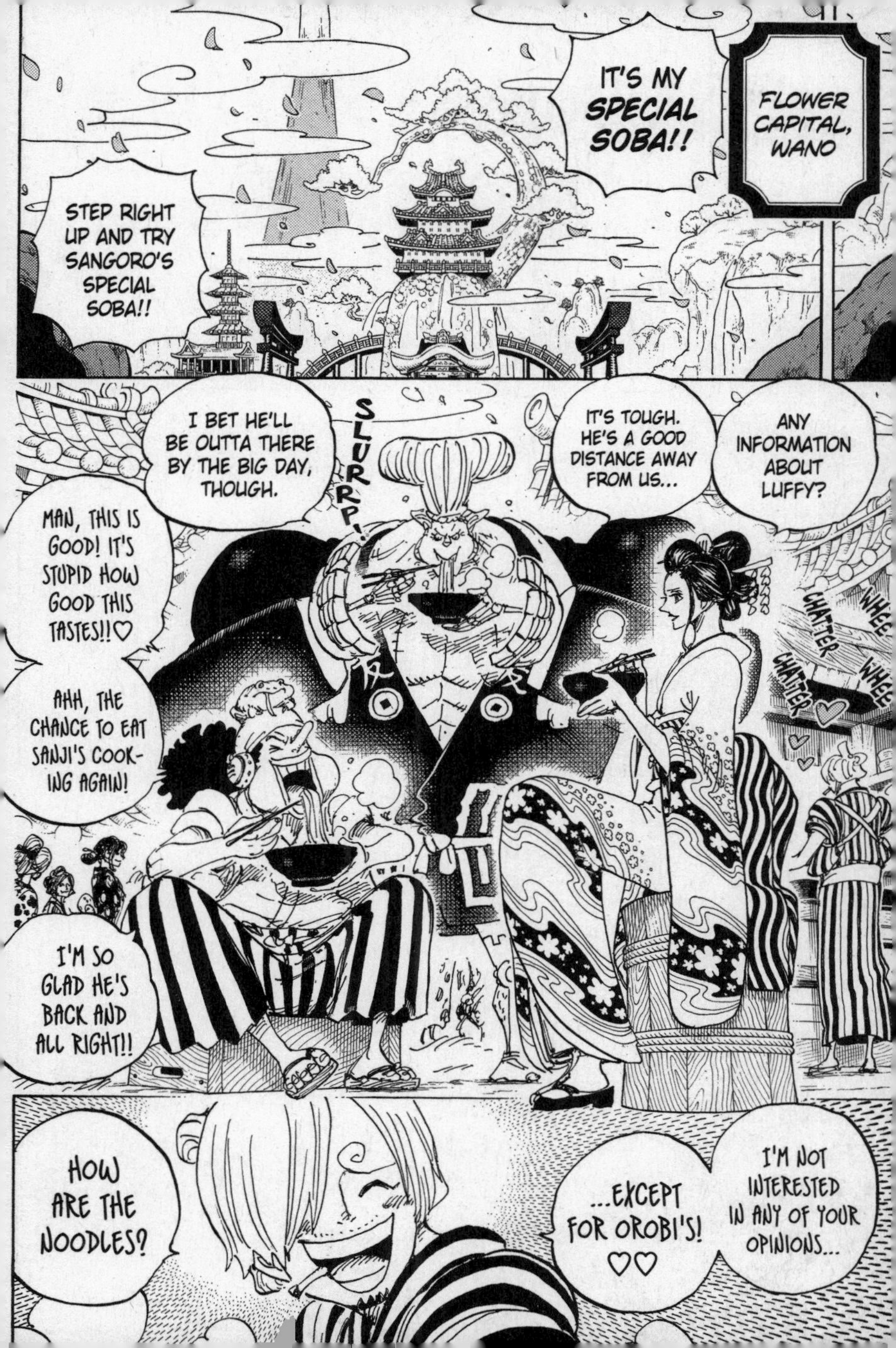
FLOWER CAPITAL, WANO
IT'S MY SPECIAL SOBA!!
STEP RIGHT UP AND TRY SANGORO'S SPECIAL SOBA!!
ANY INFORMATION ABOUT LUFFY?
IT'S TOUGH. HE'S A GOOD DISTANCE AWAY FROM US...
SLURRP!
I BET HE'LL BE OUTTA THERE BY THE BIG DAY, THOUGH.
WHEE WHEE
CHATTER CHATTER
MAN, THIS IS GOOD! IT'S STUPID HOW GOOD THIS TASTES!!♡
AHH, THE CHANCE TO EAT SANJI'S COOKING AGAIN!
I'M SO GLAD HE'S BACK AND ALL RIGHT!!
I'M NOT INTERESTED IN ANY OF YOUR OPINIONS...
...EXCEPT FOR OROBI'S! ♡♡
HOW ARE THE NOODLES?

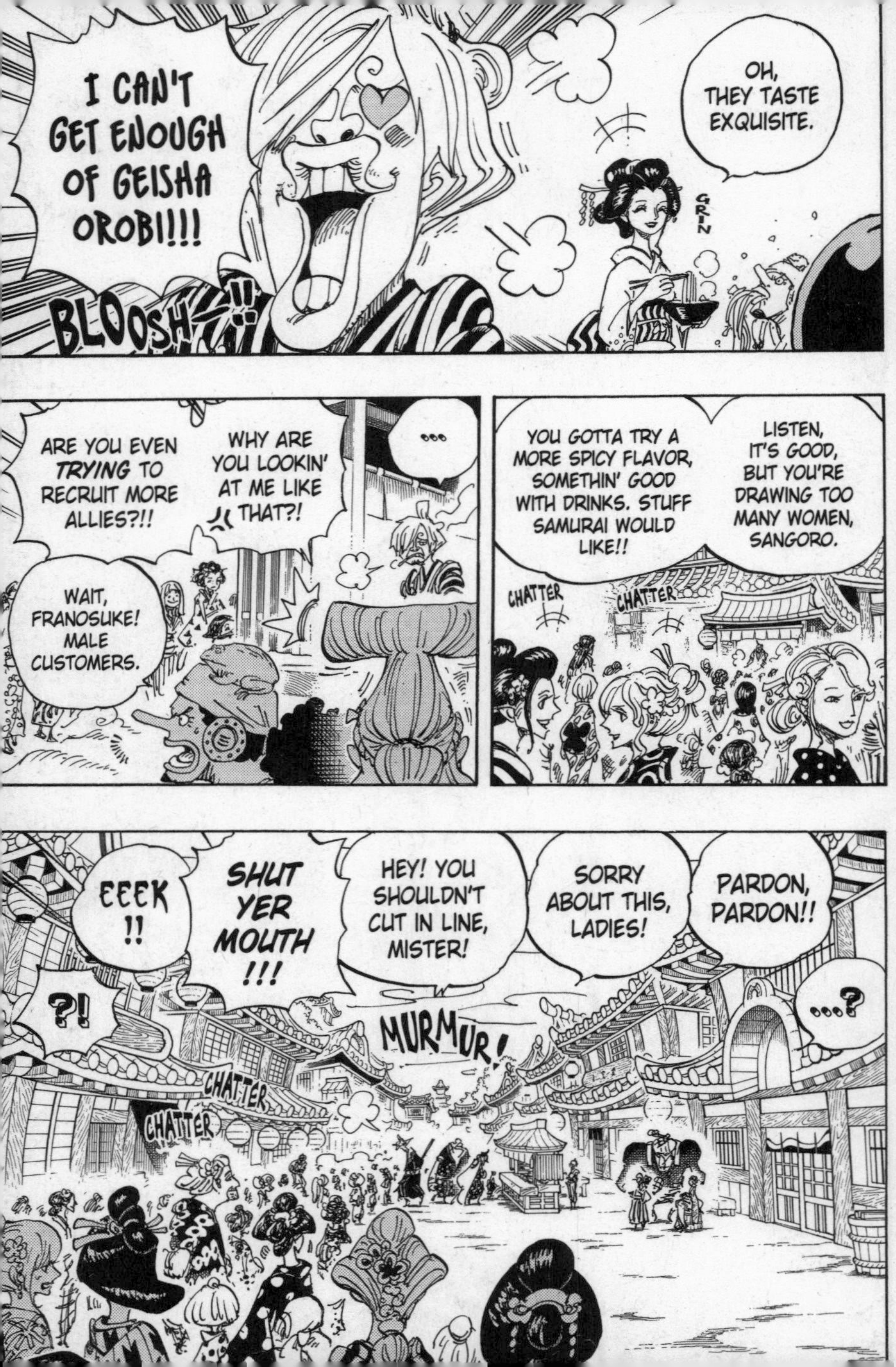
OH, THEY TASTE EXQUISITE.
GRIN
I CAN'T GET ENOUGH OF GEISHA OROBI!!!
BLOOSH !!
LISTEN, IT'S GOOD, BUT YOU'RE DRAWING TOO MANY WOMEN, SANGORO.
YOU GOTTA TRY A MORE SPICY FLAVOR, SOMETHIN' GOOD WITH DRINKS. STUFF SAMURAI WOULD LIKE!!
CHATTER
CHATTER
...
WHY ARE YOU LOOKIN' AT ME LIKE THAT?!
ARE YOU EVEN *TRYING* TO RECRUIT MORE ALLIES?!!
WAIT, FRANOSUKE! MALE CUSTOMERS.
PARDON, PARDON!!
...?
SORRY ABOUT THIS, LADIES!
HEY! YOU SHOULDN'T CUT IN LINE, MISTER!
SHUT YER MOUTH!!!
EEEK !!
?!
MURMUR!
CHATTER
CHATTER

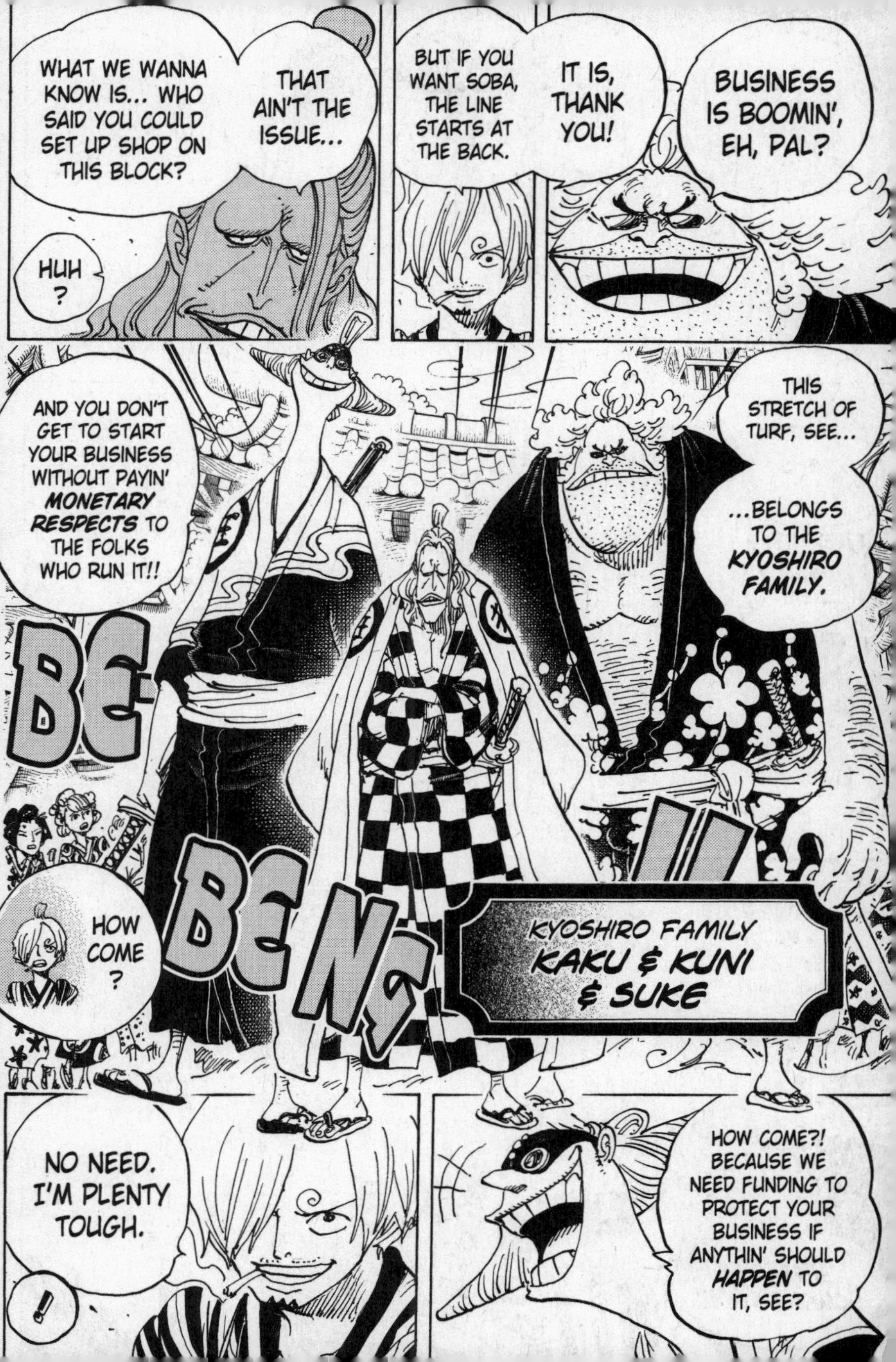

BUSINESS IS BOOMIN', EH, PAL?
IT IS, THANK YOU!
BUT IF YOU WANT SOBA, THE LINE STARTS AT THE BACK.
THAT AIN'T THE ISSUE...
WHAT WE WANNA KNOW IS... WHO SAID YOU COULD SET UP SHOP ON THIS BLOCK?
HUH?
THIS STRETCH OF TURF, SEE...
...BELONGS TO THE KYOSHIRO FAMILY.
AND YOU DON'T GET TO START YOUR BUSINESS WITHOUT PAYIN' MONETARY RESPECTS TO THE FOLKS WHO RUN IT!!
BE-
BE NG
KYOSHIRO FAMILY KAKU & KUNI & SUKE
HOW COME?
HOW COME?! BECAUSE WE NEED FUNDING TO PROTECT YOUR BUSINESS IF ANYTHIN' SHOULD HAPPEN TO IT, SEE?
NO NEED. I'M PLENTY TOUGH.
!

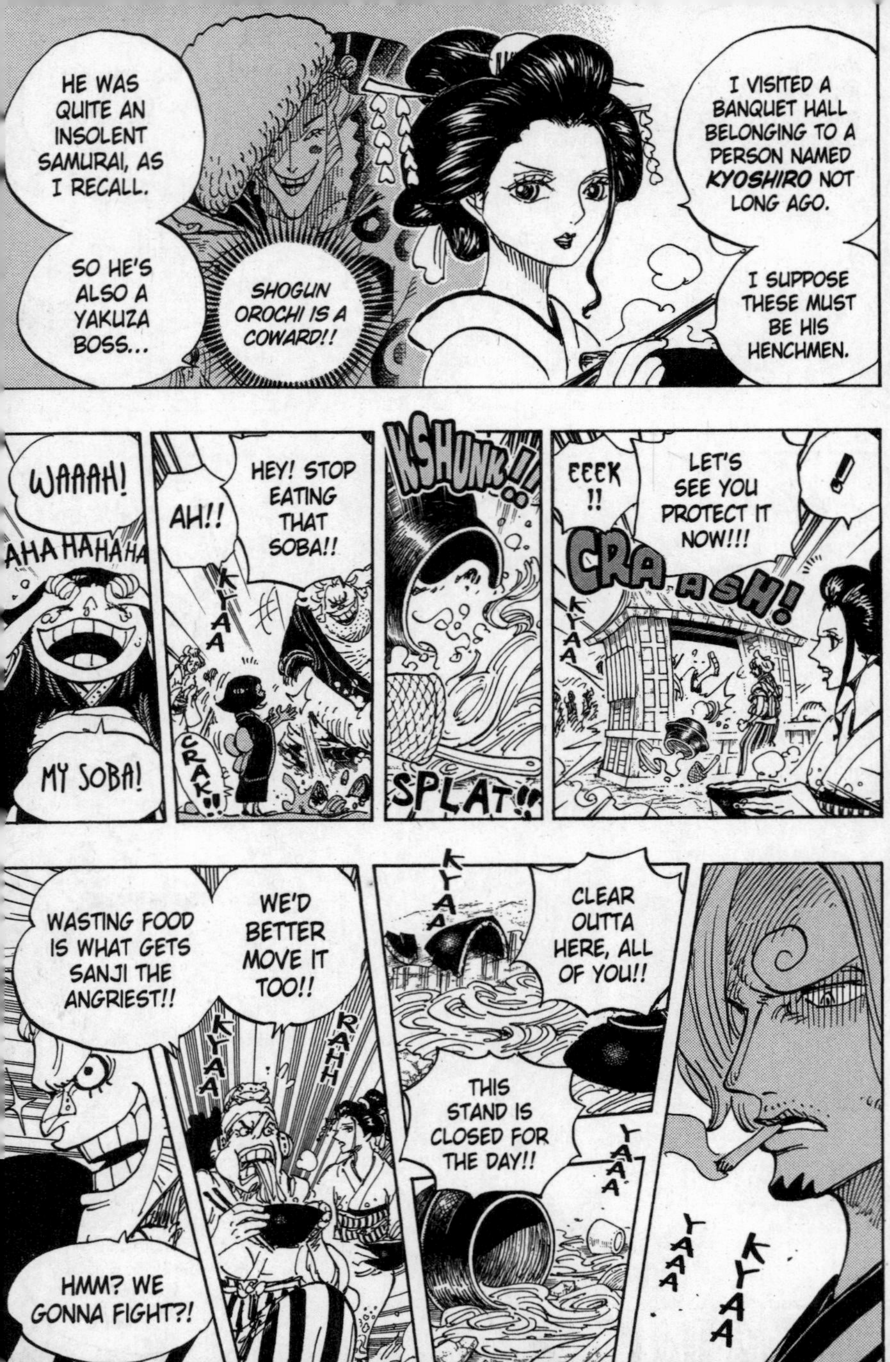
I VISITED A BANQUET HALL BELONGING TO A PERSON NAMED *KYOSHIRO* NOT LONG AGO.
I SUPPOSE THESE MUST BE HIS HENCHMEN.
HE WAS QUITE AN INSOLENT SAMURAI, AS I RECALL.
SHOGUN OROCHI IS A COWARD!!
SO HE'S ALSO A YAKUZA BOSS...
!
LET'S SEE YOU PROTECT IT NOW!!!
EEEK !!
CRA ASH!
KYAA
KSHUNK!!
SPLAT!!
HEY! STOP EATING THAT SOBA!!
AH!!
KYAA
CRAK!!
WAAAH!
AHAHAHAHA
MY SOBA!
KYAA
YAAA
CLEAR OUTTA HERE, ALL OF YOU!!
KYAAA
THIS STAND IS CLOSED FOR THE DAY!!
YAAA
WE'D BETTER MOVE IT TOO!!
RAHH
KYAA
WASTING FOOD IS WHAT GETS SANJI THE ANGRIEST!!
HMM? WE GONNA FIGHT?!

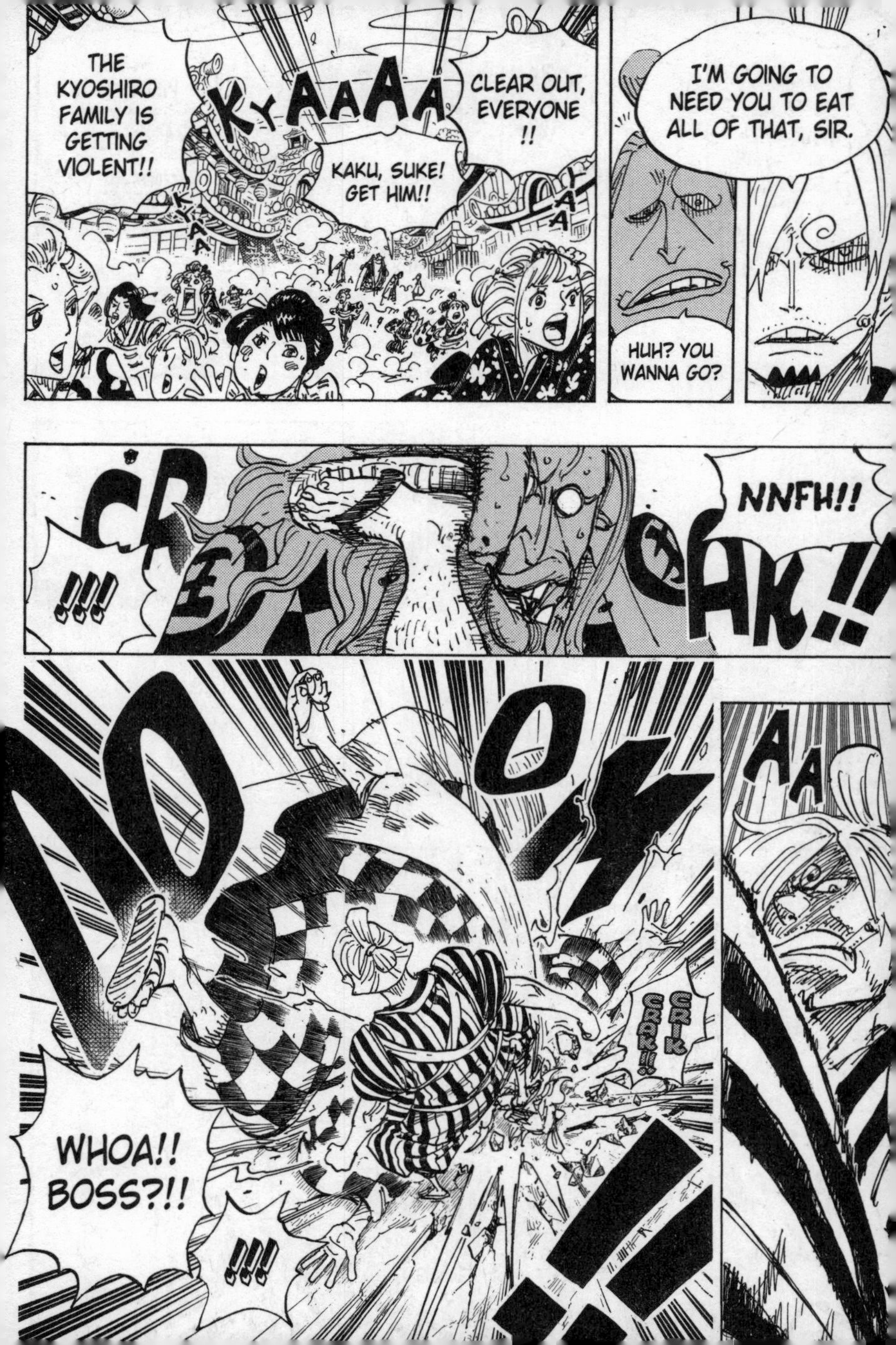
I'M GOING TO NEED YOU TO EAT ALL OF THAT, SIR.
HUH? YOU WANNA GO?
CLEAR OUT, EVERYONE !!
KYAAAA
KAKU, SUKE! GET HIM!!
THE KYOSHIRO FAMILY IS GETTING VIOLENT!!
KYAA
KYAA
NNFH!!
CR
AK!!
!!!
AA
CRIK
CRAK!!
WHOA!! BOSS?!!
!!!

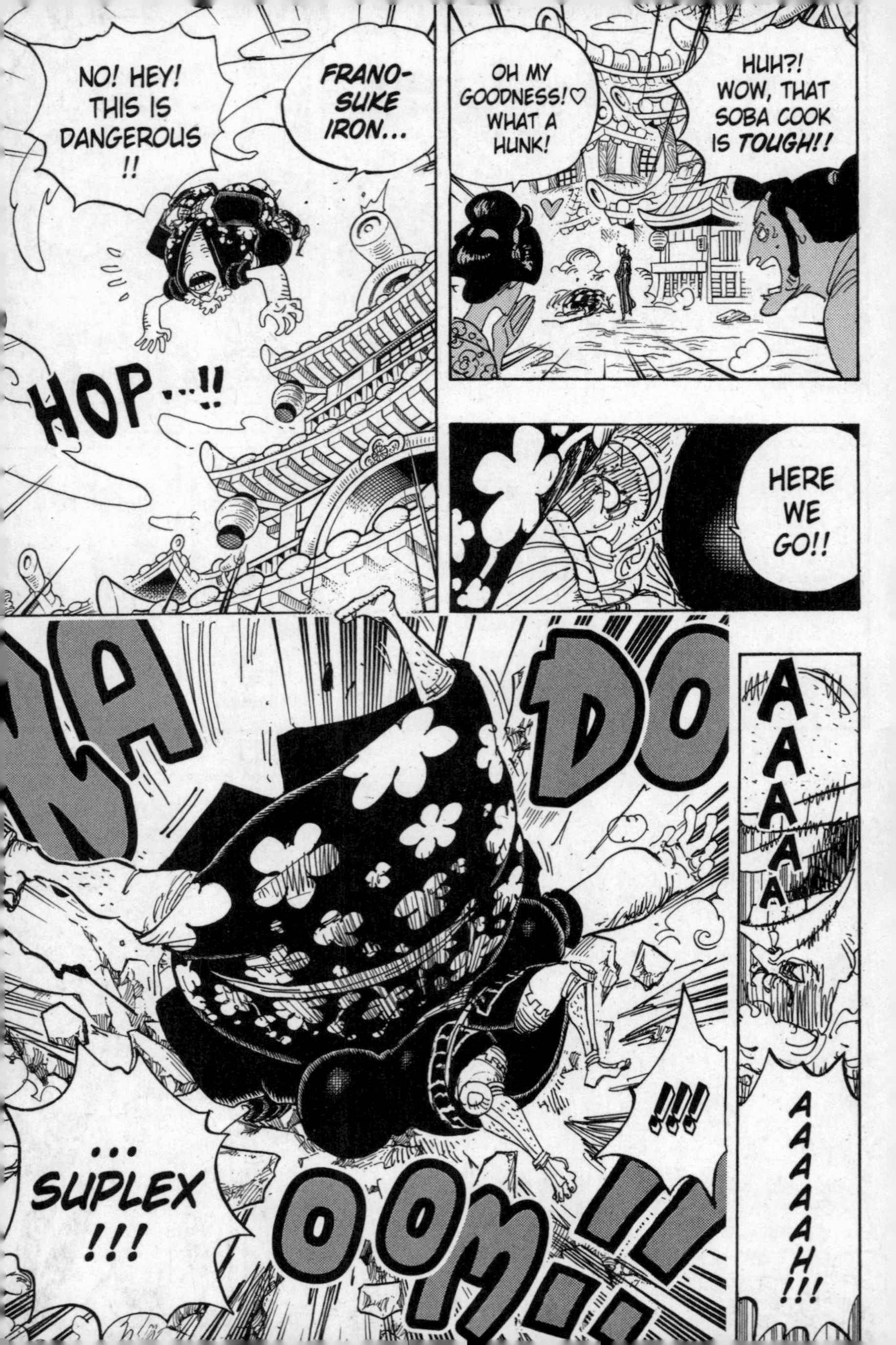
HUH?! WOW, THAT SOBA COOK IS TOUGH!!
OH MY GOODNESS!♡ WHAT A HUNK!
HERE WE GO!!
FRANO-SUKE IRON...
NO! HEY! THIS IS DANGEROUS!!
HOP...!!
AAAAA
AAAAAH!!!
DOOOM!!
!!!
HA
...SUPLEX!!!

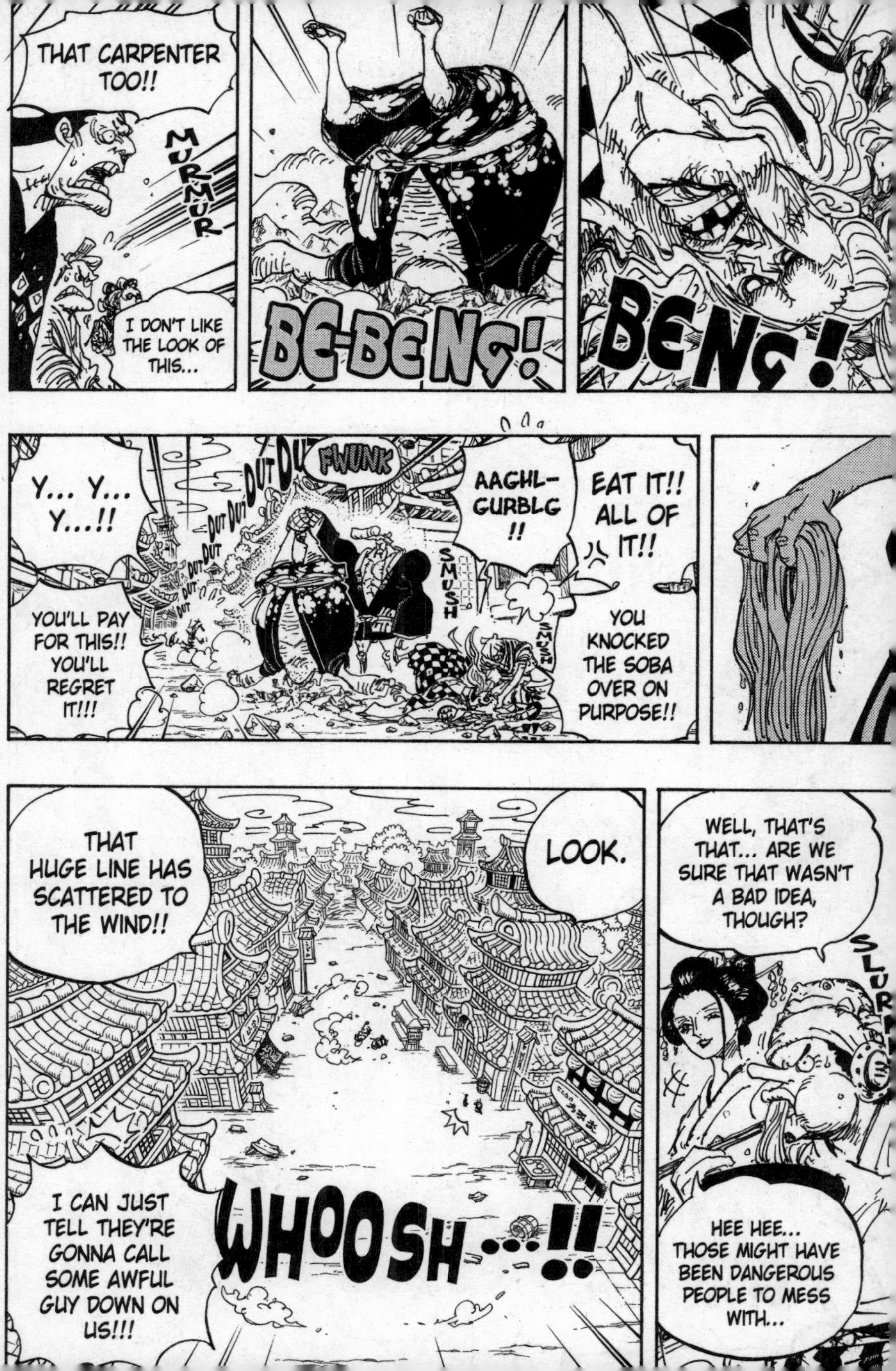
BENG!
BE-BENG!
THAT CARPENTER TOO!!
MURMUR
I DON'T LIKE THE LOOK OF THIS...
EAT IT!! ALL OF IT!!
YOU KNOCKED THE SOBA OVER ON PURPOSE!!
AAGHL-GURBLG!!
SMUSH
SMUSH
FWUNK
DUT DUT DUT DUT DUT DUT DUT DUT DUT
Y... Y... Y...!!
YOU'LL PAY FOR THIS!! YOU'LL REGRET IT!!!
WELL, THAT'S THAT... ARE WE SURE THAT WASN'T A BAD IDEA, THOUGH?
HEE HEE... THOSE MIGHT HAVE BEEN DANGEROUS PEOPLE TO MESS WITH...
LOOK.
THAT HUGE LINE HAS SCATTERED TO THE WIND!!
WHOOSH...!!
I CAN JUST TELL THEY'RE GONNA CALL SOME AWFUL GUY DOWN ON US!!!

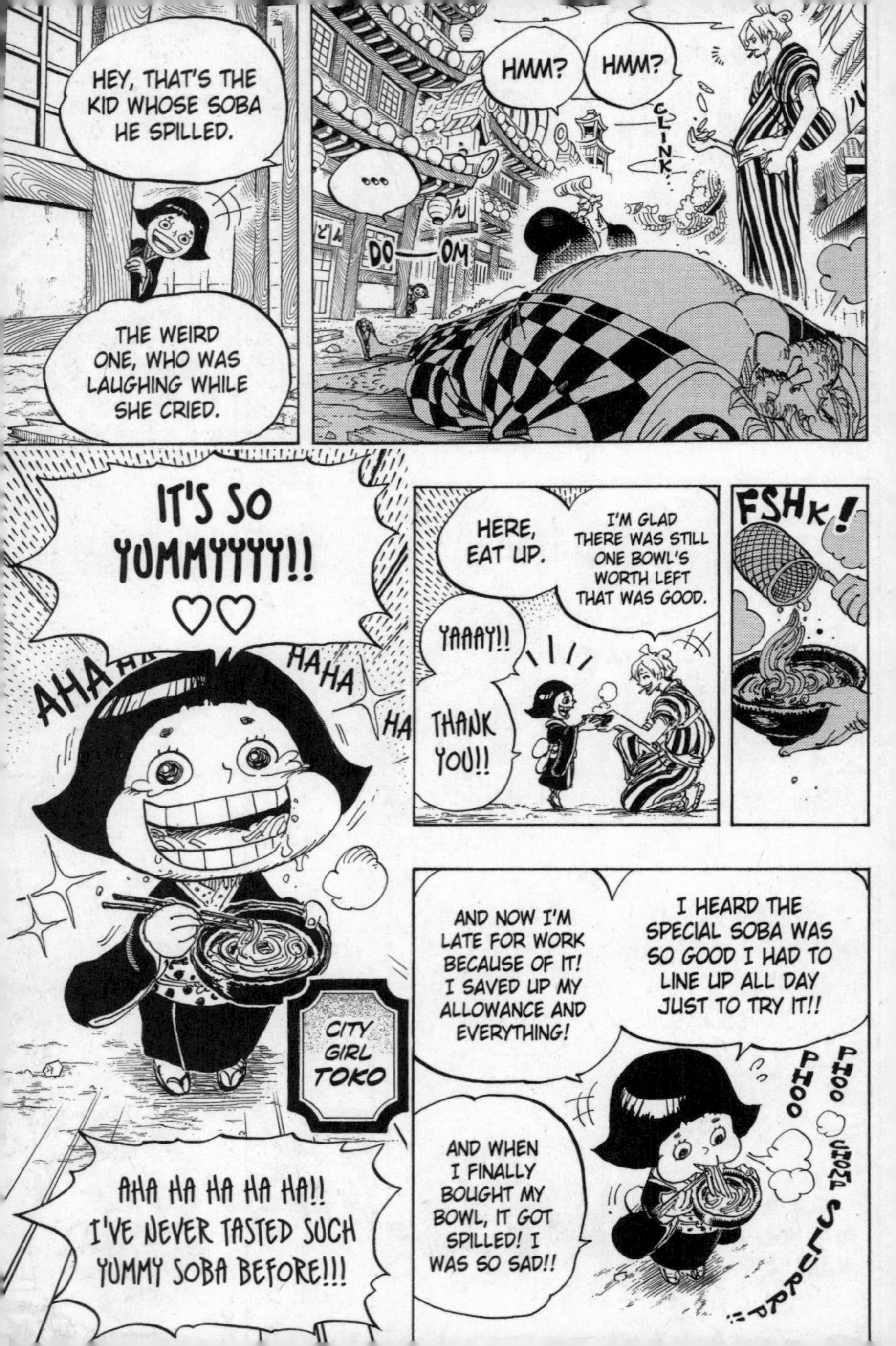
HMM?
HMM?
CLINK...
...
DO—OM
HEY, THAT'S THE KID WHOSE SOBA HE SPILLED.
THE WEIRD ONE, WHO WAS LAUGHING WHILE SHE CRIED.
FSHK!
I'M GLAD THERE WAS STILL ONE BOWL'S WORTH LEFT THAT WAS GOOD.
HERE, EAT UP.
YAAAY!!
THANK YOU!!
I HEARD THE SPECIAL SOBA WAS SO GOOD I HAD TO LINE UP ALL DAY JUST TO TRY IT!!
AND NOW I'M LATE FOR WORK BECAUSE OF IT! I SAVED UP MY ALLOWANCE AND EVERYTHING!
AND WHEN I FINALLY BOUGHT MY BOWL, IT GOT SPILLED! I WAS SO SAD!!
PHOO PHOO
CHOMP
SLURRRP!!
IT'S SO YUMMYYYY!! ♡♡
AHA HA HA HA
CITY GIRL TOKO
AHA HA HA HA HA!! I'VE NEVER TASTED SUCH YUMMY SOBA BEFORE!!!

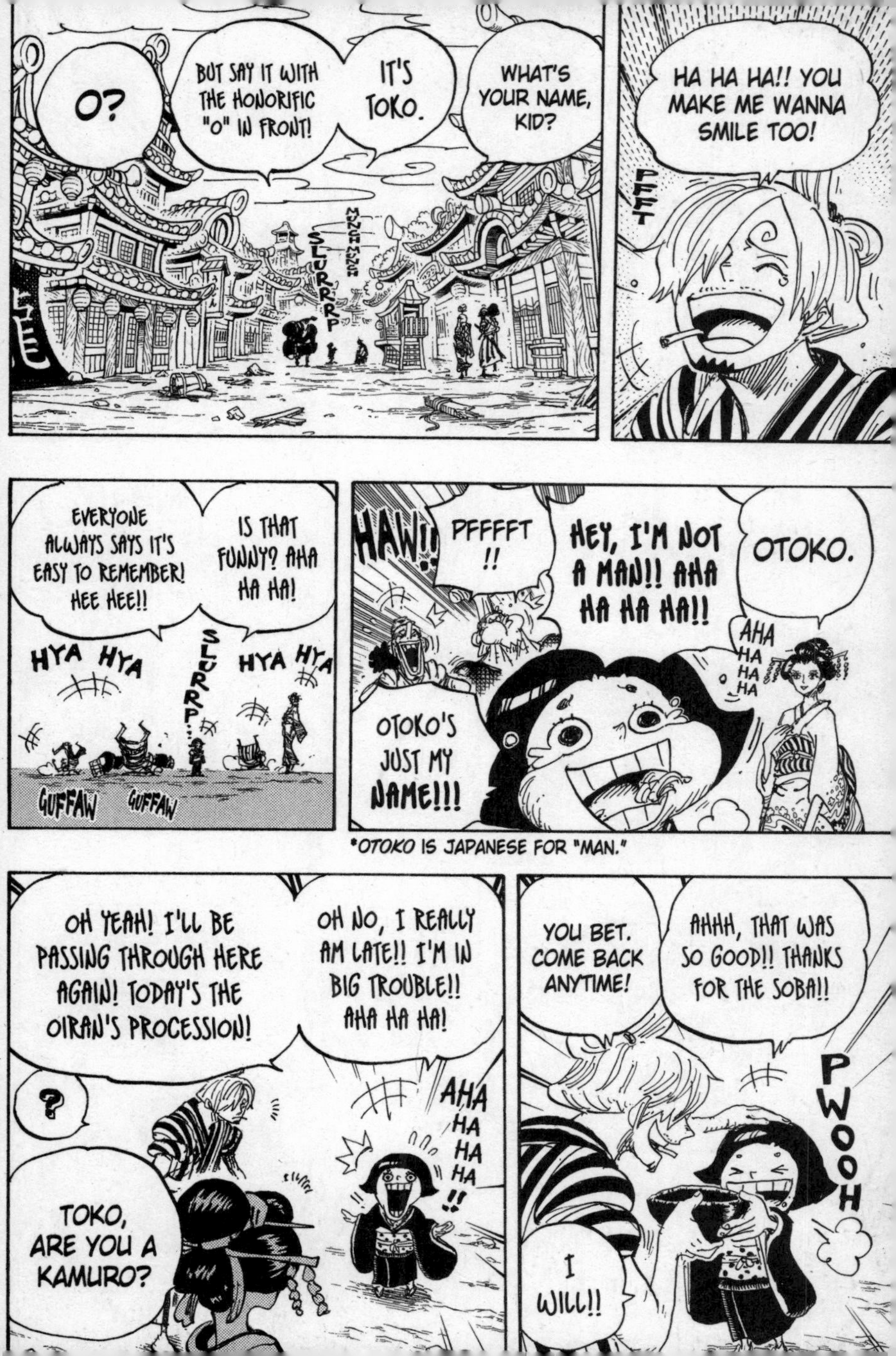
HA HA HA!! YOU MAKE ME WANNA SMILE TOO!
PFFT
WHAT'S YOUR NAME, KID?
IT'S TOKO.
BUT SAY IT WITH THE HONORIFIC "O" IN FRONT!
O?
MUNCH MUNCH
SLURRRP
OTOKO.
HEY, I'M NOT A MAN!! AHA HA HA HA!!
PFFFFT !!
HAW!!
AHA HA HA HA
OTOKO'S JUST MY NAME!!!
IS THAT FUNNY? AHA HA HA!
EVERYONE ALWAYS SAYS IT'S EASY TO REMEMBER! HEE HEE!!
HYA HYA
SLURRP
HYA HYA
GUFFAW GUFFAW
AHHH, THAT WAS SO GOOD!! THANKS FOR THE SOBA!!
YOU BET. COME BACK ANYTIME!
PWOOH
I WILL!!
OH NO, I REALLY AM LATE!! I'M IN BIG TROUBLE!! AHA HA HA!
OH YEAH! I'LL BE PASSING THROUGH HERE AGAIN! TODAY'S THE OIRAN'S PROCESSION!
AHA HA HA HA !!
?
TOKO, ARE YOU A KAMURO?

*OTOKO IS JAPANESE FOR "MAN."

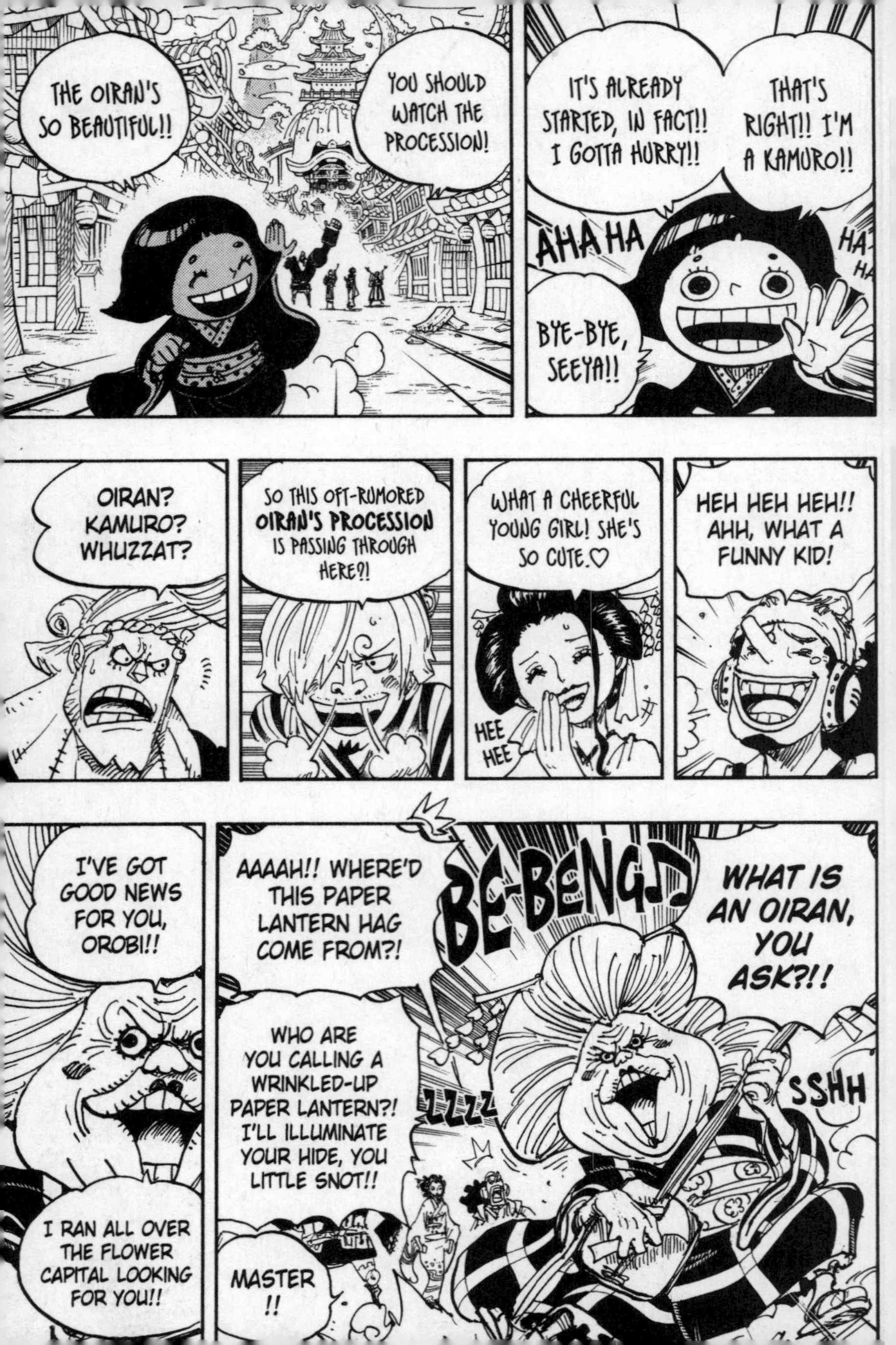
THAT'S RIGHT!! I'M A KAMURO!!
IT'S ALREADY STARTED, IN FACT!! I GOTTA HURRY!!
HA HA
AHAHA
BYE-BYE, SEEYA!!
YOU SHOULD WATCH THE PROCESSION!
THE OIRAN'S SO BEAUTIFUL!!
HEH HEH HEH!! AHH, WHAT A FUNNY KID!
WHAT A CHEERFUL YOUNG GIRL! SHE'S SO CUTE.♡
HEE HEE
SO THIS OFT-RUMORED **OIRAN'S PROCESSION** IS PASSING THROUGH HERE?!
OIRAN? KAMURO? WHUZZAT?
WHAT IS AN OIRAN, YOU ASK?!!
BE-BENG♫
AAAAH!! WHERE'D THIS PAPER LANTERN HAG COME FROM?!
SSHH
WHO ARE YOU CALLING A WRINKLED-UP PAPER LANTERN?! I'LL ILLUMINATE YOUR HIDE, YOU LITTLE SNOT!!
ZZZZ
MASTER!!
I'VE GOT GOOD NEWS FOR YOU, OROBI!!
I RAN ALL OVER THE FLOWER CAPITAL LOOKING FOR YOU!!

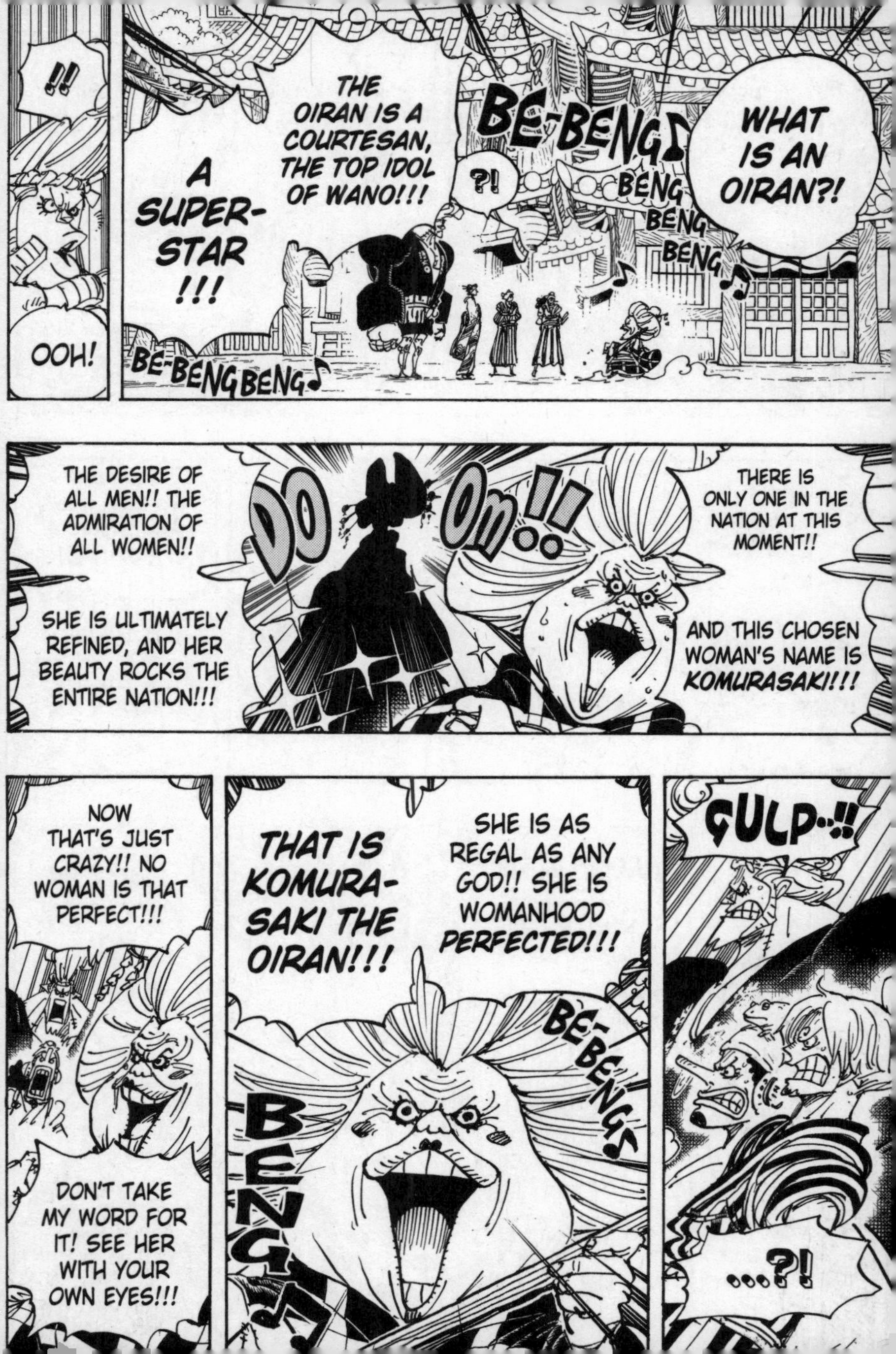
WHAT IS AN OIRAN?!
BE-BENG♪
BENG BENG BENG♪
?!
THE OIRAN IS A COURTESAN, THE TOP IDOL OF WANO!!!
A SUPER-STAR!!!
BE-BENG BENG BENG♪
!!
OOH!
THERE IS ONLY ONE IN THE NATION AT THIS MOMENT!!
AND THIS CHOSEN WOMAN'S NAME IS KOMURASAKI!!!
DOOM!!..
THE DESIRE OF ALL MEN!! THE ADMIRATION OF ALL WOMEN!!
SHE IS ULTIMATELY REFINED, AND HER BEAUTY ROCKS THE ENTIRE NATION!!!
GULP..!!
...?!
SHE IS AS REGAL AS ANY GOD!! SHE IS WOMANHOOD PERFECTED!!!
THAT IS KOMURA-SAKI THE OIRAN!!!
BE-BENG♪
BENG♪
NOW THAT'S JUST CRAZY!! NO WOMAN IS THAT PERFECT!!!
DON'T TAKE MY WORD FOR IT! SEE HER WITH YOUR OWN EYES!!!

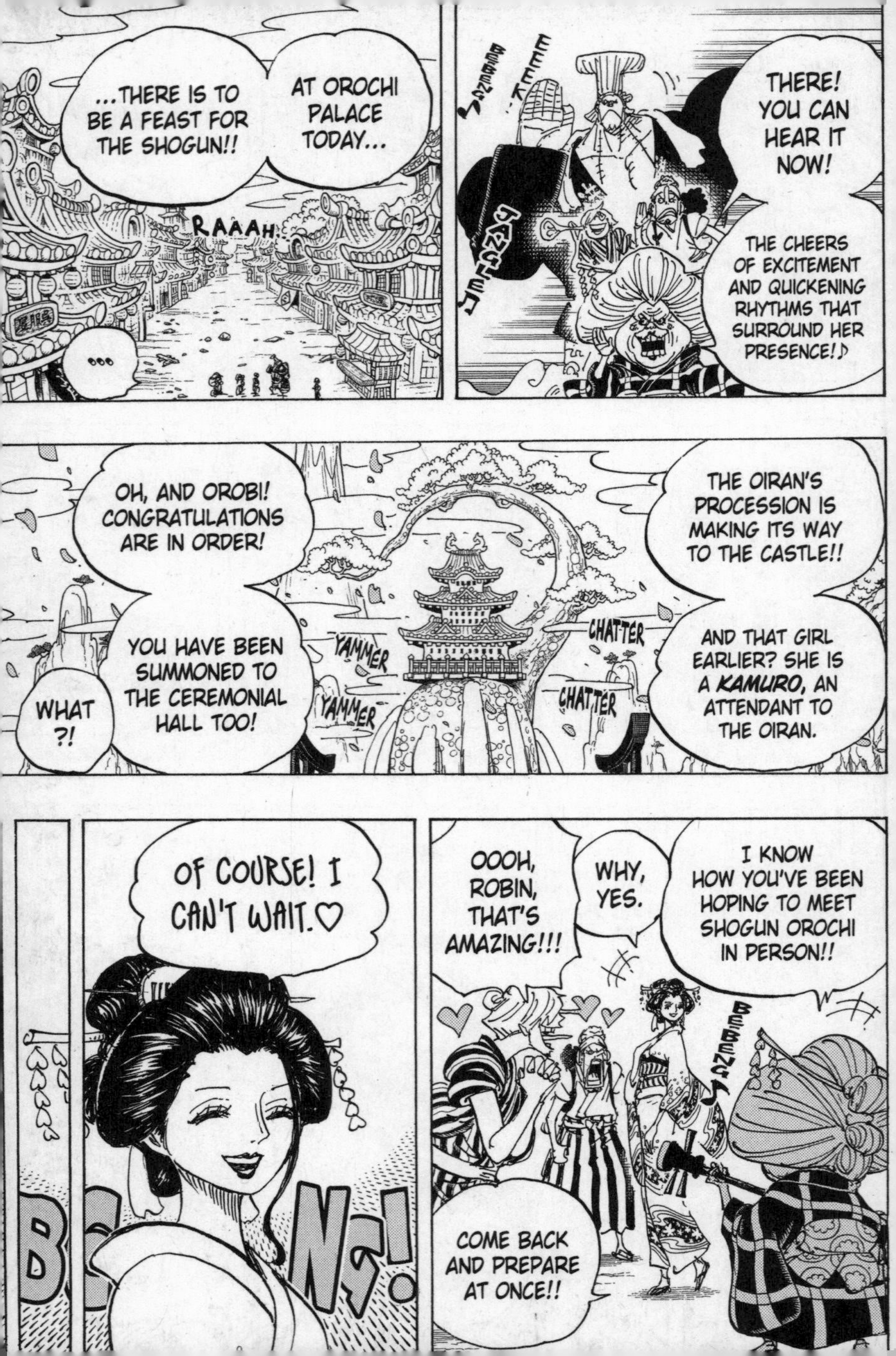

EEEEK
BEBEN
JANGLE
THERE! YOU CAN HEAR IT NOW!
THE CHEERS OF EXCITEMENT AND QUICKENING RHYTHMS THAT SURROUND HER PRESENCE!♪
AT OROCHI PALACE TODAY...
...THERE IS TO BE A FEAST FOR THE SHOGUN!!
RAAAH...
...
THE OIRAN'S PROCESSION IS MAKING ITS WAY TO THE CASTLE!!
AND THAT GIRL EARLIER? SHE IS A *KAMURO*, AN ATTENDANT TO THE OIRAN.
CHATTER
CHATTER
YAMMER
YAMMER
OH, AND OROBI! CONGRATULATIONS ARE IN ORDER!
YOU HAVE BEEN SUMMONED TO THE CEREMONIAL HALL TOO!
WHAT?!
I KNOW HOW YOU'VE BEEN HOPING TO MEET SHOGUN OROCHI IN PERSON!!
WHY, YES.
OOOH, ROBIN, THAT'S AMAZING!!!
BEBENG
COME BACK AND PREPARE AT ONCE!!
OF COURSE! I CAN'T WAIT.♡

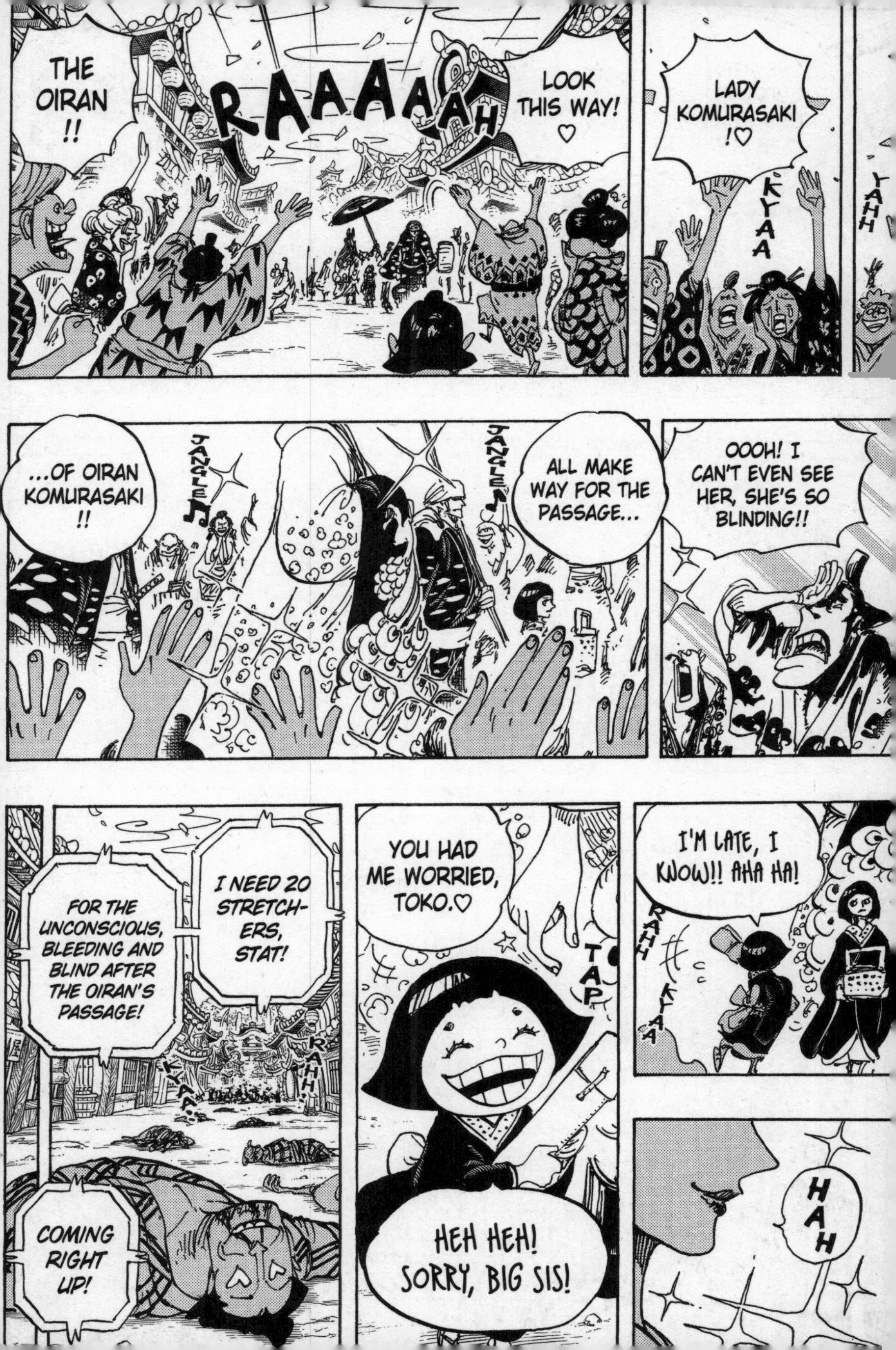
YAHH
LADY KOMURASAKI !♡
KYAA
LOOK THIS WAY! ♡
RAAAAAH
THE OIRAN !!
OOOH! I CAN'T EVEN SEE HER, SHE'S SO BLINDING!!
ALL MAKE WAY FOR THE PASSAGE...
JANGLE
JANGLE
...OF OIRAN KOMURASAKI !!
I'M LATE, I KNOW!! AHA HA!
RAHH
KYAA
HAH
YOU HAD ME WORRIED, TOKO.♡
TAP
HEH HEH! SORRY, BIG SIS!
I NEED 20 STRETCHERS, STAT!
FOR THE UNCONSCIOUS, BLEEDING AND BLIND AFTER THE OIRAN'S PASSAGE!
RAHH
KYAA
COMING RIGHT UP!

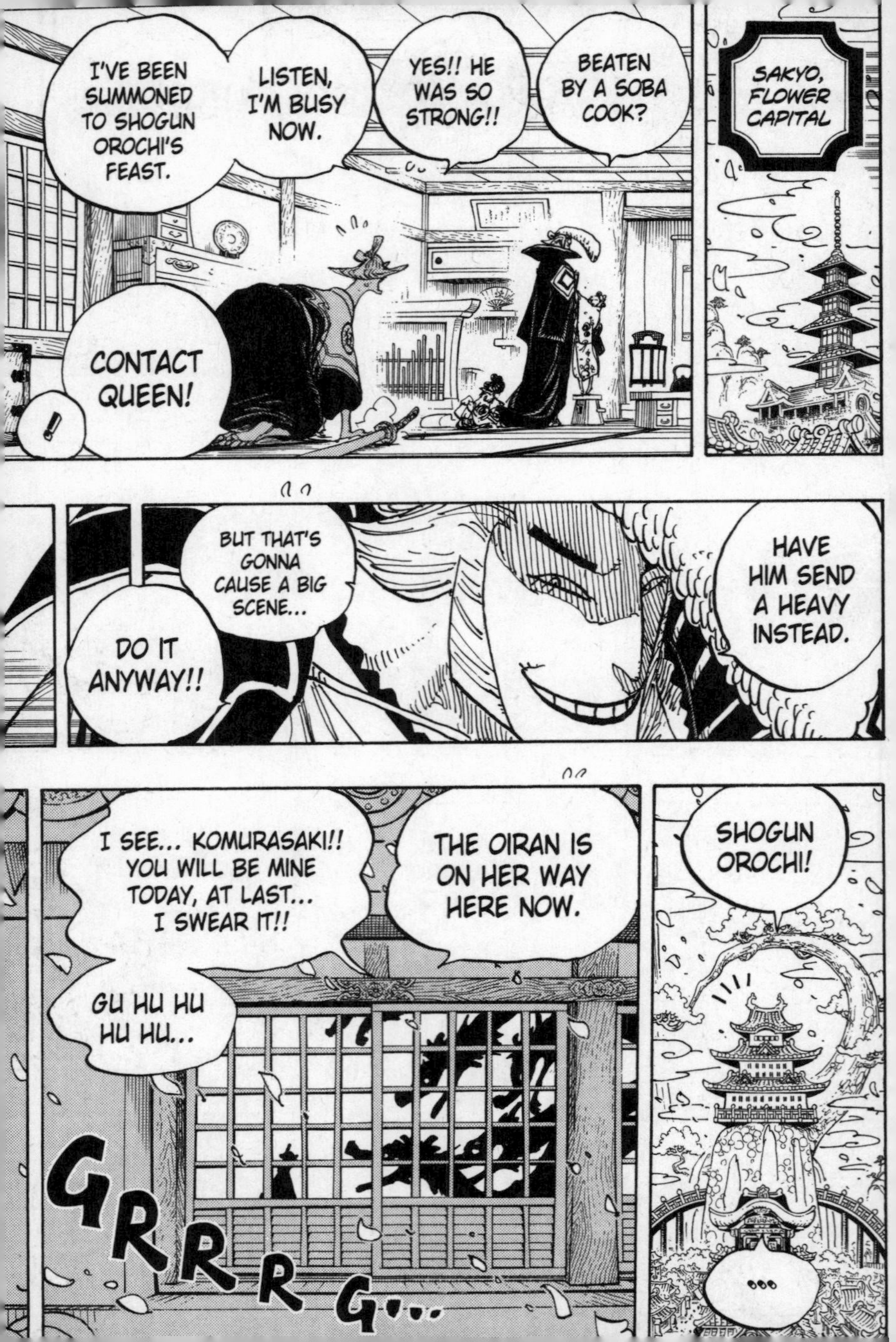
SAKYO, FLOWER CAPITAL
BEATEN BY A SOBA COOK?
YES!! HE WAS SO STRONG!!
LISTEN, I'M BUSY NOW.
I'VE BEEN SUMMONED TO SHOGUN OROCHI'S FEAST.
CONTACT QUEEN!
!
HAVE HIM SEND A HEAVY INSTEAD.
BUT THAT'S GONNA CAUSE A BIG SCENE...
DO IT ANYWAY!!
SHOGUN OROCHI!
...
THE OIRAN IS ON HER WAY HERE NOW.
I SEE... KOMURASAKI!! YOU WILL BE MINE TODAY, AT LAST... I SWEAR IT!!
GU HU HU HU HU...
GRRRRG...

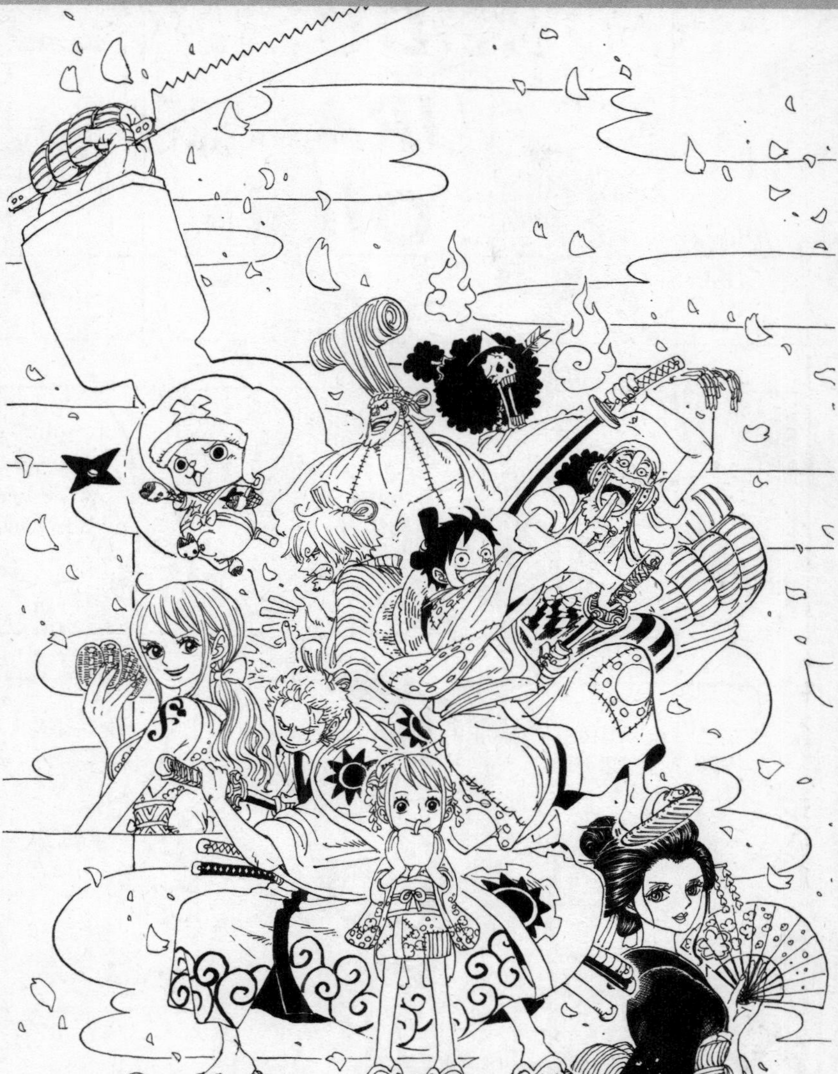

Chapter 928:
INTRODUCING KOMURASAKI THE OIRAN

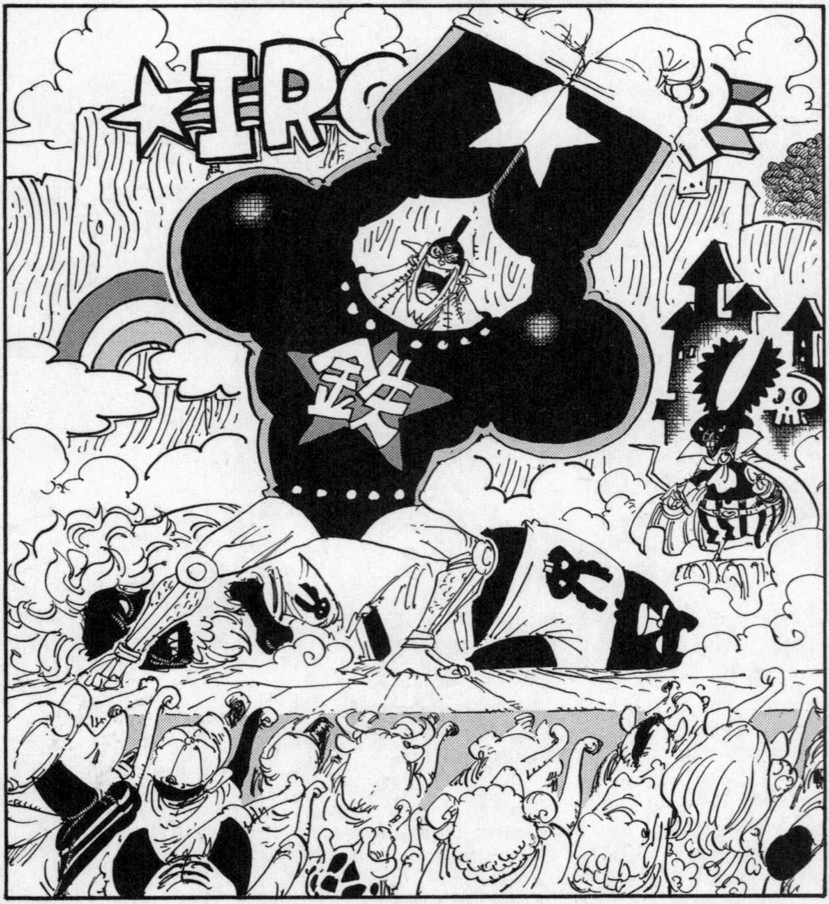
鉄

REQUEST: "THE KIDS WATCHING THE HERO STAGE SHOW LOVE FRANKY" BY FIRE YAMAMOTO

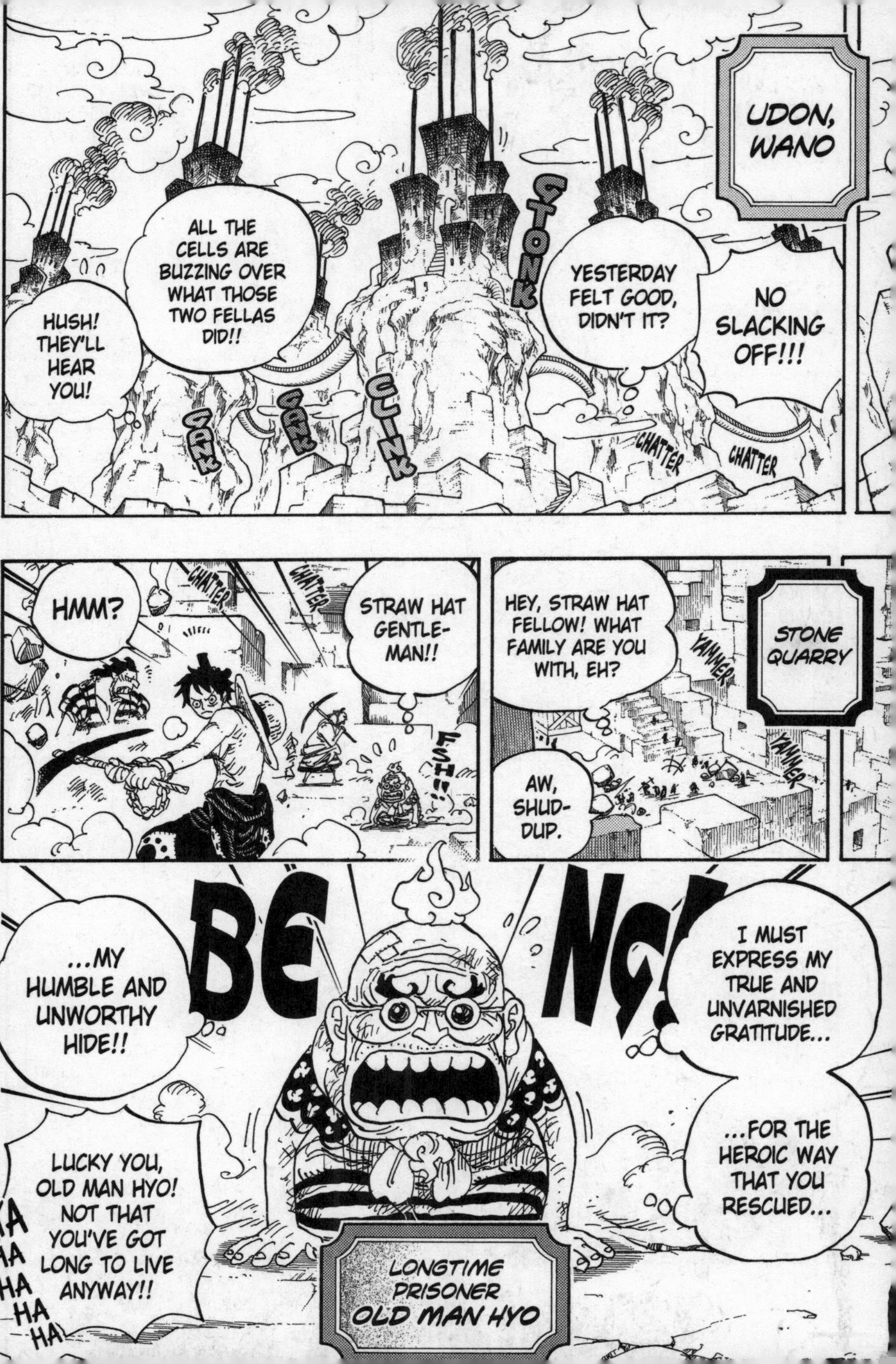
UDON, WANO
NO SLACKING OFF!!!
YESTERDAY FELT GOOD, DIDN'T IT?
GTONK
ALL THE CELLS ARE BUZZING OVER WHAT THOSE TWO FELLAS DID!!
HUSH! THEY'LL HEAR YOU!
CHATTER
CHATTER
CLINK
CANK
CANK
STONE QUARRY
YAMMER
HEY, STRAW HAT FELLOW! WHAT FAMILY ARE YOU WITH, EH?
YAMMER
AW, SHUDDUP.
STRAW HAT GENTLEMAN!!
CHATTER
CHATTER
HMM?
FSH!!
I MUST EXPRESS MY TRUE AND UNVARNISHED GRATITUDE...
...FOR THE HEROIC WAY THAT YOU RESCUED...
...MY HUMBLE AND UNWORTHY HIDE!!
LONGTIME PRISONER OLD MAN HYO
LUCKY YOU, OLD MAN HYO! NOT THAT YOU'VE GOT LONG TO LIVE ANYWAY!!
YA HA HA HA HA HA

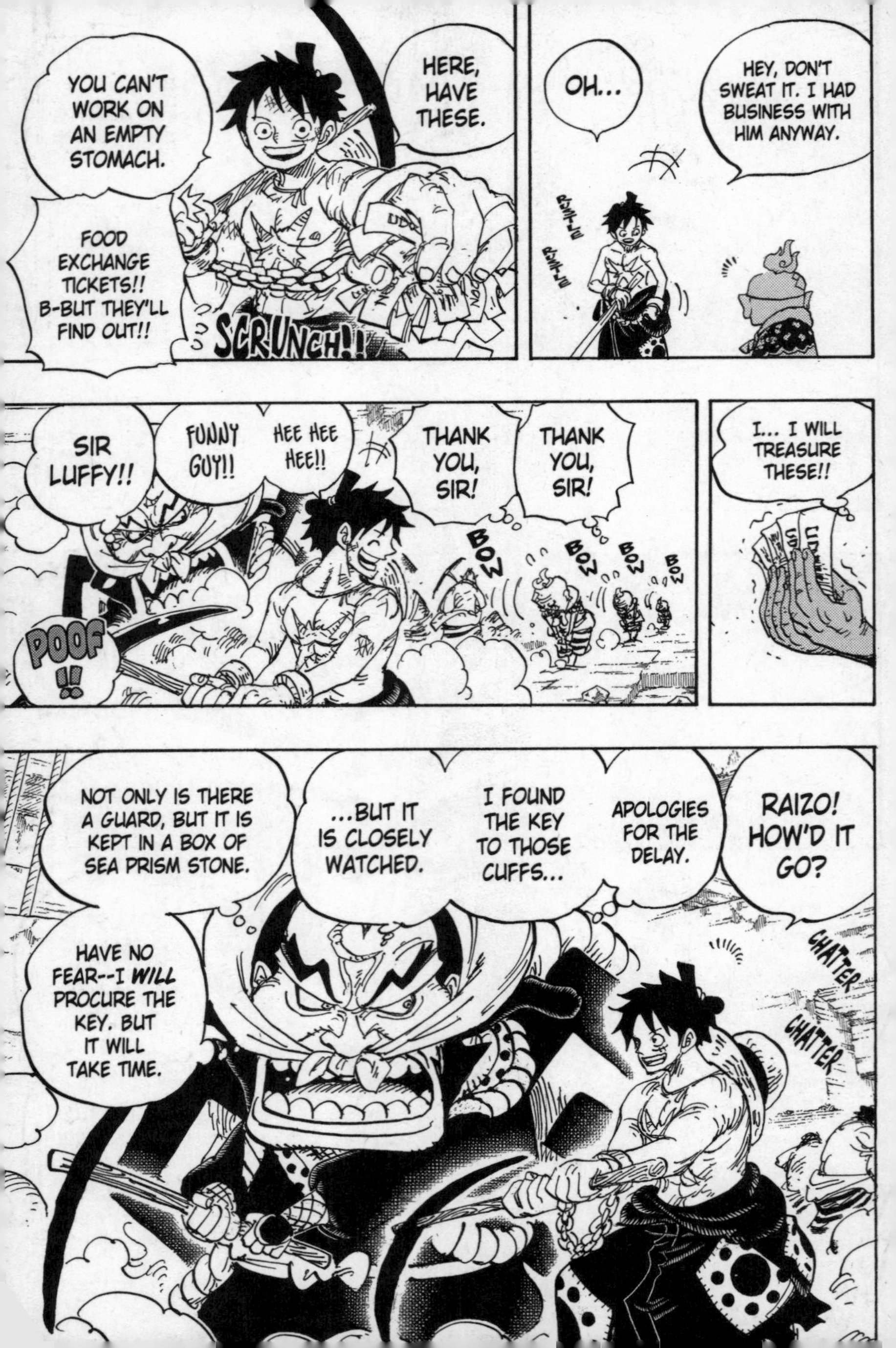
HEY, DON'T SWEAT IT. I HAD BUSINESS WITH HIM ANYWAY.
OH...
RUSTLE
RUSTLE
HERE, HAVE THESE.
YOU CAN'T WORK ON AN EMPTY STOMACH.
FOOD EXCHANGE TICKETS!! B-BUT THEY'LL FIND OUT!!
SCRUNCH!!
I... I WILL TREASURE THESE!!
THANK YOU, SIR!
THANK YOU, SIR!
BOW
BOW
BOW
BOW
HEE HEE HEE!!
FUNNY GUY!!
SIR LUFFY!!
POOF!!
RAIZO! HOW'D IT GO?
APOLOGIES FOR THE DELAY.
I FOUND THE KEY TO THOSE CUFFS...
...BUT IT IS CLOSELY WATCHED.
NOT ONLY IS THERE A GUARD, BUT IT IS KEPT IN A BOX OF SEA PRISM STONE.
CHATTER
CHATTER
HAVE NO FEAR--I *WILL* PROCURE THE KEY. BUT IT WILL TAKE TIME.

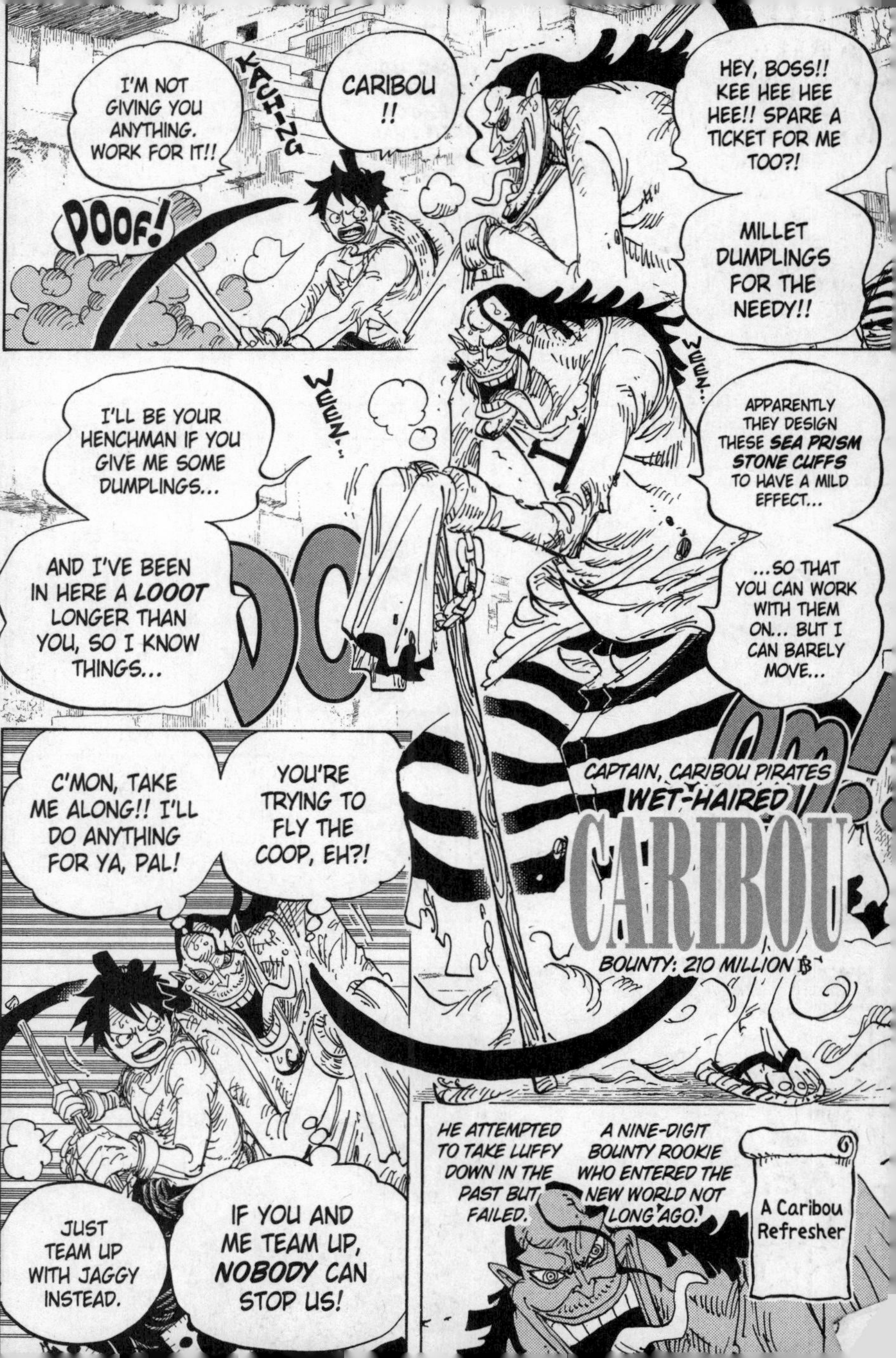

HEY, BOSS!! KEE HEE HEE HEE!! SPARE A TICKET FOR ME TOO?!
MILLET DUMPLINGS FOR THE NEEDY!!
CARIBOU !!
KACHING
I'M NOT GIVING YOU ANYTHING. WORK FOR IT!!
POOF!
WEEZ...
APPARENTLY THEY DESIGN THESE **SEA PRISM STONE CUFFS** TO HAVE A MILD EFFECT...
...SO THAT YOU CAN WORK WITH THEM ON... BUT I CAN BARELY MOVE...
WEEZ..
I'LL BE YOUR HENCHMAN IF YOU GIVE ME SOME DUMPLINGS...
AND I'VE BEEN IN HERE A *LOOOT* LONGER THAN YOU, SO I KNOW THINGS...
CAPTAIN, CARIBOU PIRATES
WET-HAIRED
CARIBOU
BOUNTY: 210 MILLION ฿
A Caribou Refresher
A NINE-DIGIT BOUNTY ROOKIE WHO ENTERED THE NEW WORLD NOT LONG AGO.
HE ATTEMPTED TO TAKE LUFFY DOWN IN THE PAST BUT FAILED.
YOU'RE TRYING TO FLY THE COOP, EH?!
C'MON, TAKE ME ALONG!! I'LL DO ANYTHING FOR YA, PAL!
IF YOU AND ME TEAM UP, **NOBODY** CAN STOP US!
JUST TEAM UP WITH JAGGY INSTEAD.

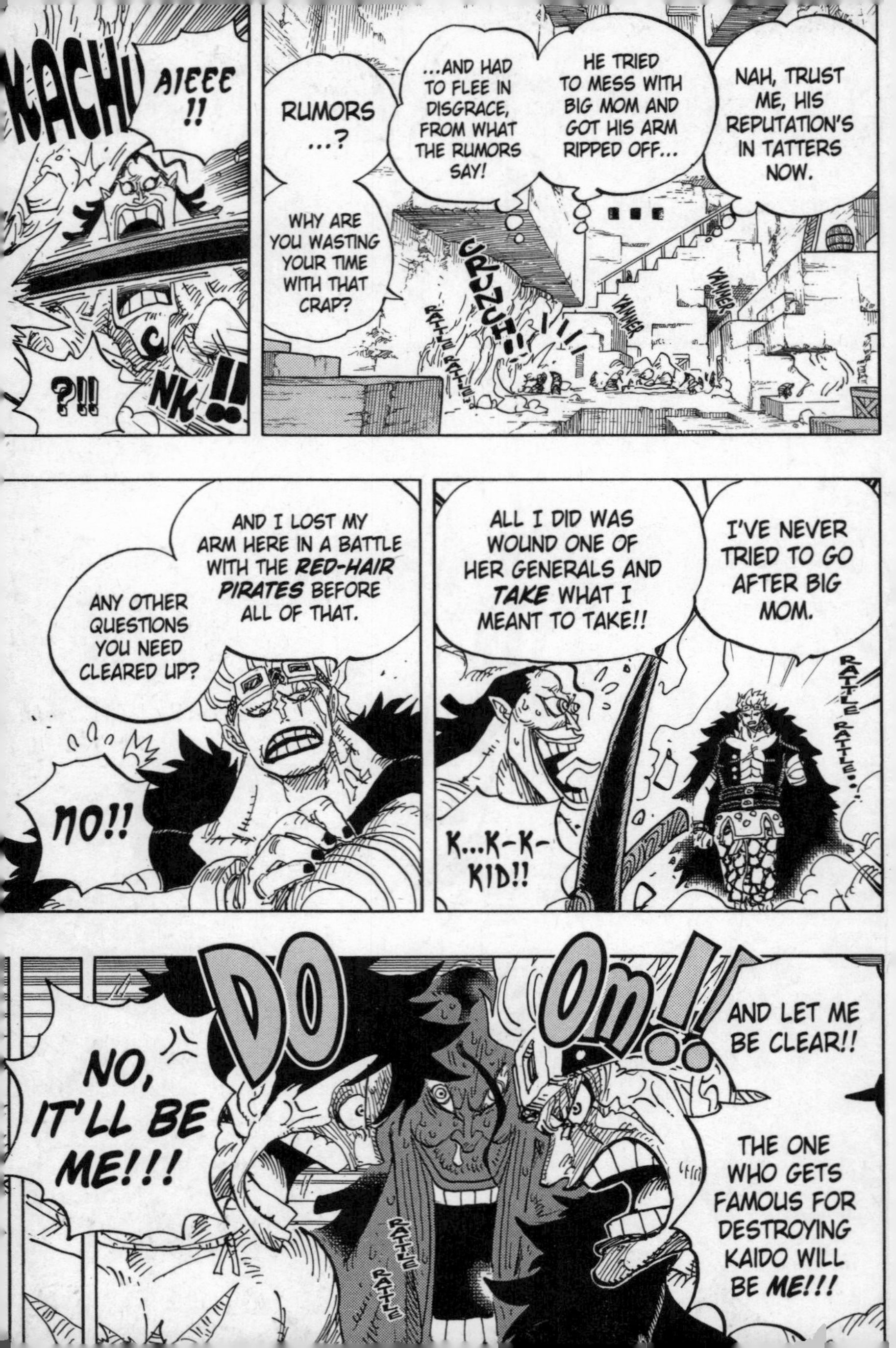
NAH, TRUST ME, HIS REPUTATION'S IN TATTERS NOW.
HE TRIED TO MESS WITH BIG MOM AND GOT HIS ARM RIPPED OFF...
...AND HAD TO FLEE IN DISGRACE, FROM WHAT THE RUMORS SAY!
RUMORS ...?
WHY ARE YOU WASTING YOUR TIME WITH THAT CRAP?
YAMMER
YAMMER
CRUNCH!!
RATTLE RATTLE
KACHU
AIEEE !!
C
?!!
NK!!
I'VE NEVER TRIED TO GO AFTER BIG MOM.
ALL I DID WAS WOUND ONE OF HER GENERALS AND *TAKE* WHAT I MEANT TO TAKE!!
RATTLE RATTLE...
K...K-K-KID!!
AND I LOST MY ARM HERE IN A BATTLE WITH THE ***RED-HAIR PIRATES*** BEFORE ALL OF THAT.
ANY OTHER QUESTIONS YOU NEED CLEARED UP?
NO!!
AND LET ME BE CLEAR!!
THE ONE WHO GETS FAMOUS FOR DESTROYING KAIDO WILL BE *ME!!!*
DOOM!!
NO, IT'LL BE ME!!!
RATTLE
RATTLE

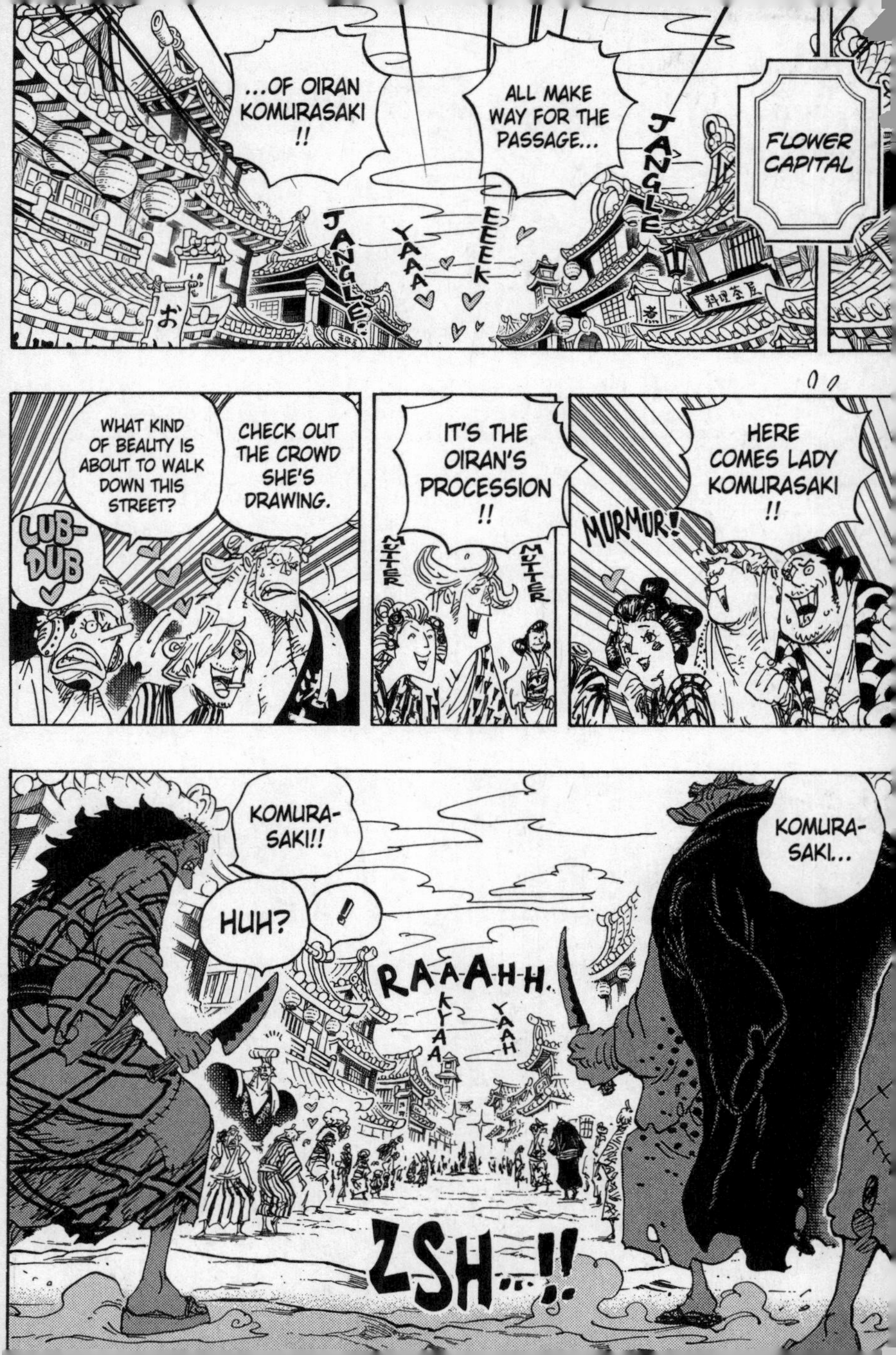
FLOWER CAPITAL
JANGLE
ALL MAKE WAY FOR THE PASSAGE...
EEEEK
...OF OIRAN KOMURASAKI !!
YAAA
JANGLE
HERE COMES LADY KOMURASAKI !!
MURMUR!
IT'S THE OIRAN'S PROCESSION !!
MUTTER
MUTTER
CHECK OUT THE CROWD SHE'S DRAWING.
WHAT KIND OF BEAUTY IS ABOUT TO WALK DOWN THIS STREET?
LUB-DUB
KOMURA-SAKI...
KOMURA-SAKI!!
!
HUH?
RAAAHH..
KYAA
YAAH
ZSH...!!

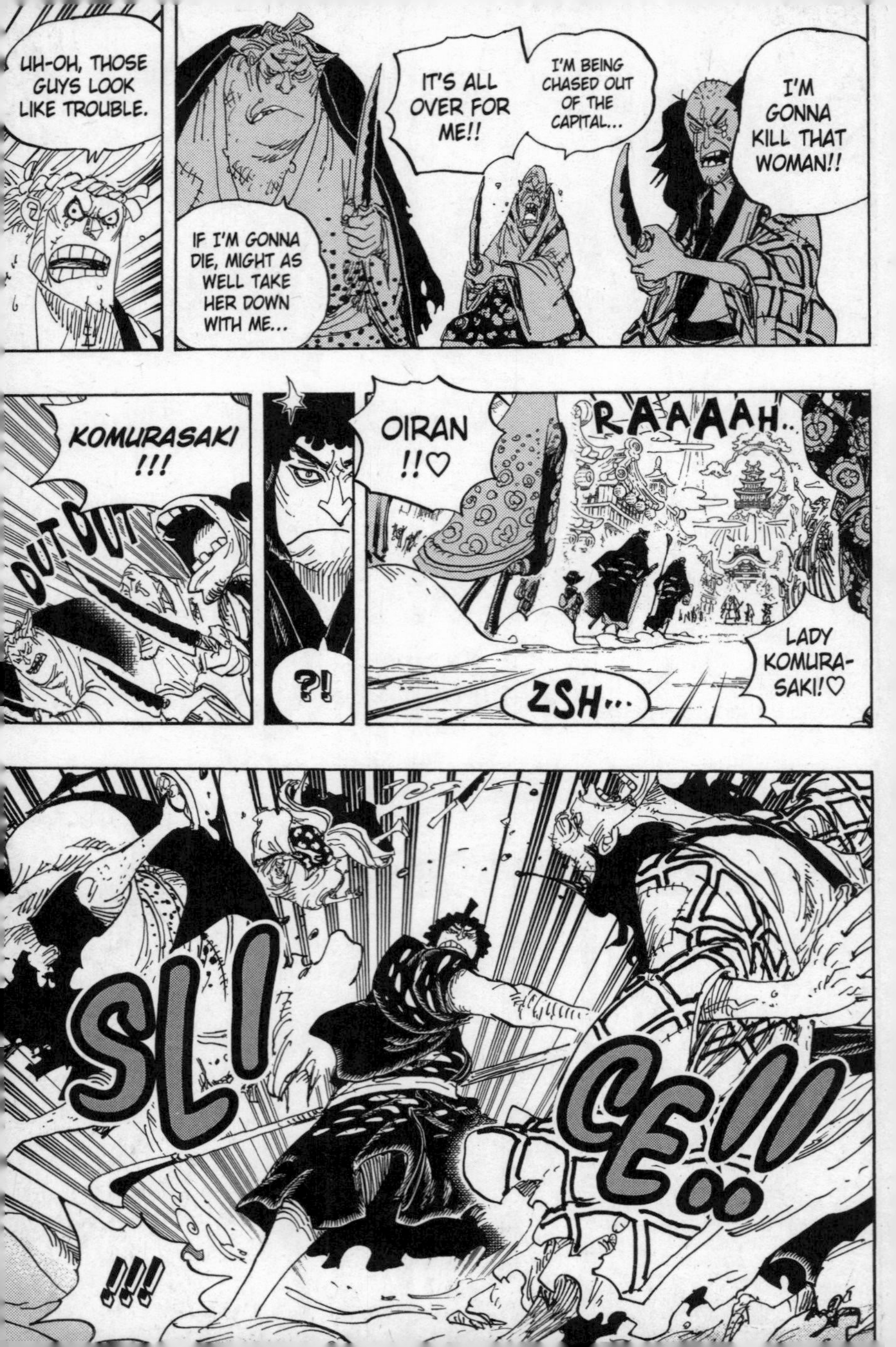
I'M GONNA KILL THAT WOMAN!!
I'M BEING CHASED OUT OF THE CAPITAL...
IT'S ALL OVER FOR ME!!
IF I'M GONNA DIE, MIGHT AS WELL TAKE HER DOWN WITH ME...
UH-OH, THOSE GUYS LOOK LIKE TROUBLE.
RAAAAH..
OIRAN !!♡
LADY KOMURA-SAKI!♡
ZSH...
?!
KOMURASAKI !!!
DUT DUT
SLICE!!
!!!

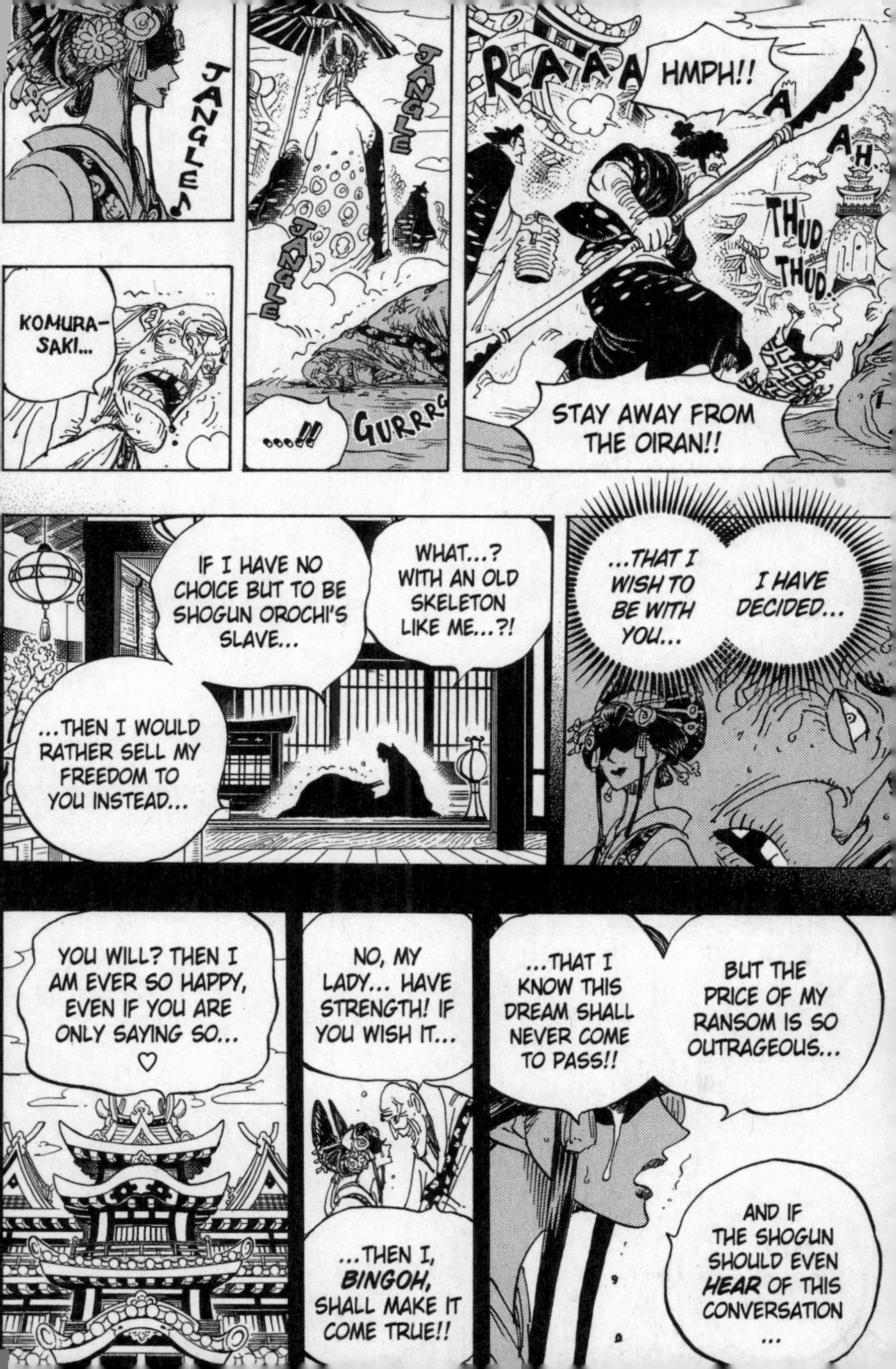
RAAAA
HMPH!!
AH
THUD
THUD
STAY AWAY FROM THE OIRAN!!
JANGLE
JANGLE
....!!
GURRRG
JANGLE!
KOMURA-SAKI...
I HAVE DECIDED...
...THAT I WISH TO BE WITH YOU...
WHAT...? WITH AN OLD SKELETON LIKE ME...?!
IF I HAVE NO CHOICE BUT TO BE SHOGUN OROCHI'S SLAVE...
...THEN I WOULD RATHER SELL MY FREEDOM TO YOU INSTEAD...
BUT THE PRICE OF MY RANSOM IS SO OUTRAGEOUS...
...THAT I KNOW THIS DREAM SHALL NEVER COME TO PASS!!
AND IF THE SHOGUN SHOULD EVEN *HEAR* OF THIS CONVERSATION ...
NO, MY LADY... HAVE STRENGTH! IF YOU WISH IT...
...THEN I, *BINGOH*, SHALL MAKE IT COME TRUE!!
YOU WILL? THEN I AM EVER SO HAPPY, EVEN IF YOU ARE ONLY SAYING SO... ♡

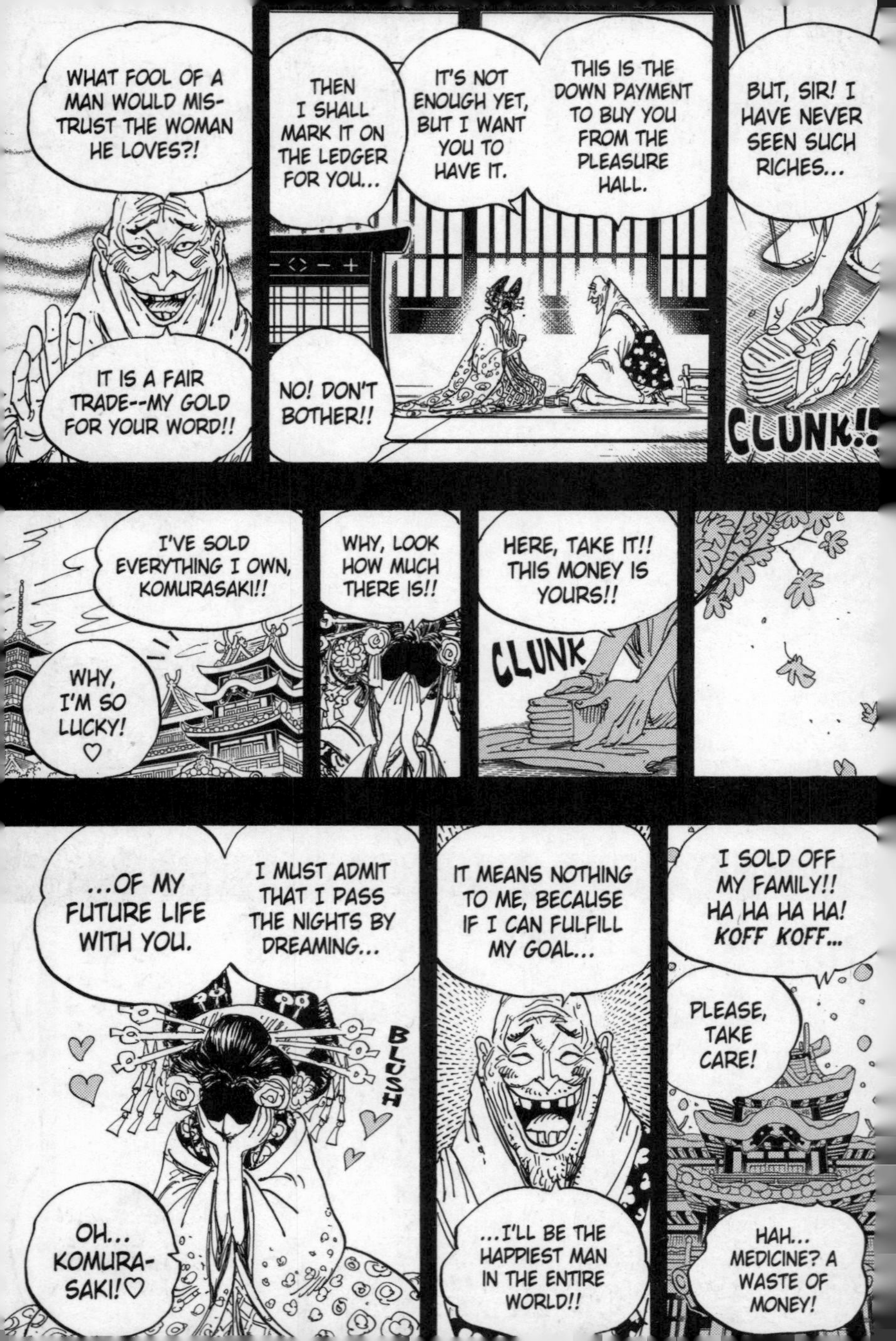
BUT, SIR! I HAVE NEVER SEEN SUCH RICHES...
CLUNK!!
THIS IS THE DOWN PAYMENT TO BUY YOU FROM THE PLEASURE HALL.
IT'S NOT ENOUGH YET, BUT I WANT YOU TO HAVE IT.
THEN I SHALL MARK IT ON THE LEDGER FOR YOU...
NO! DON'T BOTHER!!
WHAT FOOL OF A MAN WOULD MIS-TRUST THE WOMAN HE LOVES?!
IT IS A FAIR TRADE--MY GOLD FOR YOUR WORD!!
HERE, TAKE IT!! THIS MONEY IS YOURS!!
CLUNK
WHY, LOOK HOW MUCH THERE IS!!
I'VE SOLD EVERYTHING I OWN, KOMURASAKI!!
WHY, I'M SO LUCKY! ♡
I SOLD OFF MY FAMILY!! HA HA HA HA! KOFF KOFF...
PLEASE, TAKE CARE!
HAH... MEDICINE? A WASTE OF MONEY!
IT MEANS NOTHING TO ME, BECAUSE IF I CAN FULFILL MY GOAL...
...I'LL BE THE HAPPIEST MAN IN THE ENTIRE WORLD!!
I MUST ADMIT THAT I PASS THE NIGHTS BY DREAMING...
...OF MY FUTURE LIFE WITH YOU.
BLUSH
OH... KOMURA-SAKI!♡

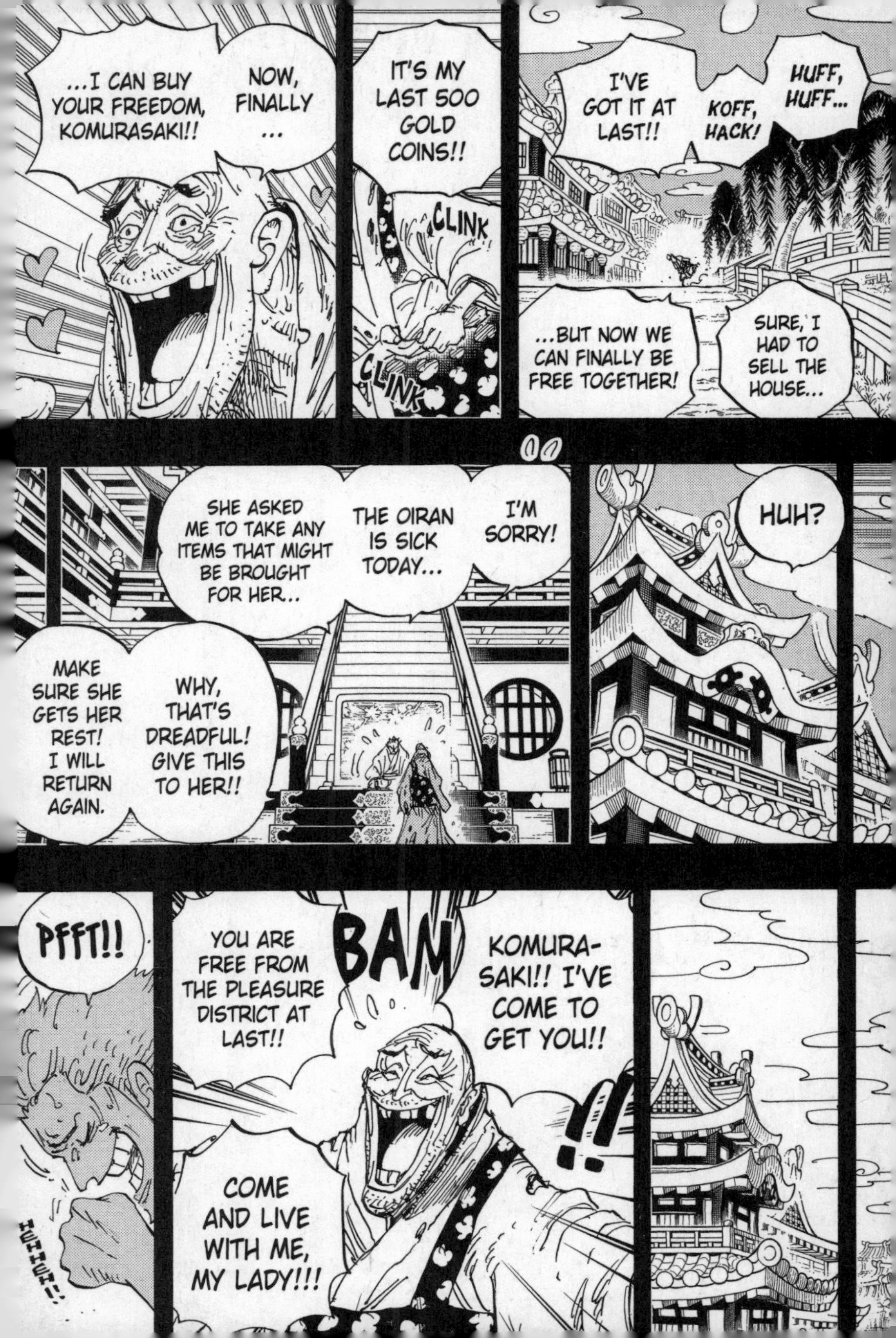
HUFF, HUFF...
KOFF, HACK!
I'VE GOT IT AT LAST!!
SURE, I HAD TO SELL THE HOUSE...
...BUT NOW WE CAN FINALLY BE FREE TOGETHER!
IT'S MY LAST 500 GOLD COINS!!
CLINK
CLINK
NOW, FINALLY ...
...I CAN BUY YOUR FREEDOM, KOMURASAKI!!
HUH?
I'M SORRY!
THE OIRAN IS SICK TODAY...
SHE ASKED ME TO TAKE ANY ITEMS THAT MIGHT BE BROUGHT FOR HER...
WHY, THAT'S DREADFUL! GIVE THIS TO HER!!
MAKE SURE SHE GETS HER REST! I WILL RETURN AGAIN.
KOMURA-SAKI!! I'VE COME TO GET YOU!!
BAM
YOU ARE FREE FROM THE PLEASURE DISTRICT AT LAST!!
!!
COME AND LIVE WITH ME, MY LADY!!!
PFFT!!
HEHHEH!!

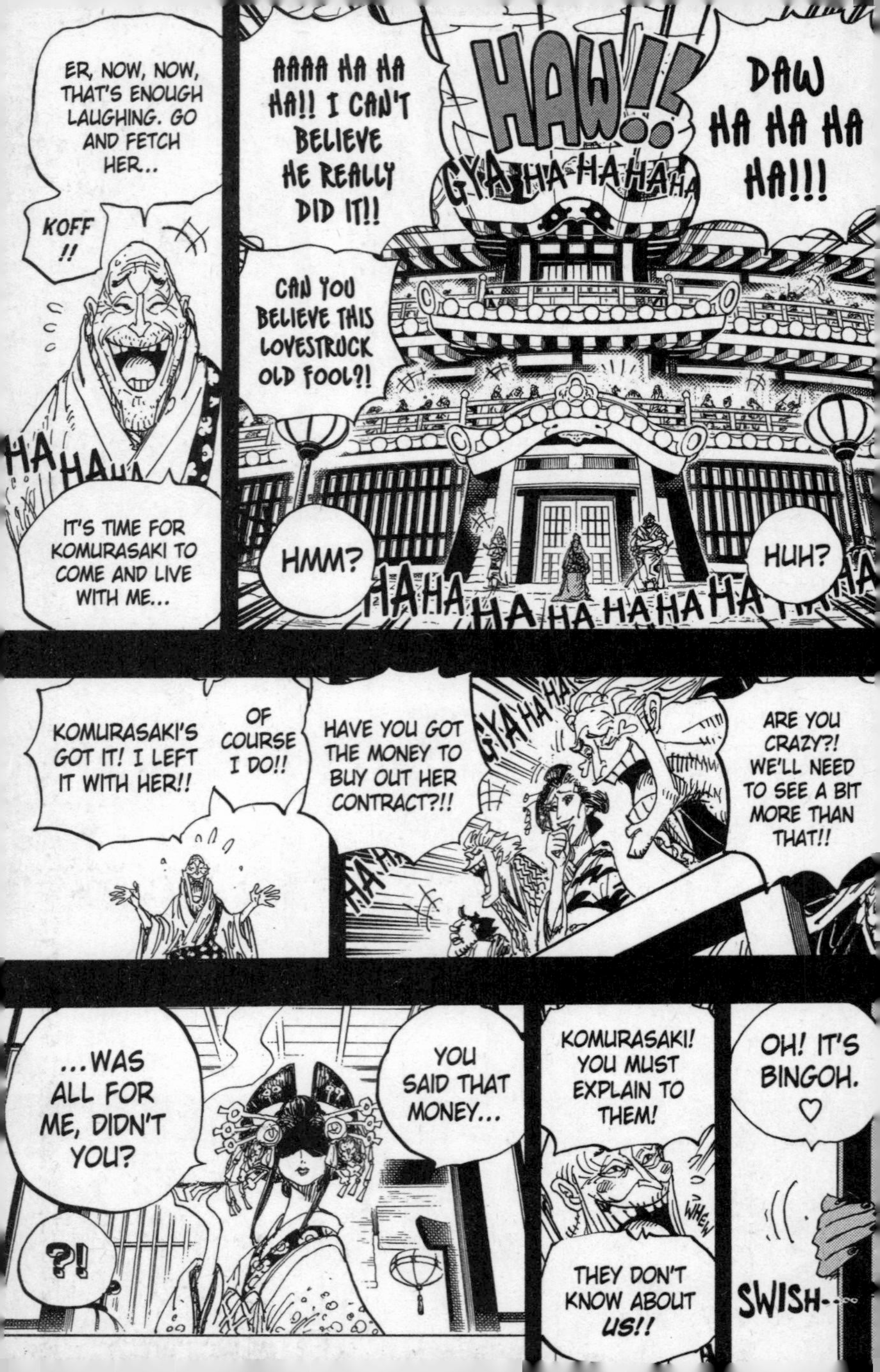
DAW HA HA HA HA!!!
HAW!!
GYA HA HA HA HA HA
AAAA HA HA HA!! I CAN'T BELIEVE HE REALLY DID IT!!
CAN YOU BELIEVE THIS LOVESTRUCK OLD FOOL?!
HUH?
HMM?
HAHA HA HA HA HA HA HA
ER, NOW, NOW, THAT'S ENOUGH LAUGHING. GO AND FETCH HER...
KOFF !!
HA HA
IT'S TIME FOR KOMURASAKI TO COME AND LIVE WITH ME...
ARE YOU CRAZY?! WE'LL NEED TO SEE A BIT MORE THAN THAT!!
GYA HA HA
HAVE YOU GOT THE MONEY TO BUY OUT HER CONTRACT?!!
HA HA
OF COURSE I DO!!
KOMURASAKI'S GOT IT! I LEFT IT WITH HER!!
OH! IT'S BINGOH. ♡
SWISH...
KOMURASAKI! YOU MUST EXPLAIN TO THEM!
WHEW
THEY DON'T KNOW ABOUT US!!
YOU SAID THAT MONEY...
...WAS ALL FOR ME, DIDN'T YOU?
?!

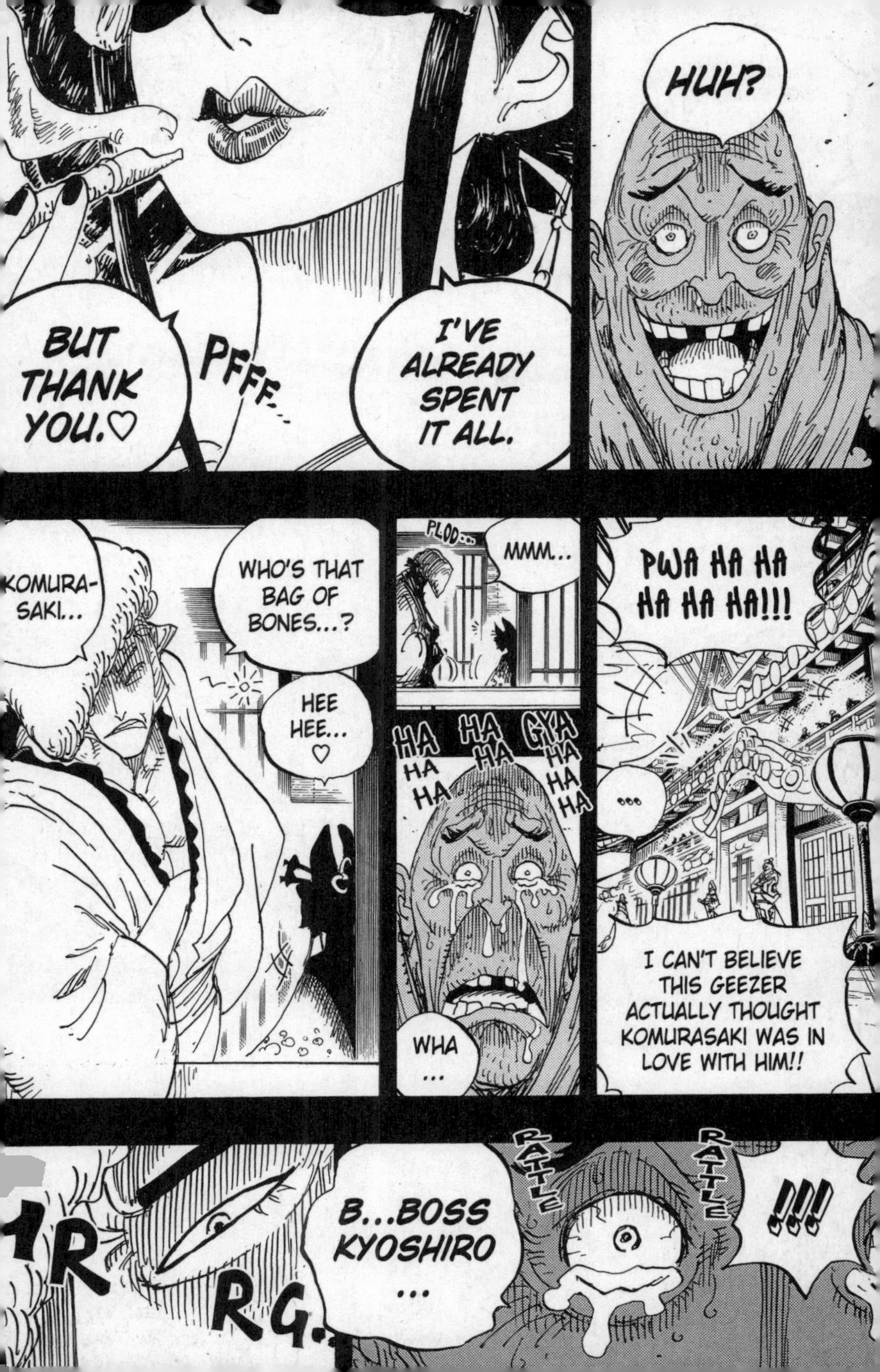
HUH?
I'VE ALREADY SPENT IT ALL.
PFFF...
BUT THANK YOU.♡
PWA HA HA HA HA HA!!!
...
I CAN'T BELIEVE THIS GEEZER ACTUALLY THOUGHT KOMURASAKI WAS IN LOVE WITH HIM!!
PLOD...
MMM...
GYA HA HA HA HA
HA HA
HA HA HA HA
WHA ...
WHO'S THAT BAG OF BONES...?
KOMURA-SAKI...
HEE HEE...♡
!!!
RATTLE
RATTLE
B...BOSS KYOSHIRO ...
R
RG...

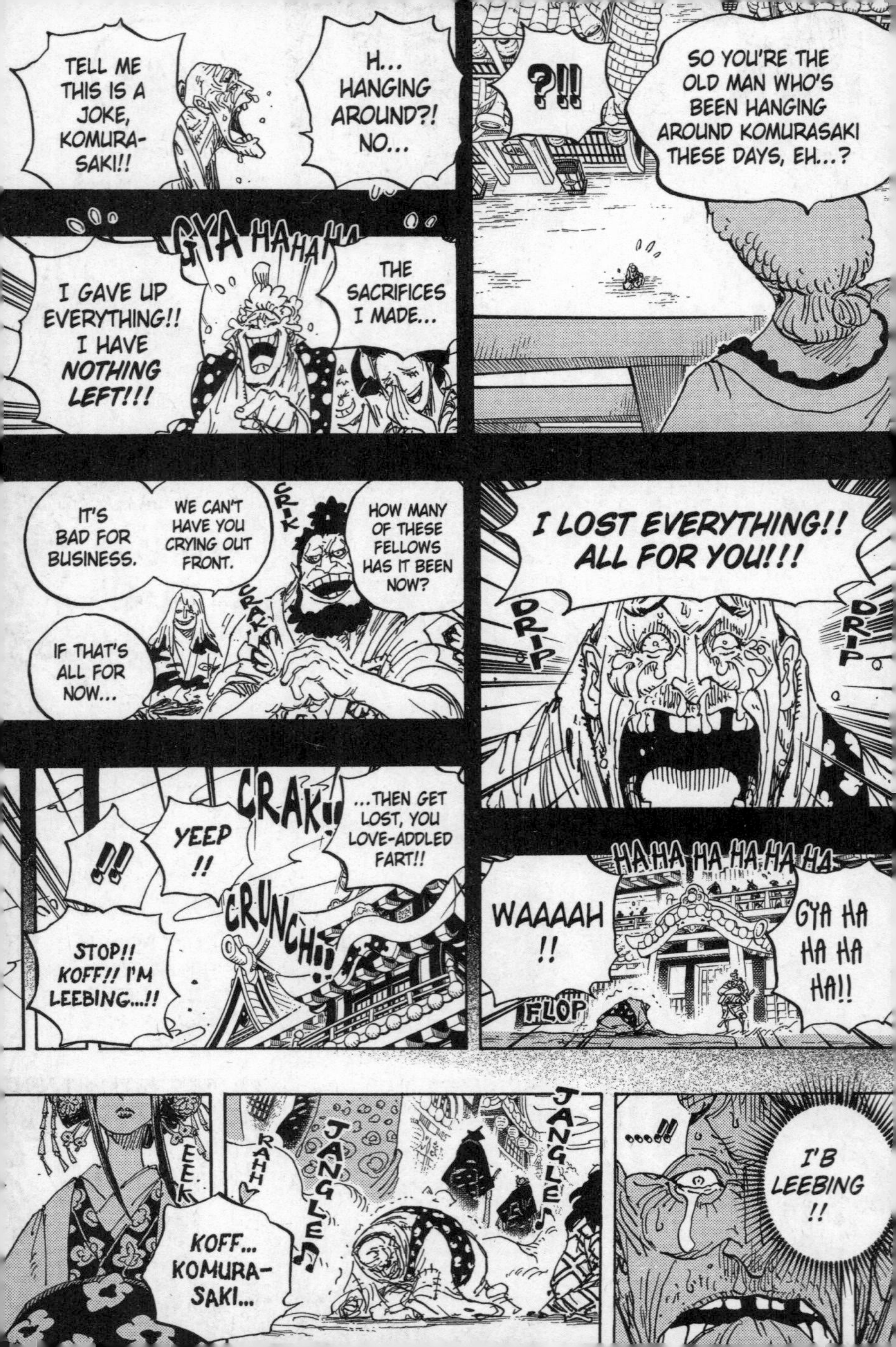
SO YOU'RE THE OLD MAN WHO'S BEEN HANGING AROUND KOMURASAKI THESE DAYS, EH...?
?!!
H... HANGING AROUND?! NO...
TELL ME THIS IS A JOKE, KOMURASAKI!!
GYA HA HA HA
THE SACRIFICES I MADE...
I GAVE UP EVERYTHING!! I HAVE NOTHING LEFT!!!
I LOST EVERYTHING!! ALL FOR YOU!!!
DRIP
DRIP
CRIK
HOW MANY OF THESE FELLOWS HAS IT BEEN NOW?
WE CAN'T HAVE YOU CRYING OUT FRONT.
IT'S BAD FOR BUSINESS.
CRAK
IF THAT'S ALL FOR NOW...
CRAK!!
...THEN GET LOST, YOU LOVE-ADDLED FART!!
YEEP!!
!!
CRUNCH!!
STOP!! KOFF!! I'M LEEBING...!!
HA HA HA HA HA HA HA
GYA HA HA HA HA!!
WAAAAH!!
FLOP
...!!
I'B LEEBING!!
JANGLE
JANGLE
RAHH
KOFF... KOMURA-SAKI...
EEEK

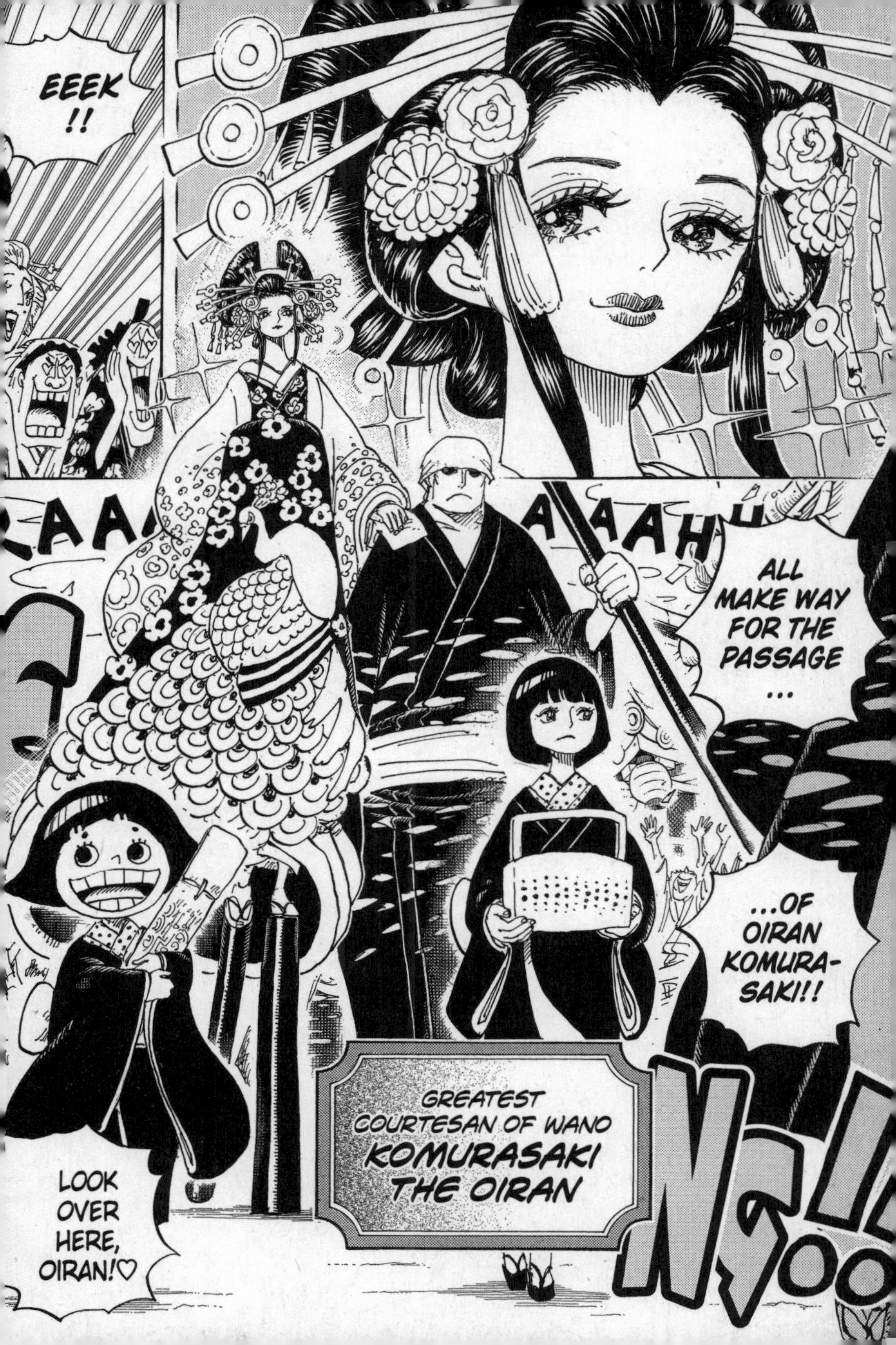
EEEK!!
ALL MAKE WAY FOR THE PASSAGE...
...OF OIRAN KOMURASAKI!!
GREATEST COURTESAN OF WANO
KOMURASAKI THE OIRAN
LOOK OVER HERE, OIRAN!♡

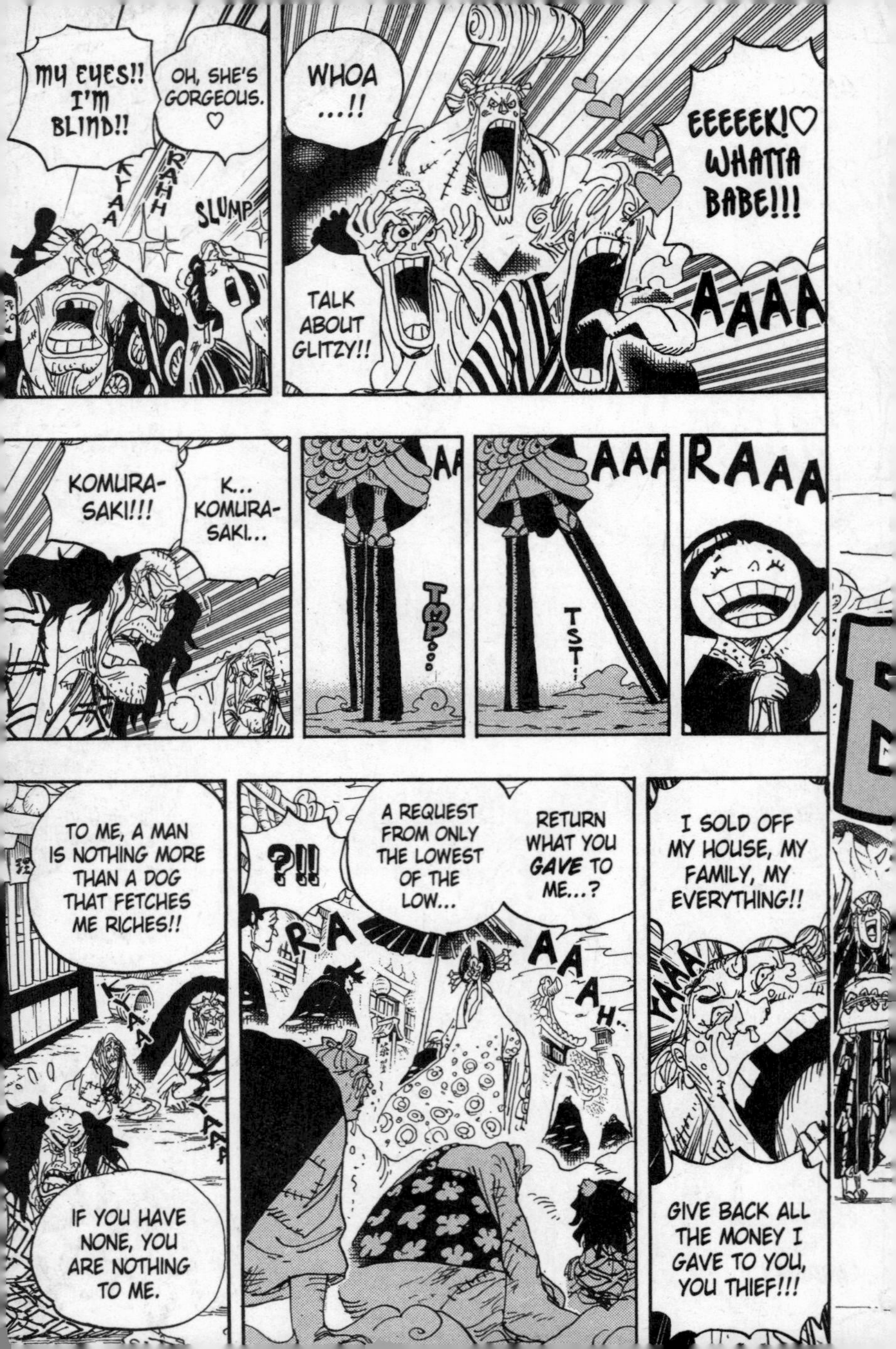
EEEEEK!♡ WHATTA BABE!!!
WHOA ...!!
AAAA
TALK ABOUT GLITZY!!
OH, SHE'S GORGEOUS. ♡
MY EYES!! I'M BLIND!!
RAHH
SLUMP
KYAA
RAAA
AAA
TST
AA
TMP
K... KOMURA-SAKI...
KOMURA-SAKI!!!
I SOLD OFF MY HOUSE, MY FAMILY, MY EVERYTHING!!
YAAA
GIVE BACK ALL THE MONEY I GAVE TO YOU, YOU THIEF!!!
RETURN WHAT YOU GAVE TO ME...?
A REQUEST FROM ONLY THE LOWEST OF THE LOW...
?!!
RA
AAAH
TO ME, A MAN IS NOTHING MORE THAN A DOG THAT FETCHES ME RICHES!!
KYAA
KYAA
IF YOU HAVE NONE, YOU ARE NOTHING TO ME.

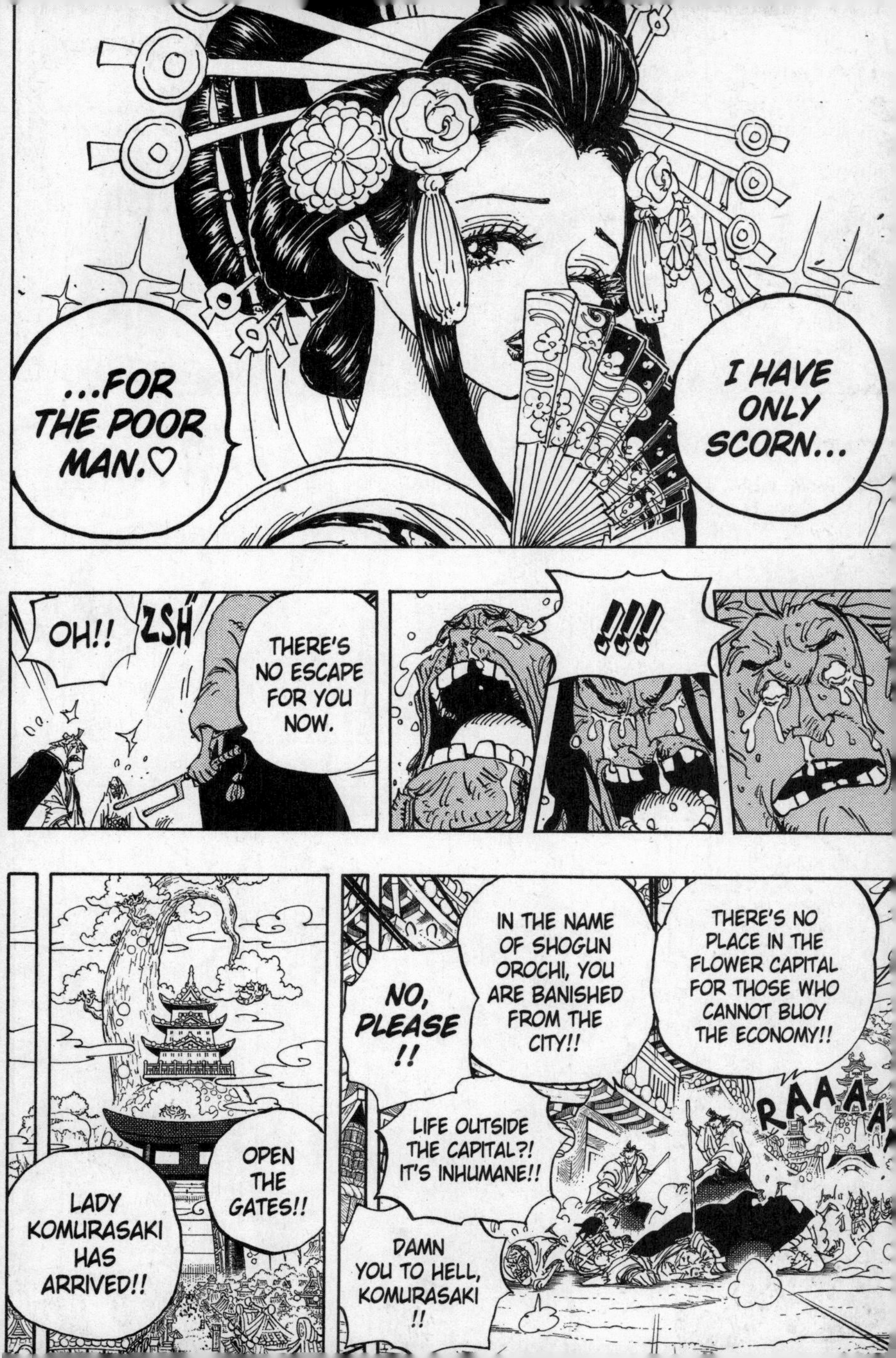
I HAVE ONLY SCORN...
...FOR THE POOR MAN.♡
!!!
THERE'S NO ESCAPE FOR YOU NOW.
ZSH
OH!!
THERE'S NO PLACE IN THE FLOWER CAPITAL FOR THOSE WHO CANNOT BUOY THE ECONOMY!!
IN THE NAME OF SHOGUN OROCHI, YOU ARE BANISHED FROM THE CITY!!
RAAAA
NO, PLEASE!!
LIFE OUTSIDE THE CAPITAL?! IT'S INHUMANE!!
DAMN YOU TO HELL, KOMURASAKI!!
OPEN THE GATES!!
LADY KOMURASAKI HAS ARRIVED!!

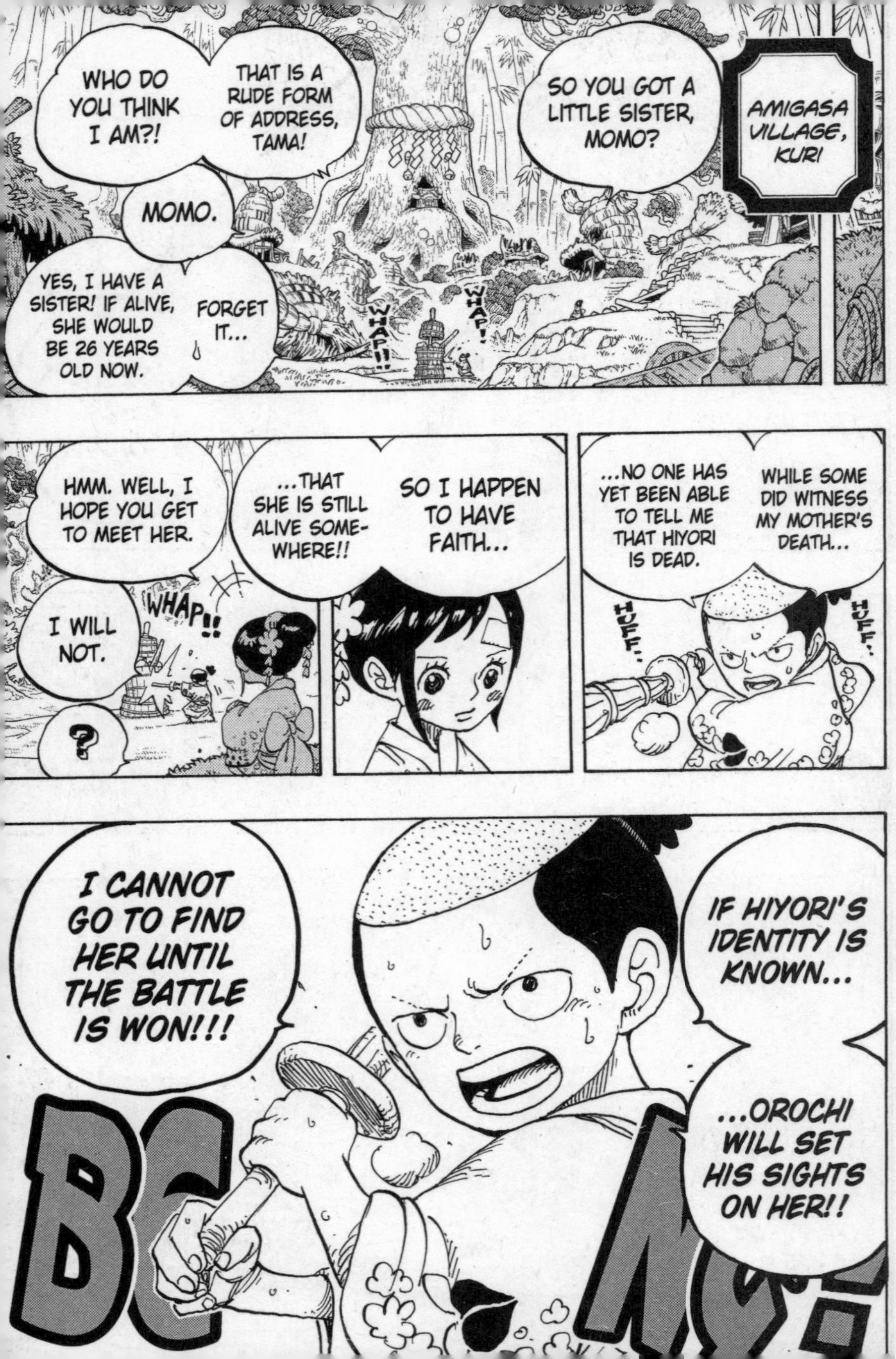
AMIGASA VILLAGE, KURI
SO YOU GOT A LITTLE SISTER, MOMO?
THAT IS A RUDE FORM OF ADDRESS, TAMA!
WHO DO YOU THINK I AM?!
MOMO.
WHAP!
WHAP!!
FORGET IT...
YES, I HAVE A SISTER! IF ALIVE, SHE WOULD BE 26 YEARS OLD NOW.
WHILE SOME DID WITNESS MY MOTHER'S DEATH...
...NO ONE HAS YET BEEN ABLE TO TELL ME THAT HIYORI IS DEAD.
HUFF.
HUFF.
SO I HAPPEN TO HAVE FAITH...
...THAT SHE IS STILL ALIVE SOME-WHERE!!
HMM. WELL, I HOPE YOU GET TO MEET HER.
WHAP!!
I WILL NOT.
?
IF HIYORI'S IDENTITY IS KNOWN...
...OROCHI WILL SET HIS SIGHTS ON HER!!
I CANNOT GO TO FIND HER UNTIL THE BATTLE IS WON!!!

KUROZUMI OROCHI

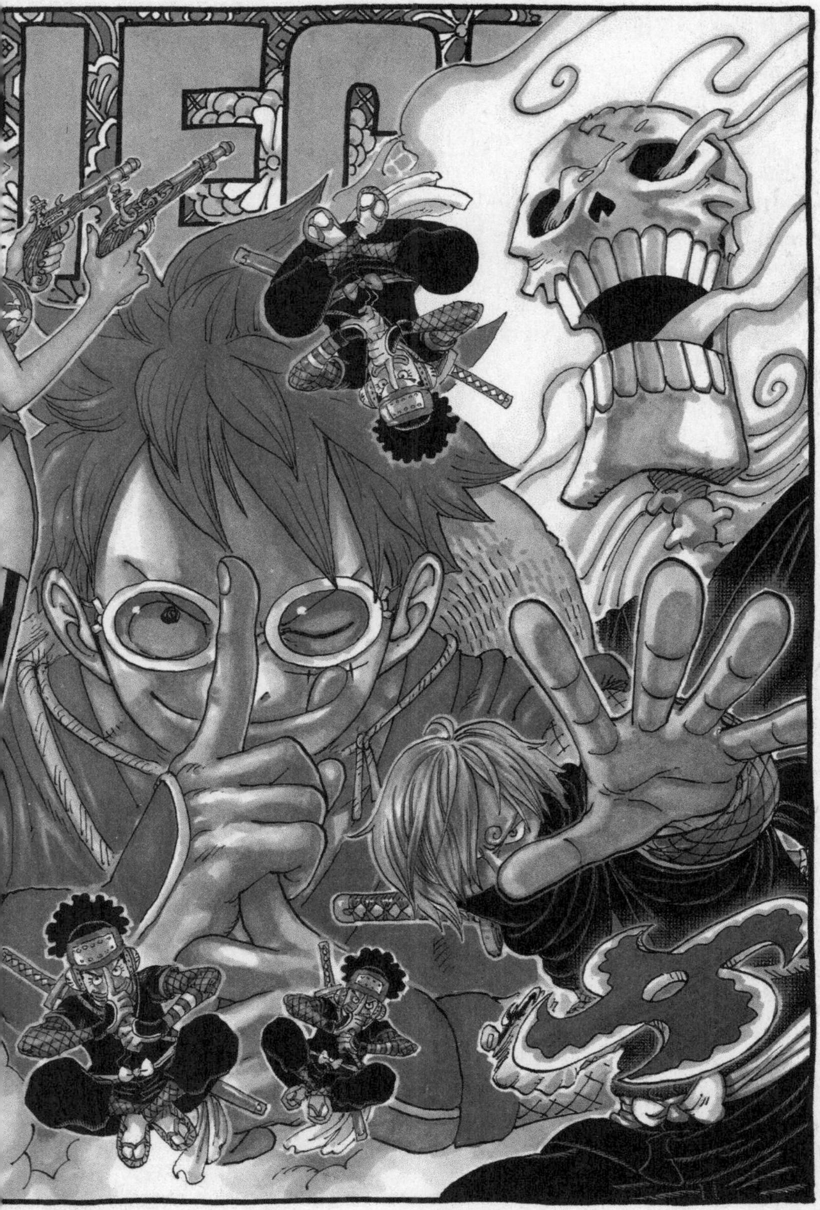

Chapter 929: SHOGUN OF WANO,

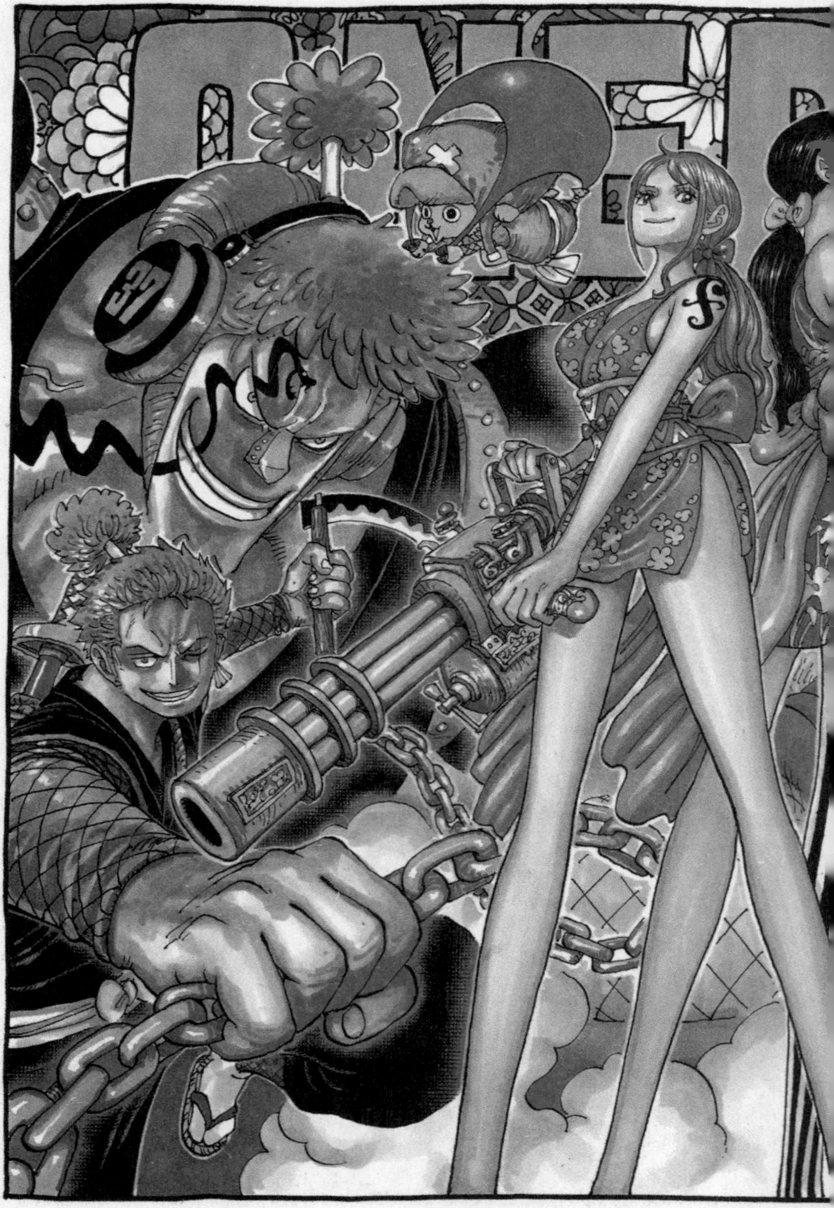
37

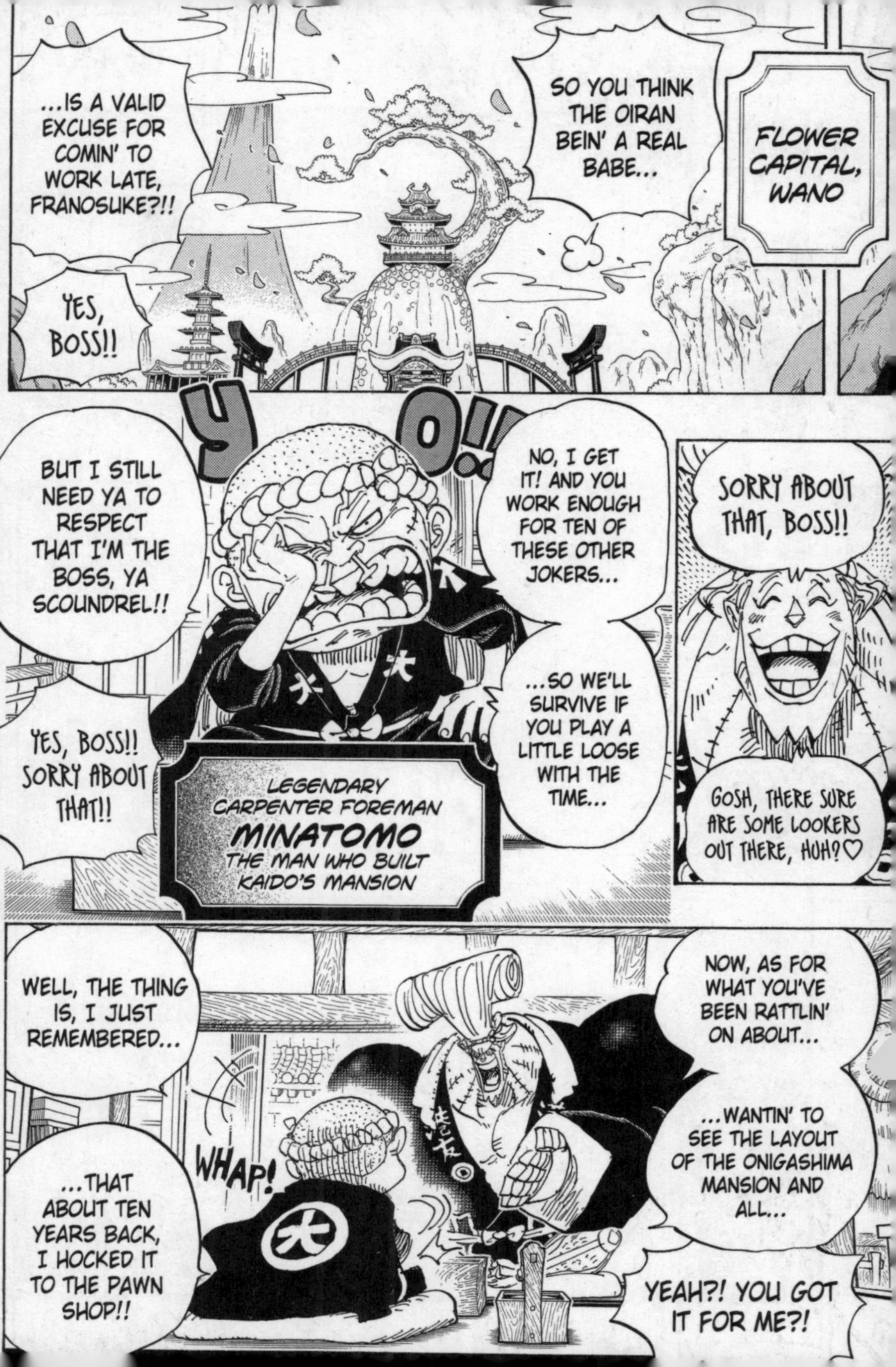
FLOWER CAPITAL, WANO
SO YOU THINK THE OIRAN BEIN' A REAL BABE...
...IS A VALID EXCUSE FOR COMIN' TO WORK LATE, FRANOSUKE?!!
YES, BOSS!!
SORRY ABOUT THAT, BOSS!!
GOSH, THERE SURE ARE SOME LOOKERS OUT THERE, HUH?♡
Y O!!
NO, I GET IT! AND YOU WORK ENOUGH FOR TEN OF THESE OTHER JOKERS...
...SO WE'LL SURVIVE IF YOU PLAY A LITTLE LOOSE WITH THE TIME...
BUT I STILL NEED YA TO RESPECT THAT I'M THE BOSS, YA SCOUNDREL!!
YES, BOSS!! SORRY ABOUT THAT!!
LEGENDARY CARPENTER FOREMAN MINATOMO THE MAN WHO BUILT KAIDO'S MANSION
NOW, AS FOR WHAT YOU'VE BEEN RATTLIN' ON ABOUT...
...WANTIN' TO SEE THE LAYOUT OF THE ONIGASHIMA MANSION AND ALL...
YEAH?! YOU GOT IT FOR ME?!
WELL, THE THING IS, I JUST REMEMBERED...
WHAP!
...THAT ABOUT TEN YEARS BACK, I HOCKED IT TO THE PAWN SHOP!!

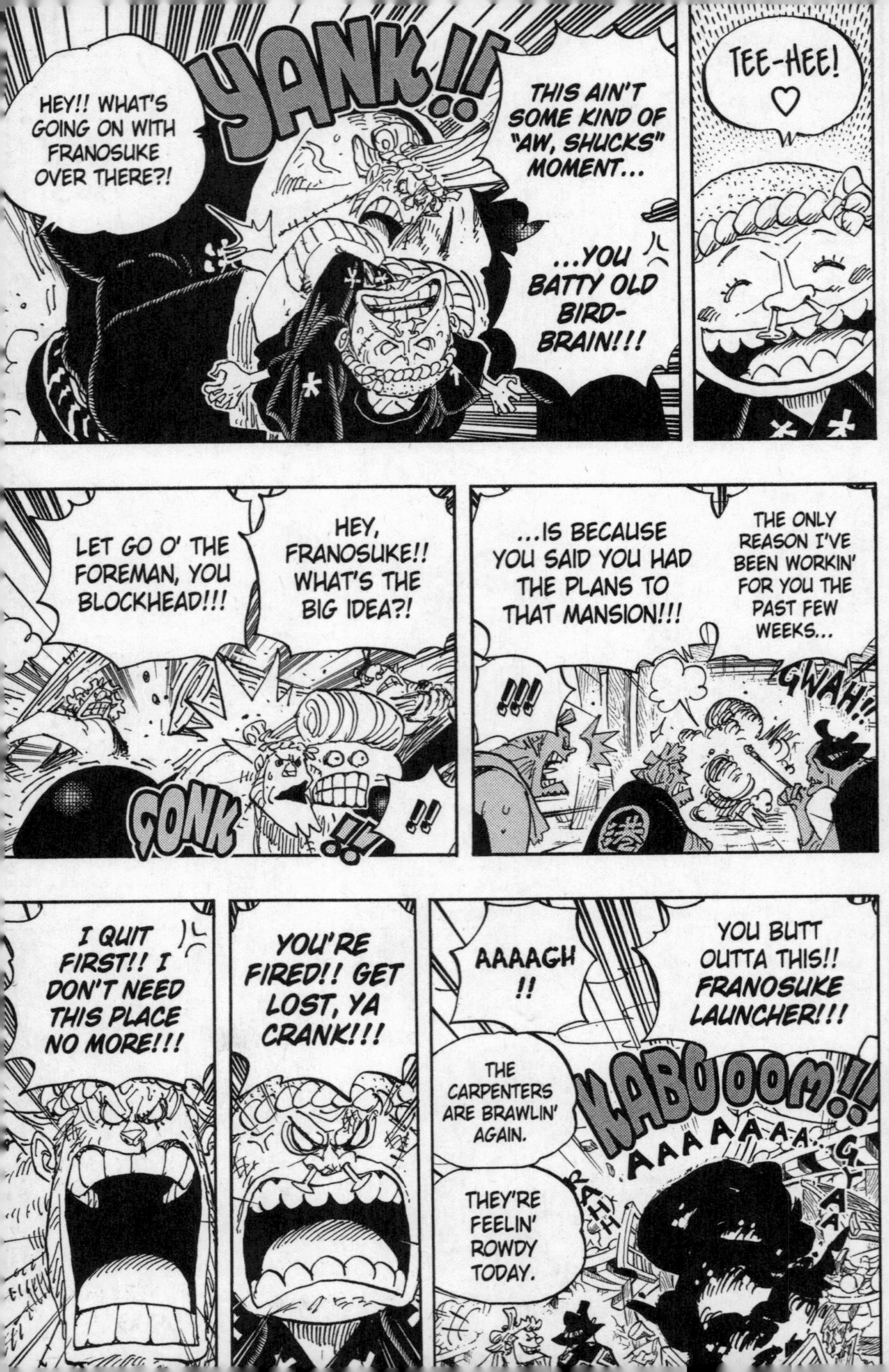
TEE-HEE! ♡
THIS AIN'T SOME KIND OF "AW, SHUCKS" MOMENT...
...YOU BATTY OLD BIRD-BRAIN!!!
YANK!!
HEY!! WHAT'S GOING ON WITH FRANOSUKE OVER THERE?!
THE ONLY REASON I'VE BEEN WORKIN' FOR YOU THE PAST FEW WEEKS...
...IS BECAUSE YOU SAID YOU HAD THE PLANS TO THAT MANSION!!!
GWAH!!
!!!
HEY, FRANOSUKE!! WHAT'S THE BIG IDEA?!
LET GO O' THE FOREMAN, YOU BLOCKHEAD!!!
GONK
!!
YOU BUTT OUTTA THIS!! FRANOSUKE LAUNCHER!!!
AAAAGH !!
KABOOOM!!
THE CARPENTERS ARE BRAWLIN' AGAIN.
THEY'RE FEELIN' ROWDY TODAY.
YOU'RE FIRED!! GET LOST, YA CRANK!!!
I QUIT FIRST!! I DON'T NEED THIS PLACE NO MORE!!!

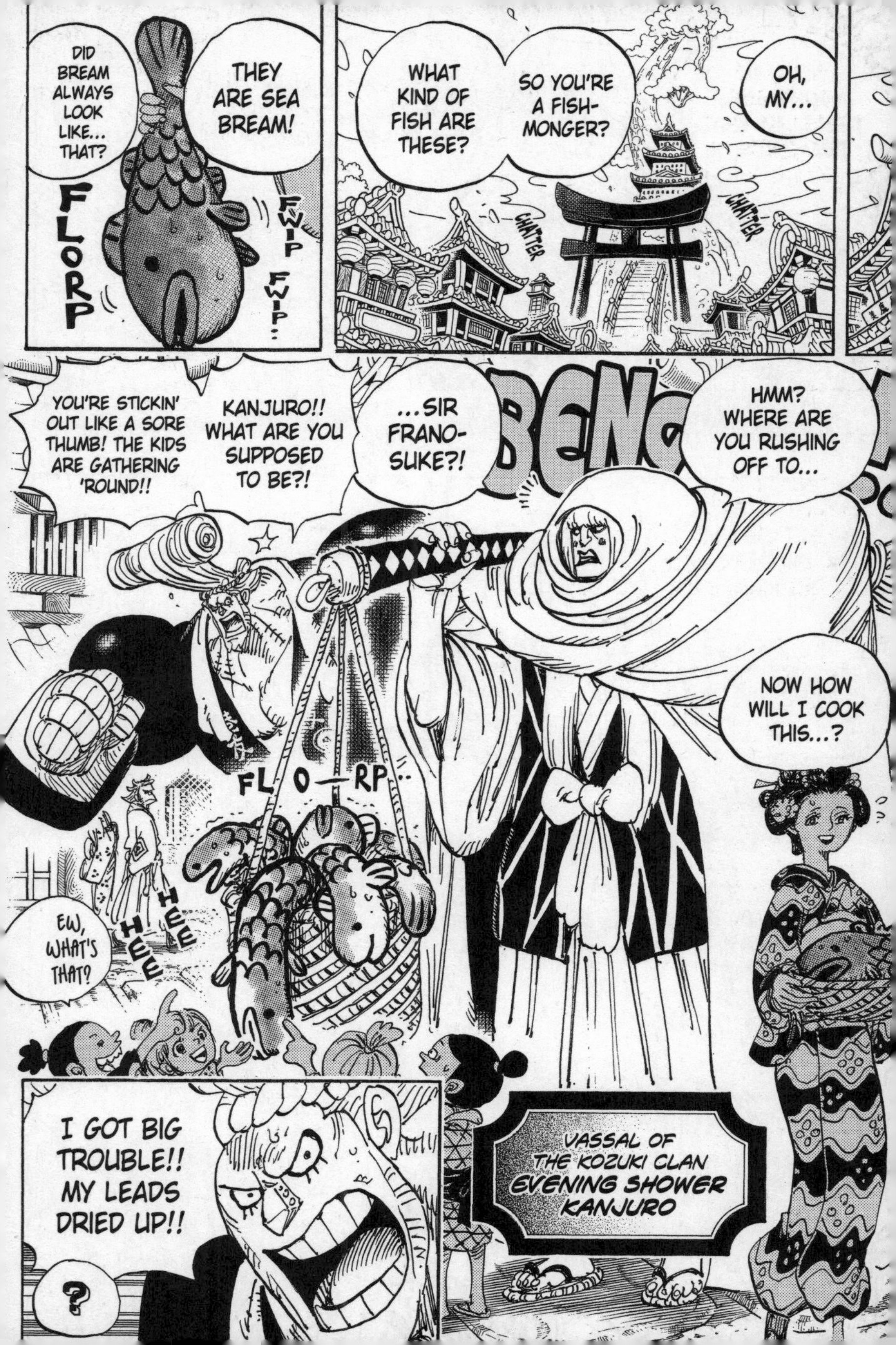
OH, MY...
SO YOU'RE A FISH-MONGER?
WHAT KIND OF FISH ARE THESE?
CHATTER
CHATTER
THEY ARE SEA BREAM!
DID BREAM ALWAYS LOOK LIKE... THAT?
FWIP FWIP
FLORP
BENG
HMM? WHERE ARE YOU RUSHING OFF TO...
...SIR FRANO-SUKE?!
KANJURO!! WHAT ARE YOU SUPPOSED TO BE?!
YOU'RE STICKIN' OUT LIKE A SORE THUMB! THE KIDS ARE GATHERING 'ROUND!!
NOW HOW WILL I COOK THIS...?
FL O—RP
HEE HEE
EW, WHAT'S THAT?
VASSAL OF THE KOZUKI CLAN EVENING SHOWER KANJURO
I GOT BIG TROUBLE!! MY LEADS DRIED UP!!
?

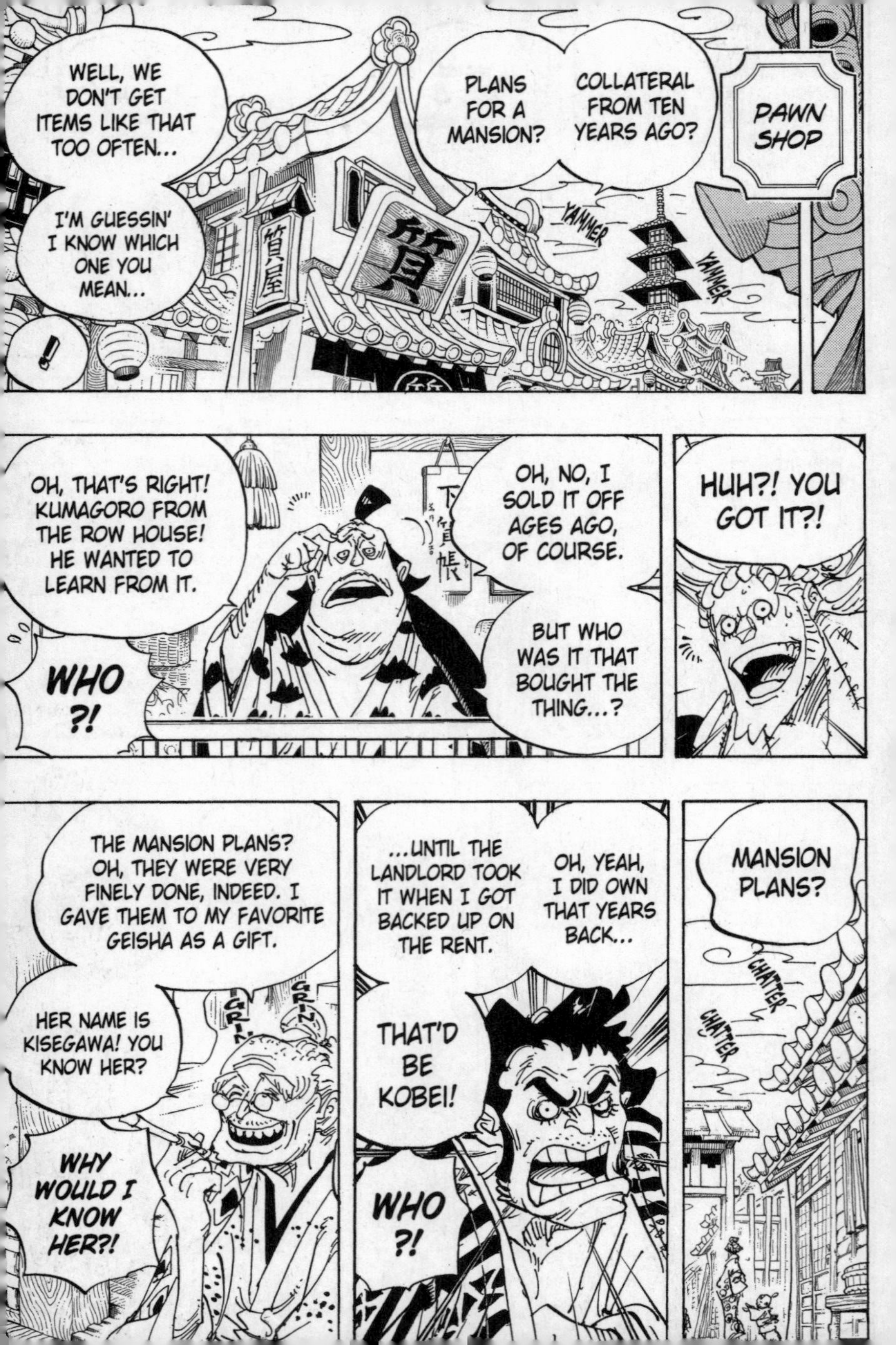
PAWN SHOP
COLLATERAL FROM TEN YEARS AGO?
PLANS FOR A MANSION?
YAMMER
YAMMER
WELL, WE DON'T GET ITEMS LIKE THAT TOO OFTEN...
I'M GUESSIN' I KNOW WHICH ONE YOU MEAN...
!
HUH?! YOU GOT IT?!
OH, NO, I SOLD IT OFF AGES AGO, OF COURSE.
BUT WHO WAS IT THAT BOUGHT THE THING...?
OH, THAT'S RIGHT! KUMAGORO FROM THE ROW HOUSE! HE WANTED TO LEARN FROM IT.
WHO ?!
MANSION PLANS?
CHATTER
CHATTER
OH, YEAH, I DID OWN THAT YEARS BACK...
...UNTIL THE LANDLORD TOOK IT WHEN I GOT BACKED UP ON THE RENT.
THAT'D BE KOBEI!
WHO ?!
THE MANSION PLANS? OH, THEY WERE VERY FINELY DONE, INDEED. I GAVE THEM TO MY FAVORITE GEISHA AS A GIFT.
GRIN
GRIN
HER NAME IS KISEGAWA! YOU KNOW HER?
WHY WOULD I KNOW HER?!

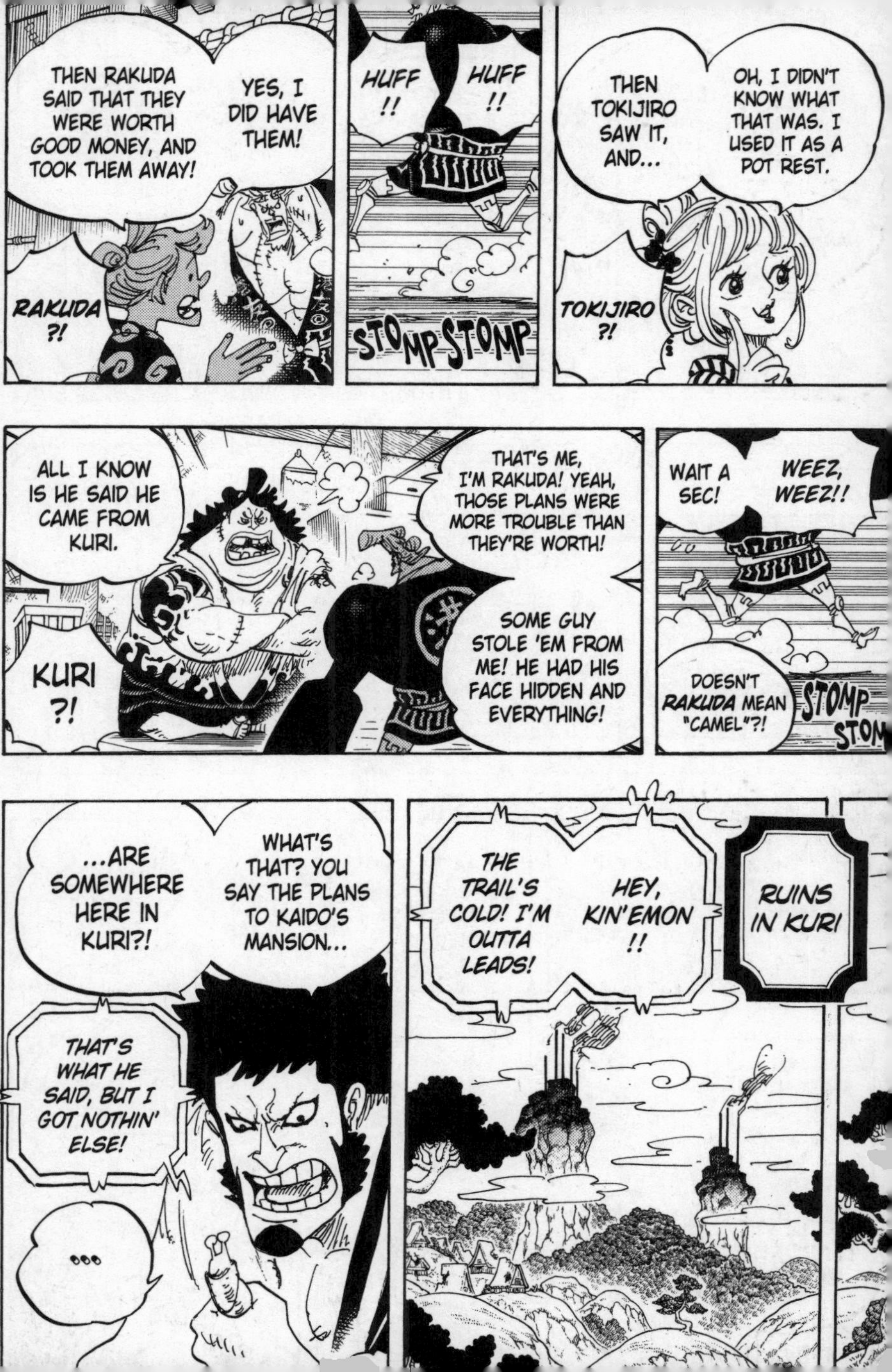
OH, I DIDN'T KNOW WHAT THAT WAS. I USED IT AS A POT REST.
THEN TOKIJIRO SAW IT, AND...
TOKIJIRO ?!
HUFF !!
HUFF !!
STOMP STOMP
YES, I DID HAVE THEM!
THEN RAKUDA SAID THAT THEY WERE WORTH GOOD MONEY, AND TOOK THEM AWAY!
RAKUDA ?!
WEEZ, WEEZ!!
WAIT A SEC!
STOMP STOM
DOESN'T RAKUDA MEAN "CAMEL"?!
THAT'S ME, I'M RAKUDA! YEAH, THOSE PLANS WERE MORE TROUBLE THAN THEY'RE WORTH!
SOME GUY STOLE 'EM FROM ME! HE HAD HIS FACE HIDDEN AND EVERYTHING!
ALL I KNOW IS HE SAID HE CAME FROM KURI.
KURI ?!
RUINS IN KURI
HEY, KIN'EMON !!
THE TRAIL'S COLD! I'M OUTTA LEADS!
WHAT'S THAT? YOU SAY THE PLANS TO KAIDO'S MANSION...
...ARE SOMEWHERE HERE IN KURI?!
THAT'S WHAT HE SAID, BUT I GOT NOTHIN' ELSE!
...

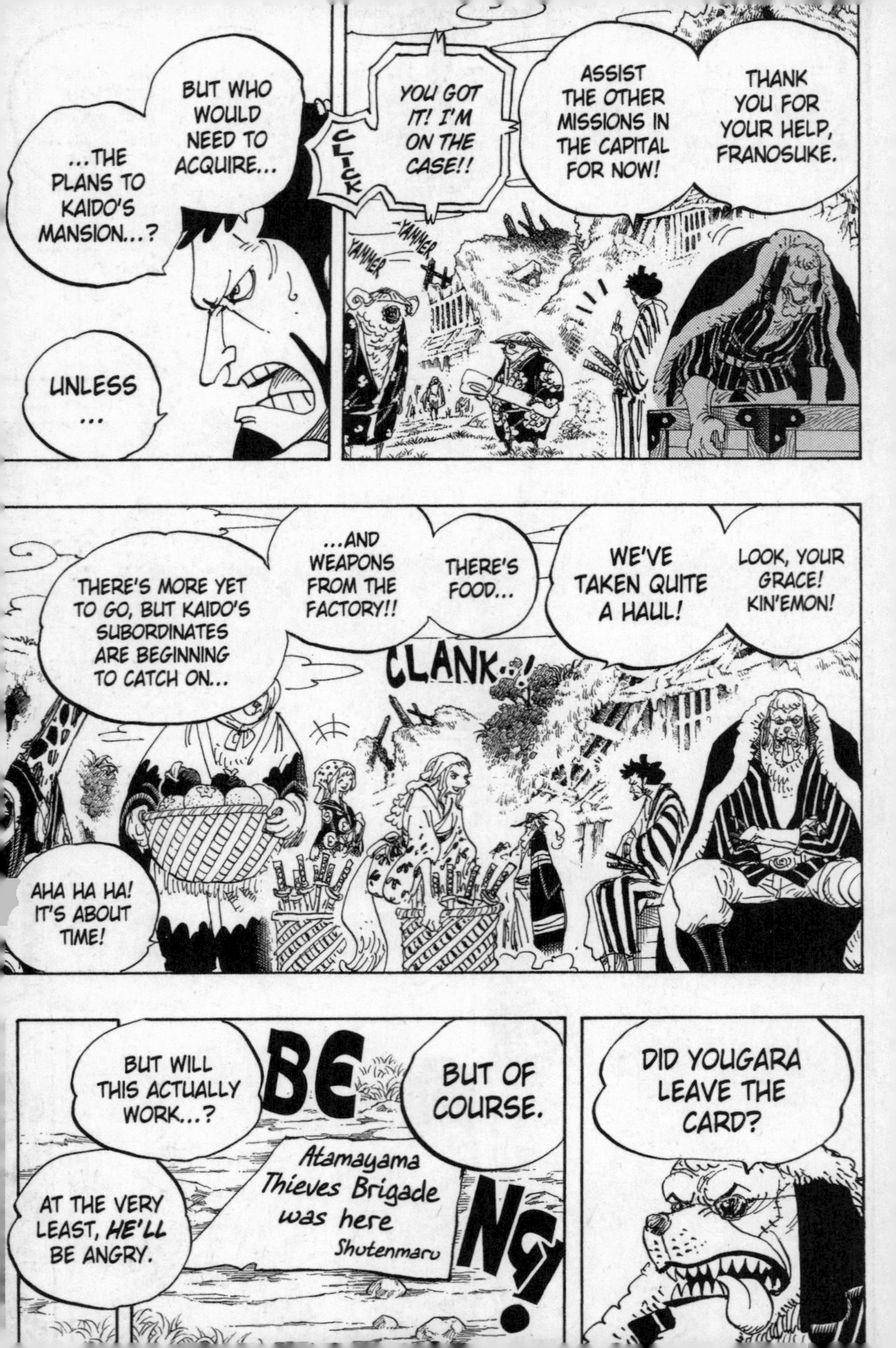
THANK YOU FOR YOUR HELP, FRANOSUKE.
ASSIST THE OTHER MISSIONS IN THE CAPITAL FOR NOW!
YOU GOT IT! I'M ON THE CASE!!
CLICK
YAMMER
YAMMER
BUT WHO WOULD NEED TO ACQUIRE...
...THE PLANS TO KAIDO'S MANSION...?
UNLESS ...
LOOK, YOUR GRACE! KIN'EMON!
WE'VE TAKEN QUITE A HAUL!
THERE'S FOOD...
...AND WEAPONS FROM THE FACTORY!!
CLANK
THERE'S MORE YET TO GO, BUT KAIDO'S SUBORDINATES ARE BEGINNING TO CATCH ON...
AHA HA HA! IT'S ABOUT TIME!
DID YOUGARA LEAVE THE CARD?
BUT OF COURSE.
BEN!
Atamayama Thieves Brigade was here Shutenmaru
BUT WILL THIS ACTUALLY WORK...?
AT THE VERY LEAST, *HE'LL* BE ANGRY.

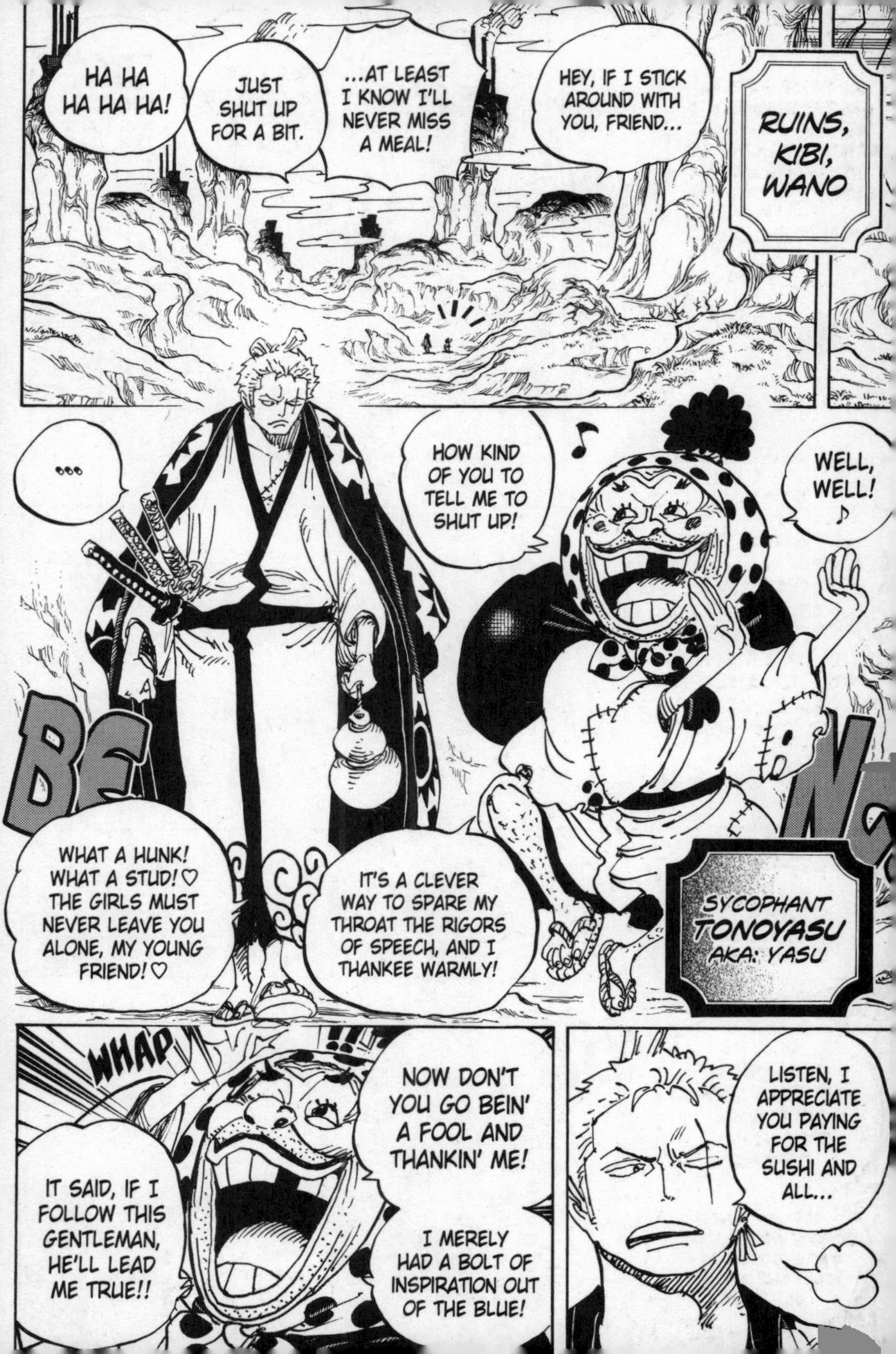
RUINS, KIBI, WANO
HEY, IF I STICK AROUND WITH YOU, FRIEND...
...AT LEAST I KNOW I'LL NEVER MISS A MEAL!
JUST SHUT UP FOR A BIT.
HA HA HA HA HA!
WELL, WELL! ♪
HOW KIND OF YOU TO TELL ME TO SHUT UP!
...
SYCOPHANT TONOYASU AKA: YASU
IT'S A CLEVER WAY TO SPARE MY THROAT THE RIGORS OF SPEECH, AND I THANKEE WARMLY!
WHAT A HUNK! WHAT A STUD! ♡ THE GIRLS MUST NEVER LEAVE YOU ALONE, MY YOUNG FRIEND! ♡
LISTEN, I APPRECIATE YOU PAYING FOR THE SUSHI AND ALL...
WHAP
NOW DON'T YOU GO BEIN' A FOOL AND THANKIN' ME!
I MERELY HAD A BOLT OF INSPIRATION OUT OF THE BLUE!
IT SAID, IF I FOLLOW THIS GENTLEMAN, HE'LL LEAD ME TRUE!!

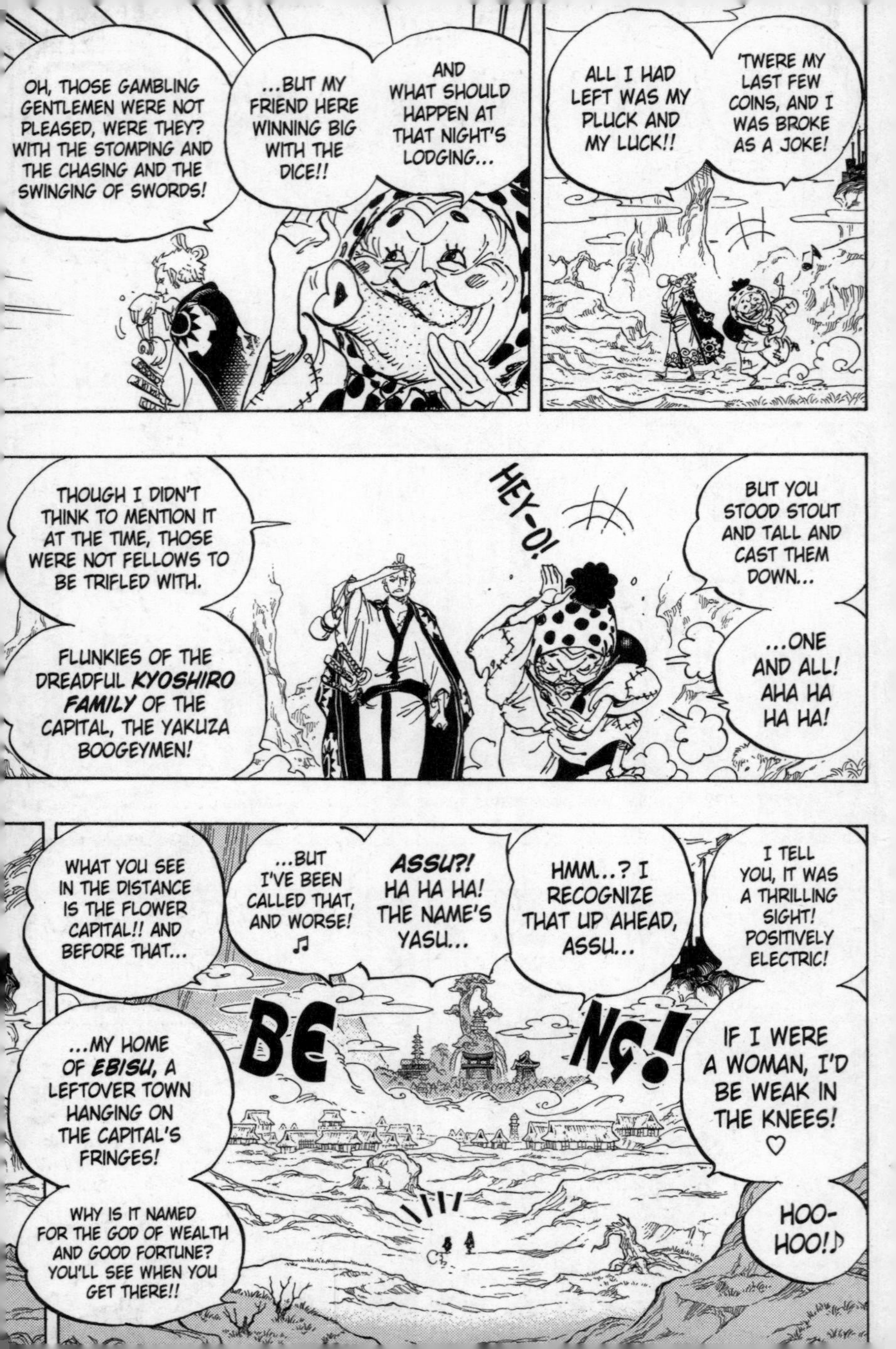
'TWERE MY LAST FEW COINS, AND I WAS BROKE AS A JOKE!
ALL I HAD LEFT WAS MY PLUCK AND MY LUCK!!
AND WHAT SHOULD HAPPEN AT THAT NIGHT'S LODGING...
...BUT MY FRIEND HERE WINNING BIG WITH THE DICE!!
OH, THOSE GAMBLING GENTLEMEN WERE NOT PLEASED, WERE THEY? WITH THE STOMPING AND THE CHASING AND THE SWINGING OF SWORDS!
BUT YOU STOOD STOUT AND TALL AND CAST THEM DOWN...
...ONE AND ALL! AHA HA HA HA!
HEY-O!
THOUGH I DIDN'T THINK TO MENTION IT AT THE TIME, THOSE WERE NOT FELLOWS TO BE TRIFLED WITH.
FLUNKIES OF THE DREADFUL ***KYOSHIRO FAMILY*** OF THE CAPITAL, THE YAKUZA BOOGEYMEN!
I TELL YOU, IT WAS A THRILLING SIGHT! POSITIVELY ELECTRIC!
IF I WERE A WOMAN, I'D BE WEAK IN THE KNEES! ♡
HOO-HOO!♪
HMM...? I RECOGNIZE THAT UP AHEAD, ASSU...
BENG!
ASSU?! HA HA HA! THE NAME'S YASU...
...BUT I'VE BEEN CALLED THAT, AND WORSE! ♫
WHAT YOU SEE IN THE DISTANCE IS THE FLOWER CAPITAL!! AND BEFORE THAT...
...MY HOME OF ***EBISU***, A LEFTOVER TOWN HANGING ON THE CAPITAL'S FRINGES!
WHY IS IT NAMED FOR THE GOD OF WEALTH AND GOOD FORTUNE? YOU'LL SEE WHEN YOU GET THERE!!

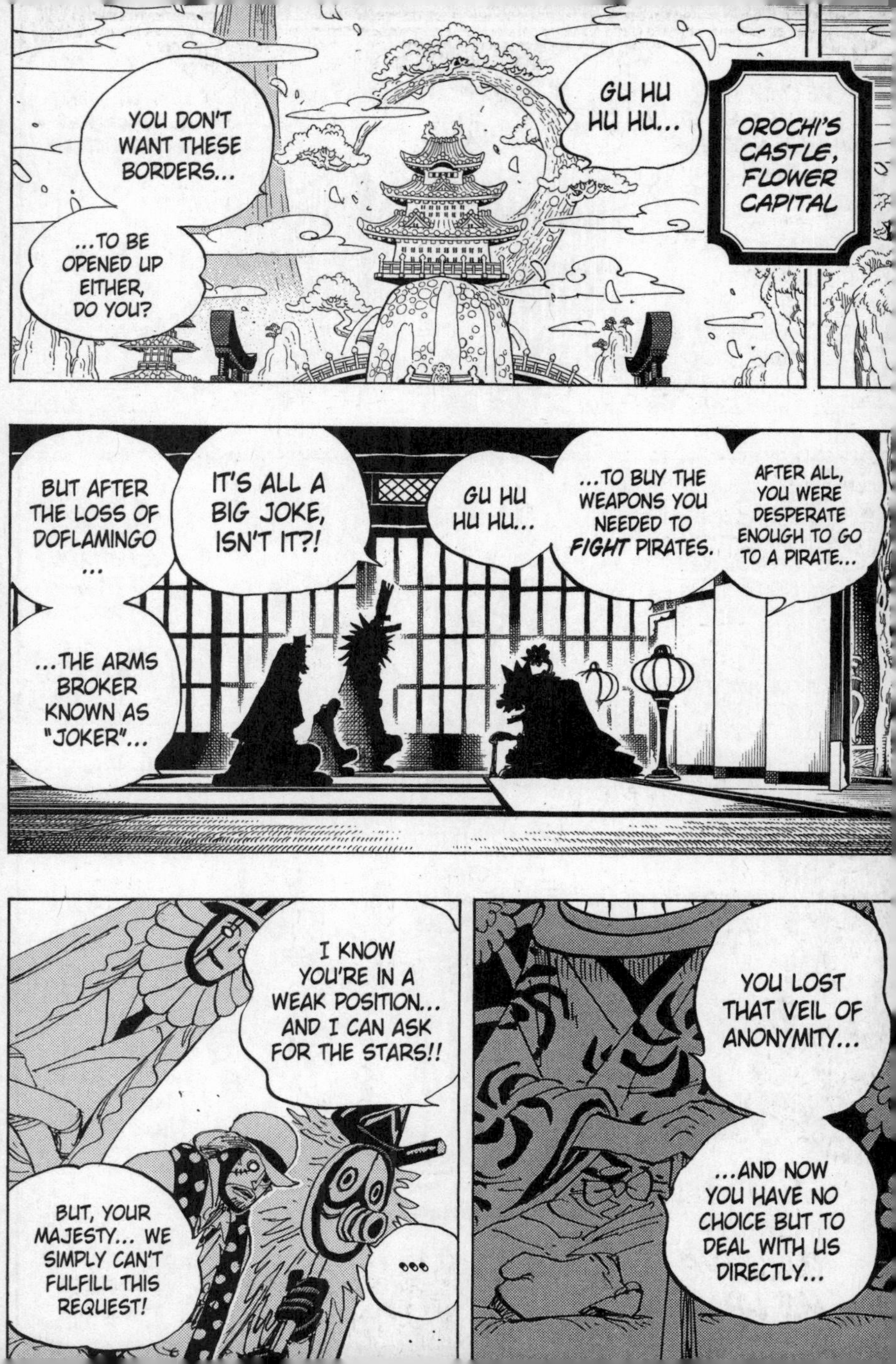

OROCHI'S CASTLE, FLOWER CAPITAL
GU HU HU HU...
YOU DON'T WANT THESE BORDERS...
...TO BE OPENED UP EITHER, DO YOU?
AFTER ALL, YOU WERE DESPERATE ENOUGH TO GO TO A PIRATE...
...TO BUY THE WEAPONS YOU NEEDED TO FIGHT PIRATES.
GU HU HU HU...
IT'S ALL A BIG JOKE, ISN'T IT?!
BUT AFTER THE LOSS OF DOFLAMINGO...
...THE ARMS BROKER KNOWN AS "JOKER"...
YOU LOST THAT VEIL OF ANONYMITY...
...AND NOW YOU HAVE NO CHOICE BUT TO DEAL WITH US DIRECTLY...
I KNOW YOU'RE IN A WEAK POSITION... AND I CAN ASK FOR THE STARS!!
...
BUT, YOUR MAJESTY... WE SIMPLY CAN'T FULFILL THIS REQUEST!

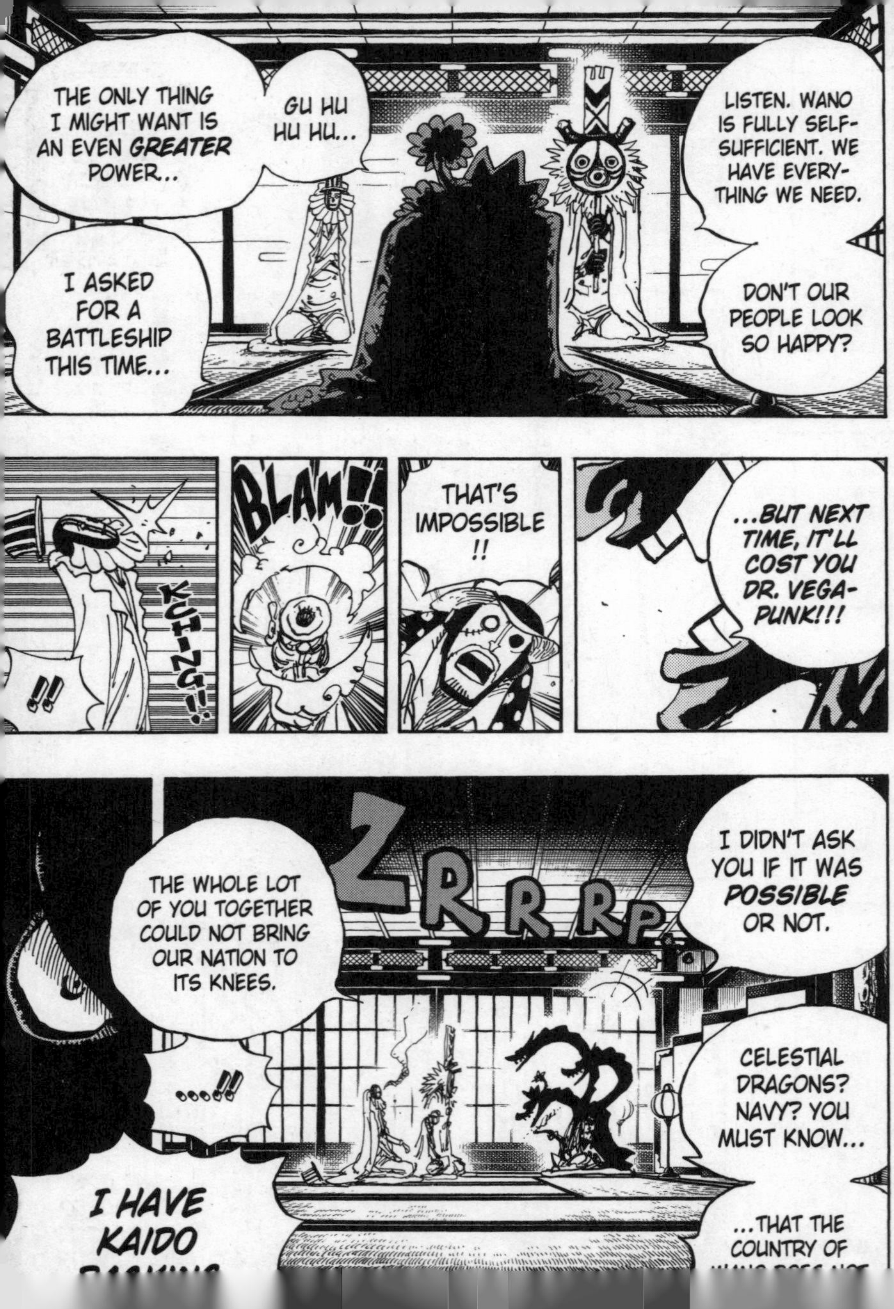
LISTEN. WANO IS FULLY SELF-SUFFICIENT. WE HAVE EVERYTHING WE NEED.
DON'T OUR PEOPLE LOOK SO HAPPY?
GU HU HU HU...
THE ONLY THING I MIGHT WANT IS AN EVEN GREATER POWER...
I ASKED FOR A BATTLESHIP THIS TIME...
...BUT NEXT TIME, IT'LL COST YOU DR. VEGAPUNK!!!
THAT'S IMPOSSIBLE !!
BLAM!!
KCHING!!
!!
I DIDN'T ASK YOU IF IT WAS POSSIBLE OR NOT.
CELESTIAL DRAGONS? NAVY? YOU MUST KNOW...
...THAT THE COUNTRY OF
ZRRRP
THE WHOLE LOT OF YOU TOGETHER COULD NOT BRING OUR NATION TO ITS KNEES.
...!!
I HAVE KAIDO

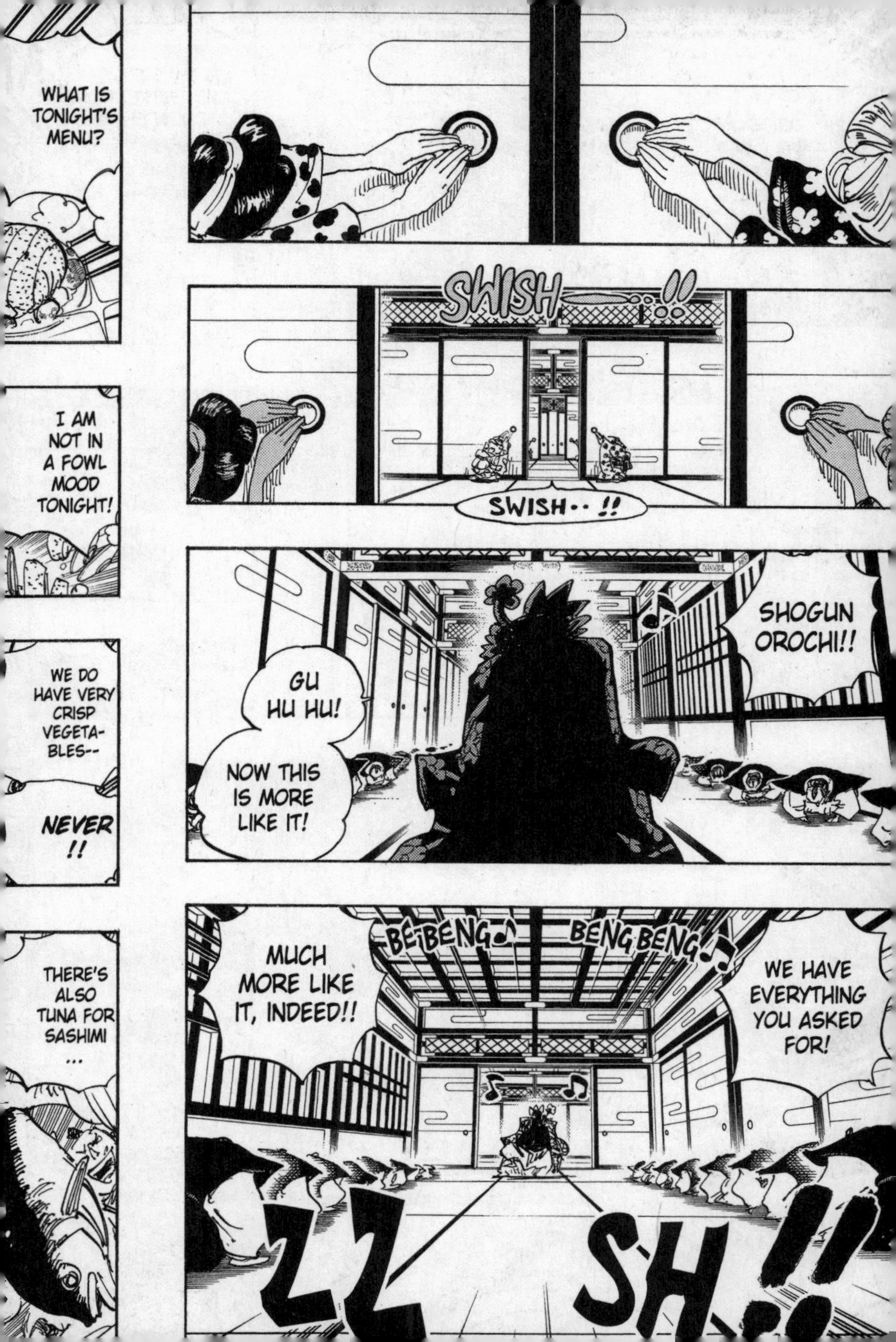
SWISH..!!
SWISH..!!
SHOGUN OROCHI!!
GU HU HU!
NOW THIS IS MORE LIKE IT!
WE HAVE EVERYTHING YOU ASKED FOR!
BENG BENG♪
BE BENG♪
MUCH MORE LIKE IT, INDEED!!
ZZ SH!!
WHAT IS TONIGHT'S MENU?
I AM NOT IN A FOWL MOOD TONIGHT!
WE DO HAVE VERY CRISP VEGETA-BLES--
NEVER!!
THERE'S ALSO TUNA FOR SASHIMI ...

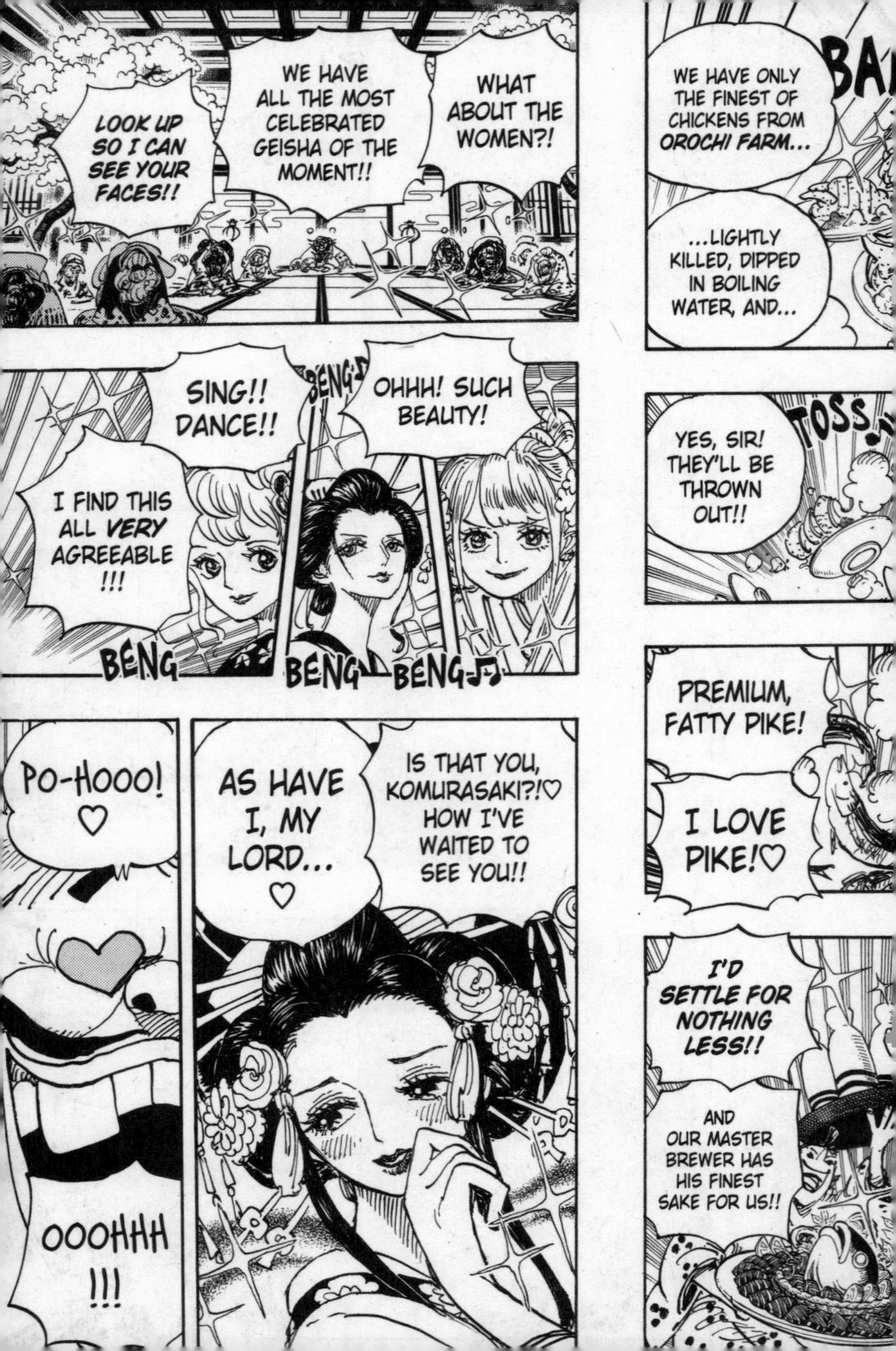
WE HAVE ONLY THE FINEST OF CHICKENS FROM OROCHI FARM...
...LIGHTLY KILLED, DIPPED IN BOILING WATER, AND...
TOSS♫
YES, SIR! THEY'LL BE THROWN OUT!!
PREMIUM, FATTY PIKE!
I LOVE PIKE!♡
I'D SETTLE FOR NOTHING LESS!!
AND OUR MASTER BREWER HAS HIS FINEST SAKE FOR US!!
WHAT ABOUT THE WOMEN?!
WE HAVE ALL THE MOST CELEBRATED GEISHA OF THE MOMENT!!
LOOK UP SO I CAN SEE YOUR FACES!!
OHHH! SUCH BEAUTY!
BENG♫
SING!! DANCE!!
I FIND THIS ALL VERY AGREEABLE!!!
BENG♫
BENG
BENG
IS THAT YOU, KOMURASAKI?!♡ HOW I'VE WAITED TO SEE YOU!!
AS HAVE I, MY LORD...♡
PO-HOOO!♡
OOOHHH!!!

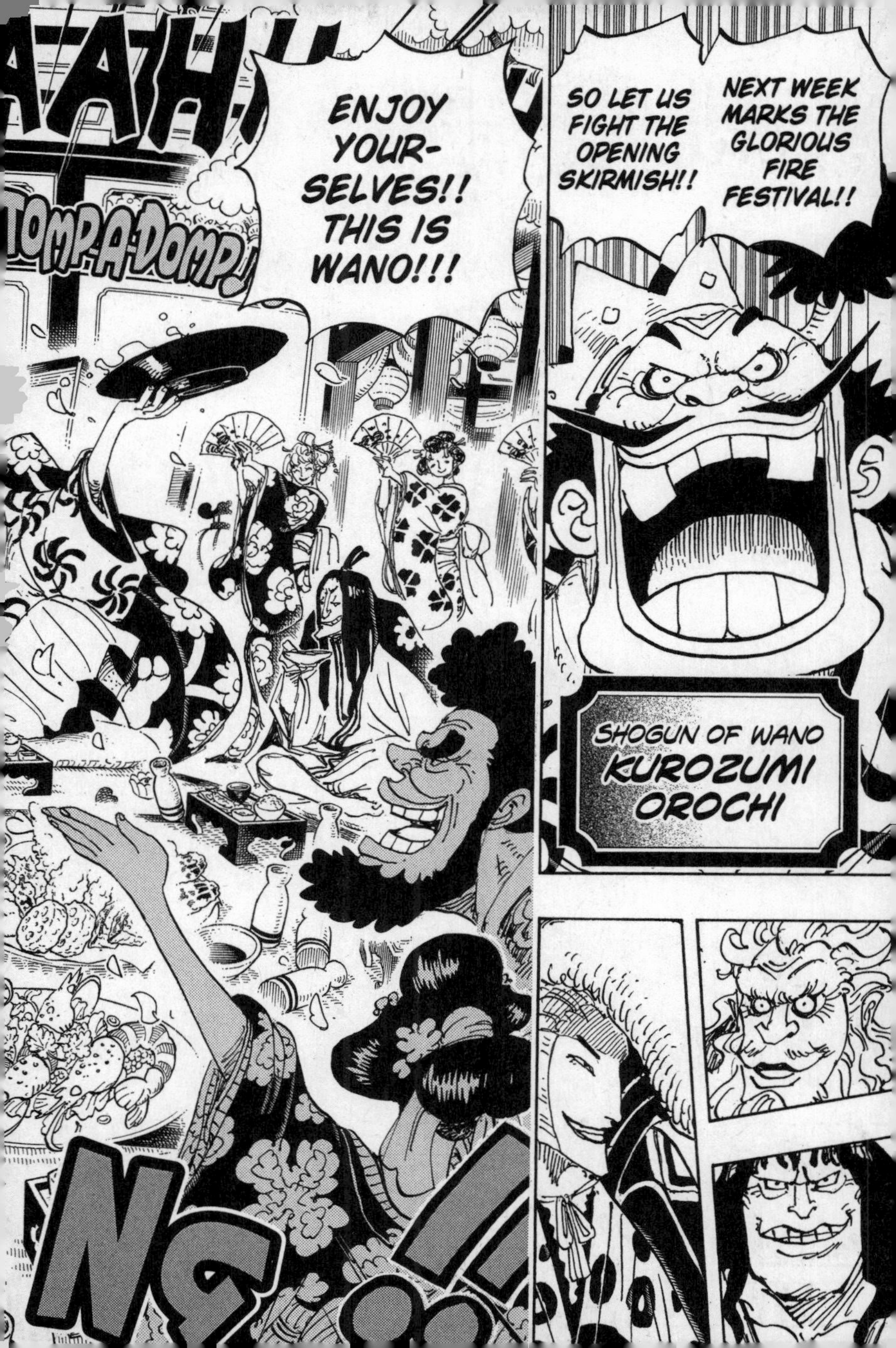
NEXT WEEK MARKS THE GLORIOUS FIRE FESTIVAL!!
SO LET US FIGHT THE OPENING SKIRMISH!!
SHOGUN OF WANO
KUROZUMI OROCHI
ENJOY YOURSELVES!! THIS IS WANO!!!
TOMP-A-DOMP!

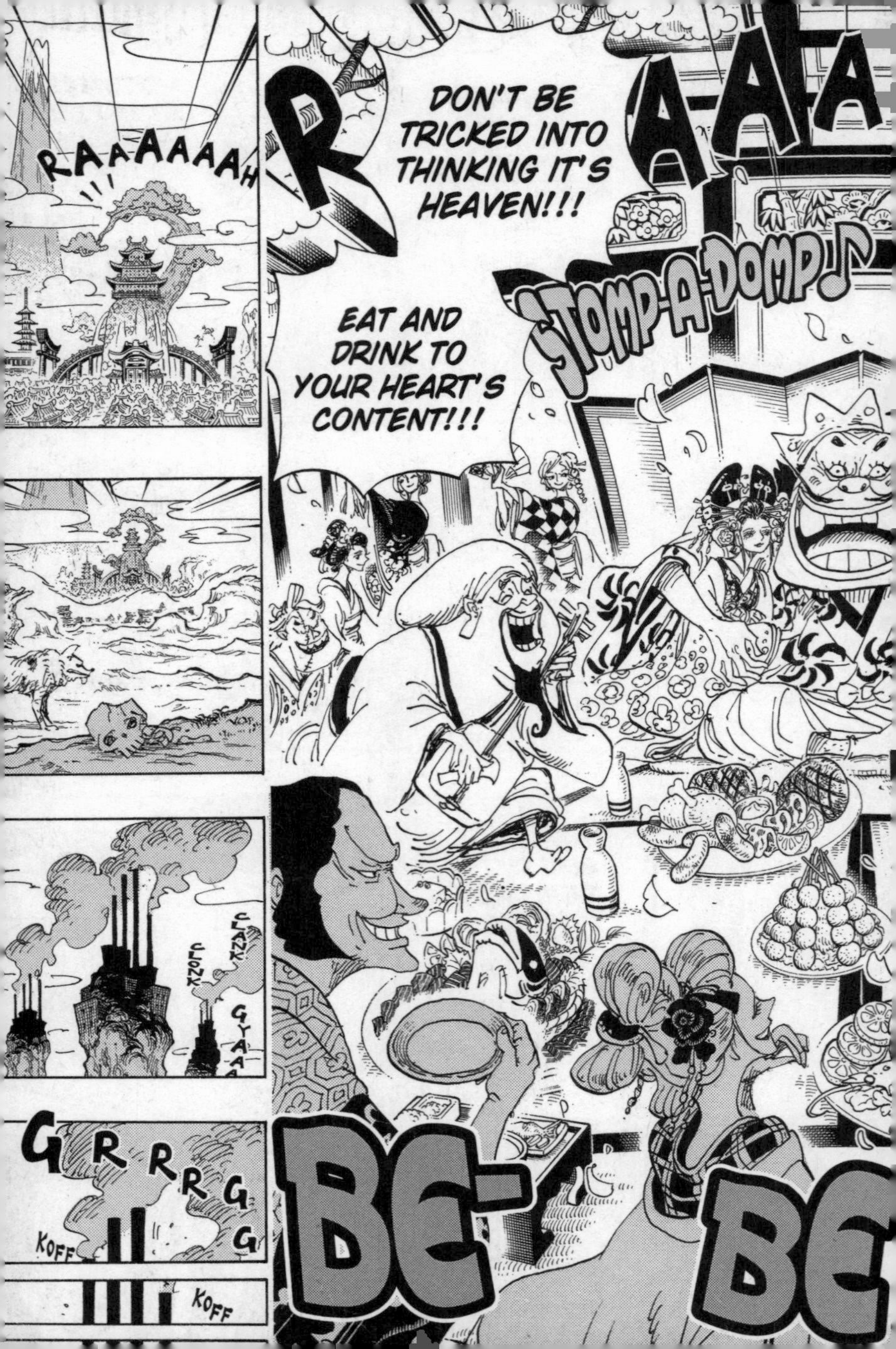
A-A-A
R
DON'T BE TRICKED INTO THINKING IT'S HEAVEN!!!
STOMP-A-DOMP♪
EAT AND DRINK TO YOUR HEART'S CONTENT!!!
BE-
BE
RAAAAAAH
CLANK
CLONK
GYAAA
GRRRGG
KOFF
KOFF

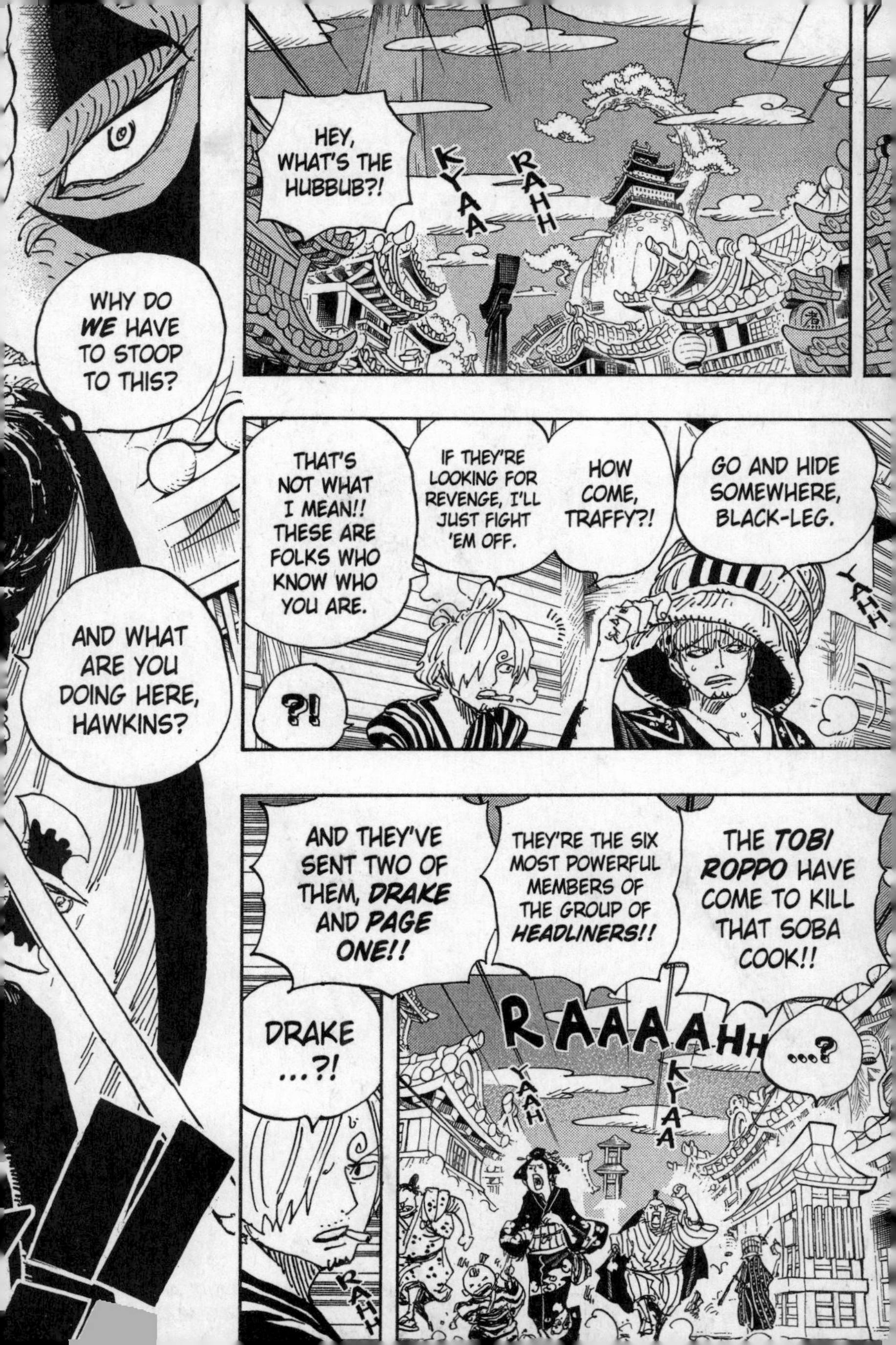

RAHH
KYAA
HEY, WHAT'S THE HUBBUB?!
YAHH
GO AND HIDE SOMEWHERE, BLACK-LEG.
HOW COME, TRAFFY?!
IF THEY'RE LOOKING FOR REVENGE, I'LL JUST FIGHT 'EM OFF.
THAT'S NOT WHAT I MEAN!! THESE ARE FOLKS WHO KNOW WHO YOU ARE.
?!
THE *TOBI ROPPO* HAVE COME TO KILL THAT SOBA COOK!!
THEY'RE THE SIX MOST POWERFUL MEMBERS OF THE GROUP OF *HEADLINERS*!!
AND THEY'VE SENT TWO OF THEM, *DRAKE* AND *PAGE ONE*!!
...?
RAAAAHH
KYAA
YAAH
DRAKE ...?!
RAHH
WHY DO *WE* HAVE TO STOOP TO THIS?
AND WHAT ARE YOU DOING HERE, HAWKINS?

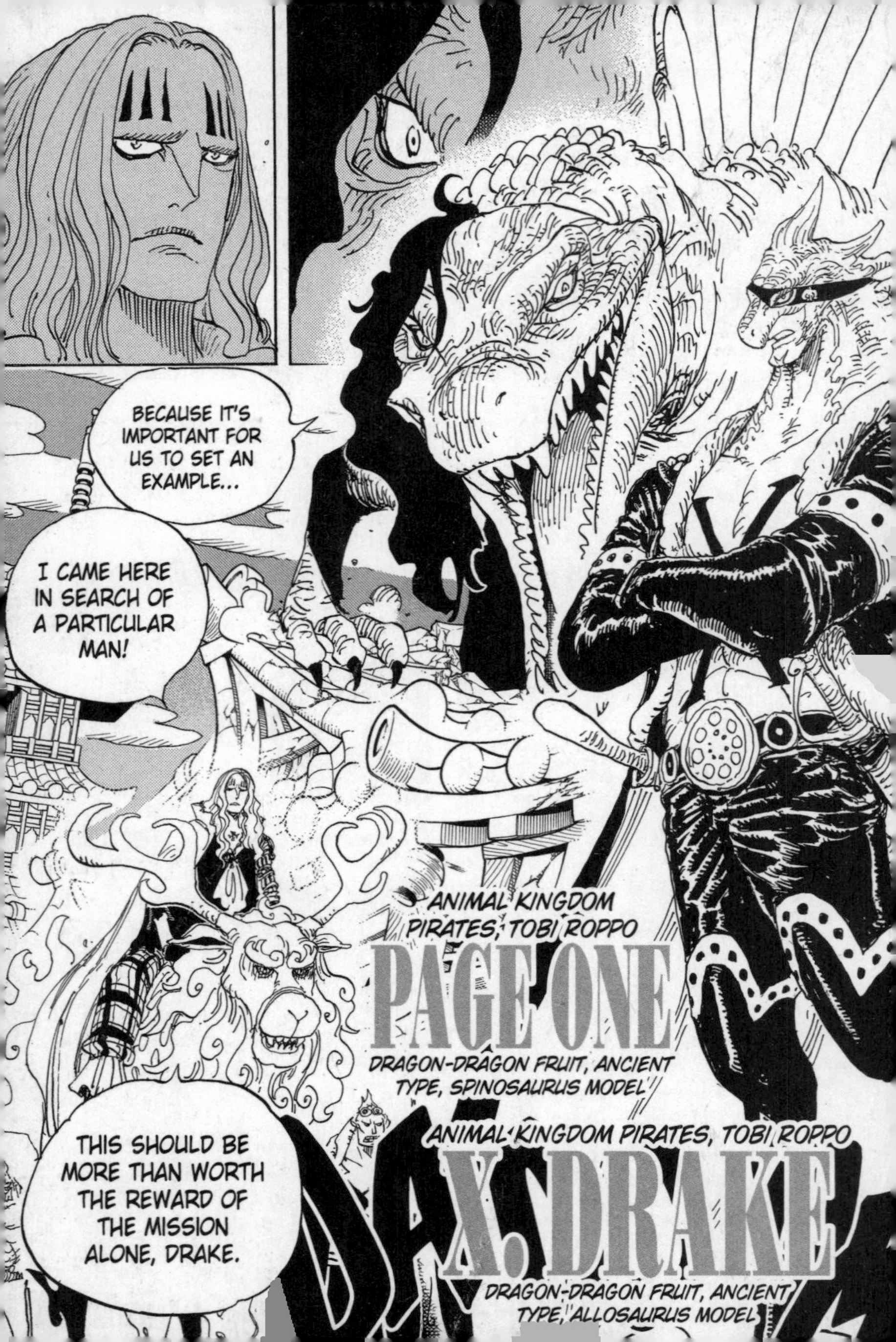
BECAUSE IT'S IMPORTANT FOR US TO SET AN EXAMPLE...
I CAME HERE IN SEARCH OF A PARTICULAR MAN!
ANIMAL KINGDOM PIRATES, TOBI ROPPO
PAGE ONE
DRAGON-DRAGON FRUIT, ANCIENT TYPE, SPINOSAURUS MODEL
ANIMAL KINGDOM PIRATES, TOBI ROPPO
X. DRAKE
DRAGON-DRAGON FRUIT, ANCIENT TYPE, ALLOSAURUS MODEL
THIS SHOULD BE MORE THAN WORTH THE REWARD OF THE MISSION ALONE, DRAKE.

SBS Question Corner

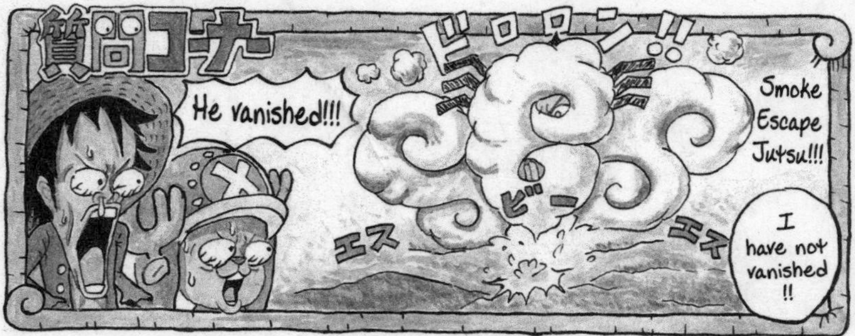

Smoke Escape Jutsu!!!
I have not vanished !!
ドロロン!!
He vanished!!!
質問コーナー

(Igarashi, Oita)

Q: Oda Sensei!! Tell us the favorite and least favorite food of the seven followers who drank from the sons' cups!!

--Princess Rabbit

A: Okay.

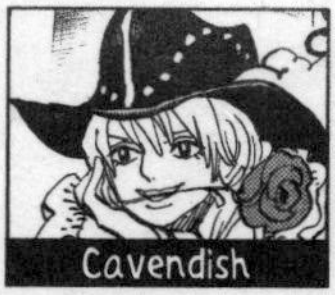

Cavendish

Likes: Roses
Hates: Ramen

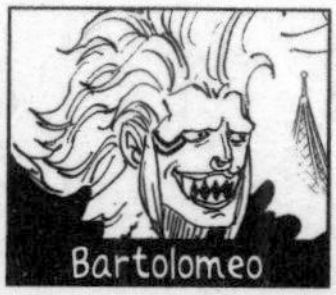

Bartolomeo

Likes: Sweets
Hates: Veggies

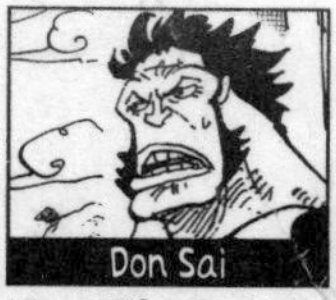

Don Sai

Likes: Wife's Cooking
Hates: Crab

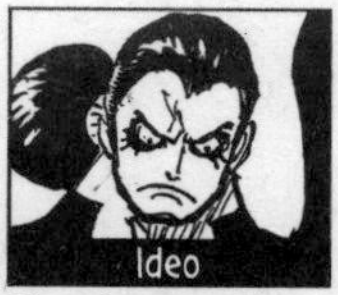

Ideo

Likes: Doner Kebabs
Hates: Pork

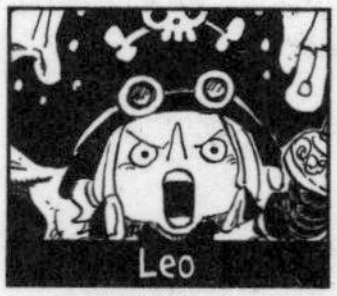

Leo

Likes: Pumpkin
Hates: Everything Spicy

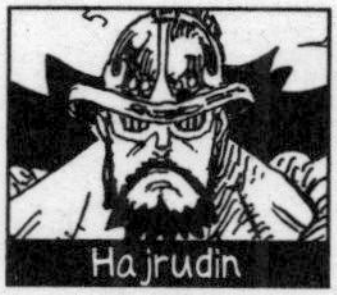

Hajrudin

Likes: Meatballs
Hates: Semla

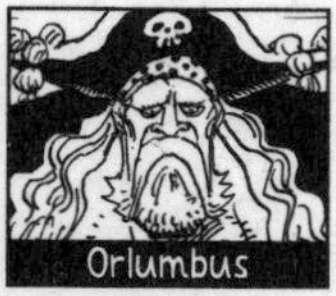

Orlumbus

Likes: Boiled Eggs
Hates: Whipping Up Whatever

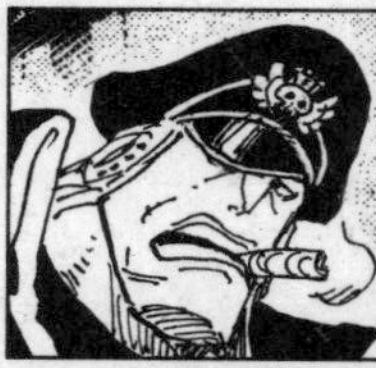

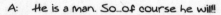

Q: So Shiryu has the Clear-Clear Fruit now. Will he use it to peep on the women's bath?

--Apoo

A: He is a man. So...of course he will!!

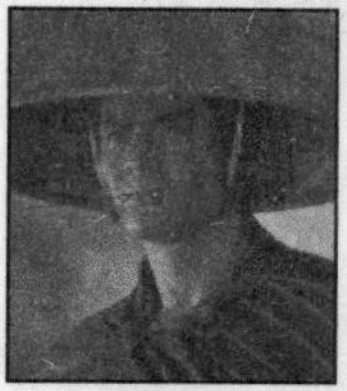

Q: It ain't got nothin' to do with me, but how does a young feller like you know about Kogarashi Monjiro? I mean, Luffy had a nice long toothpick in his mouth, so it occurred to me to ask. If you'll pardon me…

--Hiromichi "Captain" Kick (age 57)

A: I got a question from a 57-year-old! That's right! There's an old movie called *Kogarashi Monjiro* originally based on a novel, and the character always has a toothpick in his mouth! Sometimes he even spits it like a blowing dart. He's really cool. But don't try that at home, it's dangerous! Oh, and speaking of period-piece references, "Napping Kyoshiro" is also from a novel series called "Sleeping Kyoshiro."

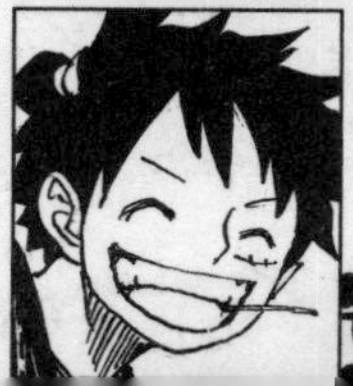

Chapter 930:
EBISU TOWN

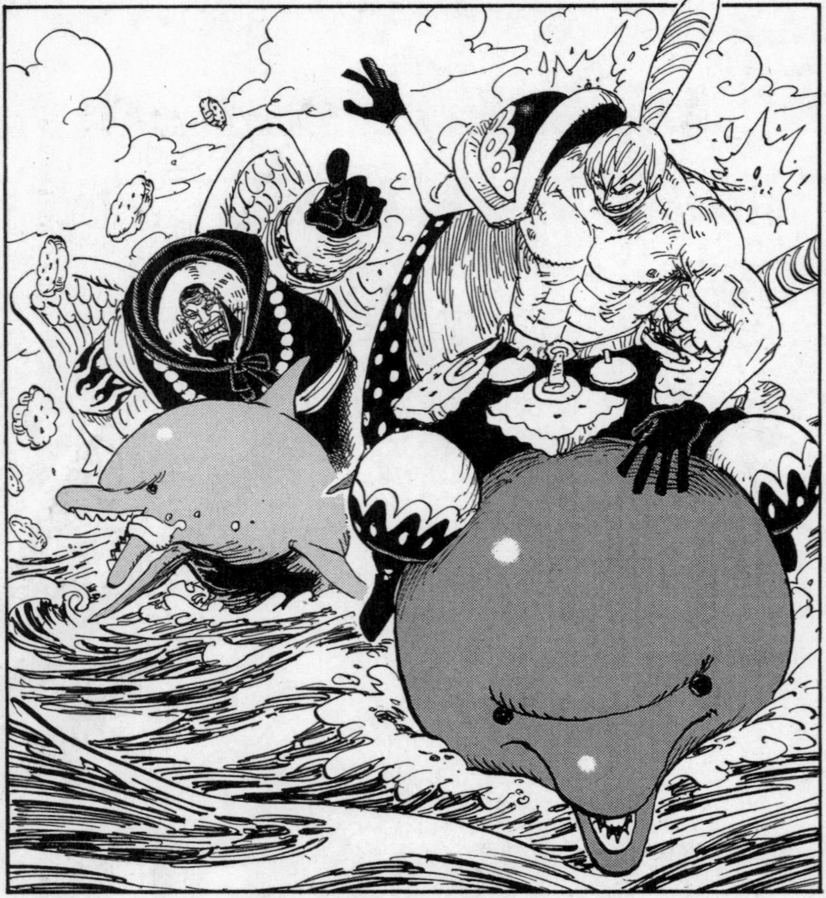

REQUEST: "UROUGE AND CRACKER
RACING ON DOLPHINS" BY OH-OH

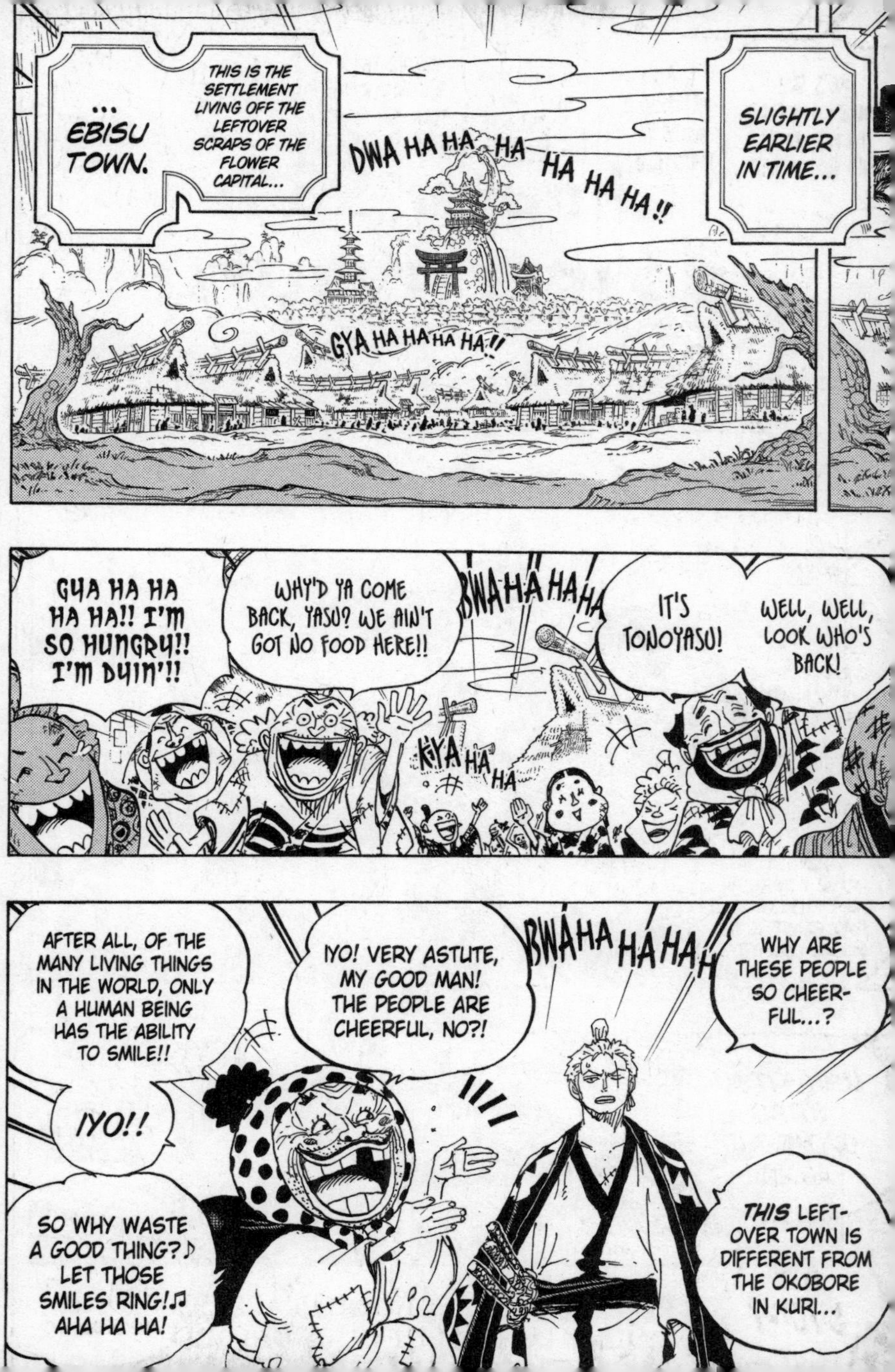
SLIGHTLY EARLIER IN TIME...
THIS IS THE SETTLEMENT LIVING OFF THE LEFTOVER SCRAPS OF THE FLOWER CAPITAL...
...EBISU TOWN.
DWA HA HA HA HA HA HA!!
GYA HA HA HA HA!!
WELL, WELL, LOOK WHO'S BACK!
IT'S TONOYASU!
BWAHAHAHA
WHY'D YA COME BACK, YASU? WE AIN'T GOT NO FOOD HERE!!
GYA HA HA HA HA!! I'M SO HUNGRY!! I'M DYIN'!!
KYA HA HA
WHY ARE THESE PEOPLE SO CHEERFUL...?
BWAHA HA HA H
IYO! VERY ASTUTE, MY GOOD MAN! THE PEOPLE ARE CHEERFUL, NO?!
AFTER ALL, OF THE MANY LIVING THINGS IN THE WORLD, ONLY A HUMAN BEING HAS THE ABILITY TO SMILE!!
IYO!!
THIS LEFT-OVER TOWN IS DIFFERENT FROM THE OKOBORE IN KURI...
SO WHY WASTE A GOOD THING?♪ LET THOSE SMILES RING!♫ AHA HA HA!

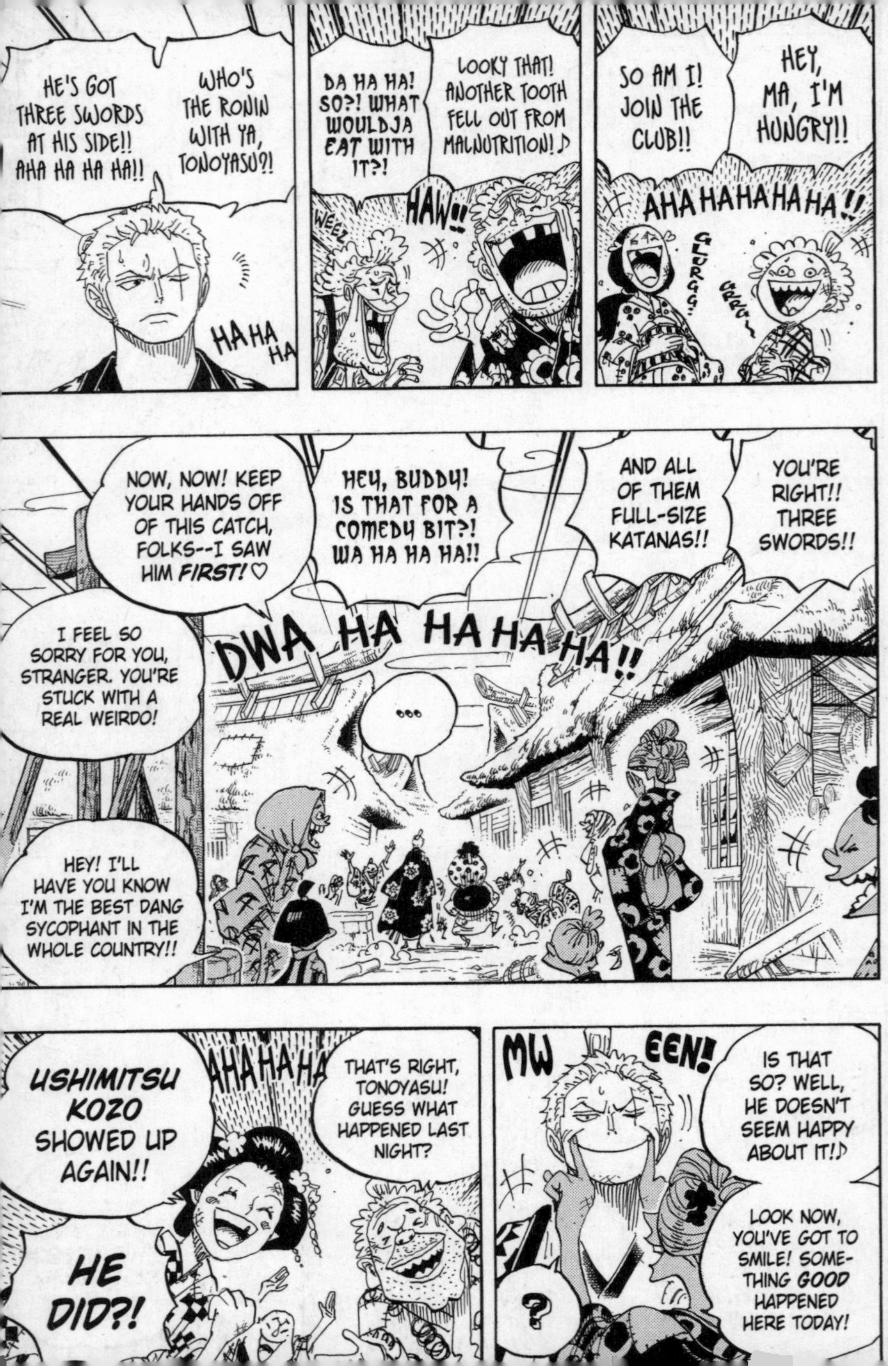
HEY, MA, I'M HUNGRY!!
SO AM I! JOIN THE CLUB!!
AHA HAHAHAHAHA!!
GLURGG!
GRRG~
LOOKY THAT! ANOTHER TOOTH FELL OUT FROM MALNUTRITION!♪
DA HA HA! SO?! WHAT WOULDJA EAT WITH IT?!
HAW!!
WEEZ
WHO'S THE RONIN WITH YA, TONOYASU?!
HE'S GOT THREE SWORDS AT HIS SIDE!! AHA HA HA HA!!
HA HA HA
YOU'RE RIGHT!! THREE SWORDS!!
AND ALL OF THEM FULL-SIZE KATANAS!!
HEY, BUDDY! IS THAT FOR A COMEDY BIT?! WA HA HA HA!!
NOW, NOW! KEEP YOUR HANDS OFF OF THIS CATCH, FOLKS--I SAW HIM *FIRST!*♡
DWA HA HA HA HA HA!!
...
I FEEL SO SORRY FOR YOU, STRANGER. YOU'RE STUCK WITH A REAL WEIRDO!
HEY! I'LL HAVE YOU KNOW I'M THE BEST DANG SYCOPHANT IN THE WHOLE COUNTRY!!
MW EEN!
IS THAT SO? WELL, HE DOESN'T SEEM HAPPY ABOUT IT!♪
LOOK NOW, YOU'VE GOT TO SMILE! SOMETHING *GOOD* HAPPENED HERE TODAY!
?
AHAHAHA
THAT'S RIGHT, TONOYASU! GUESS WHAT HAPPENED LAST NIGHT?
USHIMITSU KOZO SHOWED UP AGAIN!!
HE DID?!

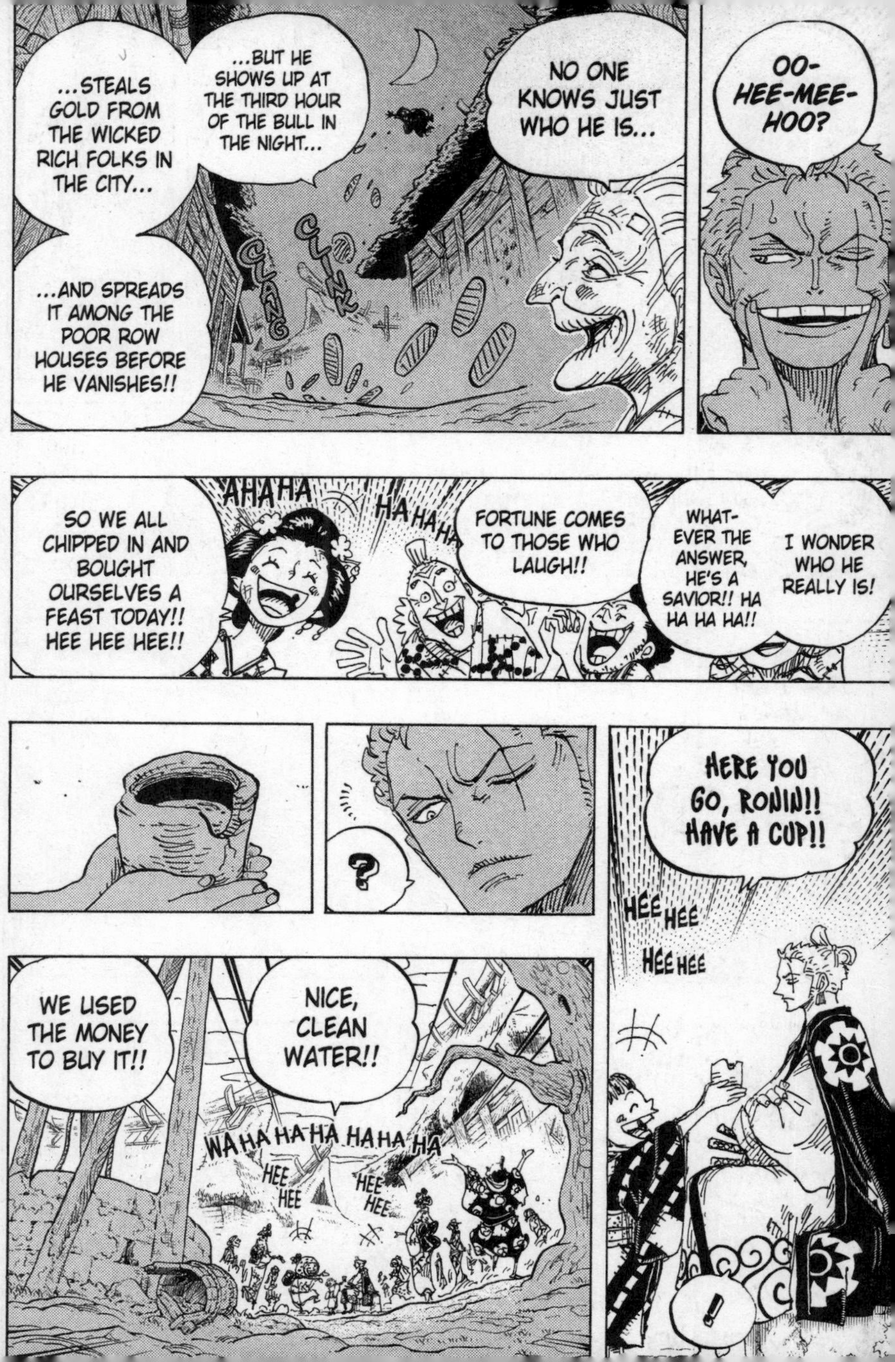
OO-HEE-MEE-HOO?
NO ONE KNOWS JUST WHO HE IS...
...BUT HE SHOWS UP AT THE THIRD HOUR OF THE BULL IN THE NIGHT...
...STEALS GOLD FROM THE WICKED RICH FOLKS IN THE CITY...
CLINK
CLANG
...AND SPREADS IT AMONG THE POOR ROW HOUSES BEFORE HE VANISHES!!
I WONDER WHO HE REALLY IS!
WHAT-EVER THE ANSWER, HE'S A SAVIOR!! HA HA HA HA!!
FORTUNE COMES TO THOSE WHO LAUGH!!
HAHAHA
AHAHA
SO WE ALL CHIPPED IN AND BOUGHT OURSELVES A FEAST TODAY!! HEE HEE HEE!!
HERE YOU GO, RONIN!! HAVE A CUP!!
HEE HEE
HEE HEE
!
?
NICE, CLEAN WATER!!
WE USED THE MONEY TO BUY IT!!
WAHAHAHAHA HAHAHA
HEE HEE
HEE HEE

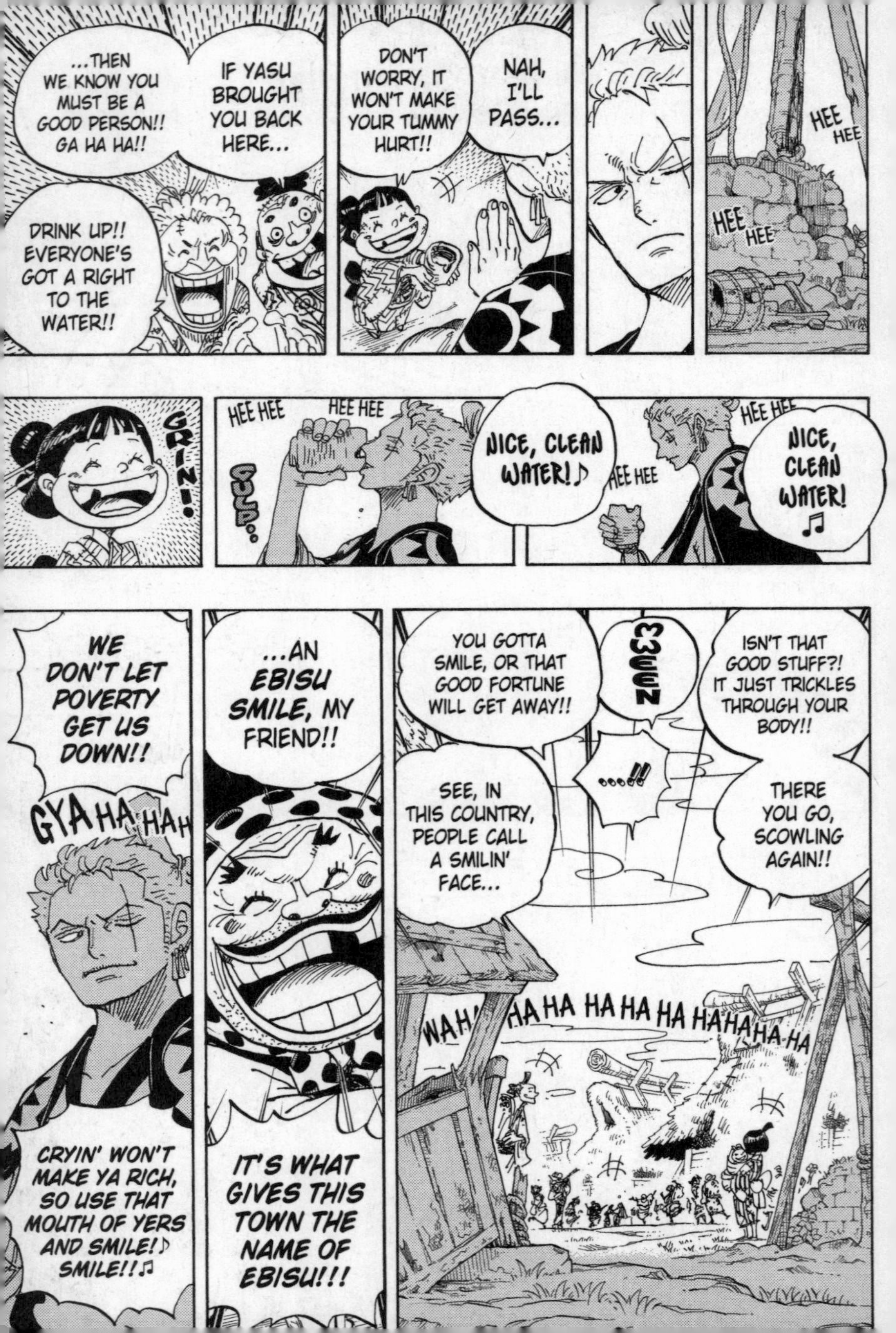
HEE HEE
HEE HEE
NAH, I'LL PASS...
DON'T WORRY, IT WON'T MAKE YOUR TUMMY HURT!!
IF YASU BROUGHT YOU BACK HERE...
...THEN WE KNOW YOU MUST BE A GOOD PERSON!! GA HA HA!!
DRINK UP!! EVERYONE'S GOT A RIGHT TO THE WATER!!
HEE HEE
NICE, CLEAN WATER! ♫
HEE HEE
NICE, CLEAN WATER!♪
HEE HEE
HEE HEE
GULP...
GRIN!
ISN'T THAT GOOD STUFF?! IT JUST TRICKLES THROUGH YOUR BODY!!
THERE YOU GO, SCOWLING AGAIN!!
....!!
YOU GOTTA SMILE, OR THAT GOOD FORTUNE WILL GET AWAY!!
SEE, IN THIS COUNTRY, PEOPLE CALL A SMILIN' FACE...
WAH HA HA HA HA HA HA HA HA HA HA HA
...AN EBISU SMILE, MY FRIEND!!
IT'S WHAT GIVES THIS TOWN THE NAME OF EBISU!!!
WE DON'T LET POVERTY GET US DOWN!!
GYA HA HAH
CRYIN' WON'T MAKE YA RICH, SO USE THAT MOUTH OF YERS AND SMILE!♪ SMILE!!♫

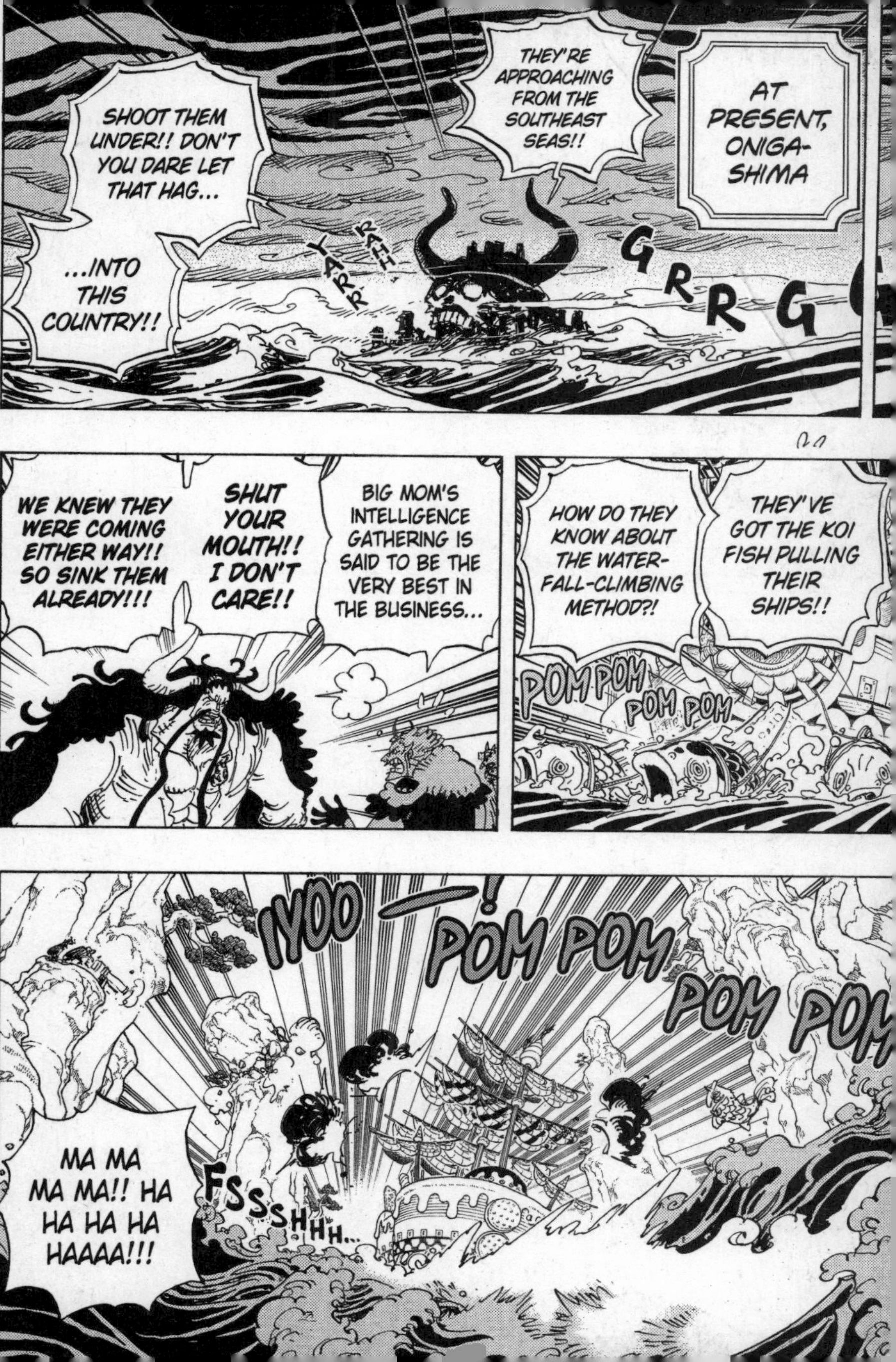
AT PRESENT, ONIGA-SHIMA
THEY'RE APPROACHING FROM THE SOUTHEAST SEAS!!
GRRRG
YARR RAHH
SHOOT THEM UNDER!! DON'T YOU DARE LET THAT HAG...
...INTO THIS COUNTRY!!
THEY'VE GOT THE KOI FISH PULLING THEIR SHIPS!!
HOW DO THEY KNOW ABOUT THE WATER-FALL-CLIMBING METHOD?!
POM POM POM POM
BIG MOM'S INTELLIGENCE GATHERING IS SAID TO BE THE VERY BEST IN THE BUSINESS...
SHUT YOUR MOUTH!! I DON'T CARE!!
WE KNEW THEY WERE COMING EITHER WAY!! SO SINK THEM ALREADY!!!
IYOO—!
POM POM POM POM
FSSSHHH...
MA MA MA MA!! HA HA HA HA HAAAA!!!

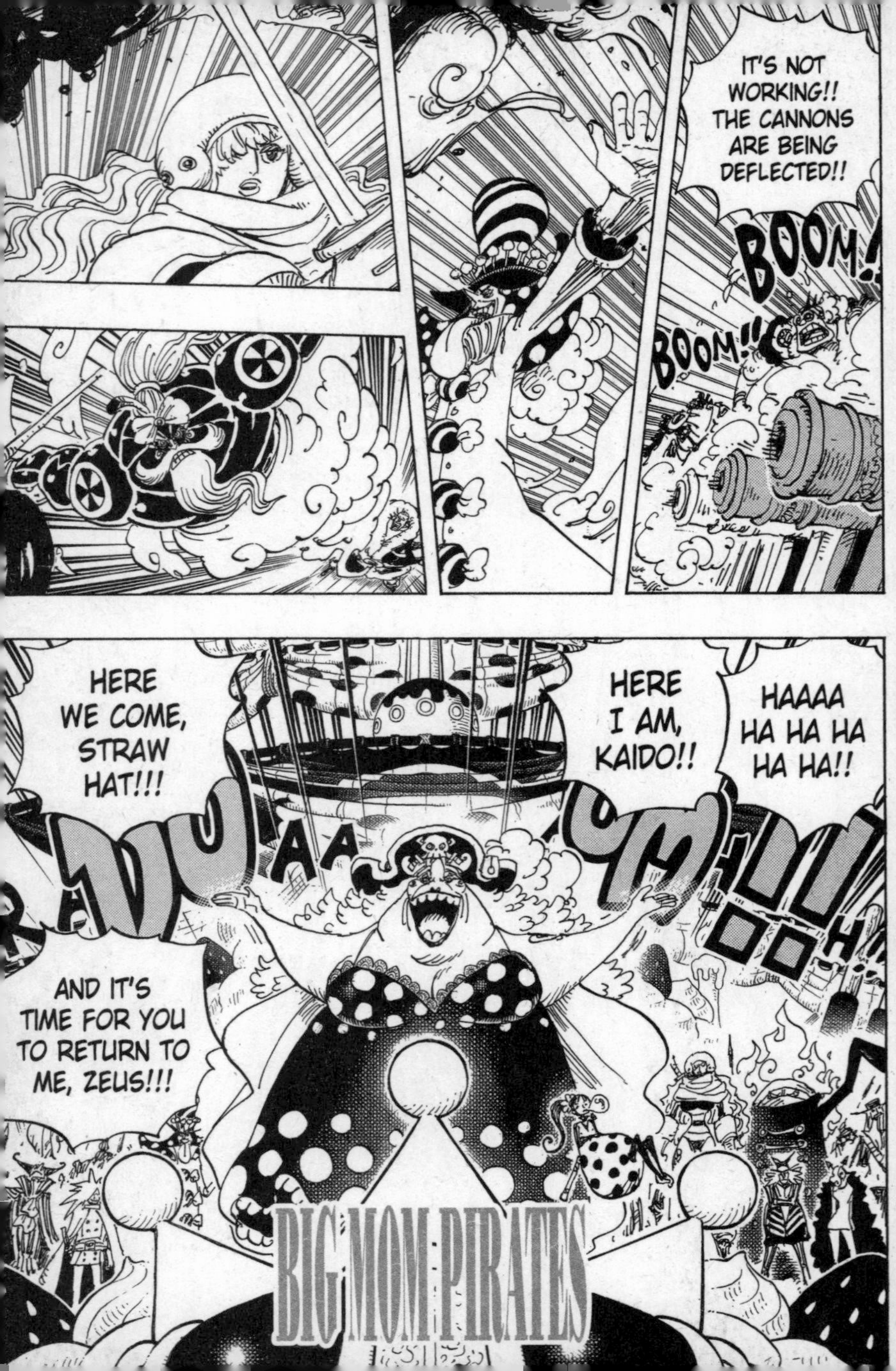
IT'S NOT WORKING!! THE CANNONS ARE BEING DEFLECTED!!
BOOM!!
BOOM!!
HAAAA HA HA HA HA HA!!
HERE I AM, KAIDO!!
HERE WE COME, STRAW HAT!!!
AND IT'S TIME FOR YOU TO RETURN TO ME, ZEUS!!!
BIG MOM PIRATES

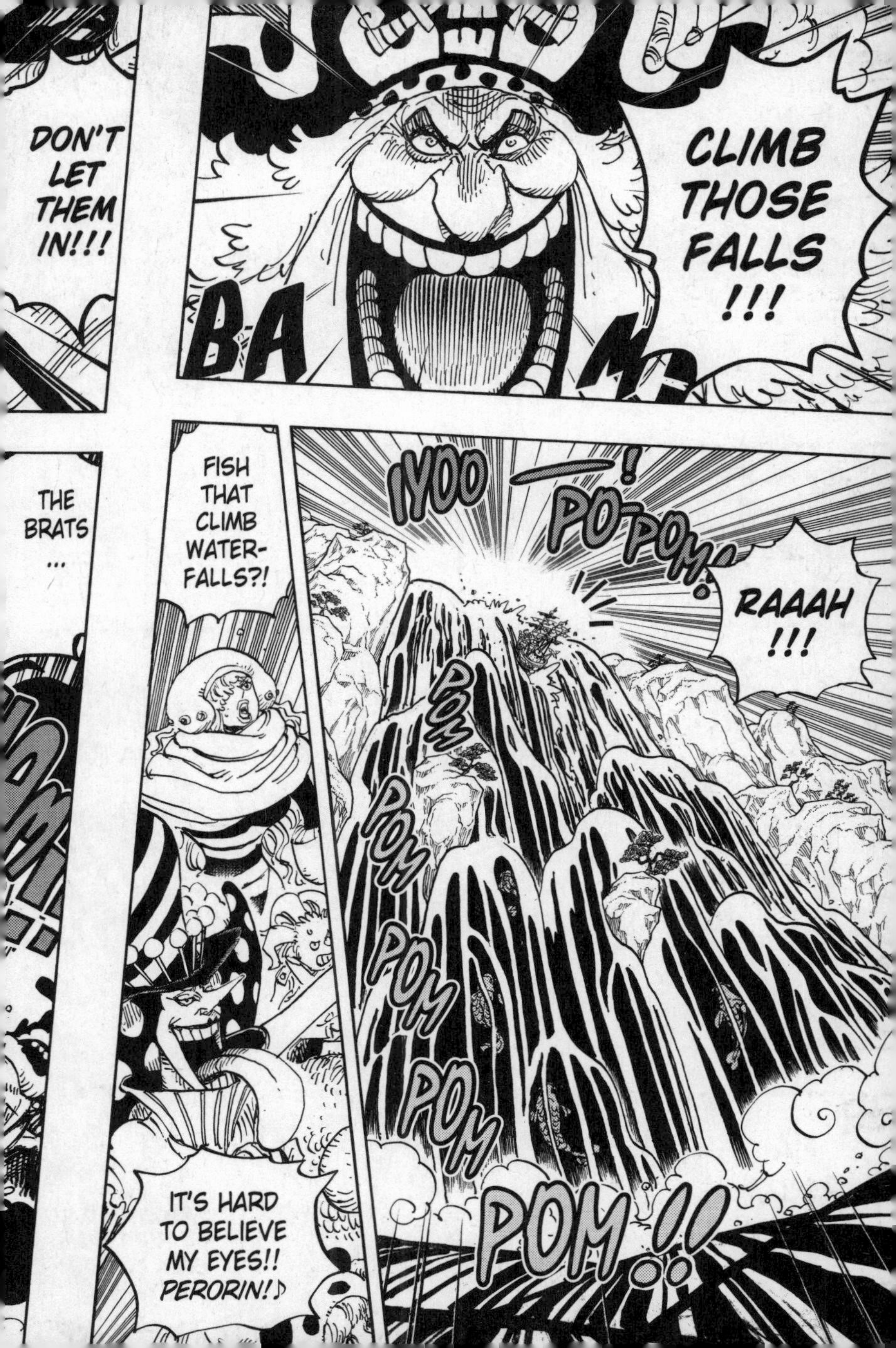
CLIMB THOSE FALLS !!!
DON'T LET THEM IN!!!
YOO —!
PO-POM!
RAAAH !!!
POM POM POM POM POM POM !!
FISH THAT CLIMB WATER-FALLS?!
IT'S HARD TO BELIEVE MY EYES!! PERORIN!♪
THE BRATS ...

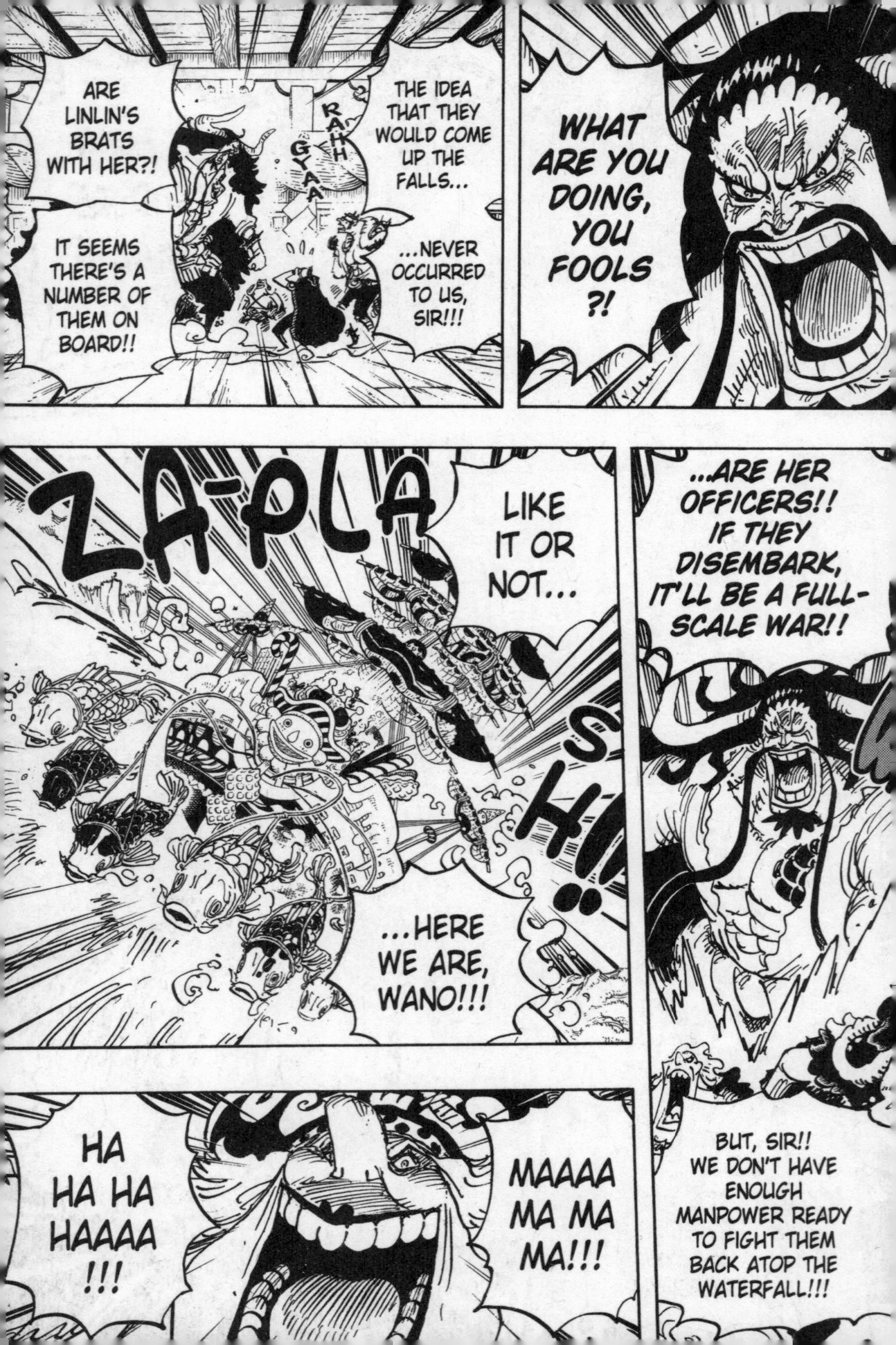
WHAT ARE YOU DOING, YOU FOOLS?!
THE IDEA THAT THEY WOULD COME UP THE FALLS...
...NEVER OCCURRED TO US, SIR!!!
RAHH
GYAA
ARE LINLIN'S BRATS WITH HER?!
IT SEEMS THERE'S A NUMBER OF THEM ON BOARD!!
...ARE HER OFFICERS!! IF THEY DISEMBARK, IT'LL BE A FULL-SCALE WAR!!
BUT, SIR!! WE DON'T HAVE ENOUGH MANPOWER READY TO FIGHT THEM BACK ATOP THE WATERFALL!!!
LIKE IT OR NOT...
ZA-PLA
SH!!!
...HERE WE ARE, WANO!!!
MAAAA MA MA MA!!!
HA HA HA HAAAA!!!

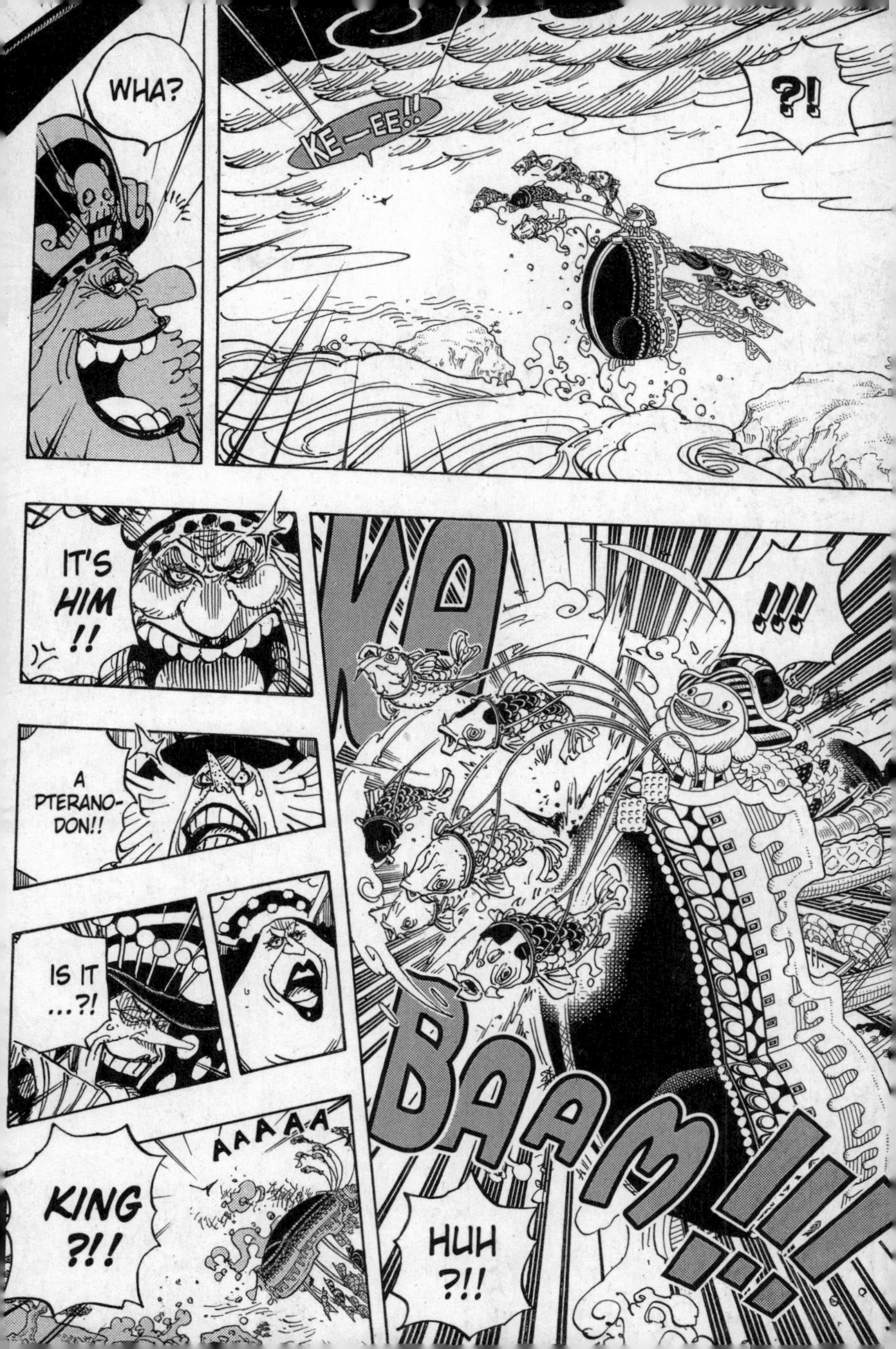
?!
KE—EE!!
WHA?
!!!
KA
BAAM!!!!
HUH ?!!
IT'S HIM !!
A PTERANO-DON!!
IS IT ...?!
AAAAA
KING ?!!

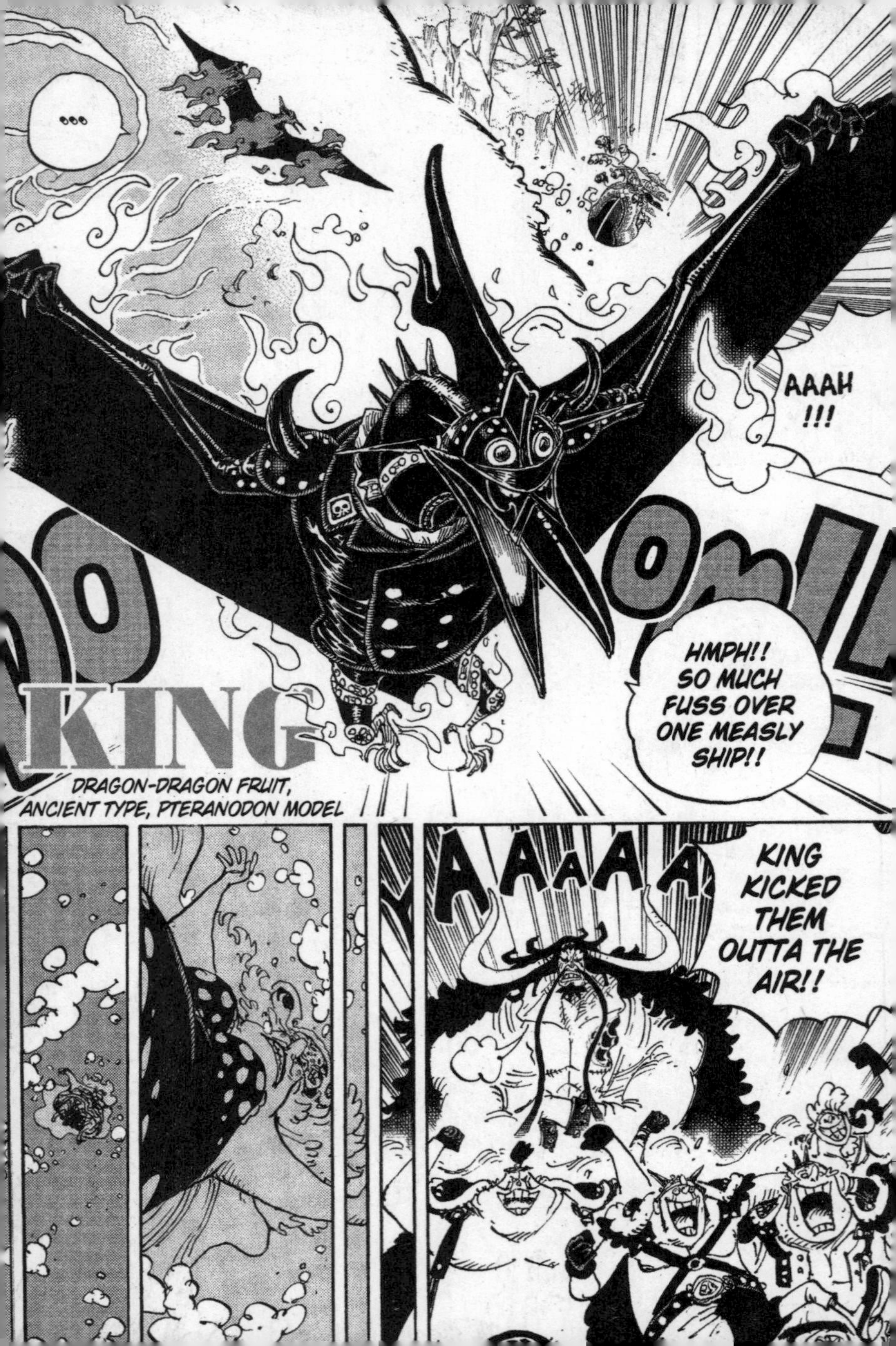
AAAH !!!
...
HMPH!! SO MUCH FUSS OVER ONE MEASLY SHIP!!
KING
DRAGON-DRAGON FRUIT, ANCIENT TYPE, PTERANODON MODEL
AAAAA
KING KICKED THEM OUTTA THE AIR!!

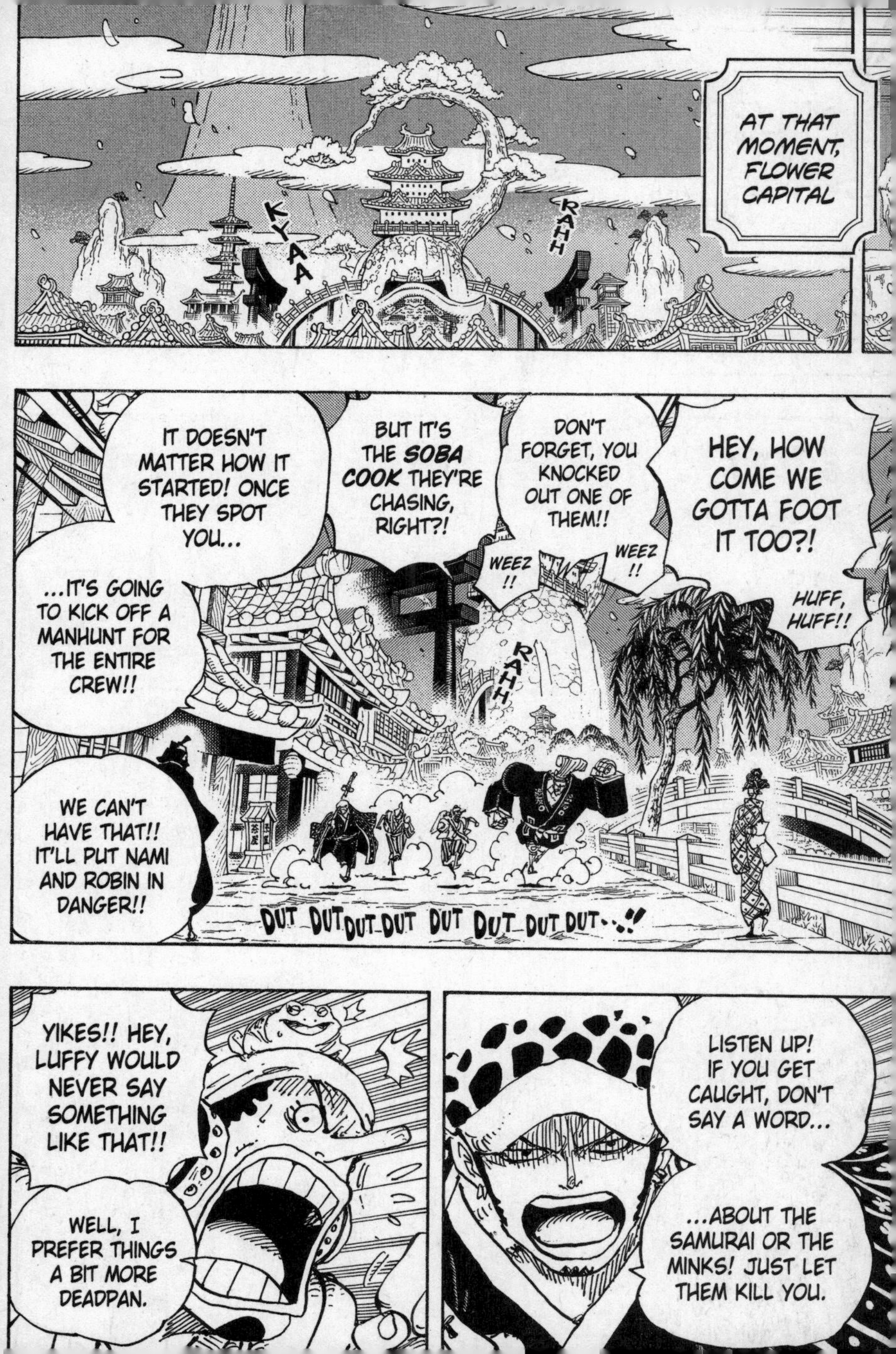
AT THAT MOMENT, FLOWER CAPITAL
RAHH
KYAA
HEY, HOW COME WE GOTTA FOOT IT TOO?!
HUFF, HUFF!!
DON'T FORGET, YOU KNOCKED OUT ONE OF THEM!!
WEEZ!!
WEEZ!!
BUT IT'S THE **SOBA COOK** THEY'RE CHASING, RIGHT?!
IT DOESN'T MATTER HOW IT STARTED! ONCE THEY SPOT YOU...
...IT'S GOING TO KICK OFF A MANHUNT FOR THE ENTIRE CREW!!
RAHH
WE CAN'T HAVE THAT!! IT'LL PUT NAMI AND ROBIN IN DANGER!!
DUT DUT DUT DUT DUT DUT DUT DUT..!!
LISTEN UP! IF YOU GET CAUGHT, DON'T SAY A WORD...
...ABOUT THE SAMURAI OR THE MINKS! JUST LET THEM KILL YOU.
YIKES!! HEY, LUFFY WOULD NEVER SAY SOMETHING LIKE THAT!!
WELL, I PREFER THINGS A BIT MORE DEADPAN.

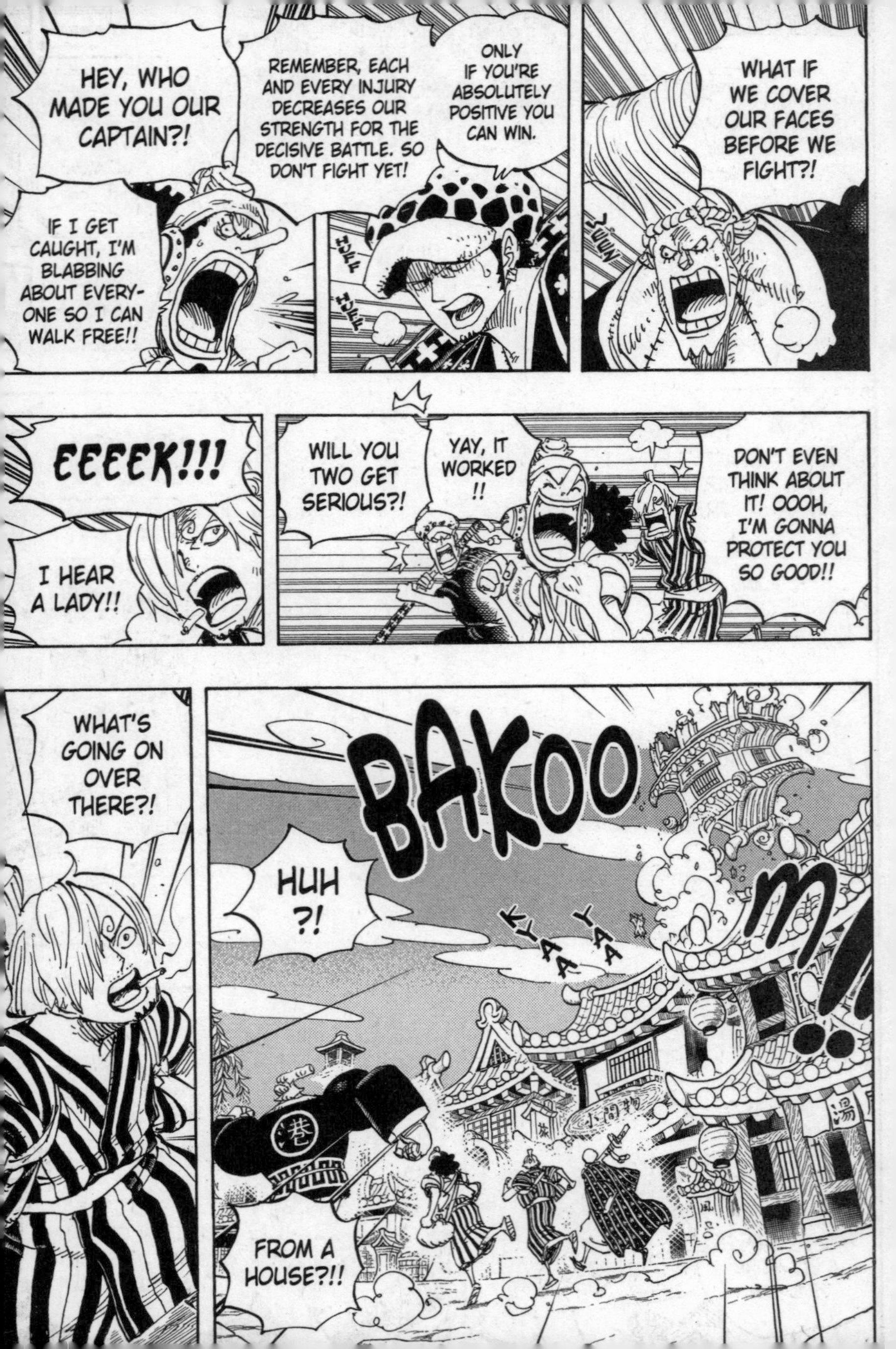
WHAT IF WE COVER OUR FACES BEFORE WE FIGHT?!
ONLY IF YOU'RE ABSOLUTELY POSITIVE YOU CAN WIN.
REMEMBER, EACH AND EVERY INJURY DECREASES OUR STRENGTH FOR THE DECISIVE BATTLE. SO DON'T FIGHT YET!
HUFF
HUFF
HEY, WHO MADE YOU OUR CAPTAIN?!
IF I GET CAUGHT, I'M BLABBING ABOUT EVERY-ONE SO I CAN WALK FREE!!
DON'T EVEN THINK ABOUT IT! OOOH, I'M GONNA PROTECT YOU SO GOOD!!
YAY, IT WORKED!!
WILL YOU TWO GET SERIOUS?!
EEEEK!!!
I HEAR A LADY!!
BAKOOM!!
HUH?!
KYAA
YAA
FROM A HOUSE?!!
WHAT'S GOING ON OVER THERE?!

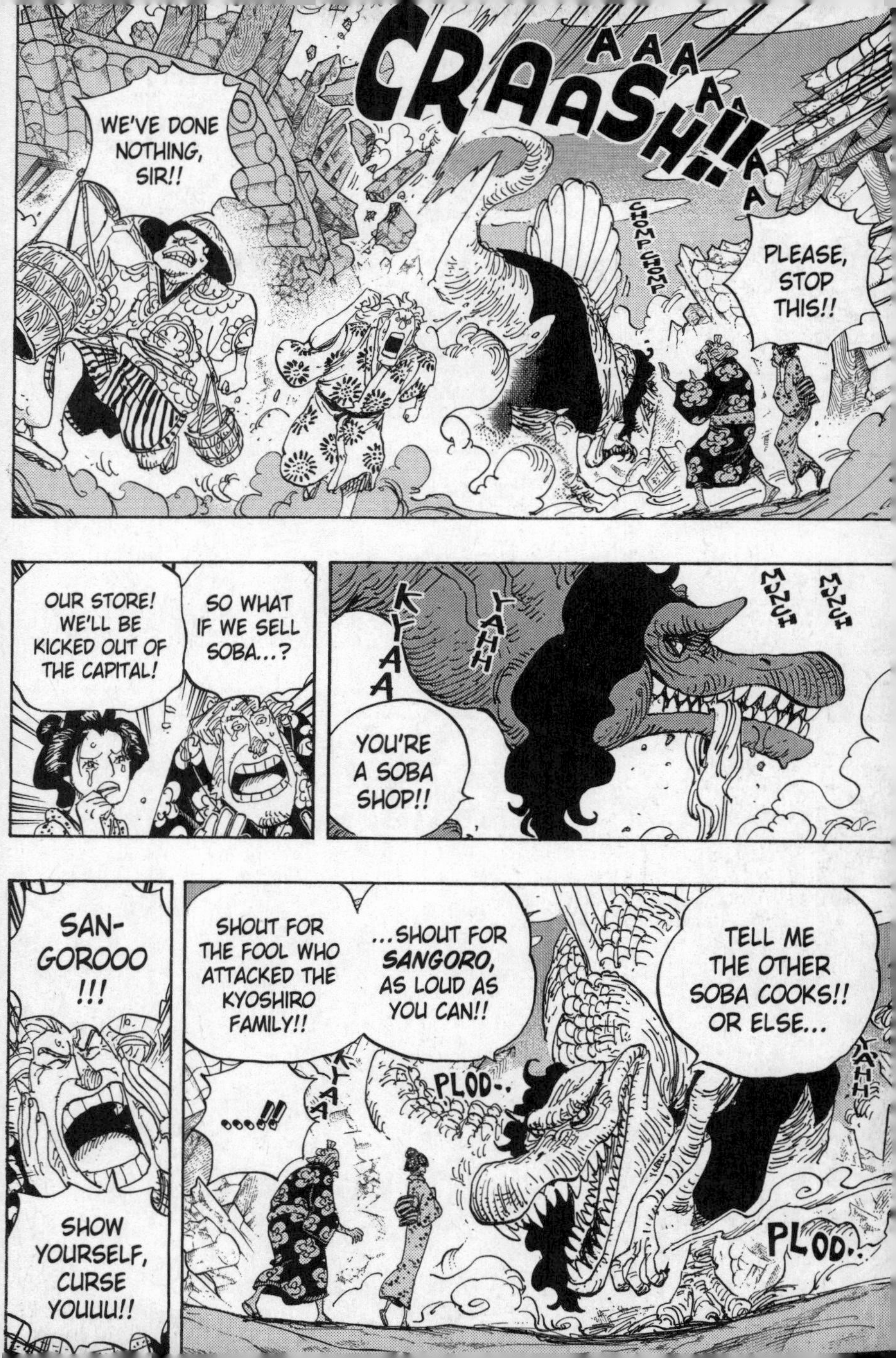
AAAAAAAA
CRAASH!!
PLEASE, STOP THIS!!
CHOMP CHOMP
WE'VE DONE NOTHING, SIR!!
MUNCH MUNCH
YAHH
KYAA
YOU'RE A SOBA SHOP!!
SO WHAT IF WE SELL SOBA...?
OUR STORE! WE'LL BE KICKED OUT OF THE CAPITAL!
TELL ME THE OTHER SOBA COOKS!! OR ELSE...
SHOUT FOR THE FOOL WHO ATTACKED THE KYOSHIRO FAMILY!!
...SHOUT FOR **SANGORO**, AS LOUD AS YOU CAN!!
YAHH
PLOD-.
KYAA
....!!
PLOD..
SAN-GOROOO!!!
SHOW YOURSELF, CURSE YOUUU!!

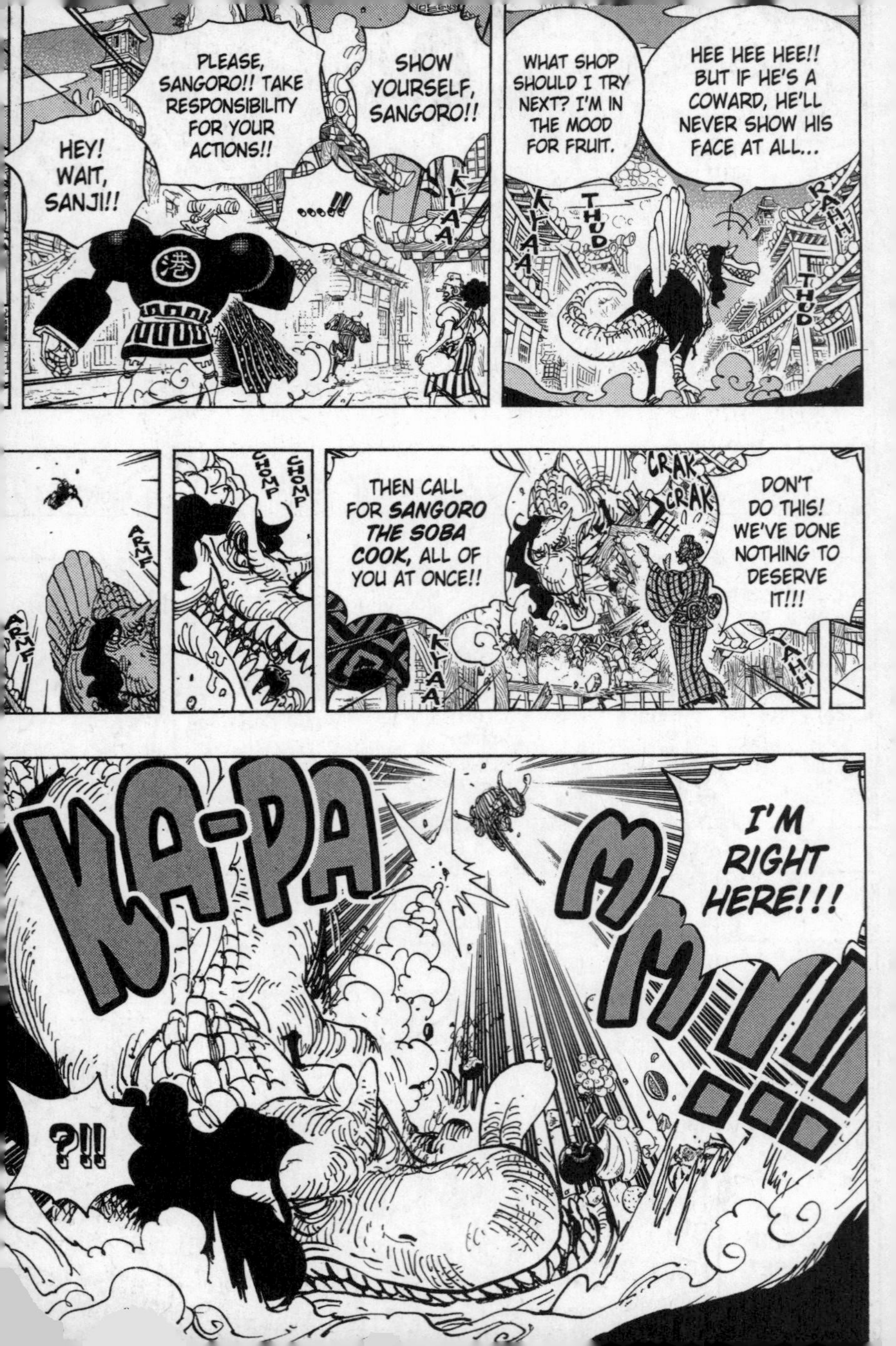
HEE HEE HEE!! BUT IF HE'S A COWARD, HE'LL NEVER SHOW HIS FACE AT ALL...
WHAT SHOP SHOULD I TRY NEXT? I'M IN THE MOOD FOR FRUIT.
RAHH
THUD
THUD
KYAA
SHOW YOURSELF, SANGORO!!
PLEASE, SANGORO!! TAKE RESPONSIBILITY FOR YOUR ACTIONS!!
HEY! WAIT, SANJI!!
KYAA
...!!
CRAK
CRAK
DON'T DO THIS! WE'VE DONE NOTHING TO DESERVE IT!!!
THEN CALL FOR ***SANGORO THE SOBA COOK***, ALL OF YOU AT ONCE!!
YAHH
KYAA
CHOMP
CHOMP
ARMF
ARMF
I'M RIGHT HERE!!!
KA-PA-MMM!!!
?!!

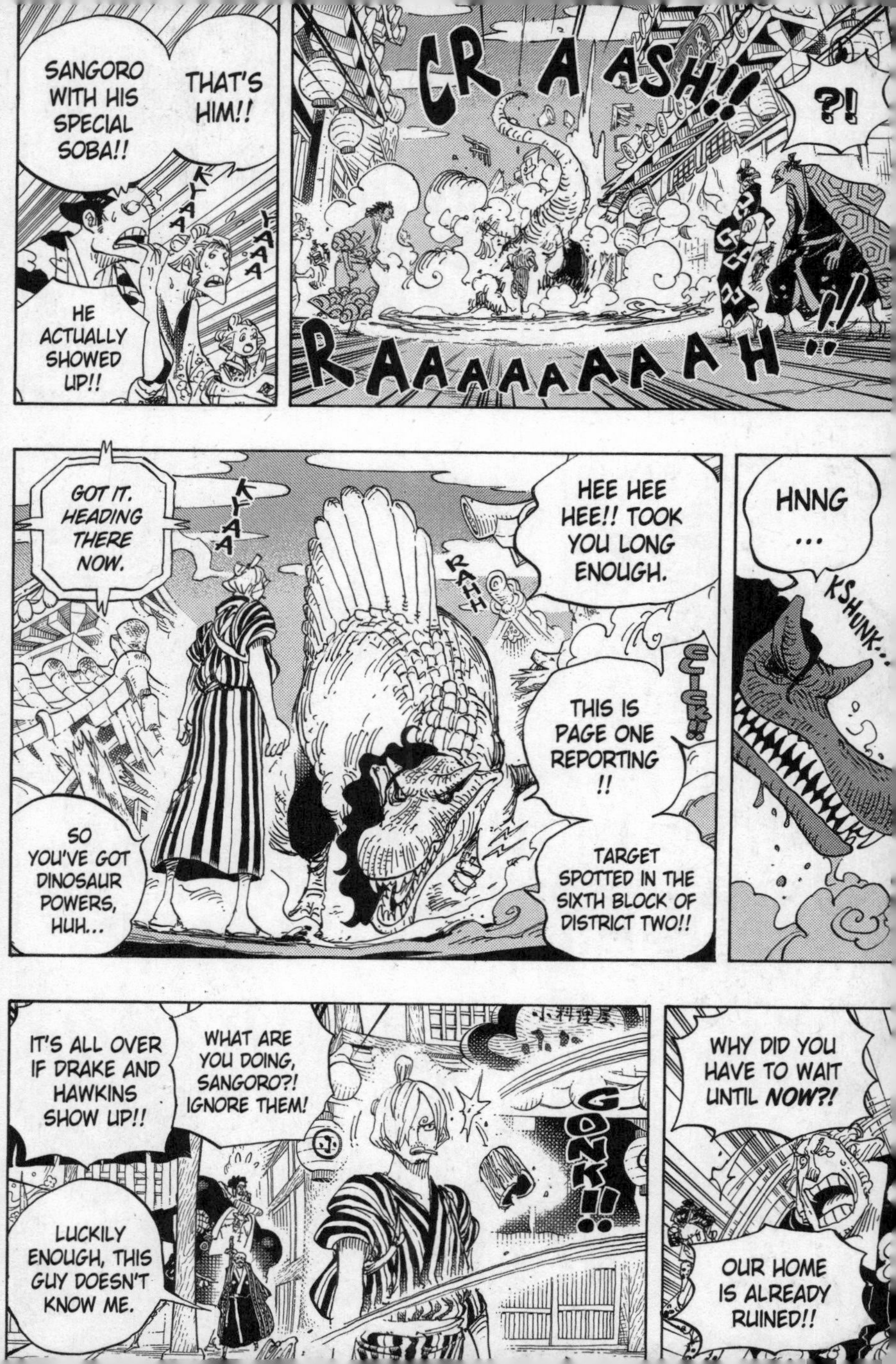
CRASH!!
?!
RAAAAAAAAH!!
THAT'S HIM!!
SANGORO WITH HIS SPECIAL SOBA!!
KYAA
KYAAA
HE ACTUALLY SHOWED UP!!
HNNG ...
KSHUNK...
HEE HEE HEE!! TOOK YOU LONG ENOUGH.
RAHH
KYAA
GOT IT. HEADING THERE NOW.
CLICK!!
THIS IS PAGE ONE REPORTING !!
TARGET SPOTTED IN THE SIXTH BLOCK OF DISTRICT TWO!!
SO YOU'VE GOT DINOSAUR POWERS, HUH...
WHY DID YOU HAVE TO WAIT UNTIL *NOW*?!
OUR HOME IS ALREADY RUINED!!
WHAT ARE YOU DOING, SANGORO?! IGNORE THEM!
IT'S ALL OVER IF DRAKE AND HAWKINS SHOW UP!!
GONK!!
LUCKILY ENOUGH, THIS GUY DOESN'T KNOW ME.

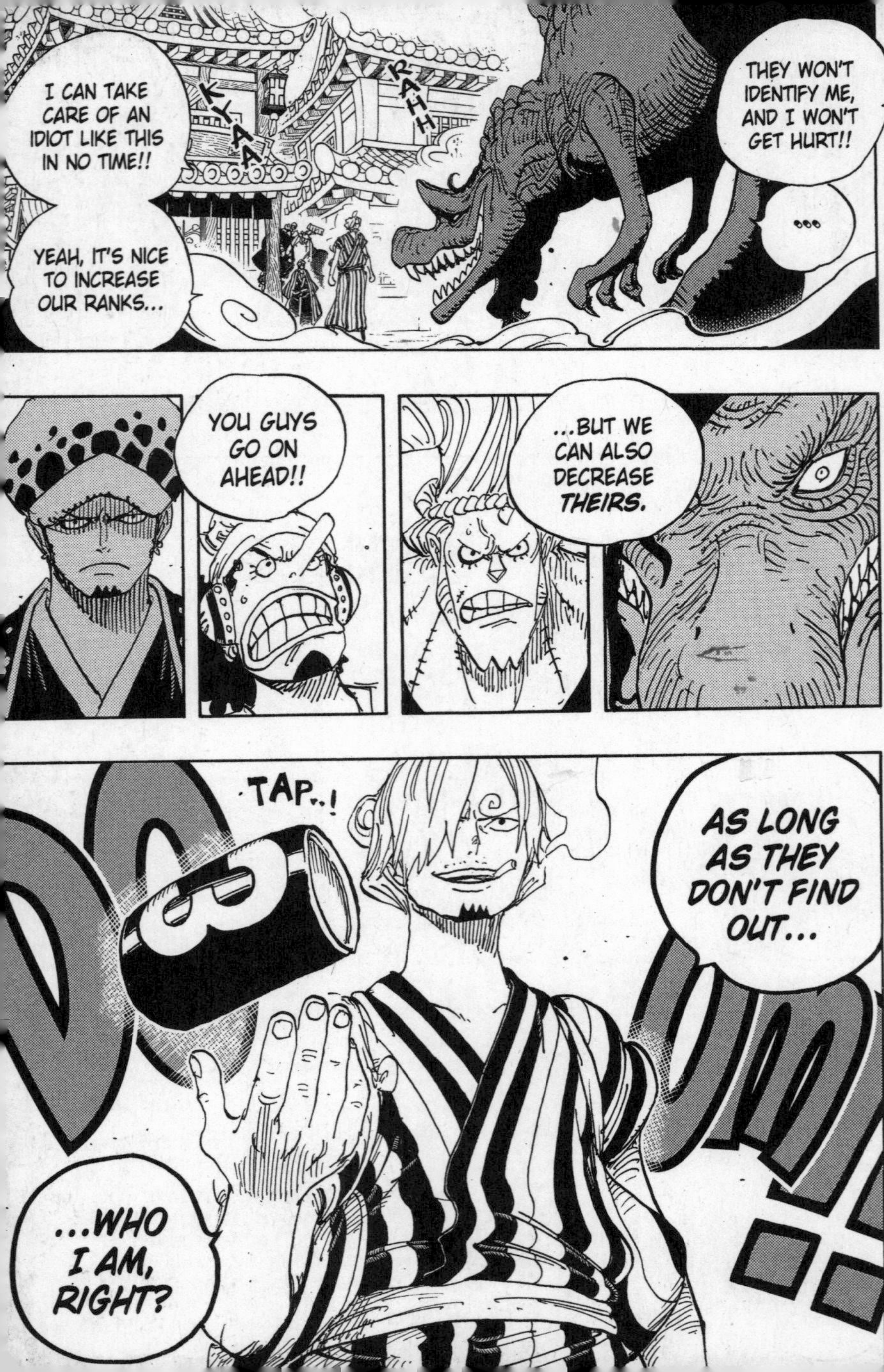

THEY WON'T IDENTIFY ME, AND I WON'T GET HURT!!
...
RAHH
KYAA
I CAN TAKE CARE OF AN IDIOT LIKE THIS IN NO TIME!!
YEAH, IT'S NICE TO INCREASE OUR RANKS...
...BUT WE CAN ALSO DECREASE *THEIRS.*
YOU GUYS GO ON AHEAD!!
AS LONG AS THEY DON'T FIND OUT...
TAP..!
...WHO I AM, RIGHT?

SBS Question Corner

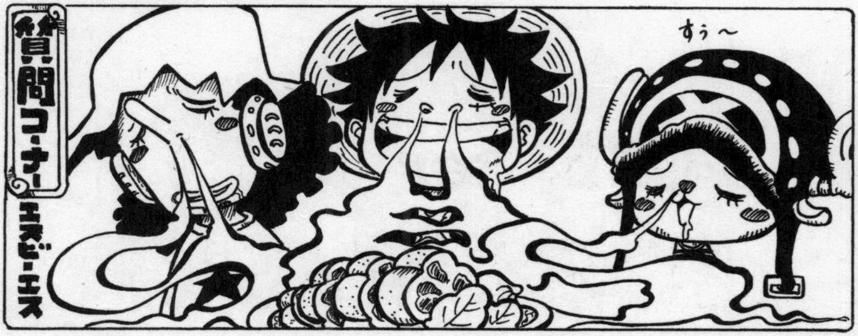
質問コーナー
エスビーエス
すぅ〜
(Michi Nakahara, Tottori)

Q: Odacchi, I have a request! If any of your readers write to say, "Please draw Nami and Robin in the future," do **not not not not not** oblige them! Please!!!

--420 Land

A: Uh... This is a bit, right? You want me to do it? Well...

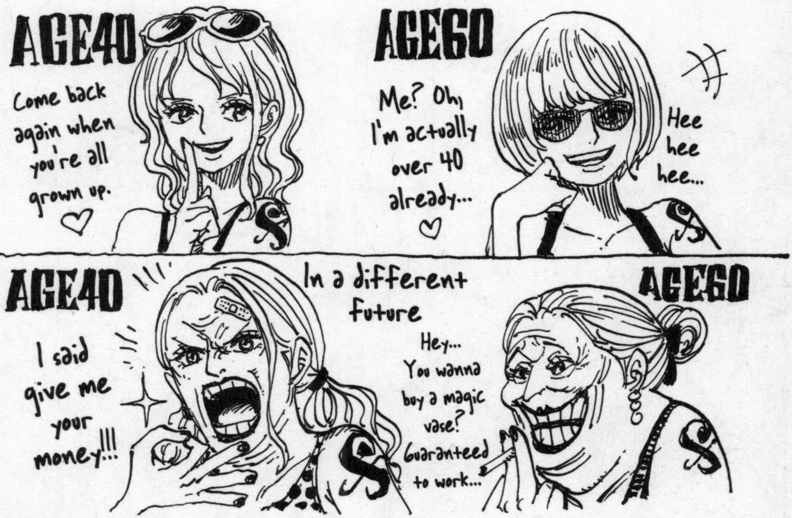
AGE60
Me? Oh, I'm actually over 40 already...
Hee hee hee...
AGE40
Come back again when you're all grown up.
In a different future
AGE60
Hey... You wanna buy a magic vase? Guaranteed to work...
AGE40
I said give me your money!!!

There, I've drawn Nami! I'll do Robin later if someone asks for her.

Q: Question for Oda Sensei!! I noticed that Sanji's beard lost one of its little prongs when the Wano arc started. Was that an intentional act to distance himself from Judge?

--Yubara

A: 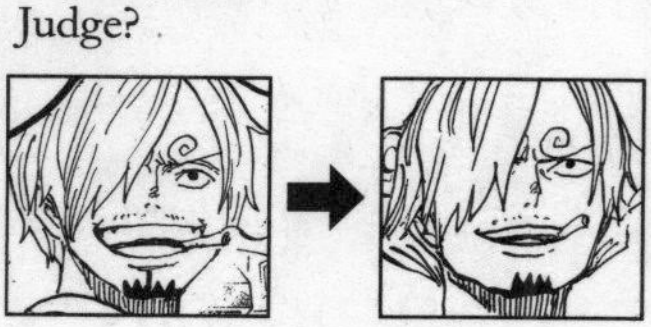

Oh! You're right! I totally forgot! I mean, he totally shaved it! How dare you, Sanji! Don't worry, I'll draw it back next time! I mean, uh, Sanji will grow it back! Oh dear! It's time! See you next SBS!!

Chapter 931:
SOBA MASK

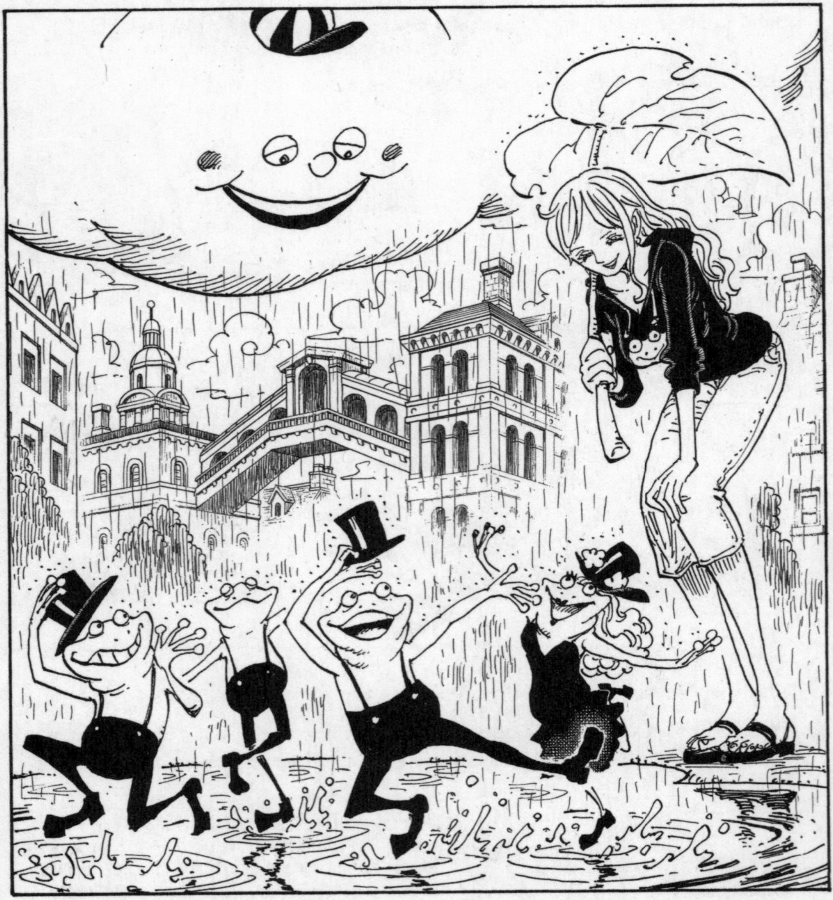

REQUEST: "FROGS TAP-DANCING WITH DELIGHT IN PUDDLES FROM NAMI'S RAIN" BY NODA SKYWALKER

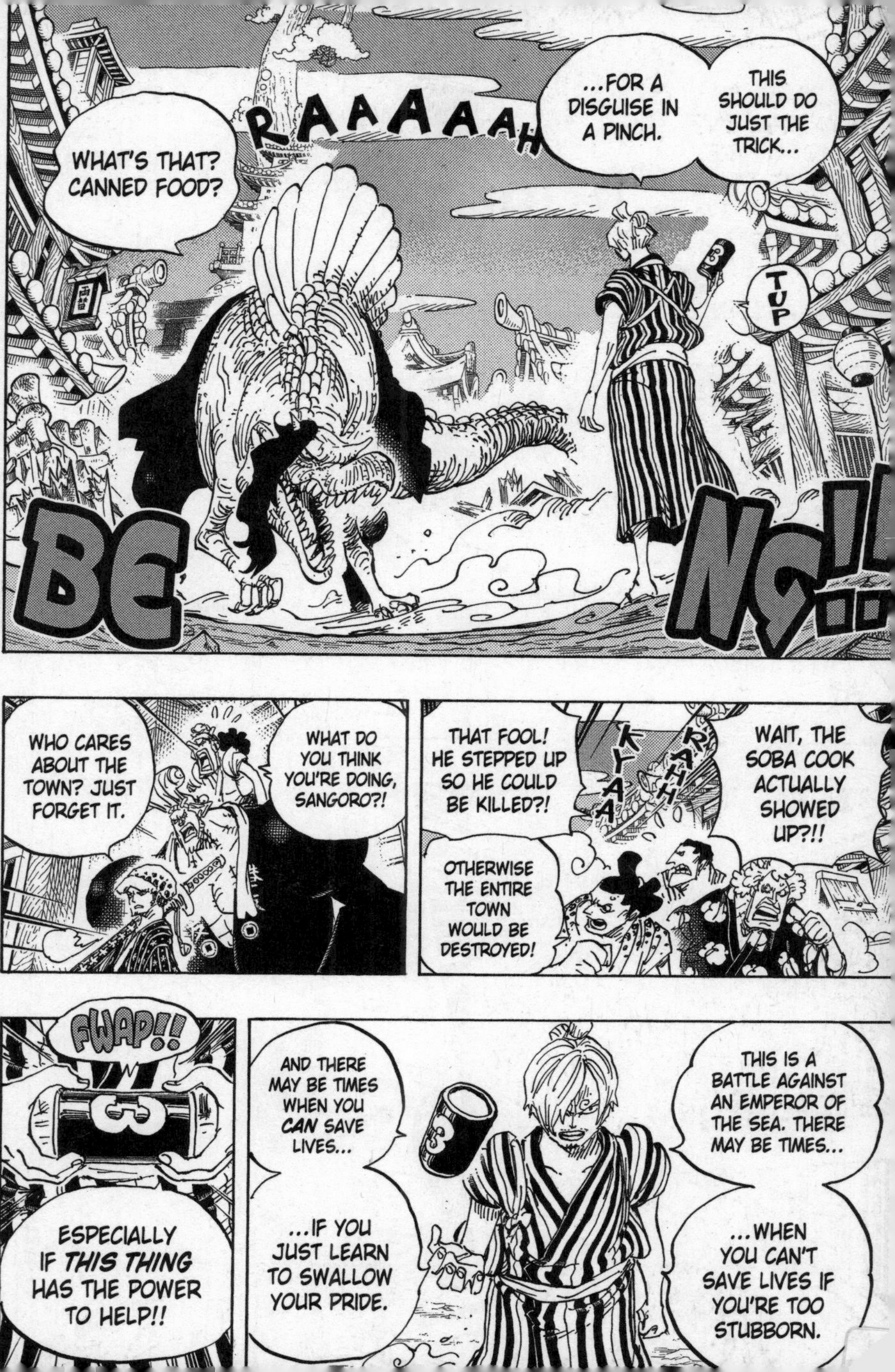
THIS SHOULD DO JUST THE TRICK...
...FOR A DISGUISE IN A PINCH.
TUP
RAAAAAAH
WHAT'S THAT? CANNED FOOD?
BE
NG!!
WAIT, THE SOBA COOK ACTUALLY SHOWED UP?!!
RAHH
KYAA
THAT FOOL! HE STEPPED UP SO HE COULD BE KILLED?!
OTHERWISE THE ENTIRE TOWN WOULD BE DESTROYED!
WHAT DO YOU THINK YOU'RE DOING, SANGORO?!
WHO CARES ABOUT THE TOWN? JUST FORGET IT.
THIS IS A BATTLE AGAINST AN EMPEROR OF THE SEA. THERE MAY BE TIMES...
...WHEN YOU CAN'T SAVE LIVES IF YOU'RE TOO STUBBORN.
AND THERE MAY BE TIMES WHEN YOU *CAN* SAVE LIVES...
...IF YOU JUST LEARN TO SWALLOW YOUR PRIDE.
FWAP!!
ESPECIALLY IF *THIS THING* HAS THE POWER TO HELP!!

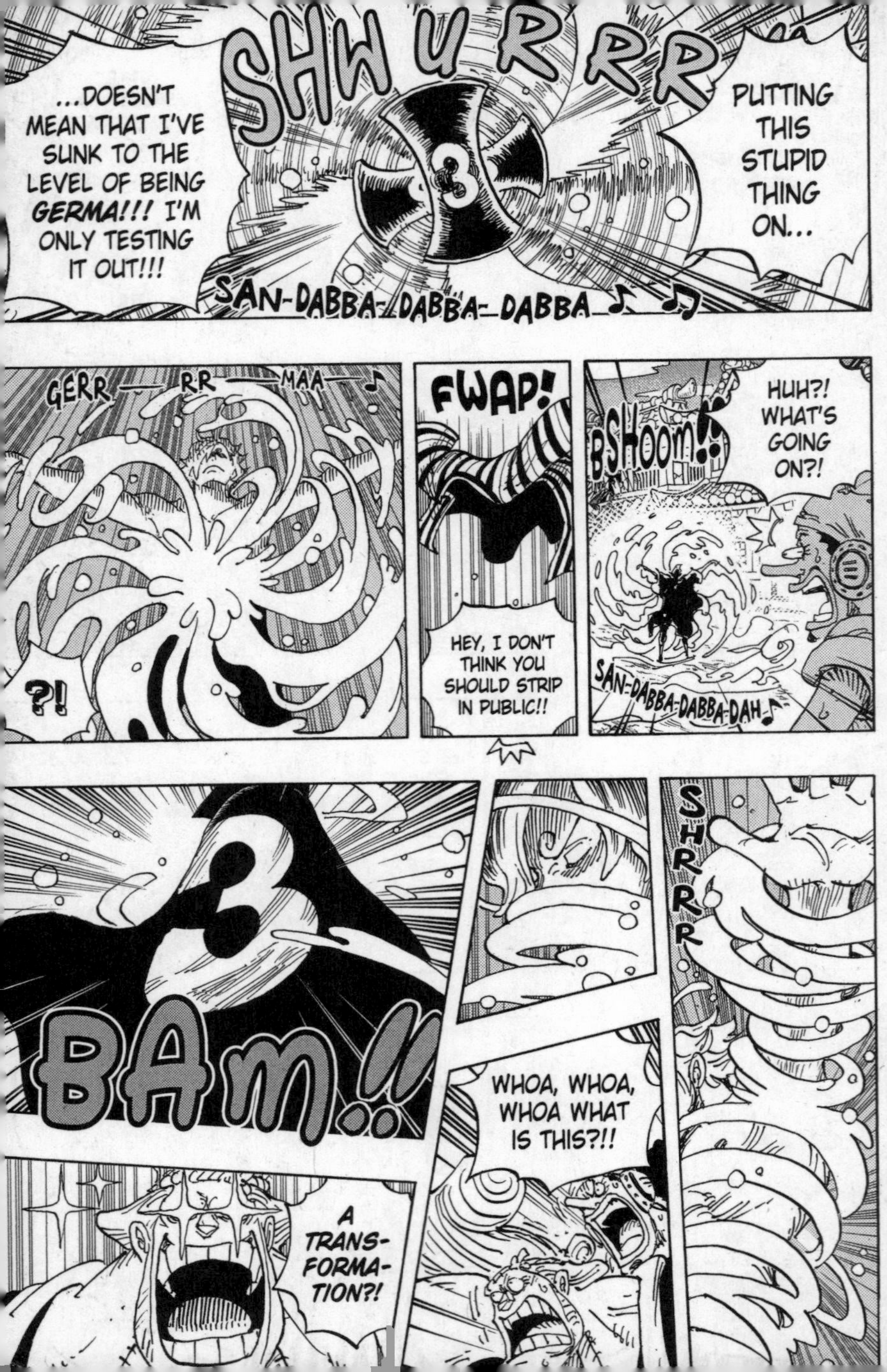
PUTTING THIS STUPID THING ON...
SHWURRR
...DOESN'T MEAN THAT I'VE SUNK TO THE LEVEL OF BEING GERMA!!! I'M ONLY TESTING IT OUT!!!
SAN-DABBA-DABBA-DABBA
HUH?! WHAT'S GOING ON?!
BSHOOM!!
SAN-DABBA-DABBA-DAH
FWAP!
HEY, I DON'T THINK YOU SHOULD STRIP IN PUBLIC!!
GERR—RR—MAA—
?!
SHRRR
WHOA, WHOA, WHOA WHAT IS THIS?!!
BAM!!
A TRANSFORMATION?!

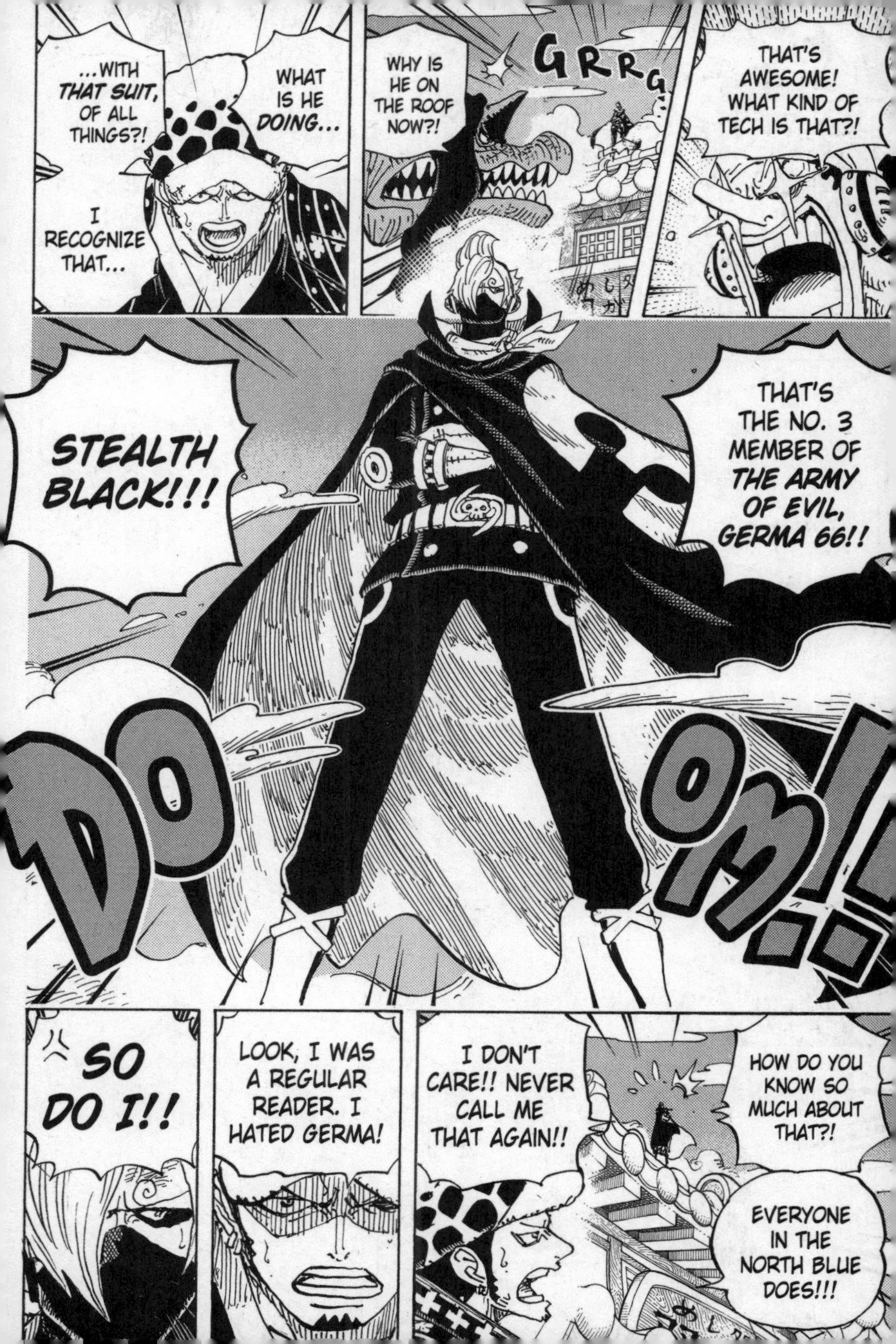
THAT'S AWESOME! WHAT KIND OF TECH IS THAT?!
GRRG
WHY IS HE ON THE ROOF NOW?!
WHAT IS HE DOING...
...WITH THAT SUIT, OF ALL THINGS?!
I RECOGNIZE THAT...
THAT'S THE NO. 3 MEMBER OF THE ARMY OF EVIL, GERMA 66!!
STEALTH BLACK!!!
DOOM!!
HOW DO YOU KNOW SO MUCH ABOUT THAT?!
EVERYONE IN THE NORTH BLUE DOES!!!
I DON'T CARE!! NEVER CALL ME THAT AGAIN!!
LOOK, I WAS A REGULAR READER. I HATED GERMA!
SO DO I!!

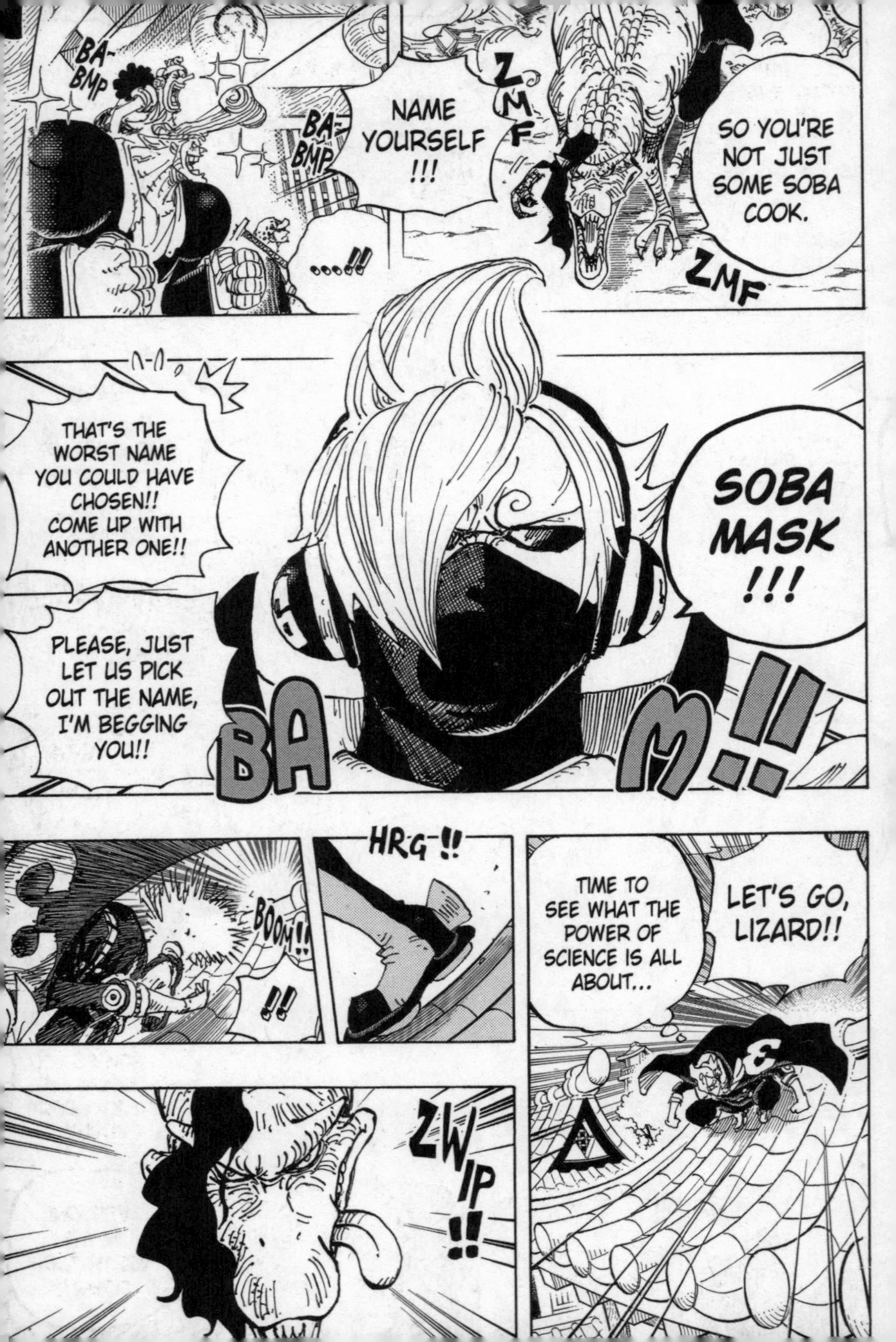
SO YOU'RE NOT JUST SOME SOBA COOK.
ZMF
ZMF
NAME YOURSELF!!!
BA-BMP
BA-BMP
....!!
SOBA MASK!!!
BAM!!
THAT'S THE WORST NAME YOU COULD HAVE CHOSEN!! COME UP WITH ANOTHER ONE!!
PLEASE, JUST LET US PICK OUT THE NAME, I'M BEGGING YOU!!
LET'S GO, LIZARD!!
TIME TO SEE WHAT THE POWER OF SCIENCE IS ALL ABOUT...
HRG!!
BOOM!!
!!
ZWIP!!

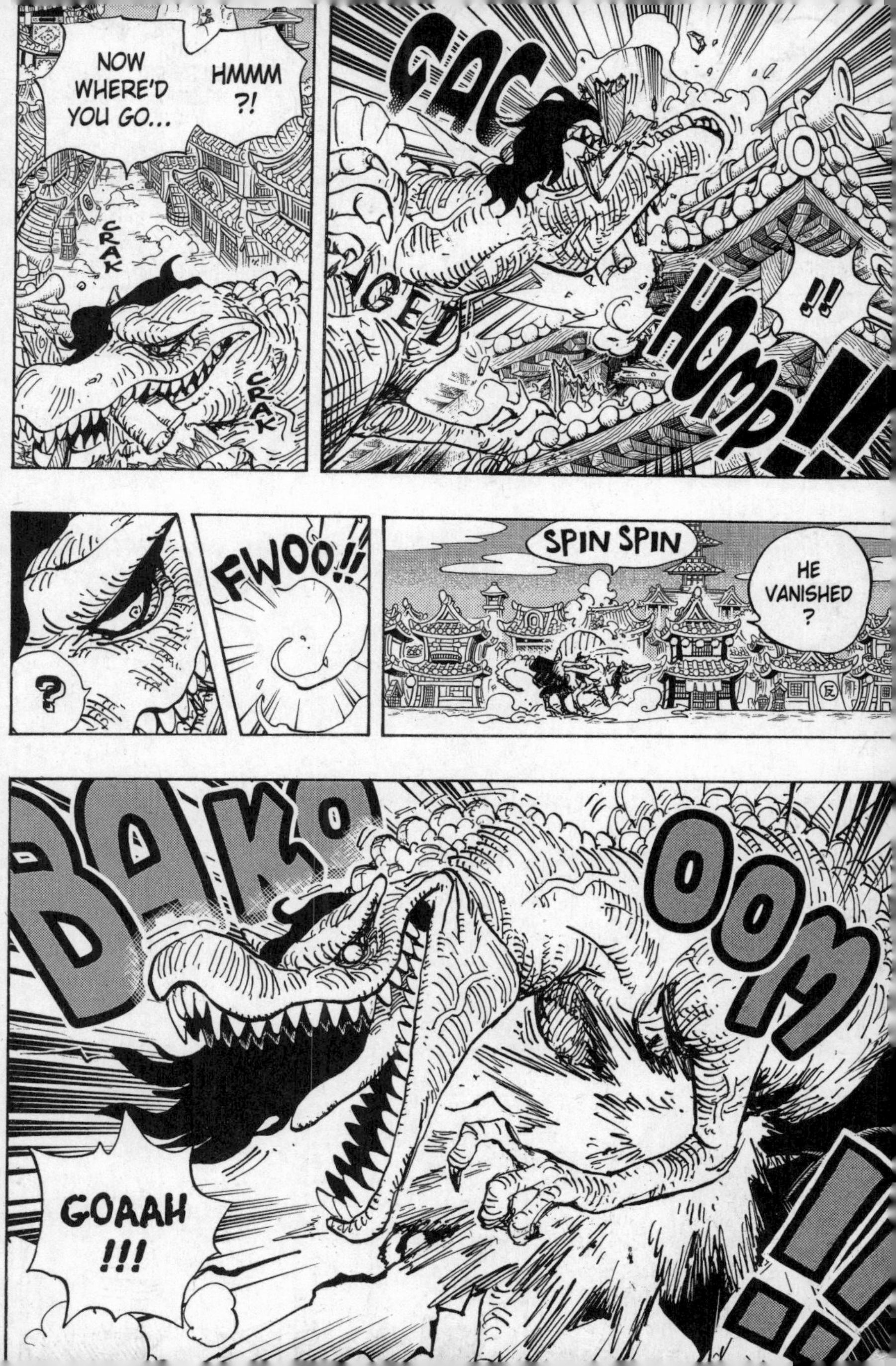
GAC
AGET
HOMP!!
!!
HMMM ?!
NOW WHERE'D YOU GO...
CRAK
CRAK
SPIN SPIN
HE VANISHED ?
FWOO!!
?
BAKOOOM
GOAAH !!!
!!

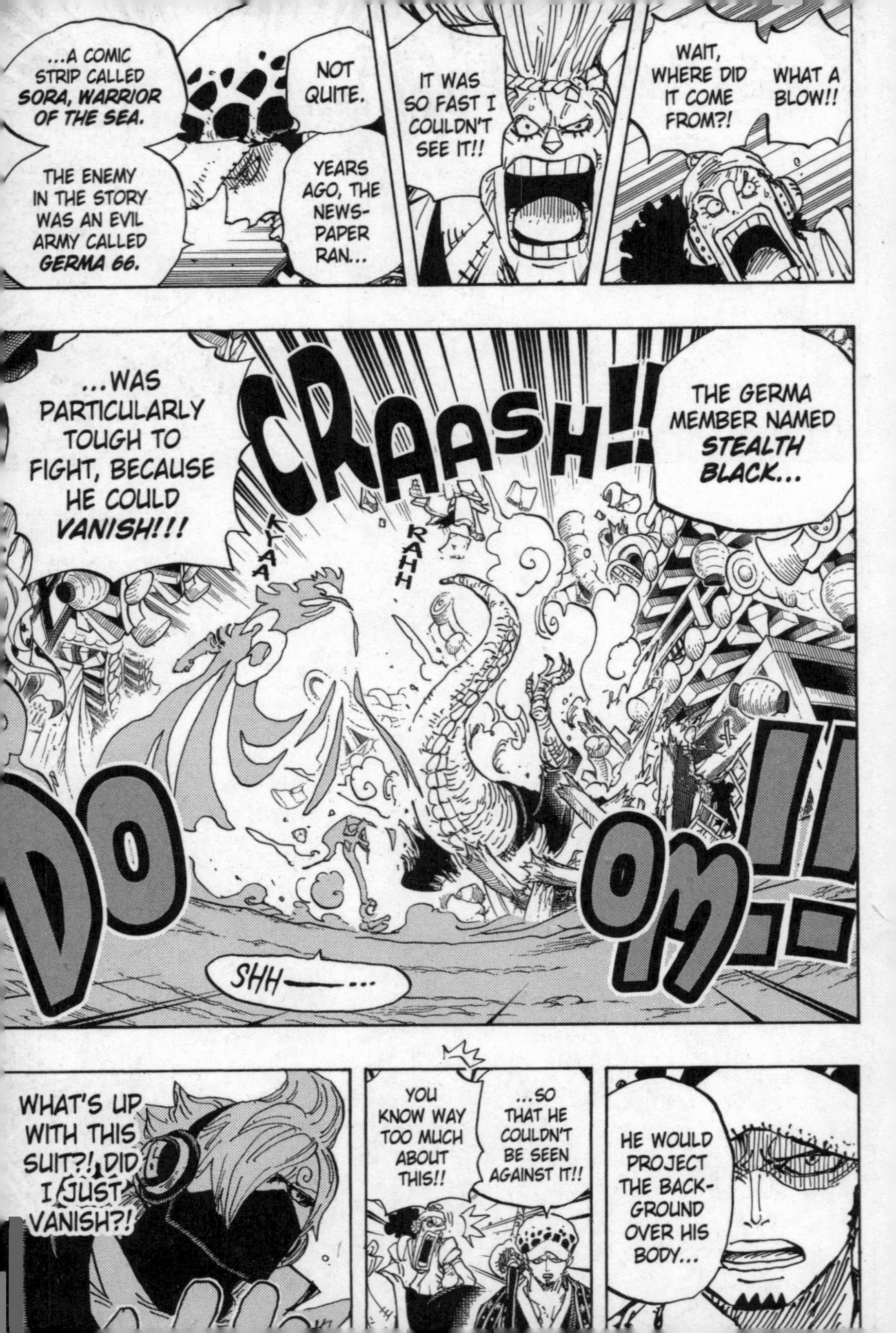
WHAT A BLOW!!
WAIT, WHERE DID IT COME FROM?!
IT WAS SO FAST I COULDN'T SEE IT!!
NOT QUITE.
YEARS AGO, THE NEWS-PAPER RAN...
...A COMIC STRIP CALLED SORA, WARRIOR OF THE SEA.
THE ENEMY IN THE STORY WAS AN EVIL ARMY CALLED GERMA 66.
THE GERMA MEMBER NAMED STEALTH BLACK...
CRAASH!!
RAHH
KYAA
...WAS PARTICULARLY TOUGH TO FIGHT, BECAUSE HE COULD VANISH!!!
DOOM!!
SHH———...
HE WOULD PROJECT THE BACK-GROUND OVER HIS BODY...
...SO THAT HE COULDN'T BE SEEN AGAINST IT!!
YOU KNOW WAY TOO MUCH ABOUT THIS!!
WHAT'S UP WITH THIS SUIT?! DID I JUST VANISH?!

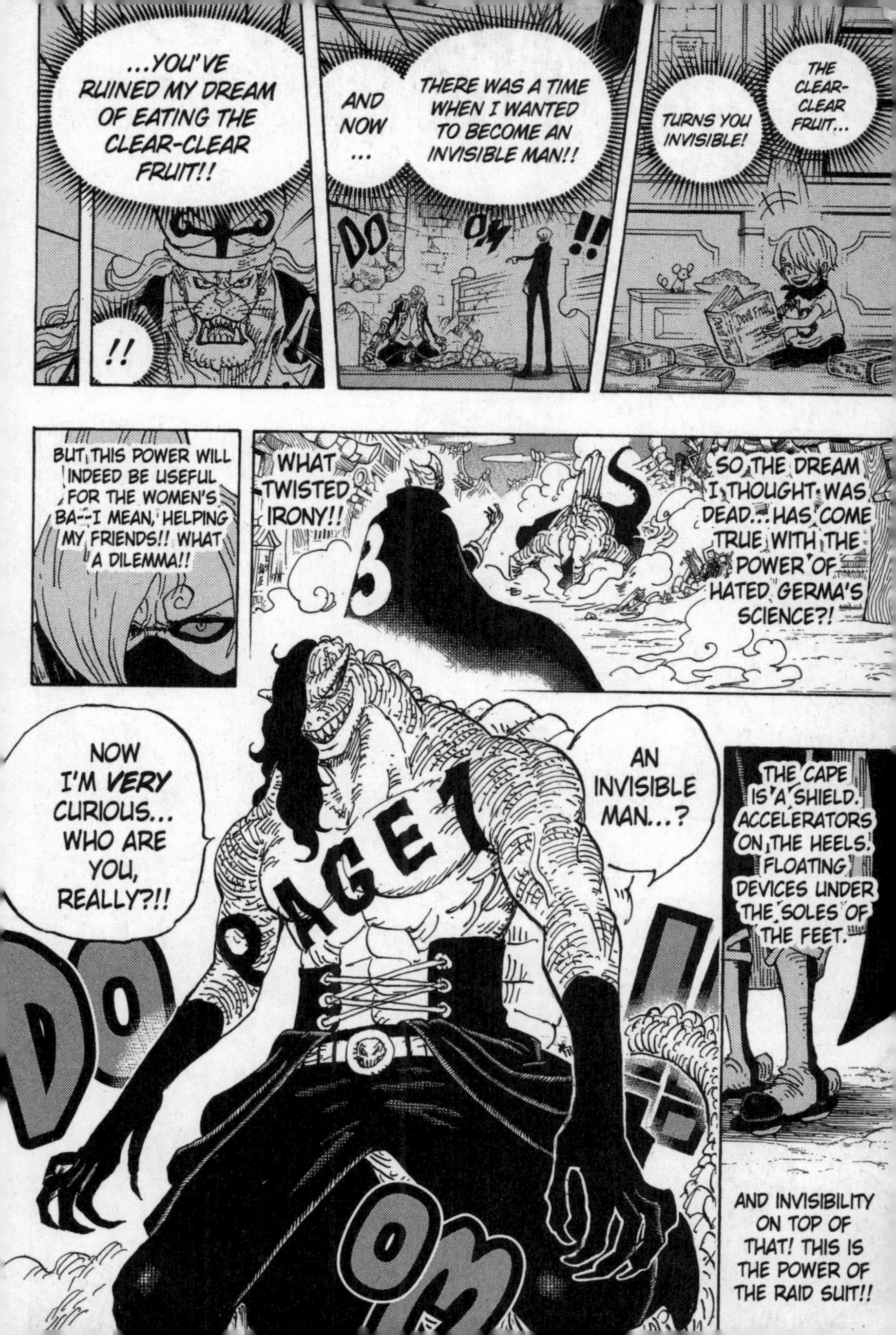
THE CLEAR-CLEAR FRUIT...
TURNS YOU INVISIBLE!
THERE WAS A TIME WHEN I WANTED TO BECOME AN INVISIBLE MAN!!
AND NOW...
DOOM
!!
...YOU'VE RUINED MY DREAM OF EATING THE CLEAR-CLEAR FRUIT!!
!!
SO THE DREAM I THOUGHT WAS DEAD... HAS COME TRUE WITH THE POWER OF HATED GERMA'S SCIENCE?!
WHAT TWISTED IRONY!!
3
BUT THIS POWER WILL INDEED BE USEFUL FOR THE WOMEN'S BA--I MEAN, HELPING MY FRIENDS!! WHAT A DILEMMA!!
THE CAPE IS A SHIELD. ACCELERATORS ON THE HEELS. FLOATING DEVICES UNDER THE SOLES OF THE FEET.
AND INVISIBILITY ON TOP OF THAT! THIS IS THE POWER OF THE RAID SUIT!!
AN INVISIBLE MAN...?
PAGE 1
NOW I'M ***VERY*** CURIOUS... WHO ARE YOU, REALLY?!!
DOOM

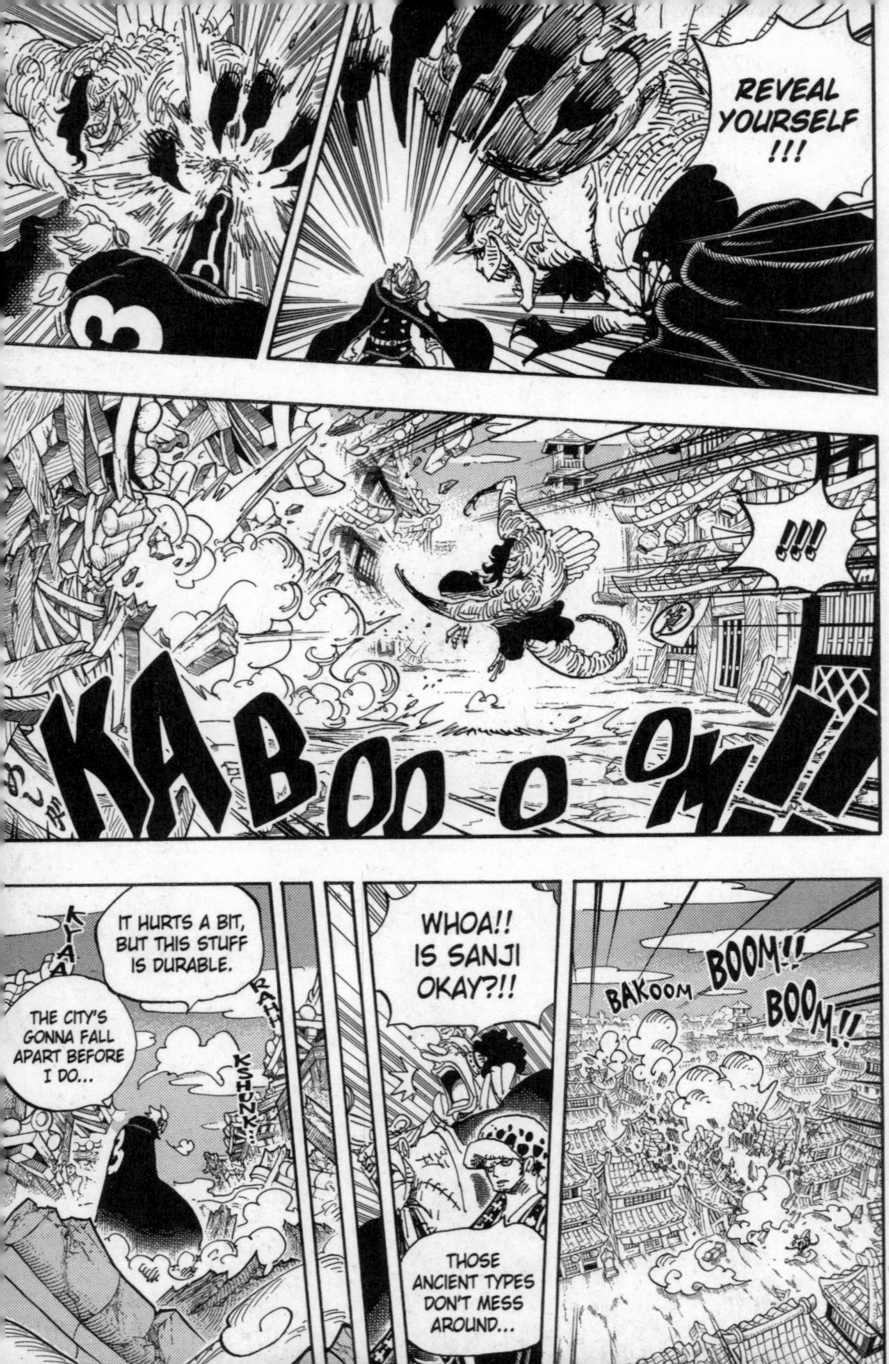
REVEAL YOURSELF!!!
!!!
KABOOOOM!!
BOOM!!
BOOM!!
BAKOOM
WHOA!! IS SANJI OKAY?!!
THOSE ANCIENT TYPES DON'T MESS AROUND...
IT HURTS A BIT, BUT THIS STUFF IS DURABLE.
RAHH
KYAA
THE CITY'S GONNA FALL APART BEFORE I DO...
KSHUNK...

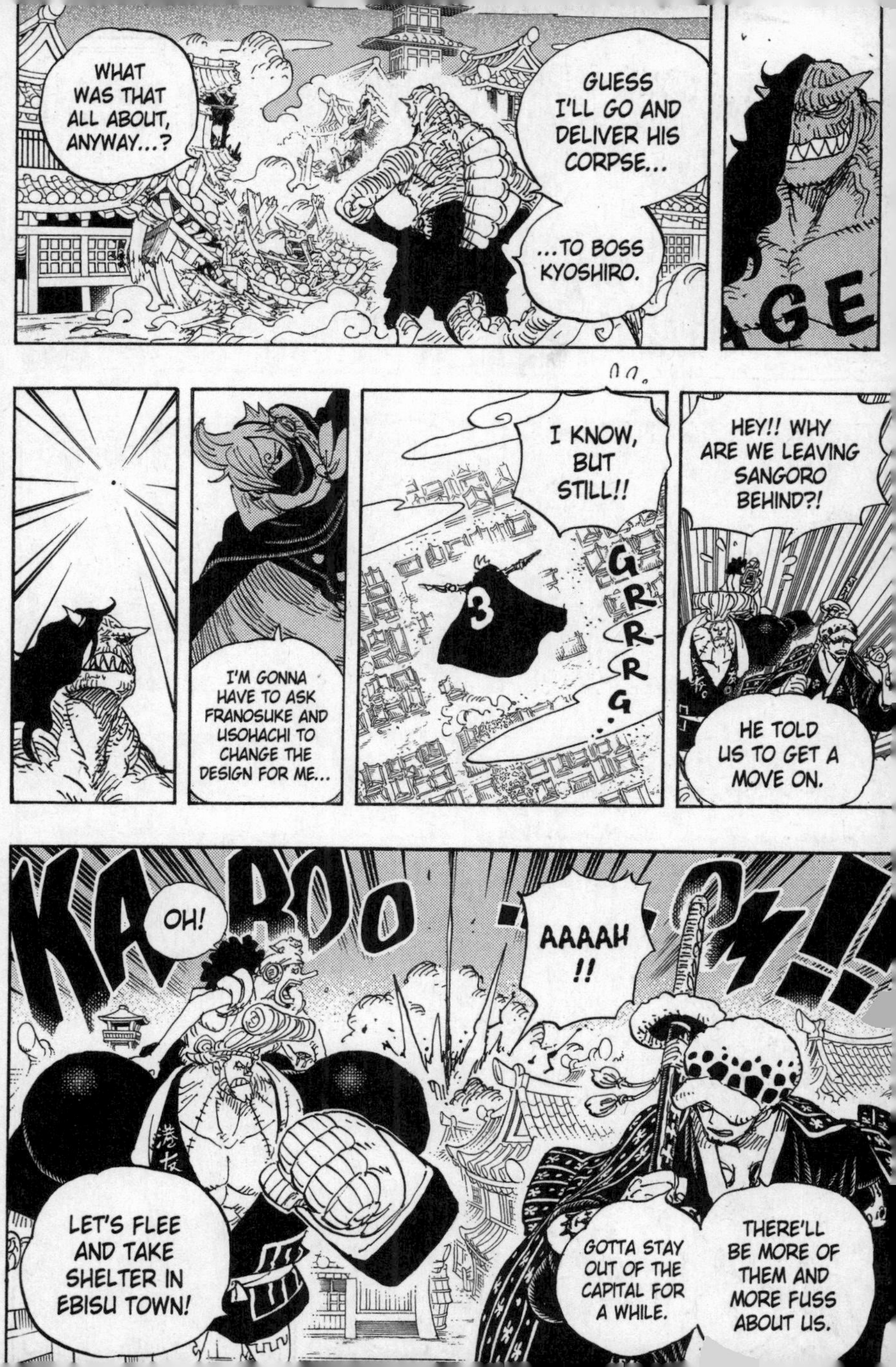
GE
GUESS I'LL GO AND DELIVER HIS CORPSE...
...TO BOSS KYOSHIRO.
WHAT WAS THAT ALL ABOUT, ANYWAY...?
HEY!! WHY ARE WE LEAVING SANGORO BEHIND?!
HE TOLD US TO GET A MOVE ON.
I KNOW, BUT STILL!!
GRRRRG...
I'M GONNA HAVE TO ASK FRANOSUKE AND USOHACHI TO CHANGE THE DESIGN FOR ME...
KABOOOM!!
AAAAH !!
OH!
THERE'LL BE MORE OF THEM AND MORE FUSS ABOUT US.
GOTTA STAY OUT OF THE CAPITAL FOR A WHILE.
LET'S FLEE AND TAKE SHELTER IN EBISU TOWN!

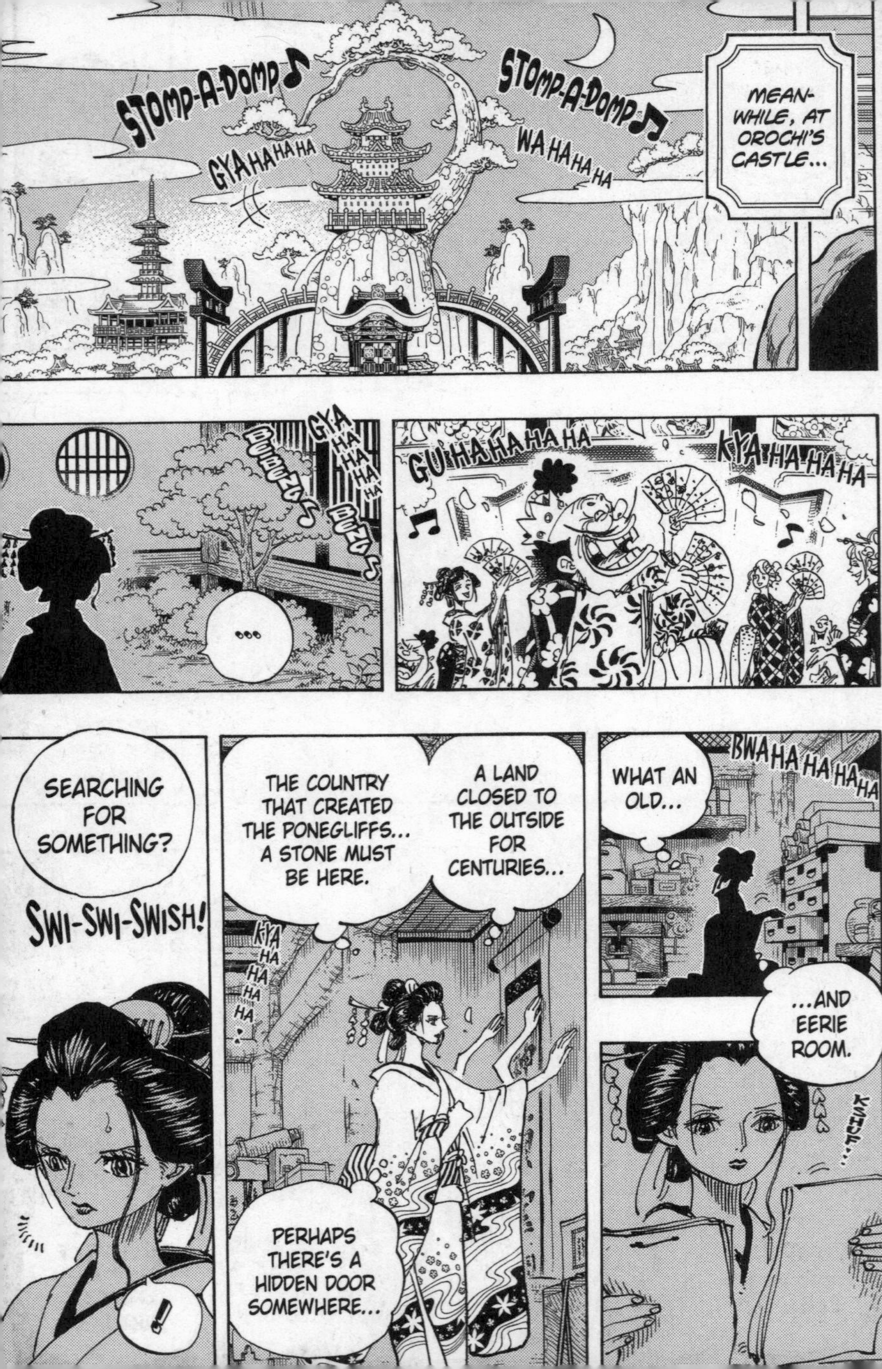
MEAN-WHILE, AT OROCHI'S CASTLE...
STOMP-A-DOMP♪
WA HA HA HA HA
GYA HA HA HA HA
STOMP-A-DOMP♪
KYA HA HA HA HA
GU HA HA HA HA
GYA HA HA HA HA
BEBENG♪ BENG♪
...
BWA HA HA HA HA HA
WHAT AN OLD...
...AND EERIE ROOM.
KSHUF...
A LAND CLOSED TO THE OUTSIDE FOR CENTURIES...
THE COUNTRY THAT CREATED THE PONEGLIFFS... A STONE MUST BE HERE.
KYA HA HA HA HA HA
PERHAPS THERE'S A HIDDEN DOOR SOMEWHERE...
SEARCHING FOR SOMETHING?
SWI-SWI-SWISH!
!

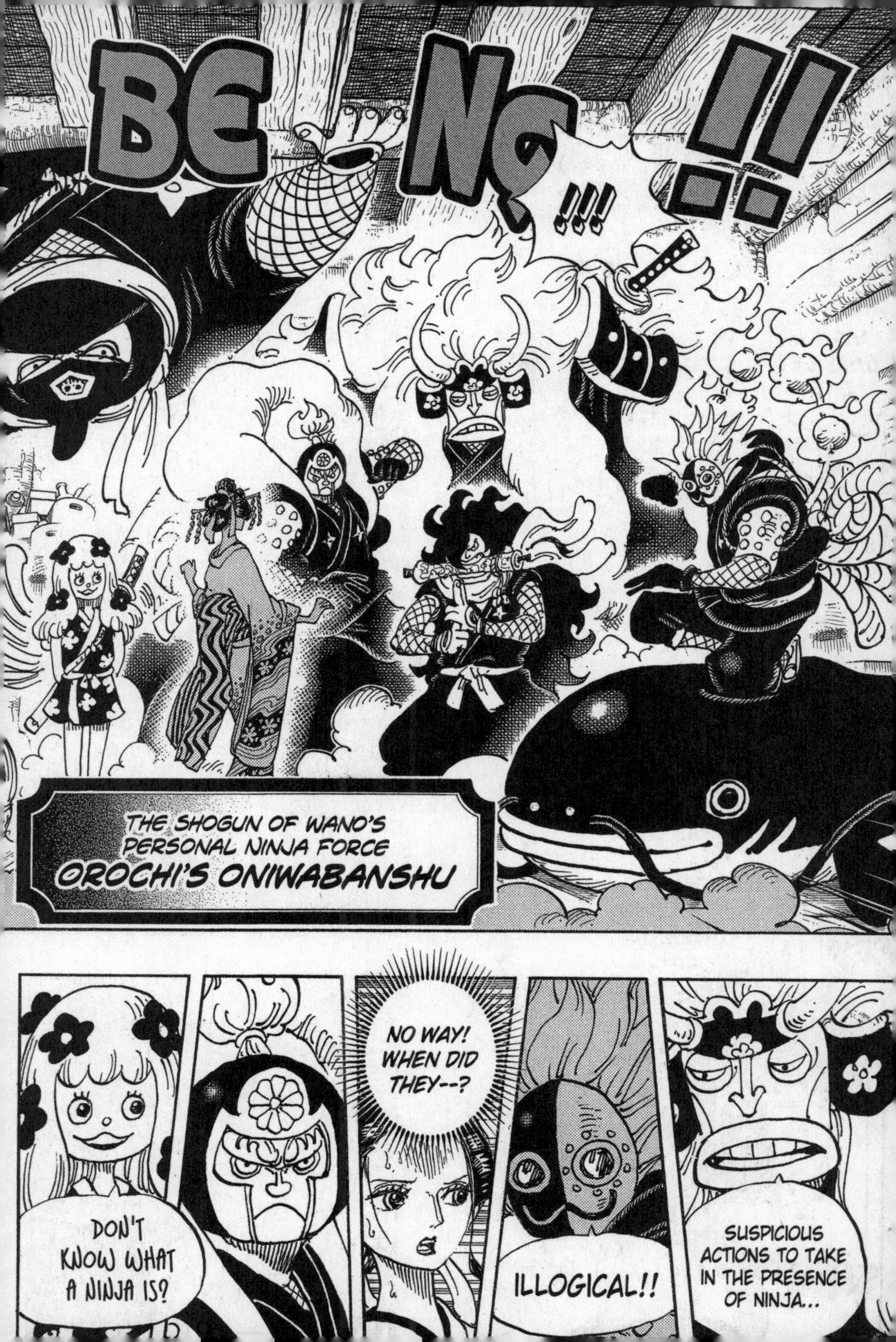
BE NG!!
!!!
THE SHOGUN OF WANO'S PERSONAL NINJA FORCE
OROCHI'S ONIWABANSHU
SUSPICIOUS ACTIONS TO TAKE IN THE PRESENCE OF NINJA...
ILLOGICAL!!
NO WAY! WHEN DID THEY--?
DON'T KNOW WHAT A NINJA IS?

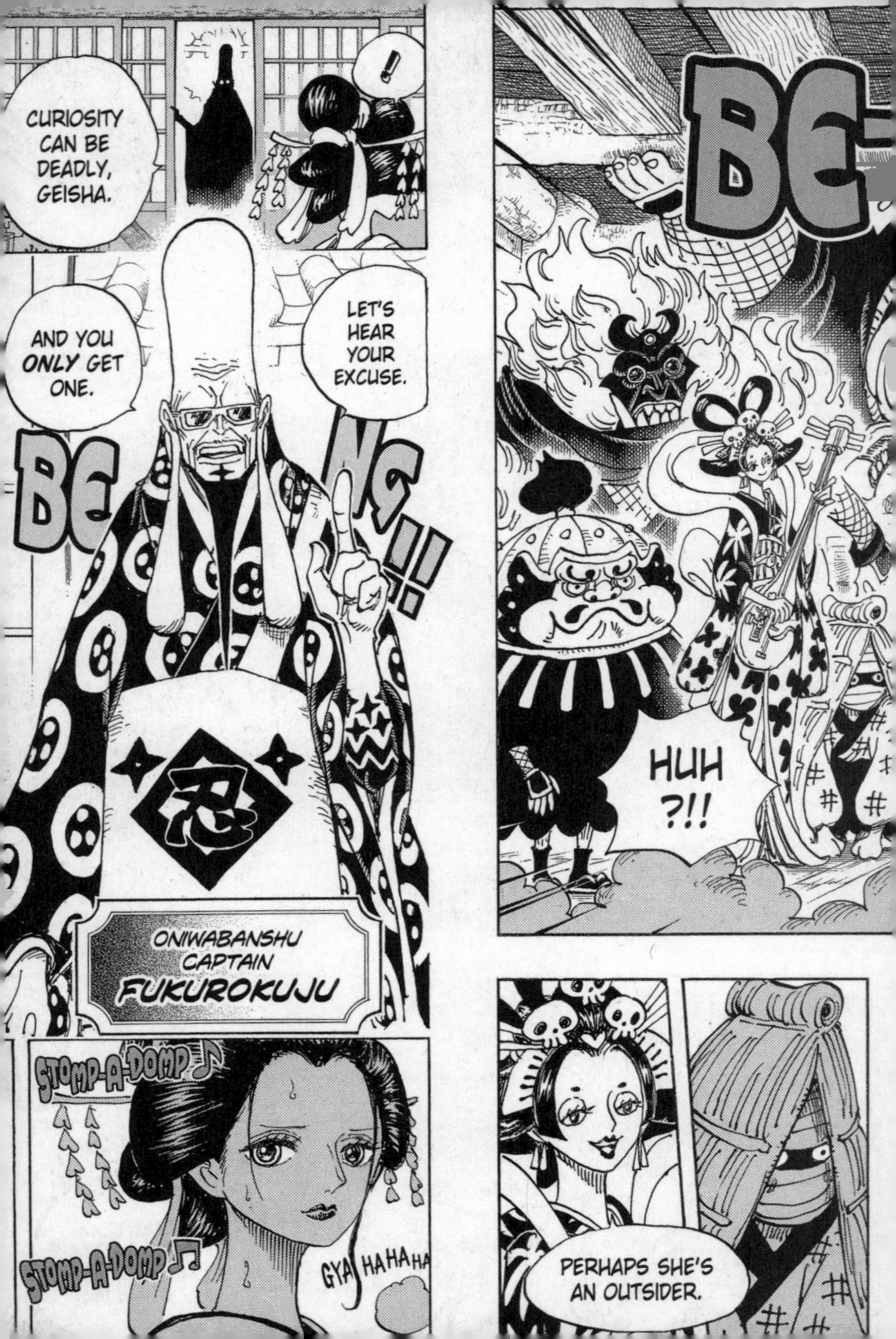
BE—
HUH ?!!
PERHAPS SHE'S AN OUTSIDER.
!
CURIOSITY CAN BE DEADLY, GEISHA.
LET'S HEAR YOUR EXCUSE.
AND YOU ONLY GET ONE.
BE
NG!!
ONIWABANSHU CAPTAIN FUKUROKUJU
STOMP-A-DOMP♪
STOMP-A-DOMP♪
GYA HAHAHA HA

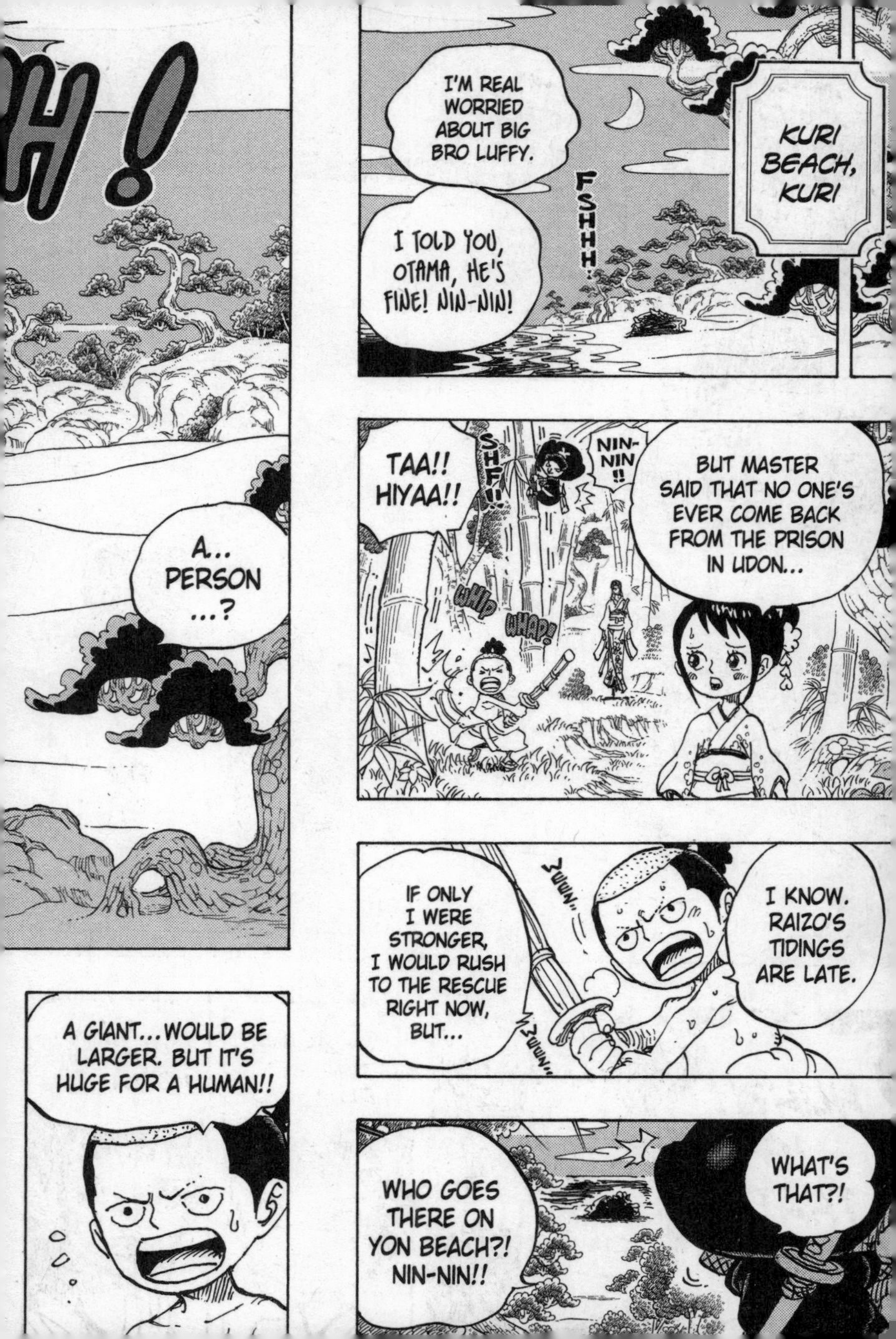
KURI BEACH, KURI
FSHHH...
I'M REAL WORRIED ABOUT BIG BRO LUFFY.
I TOLD YOU, OTAMA, HE'S FINE! NIN-NIN!
BUT MASTER SAID THAT NO ONE'S EVER COME BACK FROM THE PRISON IN UDON...
NIN-NIN!!
SHF!!
TAA!! HIYAA!!
WHIP
WHAP!
I KNOW. RAIZO'S TIDINGS ARE LATE.
WUUN...
IF ONLY I WERE STRONGER, I WOULD RUSH TO THE RESCUE RIGHT NOW, BUT...
WUUN...
WHAT'S THAT?!
WHO GOES THERE ON YON BEACH?! NIN-NIN!!
H!
A... PERSON ...?
A GIANT...WOULD BE LARGER. BUT IT'S HUGE FOR A HUMAN!!

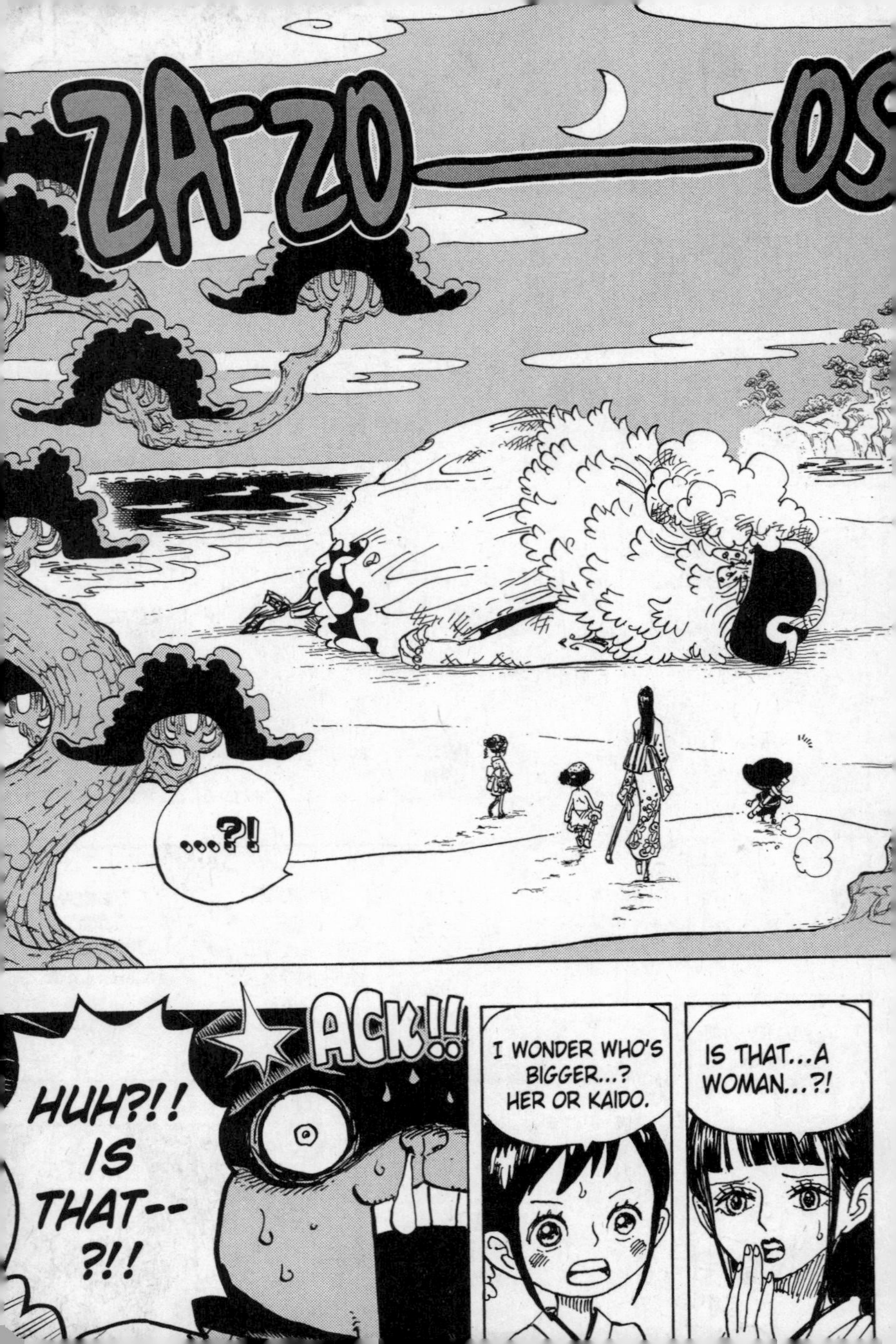
ZA-ZO——OS
...?!
IS THAT...A WOMAN...?!
I WONDER WHO'S BIGGER...? HER OR KAIDO.
ACK!!
HUH?!! IS THAT-- ?!!

IT'S BIG M...

AAAAH!!!

BA M !!

IF SHE WAKES UP, WE'RE DONE FOR!!

WE HAVE TO GET OUT OF HERE!!

DON'T SPEAK!! SHE'LL WAKE UP!!!

CHOPPER-EMON, WHAT IS THIS...

...OM!!

WHAP!!

URRGH...

KOFF!!

HAKK!!

?!!

THINK OF HER AS KAIDO!! SHE'S JUST LIKE KAIDO!!

DON'T SHOUT!! I'LL FINISH HER OFF RIGHT NOW!!

WHAT?! THIS IS THE DREADED BIG MOM?!!

CHOPPEREMON, YOU HAVE TO EXPLAIN WHAT'S GOING ON.

I'LL DO IT LATER!!!

SHING

NO... IT WON'T MATTER ANYWAY!

ASSUMING SHE CAME HERE CHASING AFTER US...!!

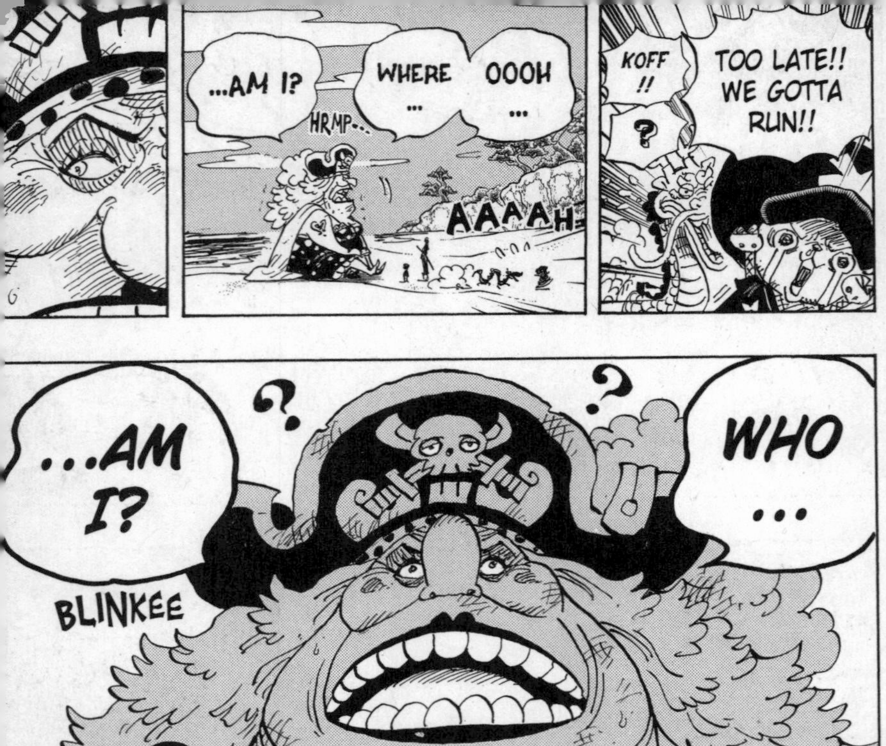
TOO LATE!! WE GOTTA RUN!!
KOFF !!
?
OOOH ...
WHERE ...
...AM I?
HRMP...
AAAAH
WHO ...
?
?
...AM I?
BLINKEE
DOOM!!

TO BE CONTINUED IN ONE PIECE, VOL 93!

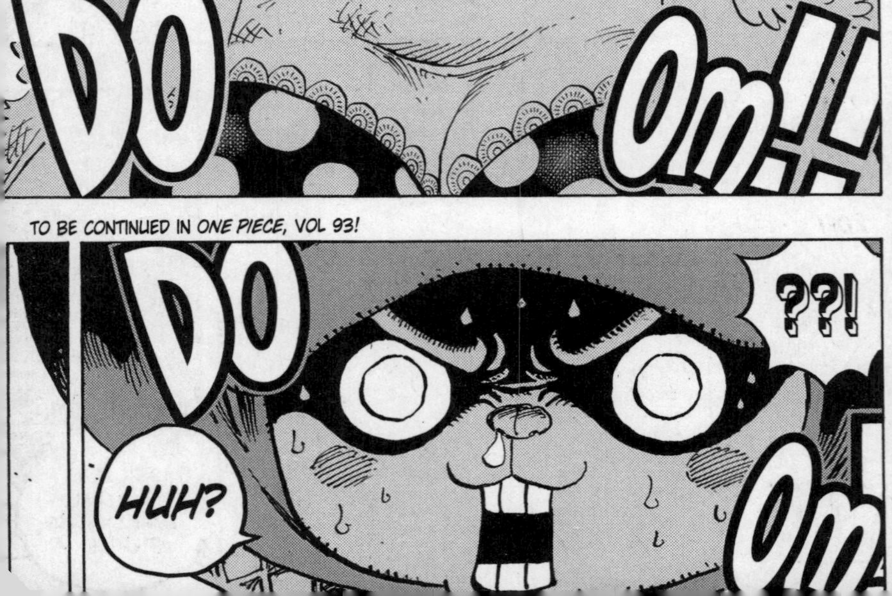
??!
DO
OM
HUH?

COMING NEXT VOLUME:

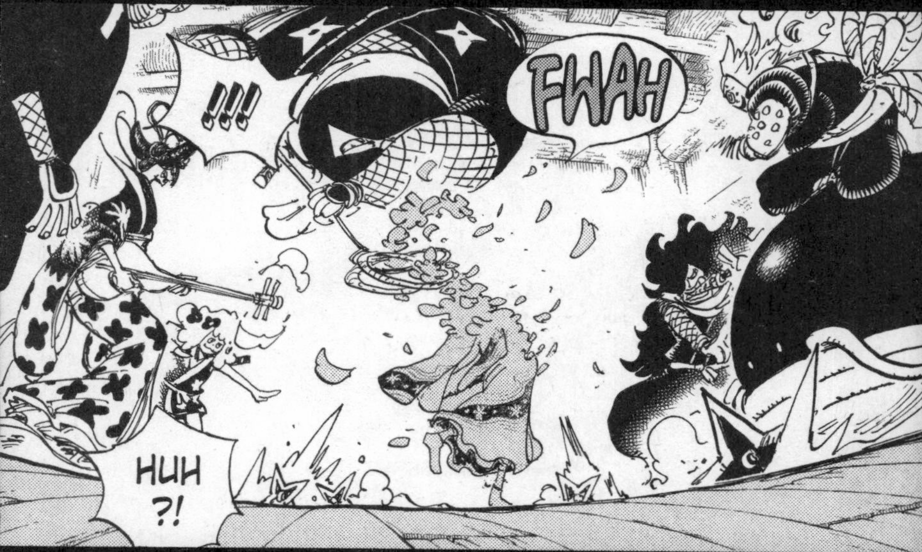
FWAH
!!!
HUH ?!

If things weren't getting crazy enough on Wano, now Big Mom has joined the fray. But there's something a little different about this Big Mom. With her memories gone, will she be friend or foe? And can Luffy break out of Kaido's prison?!

ON SALE APRIL 2020!

ONE PIECE VOL. 92
WANO PART 3

SHONEN JUMP Manga Edition

STORY AND ART BY EIICHIRO ODA

Translation/Stephen Paul
Touch-up Art & Lettering/Vanessa Satone
Design/Yukiko Whitley
Editor/Alexis Kirsch

Published by VIZ Media, LLC
P.O. Box 77010
San Francisco, CA 94107

10 9 8 7 6 5 4 3 2 1
First printing, November 2019

viz.com   shonenjump.com

You're Reading the Wrong Direction!!

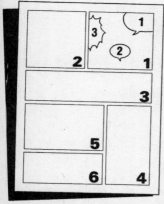

Whoops! Guess what? You're starting at the wrong end of the comic!

...It's true! In keeping with the original Japanese format, **One Piece** is meant to be read from right to left, starting in the upper-right corner.

Unlike English, which is read from left to right, Japanese is read from right to left, meaning that action, sound effects and word-balloon order are completely reversed...something which can make readers unfamiliar with Japanese feel pretty backwards themselves. For this reason, manga or Japanese comics published in the U.S. in English have sometimes been published "flopped"— that is, printed in exact reverse order, as though seen from the other side of a mirror.

By flopping pages, U.S. publishers can avoid confusing readers, but the compromise is not without its downside. For one thing, a character in a flopped manga series who once wore in the original Japanese version a T-shirt emblazoned with "M A Y" (as in "the merry month of") now wears one which reads "Y A M"! Additionally, many manga creators in Japan are themselves unhappy with the process, as some feel the mirror-imaging of their art skews their original intentions.

We are proud to bring you Eiichiro Oda's **One Piece** in the original unflopped format. For now, though, turn to the other side of the book and let the journey begin...!

—Editor